Marjorie Kinnan Rawlings

Marjorie Kinnan Rawlings

Sojourner at Cross Creek

by Elizabeth Silverthorne

The Overlook Press

Woodstock, New York

First published in 1988 by
The Overlook Press
Lewis Hollow Road
Woodstock, New York 12498

Library of Congress Cataloging-in-Publication Data
Silverthorne, Elizabeth.
Marjorie Kinnan Rawlings: sojourner at Cross Creek
Bibliography.
Includes index.
1. Rawlings, Marjorie Kinnan. 1896–1953—Biography.   2. Authors.
American—20th century—Biography.   I. Title.
PS3535.A845Z88   1988   813'.52   87-28589
ISBN: 0-87951-308-X

With love
To
My daughter Carol
who inspired and encouraged me to write
this book

Table of
Contents

Marjorie Kinnan Rawlings

Sojourner at Cross Creek

Preface

One of Marjorie Kinnan Rawlings's secret dreams was to win the Nobel Prize for Literature. Another was to have a rose named after her. Although neither of these dreams came true, they illuminate the things that were important to her.

Her temper was volatile and her generosity proverbial. Asked to describe Marjorie's personality, Jake Glisson, her friend and neighbor, said, "It was like changing channels on a television. You never knew what mood of thought, behavior, or attitude the next flick of the dial would bring."

Her husband, Norton Baskin, gave a similar description. At times she was, he said, like a "prim and proper school mistress," at others like a "bawdy Elizabethan wench," and often she was "just a struggling writer trying to find the right words to tell her story."

Though she has been dead for more than thirty years, the predominant memory of many who knew her is of her generosity. She loved to give material things but more importantly she gave of herself. Her college classmate and lifelong friend, Bee McNeil, suggested the subtitle of her biography should be "A Great-Hearted Woman." Martin Dibner, artist and author, remembers the "wise counsel, professional expertise and lavish encouragement" she gave to him when he was a struggling young writer. "I will never forget so priceless a gift, or so remarkable a woman."

She could no more help becoming involved in the personal problems of her household help or grove workers than she could help breathing. There was always a hint of sexual attraction beneath the surface of her relationships with men. She favored and cultivated friendships with achievers who earned their places by using their talents and with simple, elemental people who lived life with courage and independence. She detested self-important Babbitts, and let them know it.

Once she had left cities behind her and found her patch of frontier in north central Florida, she also found the best and most successful material for her writing. Hers was not the Florida of highways, towns, cities, and tourists, but of the hammock, the piney woods and the flatwoods, the great silent Scrub, the lakes and rivers, the marshes and prairies, sparsely populated with native Crackers. It was the Florida where a man could still make a living with an axe, a gun, and a fishing line. It was the Florida of wild orange groves and Indian wars still within the memory of living people.

Realizing it was a frontier that could not last long, she felt a compulsion to capture it on paper before it disappeared. In an indignant letter to an editor who criticized her portrayal of the Florida natives and their environment she said:

> [M]y dear sir, do not let us hustle and deny out of existence the last of Florida's frontier. The State will so soon be just like any other. Before they have been quite swallowed up, let us know and enjoy these picturesque people, pioneer remains. They are much more vital than you and I.

The basic training she had acquired as a hard-working journalist and her highly inquisitive nature enabled Marjorie to ferret out people's lives. Another quality that enriched her writing was the unusual degree to which she was able to savor the world with all of her senses. She loved the *taste* of liquor—and of good food. "I can't live without flowers," she often said and proved it by buying flowers when she was short of money for food and clothes. Trees, plants, animals were important and necessary to her sense of well-being. Her hunting dogs became house pets and constant companions; and her cats, particularly the Siamese ones, were so important to her that she carried them with her as she moved from one end of the country to the other.

Like Byron, she delighted in wild and stormy weather. And like Wordsworth, she appreciated every nuance of the changing seasons, the language of nature. Her own nature descriptions are filled with sensory information, the smells, sounds, and texture of life. "From the tangible, the intangible is deduced," she said. The intangible for her was the truth and beauty hidden behind a curtain, which the artist must draw aside.

Various articles, critical reviews, and even a movie (*Cross Creek*) have revealed facets of Marjorie's personality, but none has shown her whole. A volume of her letters (*Selected Letters*, 1983) is the best epiphany of her independent, vigorous, lively spirit. In writing her life story, I have no doubt been influenced by Marjorie's own opinions about biographies. Her last writing project, the one in which she was immersed when struck down by a fatal brain hemorrhage, was a biography of Ellen Glasgow (1874–1945), a fellow writer and friend. "I have violent ideas about biographies, and next to the dry as dust ones, I most deplore the over-intimate ones, which are always in the most appalling bad taste," Marjorie said. She had no patience with fictionalized biography or with biographers who, like carrion crow, pick the bones of their subjects to exercise their own egos. Candid and frank to a fault, she would not have wanted her other faults glossed over or ignored, and she would undoubtedly have had some choice epithets for any book that painted her in an aura of sweetness and light.

In his introduction to *Selected Letters of Marjorie Kinnan Rawlings*, Gordon E. Bigelow calls her "an extraordinary human being, warm and vital as well as gifted . . . whose career reminds one that there were liberated women in America long before the movement of the 1960s and '70s." He points out that her significant achievement as a literary artist was all the result of her own doing, "of her own talent and intelligence, her own ambition and independence of spirit, her courage and persistence in the face of reverses."

These same qualities—independence, courage, and persistence—combined with large measures of romanticism, mysticism, and an insatiable curiosity also determined the progress of her personal life.

Acknowledgments

*I*f I have succeeded in bringing Marjorie to life, it is largely because I have received such kind and abundant assistance. Norton Baskin, Marjorie's second husband, is the most perfect example of a southern gentleman. Throughout many hours of interviews, in person and by telephone and in many letters, he has shared invaluable information and insight. He has also generously shared his personal papers and letters with me. Marjorie's college mate and lifelong friend, Beatrice Humiston McNeil, has ripped up scrapbooks and yearbooks and searched her attic and closets for every scrap of material she could locate about her beloved friend, and she has shared with me excellent anecdotes about Marjorie's college days.

Henry W. Clune of Scottsville, New York, talked with me about Marjorie's life in Rochester. Jake Glisson spent the best part of a day showing me sights around Cross Creek and telling me what the people and the country were like when Marjorie lived there. Bob Lucas, a park ranger at the Marjorie Kinnan Rawlings State Historic Site, took me to the Antioch Cemetery and helped me do a rubbing of Marjorie's tombstone. Sally Morrison, another ranger, shared the insights she has gathered while living in Marjorie's Cross Creek house, tending her garden, cooking on her stove, and raising the descendants of her ducks and cats. Stephen A. Nesbitt, wildlife biologist with the Florida Fish and Game Commission, in Gainesville, Florida, gave me a delightful boat tour of Orange Lake, Cross Creek, and Lochloosa Lake, identifying the various animal, bird, and plant life for me.

Jean Kinnan Peterson of Phoenix, Arizona, provided me with pictures and family information. Martin Dibner of Casco, Maine, shared his memories and his correspondence with Marjorie. Mrs. E. F. Merrill of Rochester, New York, helped me make valuable contacts in her area. Marcia Davenport gave me her impression of Marjorie as an artist and as a friend. Patricia Fetzer read through the material concerning the trial and offered valuable suggestions as did Philip S. May, Jr.

Without the patient help of numerous reference librarians and archivists, this biography could not have been completed. It is impossible to name them all, so a few will have to represent the many to whom I am indebted. Carmen Russell, curator of Rare Books and Manuscripts, The University of Florida, has given me invaluable assistance in using the extensive collection of MKR material in her department. As always, the librarians of the Temple Public Library have given me much useful information and help. I also received much aid from the staff of the University of Wisconsin Libraries, especially in using their Historical Society Archives. Others who were particularly helpful were Robert A. Hull, public services assistant of the University of Virginia Library; Jean Preston, curator of manuscripts at the Firestone Library at Princeton University; J. Larry Gulley, manuscript librarian at the University of Georgia Libraries; Vesta Lee Gordon, assistant director for special collections at the University of Georgia Libraries; and Julia B. Campbell, public service assistant, the Beinecke Rare Book and Manuscript Library at Yale University.

Although I have received so much generous assistance, the final sifting, selecting, emphasis and conclusions (stated and implied) have been mine alone. And I only am to blame for any errors of judgment or interpretation that are to be found in this portrayal of the life of Marjorie Kinnan Rawlings Baskin.

CHAPTER · 1

Peaches

*J*ust a little over a week before Christmas 1953, a small funeral procession wound slowly up the sandy road leading into the Antioch Cemetery in north central Florida. On this warm, windy December day about sixty people gathered to pay their last respects to Marjorie Kinnan Rawlings. Among them were many who had known her for most of the quarter of a century that she had owned her farmhouse and orange grove at Cross Creek, including Martha Mickens and her husband Will, who had worked for Marjorie since she first came to Florida. With them were their daughters, Adrenna and Sissy, who had "helped out" at Marjorie's homes off and on over the years. Chet Crosby, Marjorie's grove manager, and his wife were there, as were her neighbors, the Brices and the Glissons. Longtime friends like Bob Camp, who had illustrated one of her books, and Leonard Fiddia, who had instructed her in hunting, trapping, fishing, and moonshining, were there, as was a newer friend, Gene Baro, a young writer and teacher at the University of Florida to whom she had loaned her house at Cross Creek. There were other friends from Gainesville, Jacksonville, Ocala, and other nearby towns. Some had driven over from St. Augustine, where a service had been conducted in the chapel of a funeral home by the Reverend Charles Seymour of Trinity Episcopal Church. Julia Scribner, a close friend and Marjorie's literary executor, had flown down from New York to attend both services.

Thirty years after the funeral, Norton Baskin, Marjorie's husband, still remembered the shock he had felt when he realized they were in the wrong cemetery. A few years before her death, the Baskins had attended the funeral of her friend Tom Glisson, and Marjorie, soothed by the bird chorus and the fragrance of the orange grove encircling the burial site, had told Norton, "I think I could find peace and rest here."

In his telephoned instructions to the funeral director, Norton had merely specified "the cemetery near Cross Creek," not realizing there was more than one.

"The service was nearly over," Norton recalled, "when I consoled myself that this cemetery was closer to Cross Creek and most of her Cross Creek friends were there." Then Phil May, Marjorie's attorney and their longtime friend, read the last paragraph from her book *Cross Creek*, in which she gave back her beloved spot to its original owners:

> *Who owns Cross Creek? The red-birds, I think, more than I. . . . And after I am dead, who am childless, the human ownership of grove and field and hammock is hypothetical. But a long line of red-birds and whippoorwills and blue-jays and ground doves will descend from the present owners of nests in the orange trees, and their claim will be less subject to dispute than that of human heirs.*

Houses, she said, can be owned, like nests, and fought for. But the land may only be used, not owned. We are merely tenants. "Cross Creek belongs to the wind and the rain, to the sun and the seasons . . . and beyond all, to time."

During the next weeks, Baskin anguished over the responsibility of planning an appropriate headstone for Marjorie's grave. Choosing the stone was not a problem. "She would have hated an ornate monument." He knew it must be plain and simple. But how to inscribe it? First, there was the difficulty of the names. For all her writing and business dealings she had used "Marjorie Kinnan Rawlings"—her maiden name plus her first husband's name. In her private and social life she had insisted on "Mrs. Norton Baskin" since their marriage twelve years earlier. But even more difficult than the names was the creation of an epitaph. "It was ironic," he recalled. "I felt like I was sharing the agony Marjorie had experienced as she constantly struggled to put the right words in the right place. In a few words I had to sum up the contribution she had made to the world during her fifty-seven years on it."

Marjorie Kinnan Rawlings's heritage included a mixture of predominantly Dutch, Scottish, Scotch-Irish, and English genes. One of the more colorful ancestors on her family tree was Dominie Everardus Bogardus, the first minister sent by the Dutch West India Company to head the Dutch Reformed Church in America. He arrived in New Amsterdam in the early seventeenth century in the company of the director of the colony, Governor Wouter (Walter) Van Triller. Records describe the dominie as large and strong with a "fine, broad open countenance," dark, piercing eyes, and a mouth "expressive of good humor." By all accounts he was an excellent speaker, a good shepherd, and possessed a powerful, persuasive personality.

The first church on Manhattan Island was a drafty barn of a building, and the dominie hatched a plot with the director to raise funds for a better structure for his parishioners to worship in. At a wedding celebration, after the guests had drunk enough wine to feel expansive, the two schemers passed around a subscription list. The rollicking guests tried to outdo each other in pledging funds for the new building as the dominie egged them on. When the sobered-up subscribers heartily repented the next day, they discovered there was no taking back their word. The dominie insisted they were obliged to pay what they had pledged, and a new stone church was built.

Dominie Bogardus married a pretty, aristocratic Dutch widow, Annetka Jans, who was said to be the granddaughter of William of Orange. Their first son, Wilhelm (William) Bogardus, was Marjorie's first American ancestor on her father's side. Annetka was as spirited as she was attractive. Soon after their marriage, she was accused by a disagreeable acquaintance of lifting her petticoats in an unseemly manner to display her shapely ankles. Indignant, Annetka took her case to court and proved the innocence of her behavior through the testimony of a blacksmith who had witnessed the scene. He supported Annetka's claim that she had only pulled up her skirts to save them from the mud. Annetka won her case and her accuser was ordered to retract her words publicly and to pay a fine to the poor.

The case received quite a bit of publicity, but not nearly as much as the claim by Annetka and her descendants that the land on which Trinity Church stands in New York City rightfully belonged to them. The claim arose from the fact that Annetka and her first husband had been granted sixty-two acres of land on lower Manhattan Island. When the British took over the island from the Dutch, they confirmed the ownership by Annetka and her husband. Later, however, Queen Anne granted some of this land to the Trinity Church Corporation. Following the Revolutionary War, Cornelius Bogardus laid claim to the same land that the church claimed.

After several skirmishes in which he destroyed part of the church's fence and the church officials destroyed part of his, the controversy subsided. But once again in 1830, the Bogardus heirs put forth their claims in action that occupied 130 pages of the Chancery Reports. The final opinion was against the heirs. Nevertheless, in 1925 a "society of heirs" tried again to wrest the property (or a multimillion dollar payment for it) from Trinity Church. Over the years, thousands of dollars and words have been expended concerning the Bogardus claim, but so far the church has triumphed, although it has never been able to establish a clear title to the land. Among the latter-day claimants was Marjorie Kinnan Rawlings, who gleefully supported the heirs.

Another ancestor, Mary Kinnan, exhibited great courage as well as literary talent. In May 1791, she was taken captive by a band of Shawnee Indians, who invaded her home in the valley of the Tygart River in what is now West Virginia. Mary watched helplessly as her child and her husband were scalped and killed. Then she was dragged along, by her captors, almost dead, to their village. There for four years she lived as their slave, performing the most menial labor and enduring scanty rations and frequent beatings. Through Indian traders she finally managed to get word to her brother, who helped her escape. Shortly after her rescue, she wrote a vivid account of her capture and servitude. This account, one of the few written by an Indian captive, reveals a talent for writing as well as Mary Kinnan's tenacity as a survivor. Other of Marjorie's paternal ancestors who were writers included a Methodist minister who published a work of philosophy and Marjorie's grandmother, Ethelinda Pearce Kinnan, who was a college teacher and a poet.

Ethelinda Pearce married a minister, the Reverend Asahel Simeon Kinnan, with whom she had eight children. Marjorie's father, Arthur Frank Kinnan, was their eldest child. After he graduated from Michigan State College, he served as principal of the high school at Fenton, Michigan, for four years. Here he met and married Ida May Traphagen, whose family owned a prosperous farm just outside the town of Holly, Michigan.

Ida Traphagen's ancestry also included Indian captives. Dutch Huguenots, they had settled in the early seventeenth century in the Wallkill River valley in New York in what is now Kingston, but originally was named Wiltwyck, meaning "wild Indian town." When Indians attacked the settlement and carried into captivity the wife and three children of Louis DuBois, he appealed to the settlers to help him in rescuing them and other captives. Leading thirty men, he trailed the Indians and, surprising them, managed to rescue the prisoners.

At Rhinebeck, east of Kingston on the other side of the Hudson River, a historic old stone building called Beekman Arms claimed to be the oldest hotel in America. The original stone portion of the building with its unusually thick walls of native fieldstone was built by William and Arent Traphagen in 1700 and remained in their possession until 1769. The inn was an important stopping place in the days when coaches were the only means of land transportation on the old Albany trail, and George Washington was one of its frequent guests.

The DuBois and Traphagen families were united by the marriage of Catherine DuBois and Abraham Traphagen in 1788. In the early nineteenth century the couple moved to Michigan. Their land, in Oakland County, was pretty much a wilderness, with the nearest trading post, Pontiac, a three-day trip in a two-wheeled cart drawn by oxen. Often the men had to blaze a trail with an ax, and a stockade had to be built around the farm to keep out marauding animals. The Traphagens' grandson, Abram or Abraham, married Francis Beardslee Osmun when he was twenty-five. Her father owned one thousand acres of land near Pontiac, and there is a street in the city of Pontiac named Osmun Street. When the first farmhouse that he built for his bride, near Holly, Michigan, burned, Abram built her a much larger one. It was this house and the farm and dairy connected with it that would become an important part of Marjorie's childhood experiences.

When Abram and Francis Traphagen's daughter, Ida, left the farm to marry Arthur Kinnan, the young couple moved to Big Springs, Texas, where Arthur had an offer to become superintendent of public schools. Ida Kinnan taught in the high school, and they lived in Big Springs for two years. In 1889, Arthur Kinnan obtained an appointment as a member of the Examining Corps of the U. S. Patent Office, and the Kinnans moved to Washington, D. C. Here Arthur rose by competitive examinations to the position of principal examiner in the Patent Office in charge of the Division of Electricity, an office he held until his death. In 1895, the year before Marjorie was born, he obtained his law degree from George Washington University. He also acquired a dairy farm on the outskirts of Washington, in the Rock Creek area of Maryland. It was his hobby and his retreat, although it was only ten miles from their home in the Brookland suburb of Washington. After she was grown, Marjorie remembered that this farm was where her father's "heart and mind lived."

Apparently a man of tremendous energy, Arthur Kinnan found time to participate in politics, campaigning vigorously for his favorite candidates. He strongly supported President McKinley. He formed a friendship with Robert La Follette, who served as a U.S. Congressman (1885–1891), governor of Wisconsin (1901–1905), and as U.S. Senator (1906–1925). He ran for president on the Progressive Party ticket in 1924, polling five million votes. This friendship grew to include the other members of the Kinnan and La Follette families and was to have an influence on Marjorie's future.

While her husband was rising in the patent office, managing his farm, and dabbling in politics, Ida Traphagen Kinnan was setting up a model household in the somewhat stuffy and formal atmosphere of turn-of-the-century Washington, D. C. Visitors never found a speck of dust, a limp curtain, or a spotted windowpane in her home. She joined the embroidery club and competed with the other members to see who could serve the daintiest morsels with the most artistic flair, while maintaining the illusion of its all being done with no effort on the part of the exhausted hostess.

Into this setting, on August 8, 1896, Marjorie was born at the tail end of the American Victorian period. Some of her features—the round cheeks, the tiny mouth, the blue eyes—never changed. But the light-colored hair would become a dark brown as she grew older, and the delicate peaches-and-cream complexion would fade a little as she aged.

A cherubic Dutch doll, she delighted her parents, grandparents, and numerous aunts and uncles. When Marjorie was two, her father wrote to his mother that she was growing sweeter and prettier every day and that she was a "little mimic" who attracted the attention of total strangers in the street. While Ida visited relatives in the spring of 1899, Arthur delighted in caring for his little daughter, who "stuck to him like a burr." He wrote Ida, "She is the joy of my life. I never knew I had so much love in my heart." His nickname for her, Peaches, was adopted by her adoring aunts. In later years, Marjorie tried to shake it off but never quite succeeded.

One of the things Marjorie loved best was to go with her father to visit the dairy farm. It was here that he shared with his daughter his appreciation and love of the land, its creatures, and every growing thing. One day when Marjorie found him alone, talking while working at his planting, he explained to her that he was talking with "the maker" of both them and the plants.

He was creative and inventive in his farming and dairy projects. For the U. S. Department of Agriculture, he conducted experiments with the inoculation of seeds, rotation of crops, and the planting of alfalfa to enrich depleted land. He installed a hydraulic pump to carry water uphill to the dairy barn from an ice cold spring. He began the farm with ordinary grade cattle; as he could afford it, he bought registered cows and a registered Holstein bull named "De Kalb Second's Paul De Kalb No. 2's Ormsby." When calves were born eligible for registration, Marjorie was allowed to help draw in the calves' markings on the diagrams in the registration charts.

Sunday afternoons the family went driving in a two-seated surrey with a fringe on top, pulled by Dan, one of the farm horses. Summers they lived in a cluster of tents on the farm in a flowering locust grove—to the dismay of Ida and the joy of Marjorie. The large sleeping tent had a wooden floor and partitions. There was also a dining tent, a cooking tent, and a country outhouse. Mosquito netting protected the sleepers or diners in the tents while still allowing the air to circulate.

Only three strands of barbed wire and a stile separated the campers from the dairy herd. Sometimes the big bull broke loose and the cry "De Kalb is loose!" went up as he rampaged across the pasture, creating excitement and occasional nightmares for the young girl. Marjorie was lulled to sleep at night by the sounds of the cows chewing their cuds, snuffling over the fence, or dropping down heavily to rest.

She enjoyed driving with her father in a smaller buggy behind Old Dan to Frederick, Maryland, to buy mules or cattle. But rambling with him along the brook that ran through the woods and sharing his dream of building a house beside the brook was even better. Her father taught her his extensive animal lore and passed on to her his understanding of and love for birds. In the evenings, walking home from the station, when he reached the foot of their hill he began a special birdlike whistle that was a signal to Marjorie, who raced down the hill to meet him.

When Marjorie was four, a second child, Arthur Houston, was born to the Kinnans, and from the beginning she considered him to be "hers." Her attitude toward her little brother was always warm, loving, and more than a little maternalistic—even when he became a tall, middle-aged man. He, too, called her Peaches, and as soon as he could toddle, she shared the pleasures of the farm with Artie, as he was called. Together they learned to swim in Rock Creek and tried to catch the tiny fish in it. They rode bareback on the patient work horses and spent long hours exploring the wooded area surrounding the crops.

The second farm in Marjorie's childhood was her maternal grandparents' Michigan farm. Here, on two hundred acres, Abe and Fanny Traphagen raised navy beans, wheat, and apples as their cash crops. In addition, they raised bountiful crops of vegetables for home use. The smokehouse was always filled with choice hams and sausages, and behind it lay beehives and a watermelon patch, where the only rules were that greedy grandchildren should learn to identify the ripe melons and not waste the crop by cutting green ones and that they should not make themselves sick by overeating.

The order and lavishness of this farm made an impression on Marjorie that remained with her all her life. When she was forty-two she visited Michigan again and wrote an article for the Centennial Anniversary Edition of the Holly *Herald*, describing in vivid detail her memories of life on the Traphagen farm. The barns were clean enough for humans to live in. The woodshed held neatly ordered stacks of kindling and furnace wood. Storerooms and the cellar held barrels of hickory nuts and apples, shelves of canned fruit and vegetables, jams and jellies and crocks of pickled pork, honey, brandied peaches, apple butter, and various relishes. Tempting odors came from cookie jars filled with molasses, sugar, and hickory-nut cookies; and mingling with the smells were platters of raspberry tarts and cakes on high-stemmed, covered glass plates.

The noon meal, which was gargantuan, was followed by a "light" supper, although the lightest might include pickled pork fried to golden crispness, new potatoes with milk gravy, poached eggs, the leftover noon meats of chicken, roast lamb, pot roast of beef, baked beans, salt-rising bread—and hot biscuits, for fear the meal should seem too casual. The table also included pickles, jams, jellies, relishes, and an assortment of cakes: pound cake, jelly roll, nut cake, chocolate layer cake.

As she savored the eggs she herself had gathered in the sweet-smelling hayloft and the roasting ears picked only minutes before they appeared on the dinner table, Marjorie learned to appreciate the taste of truly fresh food. It was only after she acquired her own superb Jersey cow at Cross Creek that she again tasted cream and butter to equal that of her grandparents' farm. As an adult, Marjorie became a noted cook and author of a best-selling cookbook. And even when, in the interest of saving her time for her writing, she turned over meal preparation to her household help, she never gave up making jams and jellies, an art she considered truly creative.

These early memories would be drawn on in her last novel, *The Sojourner*, which is set on a northern farm. The fact that the farm was almost totally self-sustaining was only appreciated much later when she came to realize that the stock were fed entirely by feed grown on the place. There were oats for the plow horses, corn and fodder for cows and hogs and chickens, silage for winter use. Wood for fuel and warmth came from the timbered forty acres, and the only items that had to be purchased for human consumption were coffee, tea, sugar, and spices.

In *Cross Creek*, in the chapter titled "The Evolution of Comfort," Marjorie gave an almost lyrical description of the outhouse on her grandparents' farm. It was papered with beautiful colored pictures of reigning queens:

> *Alexandra was magnificent. Wilhelmina was demure and very pretty in pale pink with a pearl and diamond crown. I cannot look today at the news pictures of the stout housewife in tweeds on a bicycle and believe that it is the same woman. The queen of Norway I recall as rather austere, the queen of Italy as blackly horselike. But all were queens, in full color, in décolleté and jewelled diadems. The building had a door with crescent windows and it stood discreetly behind a hickory tree and was reached by a high trim boardwalk bordered with marigolds.*

In her article for the Holly *Herald*, Marjorie called an apple orchard the "most beautiful and satisfying source of income a man can possess, after an orange grove." She never forgot the loveliness of the pale apple blossoms that later became the heavy, various-colored fruit—red Baldwins, pink-stained snow apples, sweet as honey, wax green greenings, golden sheep's nose, banana apples, and golden russets. The orchard was always for her a thing of grace and beauty, even in winter when the "bare gray trunks and limbs were as lovely as a Japanese drawing" against the snowy fields. A special treat was to jog along in the wagon with her grandfather, taking a load of apples to market in Flint on crisp October days, while he stirred her childish imagination with tales of Indians and Gypsies in the old Michigan days.

Marjorie loved her plump, laughing mischievous grandmother with the bottomless cookie jars, but she had a special feeling for her gaunt, taciturn grandfather, who resembled another Abe—Lincoln. He haunted her all of her life because she felt she had not understood him. As early as her college days she tried to express her feelings about him in a poem called "Grandsire." It ended:

> *where bronzed wheat and emerald corn make tapestries*
> *Where Grandsire bade the land bring forth, his ancient*
> *triumph is.*
> *when moonlight lies on blossoming apple trees,*
> *The scented night, the fertile earth, are still, past dying, his.*

Toward the end of her life, in *The Sojourner*, she would again pay tribute to her grandfather by basing her protagonist on him.

As Arthur Senior became more affluent, he took the family to Maine for summer vacations. They stayed at Harpwell Center and he sometimes raced his little catboat, named *The Marjorie*, at Bar Harbor, once or twice winning races with it. A few months before she died, Marjorie described in a letter to her friend Martin Dibner an incident that had occurred during one of these summer vacations. One afternoon, watching her father moor the boat and row ashore in a dinghy, Marjorie cried out to join him. It was low tide, so he rowed the dinghy in by the steps of the wharf, and her mother took her as far down the steps as possible and dropped her into her father's arms. Something was wrong with the balance, and although Arthur cut his hands badly on barnacles trying to hold the dinghy close to the steps, it overturned. Since the day had been stormy, Arthur was in heavy oilskins and rubber boots, but he said quietly, "Put your arms around my neck." She did so, clinging to him without fear until they were rescued and rowed to shore. Then she recalled:

> [B]efore I was stripped and dressed in my nighty, to be given
> supper in bed, I had an egg-nog with something strong and

pungent in it, and perhaps that is why to this day I like strong and pungent drink. For it was part of safety, and although for days I heard people speak of our danger, I knew there had never been any danger at all.

The ocean made a lasting impression on the sensitive young girl, and in the last year of her life she still remembered the placid cove at Harpswell Center and the great rocks and boulders below the pine forest where the sea roared in with spray and tumult and with a satisfying angry sound. She described to Dibner her memory of bathing in ocean water so cold that it burned, in great "cover-all bathing suits" and long black stockings, on pebbles that hurt her feet. At low tide they walked across the flats to an island where they picked wild raspberries. And from the same flats they dug clams whose smell mingled with that of the grayish mud. They all picked enormous blueberries and ate them two or three times a day with thick yellow cream, and there were lobster roasts, with the sweet lobster smell mixed in the steam with clam juice and fresh garden corn.

One day they went to a fair at Harpswell Center, where the six-year-old Marjorie was impressed with the "rows and rows of glittering jellies and prize fruits and vegetables." But above all she admired a hand-pieced quilt with sunrays in it, "surely the most beautiful thing ever made by the hand of woman."

Her ability to respond intensely to nature with all of her senses was extraordinary from a very early age. When she was about ten, she had an experience on a glorious April day that she never forgot:

I was standing under a tree. The sun shone through the leaves and a soft breeze caused the light and shadow around me to shift and change. There was a stillness . . . and with it came a feeling of ecstasy and regret—a lifting sensation but tinged with sadness. It was a definite premonition of maturity.

She knew that someday, somehow, she would have to find an outlet to use that experience and that feeling. Years later she found a way to use it in *The Yearling*.

During her adult life, Marjorie's acquaintances were often surprised by seeming contradictions in her personality. Aside from the influence of her heredity, the seeds of her duality of personality can be found in the environment in which she grew to maturity. On the two farms she lived a life that was free, natural, and unhampered by formal behavior. But Ida Kinnan, like other mothers of the period, wanted her daughter to be a little lady, and in the city, she dressed Marjorie in ruffles and frills and enforced, as far as she was able, ladylike behavior. Recalling those fancy outfits and stilted manners, Marjorie remembered she felt herself "a nasty little hypocrite," although she endured them for the sake of peace. Acquaintances, including Marjorie's college friends and Norton Baskin, remembered Ida Kinnan as elegant and strict, but also as a devoted mother. While she learned her mother's housekeeping skills and eventually surpassed her in cooking ability, Marjorie rejected the intense perfectionism that kept Ida from enjoying her own parties and sent her to bed with sick headaches after they were over. Marjorie expressed this rebellion in an article written years later, which she titled, "I Sing as I Cook." She also expressed it in her style of entertaining, which was warm and informal.

Nevertheless, her mother's influence in matters of behavior was never to be shaken off entirely and sometimes surfaced in later years to contrast oddly with the free spirit that Marjorie wanted to be. Her sometimes painfully sensitive conscience, too, was developed, and perhaps overly developed, as a child. She attended services at the Baptist church with her parents, and although she later rejected organized religion, she was so conscientious that she was often tormented by what she thought were sins of omission or commission on her part.

The Edwardian period (1901–1910, during the reign of Edward VII) was a time when things as well as people were often not what they seemed. Seashells, toothpicks, porcelain, hair, and other objects were twisted and forced into strange pictures, gaudy vases, unnatural animals, and ugly bracelets. Food, too, came in many disguises. One of Ida's specialities was a cake that resembled a watermelon, presented at Marjorie's fifth birthday party. It was pink inside with chocolate blobs for seeds and iced with a delicate green frosting.

It turned out to be a memorable party in other ways, as Marjorie observed in *Cross Creek Cookery*. All the members of her kindergarten class and some additional juvenile neighbors were invited. Perhaps to teach generosity, her parents decided that instead of bringing gifts, each child should receive one. The tissue-wrapped presents were tied with silk ribbons to the limbs of one of Arthur Kinnan's imported French pear trees, which had slender branches within reach of the small-sized guests. After games were played on the lawn, the children were invited to approach the tree one by one and pluck a gift from it. Instead, they rushed pell mell to the tree in a pack and literally tore it limb from limb. Order was restored only by threats that ice cream and watermelon cake would be served only to those behaving in a decorous manner.

From her early years, Marjorie showed a strong preference for the company of males over females. This natural inclination was reinforced by experiences with a neighboring playmate, who was three years older than Marjorie. Sarah Pretty belonged to a glamorous family, and one of her older sisters impressed Marjorie by learning to faint in an amateur play. Trying to imitate her (falling straight backward onto a hard floor), Marjorie almost knocked herself out. One day borrowing her big sister's theatrical paints, Sarah made up herself and tag-along Marjorie, telling her, "We shall both become actresses. Of course I shall be much better than you." The adoring Marjorie accepted both statements as being right and true. The only bit of superiority Marjorie was allowed to feel by Sarah was when they would begin to play paper dolls, and Sarah would say to her much more imaginative playmate, "Now start the story. . . ."

Once Sarah tied Marjorie to a tree and left her for hours, and on another occasion she beat Marjorie's head against a chest of drawers in a fit of anger. But this physical abuse did not appear to hurt Marjorie nearly so much as an occasion when she felt herself emotionally betrayed. Sarah's paper dolls came from elegant magazines sent to her by an older sister who was a fashion designer. Marjorie's came from ordinary women's magazines. So one day, when Sarah offered to trade paper dolls, Marjorie was thrilled that her adored Sarah cared enough for her to make this generous offer.

When the exchange was completed, Sarah laughed fiendishly and pulled out a brand new super elegant set of paper dolls that her sister had sent, gloating that now she had Marjorie's (fairly new) paper dolls and her superior ones while Marjorie had only one worn set. Well past fifty, Marjorie remembered the incident vividly and described it to her friend, Bee McNeil, telling her that she had decided that Sarah Pretty was to be the secret name of one of her cats—one that was particularly self-centered and conniving. Although this childhood incident was a seemingly minor revelation out of the many that led Marjorie to use the theme of betrayal as a dominant motif in her writing, it was an indelible one.

A happier memory remained with her from about the same time. When she was seven, her first "true love," Jimmy Monahan, gave her his precious cat's eye taw while they were playing marbles. She realized how much he valued the marble as his shooter and was impressed by his generosity. This time there were no tricks.

Marjorie's quick imagination and dramatic flair combined to make her the source for dramatic entertainment in her neighborhood. After the strenuous running games in the long summer twilights, when the red-glass gas lamps had been lit all along their street, the neighborhood children gathered around her on the cool steps of the Baptist church. A runner was sent up the street to call to the stragglers, "Marjorie's going to tell stories!" and she, with a smug sense of being in control, refused to begin until everyone was there.

Her one rule in selecting her audience was that they all be *boys*, Marjorie told Maxwell Perkins. No girls were allowed to listen to her tall tales. She was celebrated among her fans for her imitation of a wolf howl, but there was one rather sensitive young boy named Jimmy who shrieked every time he heard it. Consequently, she would preface certain stories by saying sternly, "You'll have to take Jimmy home now—there's going to be a wolf in the next one."

By the time she was six, Marjorie had learned to write well enough to compose verses on brown wrapping paper with a stubby pencil. They were all dedicated to her father. Once when she rhymed "candy" with "auntie," her father told her she must have a little poetic license. Thinking it was something she would have to purchase at the post office, she began saving her pennies.

"The Bluebirds," a poem written when she was in the first grade, won compliments from her teacher. Thereafter, whenever there were guests at home, she was called upon to read it aloud. The applause and compliments that followed the readings convinced her that she had found her vocation. Reading it again years later, Marjorie concluded that their pleasure in this story reflected the "low minds" of the adults. The story ended, "Miss Bluebird and Mr. Bluebird were married. They were very happy. The next day to their great surprise there were four little bluebirds in the nest."

Her parents encouraged both her precocious reading and her writing efforts. Women's suffrage and more freedom for women in general were popular themes of the day, and Ida Kinnan, who had enjoyed a career as a teacher before the birth of her children, wanted her daughter to have every opportunity to develop her talents. When Marjorie got a glazed look of concentration, her mother would say, "If you have an inspiration, you may go and write." Naturally Marjorie, the little actress, soon learned this was an easy way to get out of dusting furniture and drying dishes. As an adult, she sometimes found herself using the same technique for avoiding housework.

Marjorie's second writing success came at the age of eleven when she won a two-dollar prize for a story on the Sunday children's page of the Washington *Post*. Other prizes followed for her literary contributions to the *Post*, including a gloomy poem intended to honor James Whitcomb Riley. For her early writings, she used the pen name "Felicity."

Marjorie and Arthur Junior attended Western High School in Washington, and in her junior year Marjorie served as assistant editor of the high school magazine. The same year she entered a child authorship contest sponsored by *McCall's* magazine and her short story won second prize, seventy-five dollars. Her entry, "The Reincarnation of Miss Hetty," was published in the August 1912 issue of *McCall's*. The judges criticized her overuse of adverbs and clichés and questioned her attempts at dialect: "Me lives at orphan 'sylum"; "Hain't got any folkses"; and "He likes yer—he's awaggin' of his tail!" But they praised her nature description:

in Miss Hetty's prim, old-fashioned garden, with its wealth
of sweetness, the bees droned busily, the steady hum and buzz
the only sound that broke the quiet, save when now and then
a wood-thrush called to his mate from the lilac bush.

Marjorie grew up between the time of the Spanish-American War and World War I. Civil War veterans still held annual meetings and parades in the nation's capital. By the time she entered her teens, automobiles shared the streets with horse-drawn carriages, but the carriages were still considered superior transportation by many to the noisy, smelly, undependable horseless machines. However, everyone in Washington agreed in praising the grand new railroad station that was completed in 1909. Aerial navigation was an exciting topic for conversation, but some doubted whether it was a good thing for nations to be brought so close together by this swift means of travel. After the passengers and crew of the S. S. *Republic* were saved in the first sea rescue using radio, there was much conjecture about the future of this invention. But the first regular radio broadcasts wouldn't begin until 1920, and by that time Marjorie was a college graduate and married woman.

The reappearance of Halley's comet in 1910 aroused some superstition and fear of dire events to follow. And between 1908 and 1912, Washington, D.C., residents, as well as the rest of the world, focused their attention on the North and South Poles as various explorers raced to be the first to reach these remote and forbidding destinations.

Living in the nation's capital and having a father who was interested in politics undoubtedly made the Kinnan children unusually aware of current events. Although it was fashionable to laugh at the boisterous behavior of President Theodore Roosevelt and to complain of Teddy's cocksure ways and of the "din" he made, he was a constant source of interest. Under Roosevelt's leadership the United States came to realize its position and responsibility as a world power. A treaty was signed with Panama to allow the United States to build the Panama Canal to connect the Atlantic and Pacific oceans; a settlement of the disputed boundary between Alaska and

Canada was reached; and Russian and Japanese delegates met at Portsmouth, New Hampshire, and agreed on peace plans to end the Russo-Japanese War.

Determined to give farmers and workingmen "a square deal," Roosevelt fought for "trust-busting" reforms to stop the monopolies that were stifling free competition. Railroads were reformed and the Standard Oil trust was busted. The nation was being made conscious of the need for conservation of its natural resources.

Roosevet's daughter Alice ruled Washington society and was in her glory while Marjorie was in high school. To the young girl, she was a glamorous figure, defying the stuffy rules of polite society, as women began to clamor for the right to vote. This became the subject of meetings, marches, occasional violence and endless debate, and was constantly in newspaper headlines. There was a marked increase in the appearance of women who carried gold and silver cigarette cases and were seen smoking in public places. Men wore frock coats and tall silk hats, while the women went from enormous wide-brimmed hats and flaring gored skirts that swept the streets to hobble skirts that endangered their balance. Ostensibly, cosmetics were still taboo (but were nevertheless discreetly used).

Although William Howard Taft was dubbed Teddy Roosevelt's "crown prince" and was his hand-picked successor, he lacked the leadership and charisma of his friend. Progressives considered him weak and conservative. During his term a constitutional amendment was approved by the states permitting Congress to levy an income tax. Another amendment provided that the people (instead of state legislatures) should elect U. S. Senators. In 1912 the loss of the supposedly unsinkable *Titanic* shook Americans' faith in any kind of guarantee of safety. As the stories of bravery and tragedy trickled in, the news of the sinking overshadowed every gathering in Washington for weeks. Enrico Caruso and Lillian Russell were among the most popular entertainers of the time. And Henry Ford was mass-producing about one thousand flivvers a day.

In 1913 a personal tragedy struck the Kinnan family and made them oblivious for a time to whatever else might be happening in the world. Arthur Kinnan became ill and died from a kidney infection.

He had never been able to build his dream house by the brook on the Maryland farm. The loss of her adored father was the first deep tragedy and the greatest betrayal in Marjorie's young life. She remembered always the "great and terrible stillness" that seemed to cover the earth on the day he died.

CHAPTER · 2

Marjorie
Kin-NAN

Marjorie was a senior in high school when her father died. Among her classmates were children of U. S. representatives and senators, one of President Taft's nephews, and Bob and Phil La Follette, sons of her father's friend, Senator La Follette. Marjorie later said that "Battling Bob" La Follette, a liberal politician who kept Wisconsin in the headlines, made her family "Wisconscious." Before he died, Arthur Kinnan had planned to send both his children to the University of Wisconsin. Consequently, as soon as Marjorie graduated from high school, Ida Kinnan decided to move to Madison, as she too was convinced that Marjorie and Arthur could get good college training at the university there, which had an enrollment of about four thousand students. So that summer the small family—mother, sister, brother—settled into a comfortable apartment by Lake Mendota near the campus.

In September 1914 Marjorie entered the University of Wisconsin as an English major. During registration another freshman, Beatrice Humiston, noticed a "cute" girl in a brown suit, white gloves, and high heels. Observing her blue eyes, dark brown hair, and rosy cheeks, Beatrice thought, "This is the way a girl ought to look." She also had a premonition that she was seeing someone "special."

Later the two girls met at tryouts for Red Dominos, the women's drama club. Both made it into the club, and they began a lifelong friendship. Marjorie found a soulmate in Bee, who as a child had put worms in a robin's nest to help the robin parents with their feeding chores. In addition to being stage struck, they shared a delight in animals, flowers, books, writing, and having fun. Both were attractive and popular. The war in Europe seemed very far away during their first two college years, and the days were crammed with new adventures, with laughter always lurking just below the surface of the most solemn events.

On an assignment to judge a high school declamatory contest, they found hilarity in being assigned to the "saloon suite" of their tiny hotel. At Wisconsin the men students drank beer, smoked, and swore, but ostensibly the women students did not. Their behavior was carefully monitored, and a young woman who wore lipstick was likely to be "spoken to" by the dean of women. A young lady did not listen to (much less tell) risqué stories. Once Bee and Marjorie found themselves trapped in the back seat of a car with Harold, who was known as a "sissy" whose mother made him do embroidery. When Harold began telling them naughty stories, they were shocked. Bee hung out the window, looking at the tires, and left the dauntless Marjorie to cope with the situation. The incident became more grist for their perpetually turning mirth mill, which ground the foibles and quirks of professors, their wives, fellow students, and above all, themselves, into humorous anecdotes.

Marjorie and Bee appeared in a number of plays together. One of these was 'Op-O-Me Thumb, a one act play, in which Bee played the lead and Marjorie played a maid. On the same program, in another one-act play, was Freddy Bickel, who later transformed into the actor Fredric March. Marjorie also appeared as a maid, named Tweeny, in J. M. Barrie's The Admirable Crichton, and she and Bee together made Alfred Kreymborg's whimsical Lima Beans famous on campus. In her junior year Marjorie appeared as Pierrot in a Union Vodvil performance, looking captivating in her ruffled costume with short skirt that revealed her attractive legs.

Gertrude Johnson, the speech and drama coach at the University of Wisconsin, was noted for her excellence as a teacher and for her temperamental outbursts. As one former student put it, "She lashed her tail at every little thing." She was middle-aged and unmarried and teaching drama was her life. She appreciated talent and dedication. Recognizing the sincere devotion of Marjorie and Bee to the stage, she encouraged them at the same time she intimidated them. Under her direction, both young women wrote successful plays. Marjorie's was a pantomime fantasy called *Into the Nowhere*, which a classmate set to music. It was popular on the Wisconsin campus, and was also performed by drama groups at other colleges and universities. Marjorie and Bee each formed enduring friendships with Gertrude Johnson.

In her classes, Marjorie politely but firmly corrected her professors, "It's not KIN-nan; it's Kin-NAN, please," until they got it right. She was a bright, articulate student, who did her share of "bucking," as studying was called. She shone particularly brightly in her literature and creative writing classes. Languages came easily to her, and she found learning Latin, German, and French "easy as pie." She even wrote some poetry in French.

In 1916 she received the school's Sophomore Honors, which was an award given as "an incentive to continued achievement." And in recognition of her outstanding scholastic record she was one of only fifteen women elected to Mortar Board, an honor society. In her junior year she was elected to Phi Beta Kappa.

Marjorie studied writing under William Ellery Leonard, whose abilities as an educator, poet, translator, and critic were significant enough to gain him a listing in the *Encyclopaedia Britannica*. Leonard recognized Marjorie's talent and encouraged her, especially in writing poetry. Eventually one of her college poems, "The Monastery," was published in an anthology called *Poets of the Future*. Some of her poems, such as that one, showed the influence of her studies of Robert Browning's dramatic monologues and of English Renaissance and seventeenth-century poets. Others reflected her own unique humorous streak.

After she had her tonsils removed, she wrote a poem called "The Miracle," in which a nurse brings a tonsillectomy patient a newborn baby, just as the patient struggles up to consciousness from the anesthetic. The surprised young woman accepts the baby as a "miracle," until a distraught intern dashes in crying to the nurse:

> *My God! My God! What have you done!*
> *The infant here? This girl's a tonsil case!*
> *It goes to Mrs. B____ in forty-one!*

During her junior and senior years Marjorie held several positions on the staff of *The Badger*, the school yearbook, serving on the "satire board," as woman's editor, and as a special feature editor. The praise of her teachers and her success in all of her literary endeavors in college confirmed the expectation she had formed early in childhood that she would become a famous writer.

As an associate editor of the Wisconsin *Literary Magazine*, commonly known as the *Lit*, she worked with an unusually talented group of students, including Ernest L. Meyer, who became a successful journalist, and Esther Forbes, who later won a Pulitzer Prize and a Newberry Medal for her writing. Also on the *Lit* staff was an attractive young man from Rochester, New York, named Charles Rawlings. His blond good looks and off-hand charm caught the attention of many of the women students. He had a love of the sea and of boats and a flair for writing about them.

The *Lit* staff often worked late into the night, and after midnight "lunches" they sometimes spent the hours until dawn talking about literature, life, love, and the future. Marjorie wrote editorials, articles, short stories, poems, and book reviews for the *Lit*.

When Vachel Lindsay visited the campus, she interviewed him and wrote an editorial praising poetry as "food for the soul." She urged her readers who thought they didn't care for poetry to begin with Vachel Lindsay and to try other moderns. "Read them aloud," she urged. "Read them in different moods . . . and see if it [poetry] doesn't satisfy something that beer or canoeing won't touch. Expand your poetry reading as widely and as fast as you can. See if your soul doesn't grow. Just see!"

As a student, Marjorie was slender, well-dressed, witty, pretty, and outgoing. She formed lasting friendships with men and women. She also attracted men who were interested in dating her and in "fussing," the slang predecessor of "necking," "petting," and "making out." Picnics, canoeing, dances, parties, all-night literary talk sessions, and writing and drama activities crammed her days and her nights. Neither she nor her fellow *Lit* editor, Chuck Rawlings, was interested in becoming serious about anyone. He too had a busy social life and liked to spend his leisure moments on the lake. Their mutual interest in writing and their appreciation for each other's talent drew them together. Youth, propinquity, and a strong romantic streak in each of them led to an increasing emotional bond. His affectionate nickname for her was Skinny. Gradually he came to be recognized as her "beau" by other students, and he soon began to have an influence on her behavior and on her thinking.

Although she belonged to the Kappa Alpha Theta sorority, Marjorie's feelings about these exclusive clubs were mixed. When the Thetas pledged themselves to earn five dollars each toward new furniture for the Theta house, Marjorie wrote a short poem of four lines and sold it to a magazine to earn her five-dollar contribution. But later she was active in a group that rebelled against "snobbish" Greek letter societies. She worked actively with the group until the last minute when she would have had to turn in her pin. Then, at the persuasion of Chuck Rawlings, who warned her not to "socially blight" herself, she withdrew from the rebel group in great distress of mind and floods of tears, and remained in the sorority.

Chuck himself was quite fond of the fraternity atmosphere. He was an avid bridge player, who had "no respect" for anyone who did not play the game well, so it was probably he who taught Marjorie to play.

During Marjorie's four years at Wisconsin, as the war in Europe escalated, military activities became increasingly a part of the school's curriculum. Freshmen and sophomores performed competitive drills, and a military band was formed to discover and develop musical talent for the armed forces. To give its members experience in public performances, the band gave Sunday afternoon concerts on the campus.

When the United States declared war on Germany on April 6, 1917, three hundred male students immediately withdrew from their academic courses at Wisconsin and entered a course of intensive military training set up by the university to prepare them to receive commissions in the army. Many promising students left the campus to join the war. Among them went Freddy Bickel, who dropped out of the spring play for which he and Bee and Marjorie were rehearsing, to go to officers' training camp. Another student, Art Nielsen, also left the university. In later years he remembered his alma mater generously by giving it indoor tennis courts, after he had made a fortune in television program rating.

The students' vocabularies soon included new words and phrases such as *doughboy, mustard gas, hun, boche, khaki, puttees, shell shock, shrapnel, dogfight, cooties, Big Bertha, no man's land,* and *Zeppelin.* Everyone tried to "hooverize"; that is, to help the war effort by following U. S. Food Administration Bureau director Herbert Hoover's advice to be frugal. Meatless days, wheatless days, and eggless days were observed. The country's manufacturing energy was directed toward war needs, and new clothes were frowned upon. The students sang sad songs like "Keep the Home Fires Burning"; chin-up songs like "Pack up Your Troubles in Your Old Kit Bag"; and funny songs like "Tillie's Tilling Beans for Belgium" and one beginning "Today is Tuesday, Tuesday beans" and ending "And all the German mothers, we wish the same to you." A popular comedy at the Grand Theater in Madison was *Kicking the Germ out of Germany.* A community sing in honor of General Pershing's birthday was held in Madison, and a patriotic parade of fifteen thousand soldiers took one and a half hours to pass.

The mood on campus became darker as the war ground on and the casualty lists lengthened. The sickening reality that many of their classmates were gone forever or maimed for life was brought home to the students by the long Honor Roll in the *Badger* of 1918. For the remaining students, the lighthearted spirit of their earlier college days had vanished. Marjorie wrote her senior English thesis on paganism in English poetry, and like the other students scanned the daily Madison papers for news of their classmates who were in the war.

But youth and the excitement of beginning what she called "the fight of life" combined with spring and being in love made it impossible to mope. Bee looked up from her studying one warm day in May toward the end of the semester to see Marjorie coming into the library looking slim and pretty, happy and confident and stylish in a dress of burnt orange that set off her naturally high color. She was glowing with happy plans for her day and for her future. In the afternoon she would go swimming in Lake Mendota from the Chi Psi pier with Chuck and in the evening she would sit under a tree at the outdoor theater, waiting for her cues in the rehearsal for the senior play.

Marjorie seemed to have every reason to be pleased with herself and her prospects. She had made an enviable record in college, not only scholastically, but also in her extracurricular activities. And she had made many friends and achieved recognition by being chosen to appear in the *Badger's* portfolio of "Representative Women." This selection was based on: "Spirit—that indescribable something . . . which makes her live and glow"; "Competency—proving to be adequate, capable, fitting in where most needed"; and "Womanliness —"the power to stand for the best" and having proved to have "a deep and lasting personality." Her success in dramatic activities was gratifying, but her achievements in all of her writing efforts was even more so, for they seemed to point to a successful career as a writer.

The most important source of her happiness that spring was her understanding with Chuck that, when circumstances permitted, they would be married. "No woman," Marjorie would say, "was ever more in love than I." They had much in common. Chuck was as intellectual as Marjorie, as well-read, as articulate. He took delight in questioning any girl companion, usually to her dismay, with "Have you read . . . ?" And he was as intolerant of the halfhearted reader as he was of the indifferent bridge player. He was as fond of poetry as Marjorie and as knowledgeable about it. With his regular features, sturdy build, and high color, he was easily one of the three or four handsomest men on the campus, and many a woman student would gladly have changed places with Marjorie. When Chuck broke his leg in a car accident, Marjorie was deeply concerned until he was well on the way to mending, although she confided in Bee that she "secretly" felt a sense of relief that his condition would at least delay his entry into the service.

Their class was graduated in the spring of 1918 with as little pomp and circumstance as possible, and Chuck felt that in spite of a "twisty knee" he had to get into the war. He spent the summer at home in Rochester trying to get a commission in the army. Despite the influence of family friends and business associates of his father, who was part owner of a shoe factory, the commission did not come through. And Chuck was enrolled—with some feeling of chagrin—as a buck private. After basic training, he was scheduled to be stationed at Camp Upton on Long Island.

Many-paged love letters filled with physical longing for each other traveled daily between Rochester and Madison, where Marjorie was preparing to begin a career in the writing world of New York City. Marjorie told him, "You *are* all of my body and thought. I don't need to tell you, but I love to say it to you, knowing you want to hear it," and she thanked him for his "golden" love letters. He wrote to her:

> *Sweetheart, I would rather have you to-night, close to me and loving me closely—be able to kiss you, tenderly, and feel your cool hand in mine, than live. With my arms out-stretched and grieving in their desire, I want you,* want *you,* want *you to love. I'm like a mad spendthrift that is mad to throw his gold. I crave to spend my moments of hearing your voice in my ears, your hand in mine, spend my flesh against yours. . . .*

and another letter ended:

> *I wonder just how cool and wonderful your lips are to-night. I would give most anything . . . to gather you in and kiss you once; slowly and caressingly, like I think the foundation of our love really is. I love you, dear, dear sweetheart; slowly and surely and deeply. Good night. May all the stars guard you from harm.*

Marjorie's mother, Ida, accompanied her to New York to help her find suitable living quarters and to see her settled in a respectable job. En route to New York, Marjorie and Ida went by way of Rochester to visit the Rawlings family. Chuck, who loved his hometown and had a warm, close relationship with his family, was delighted to be able to show them to Marjorie and Marjorie to them. His parents, who had three sons but no daughters, were charmed with Marjorie. Charles Rawlings, Senior, immediately called her "daughter" and referred to her as "our wonder girl." Later, his letters were signed "Daddy." Although a bit more reserved, Mrs. Rawlings also expressed affection for her eldest son's future bride and signed her letters "Mother Rawlings."

Ida Kinnan was considerably less enthusiastic about the engagement. She thought Marjorie too young to marry and had doubts that Chuck would become a husband who could support a wife at the level to which she held ambitions for her daughter. Marjorie told Chuck that her mother made some "horrid comment" every time his name was mentioned, that she called him a fool, and that she complained, "This Chuck business makes me tired." Although her mother kept her "sick at heart" with such comments, Marjorie told him she knew her mother worshiped her "or rather the part of me that can do creditable things."

In spite of their arguments over Chuck, Marjorie and her mother enjoyed seeing the sights of New York together and taking in movies and plays. For six dollars a week, they found a cozy little single room for Marjorie with kitchen privileges, in an apartment on Morningside Drive. The landlady assured Mrs. Kinnan that although the girls had to entertain their gentlemen callers in their rooms, it was all perfectly proper, as everyone was going back and forth in the hall constantly.

Marjorie's high spirits drooped a little as finding a job to her liking proved difficult. Proofreading jobs that paid $18.00 a week were available, but she felt she had to make at least $25.00 a week to live decently in such an expensive city. Her mother began to urge her to give up the struggle and come home to Madison with her, but Marjorie had no intention of being defeated by the big city. Reluctantly Ida Kinnan helped Marjorie settle in the Morningside apartment and returned to Madison, leaving her daughter still jobless, but with $60.00 to tide her over until she found employment.

On her job-seeking rounds, Marjorie carried a briefcase filled with her short stories, poems, and copies of her editorials and book reviews that had been printed in the Wisconsin *Lit*. She learned to know the city well as she rode subways and elevateds uptown, downtown, and crosstown. One day a thief snatched her new purse with the $60.00. But, as Marjorie afterward said wryly, "He was discerning enough to ignore the briefcase."

Alone, jobless, and flat broke, Marjorie walked from upper New York to the offices of the *New Republic* on West 21st Street. She had a letter of introduction from one of her college professors to a woman editor at the magazine. The editor listened to her story, dried her tears, and loaned her $20.00. "But I'm a stranger to you," Marjorie said, "Suppose I can't pay this back?"

"If you don't, it won't matter," the editor replied. "Some day you'll have a chance to give a lift to some other young writer."

Marjorie did eventually pay the loan back, but she never forgot the kindness. In later years the remembrance of it was enough to stifle her impatience with beginning writers who asked her endless, often unanswerable questions about their careers.

Quarantined at Camp Upton by the devastating flu pandemic, Chuck was frantically worried about Marjorie. His salary was being sent to his parents to keep for him so he and Marjorie would have a nest egg when he got out of the army. He begged her to keep herself "safe" by going home to Madison, or to Rochester, or at least to write to his parents for financial help, which he was sure they would be happy to give her. But she refused to do any of these things and continued to knock on the doors of magazine publishers—with no luck.

The $20.00 was completely gone when a college friend got her a job as writer and editor for the War Work Council at the national headquarters of the Y.W.C.A. in New York. The job was not the kind of work she had hoped to find, although it did involve some writing for the Y.W.C.A. newsletter and magazine. Much of it, however, involved such tedious chores as getting out the bulletin and clipping material from papers and magazines to file. But she did the work conscientiously and well enough to be promoted within the department of publicity and education.

In her spare time she consistently tried with little luck to sell her short stories and poetry. When she sold a "trashy" story to *Young's*

Magazine for $15.00, she told Chuck it was "manna from heaven." With the proceeds from another sale to *Snappy Stories* she bought an incense burner. And even though her salary barely covered the necessities, she spent some of it on flowers to keep in a pretty vase that Mrs. Rawlings had given her. Flowers remained one of life's necessities.

She enjoyed window shopping the Fifth Avenue stores, and described for Chuck a black velvet dress embroidered in orange and yellow with a matching hat that she yearned for "passionately." But she didn't even dare to go in and price them. As often as she could, she sent candy, cakes, and other little treats to Chuck.

It was tantalizing to both of them to be so close and yet to be so effectively separated. Chuck had difficulty getting weekend leaves and sometimes did not have enough money to come into the city even when he was free. Phone calls were expensive luxuries, so long love letters bridged the few miles between them. They poured out their frustrations, aches, and pains to each other. A letter soaring with rapture and vows of eternal love might be followed by one sunk in the depths of despair and doubt.

Although Chuck was romantic and moody himself, he was bewildered by Marjorie's outbursts of blind rage when his letters were too casual or too cynical or when she thought he was taking her for granted. Ida Kinnan's judgment that Marjorie reacted "hysterically" to Chuck's behavior must at times have seemed correct to him.

When she was worn out from job hunting, broke, depressed over rejections of her writing efforts, or feeling bad physically, she took it out on Chuck—either by crying on his shoulder (which he liked) or by blowing up at him over some minor matter. She understood her own behavior, realizing that she read too much into and between the lines of his letters when she was suffering from "nerves" or in a down mood. She told him:

> *I wish I was normal and cow-like and grass chewingly contented, no matter what happened. But the trouble with me is, I act like a nut when nothing happens! Give me a real mess, or tragedy, and I come through with flying colors—and then*

I get cry-baby and unhappy—out of the air! It's bad enough to live with yourself when you're a nut—but it must be awful for someone else!

But her insight into her behavior didn't give her control over it. In reply to a letter in which he told her he had decided not to get upset and hurt over their misunderstandings and was resolved not to "worry," she fired off an eighteen-page letter, berating him for his callousness, telling him she felt she could no longer count on him, and "damning" him to "Palestine and back again" for his attitude. She ended by threatening to dissolve their relationship. Early the next morning, before the letter arrived, he received a telegram: "UTTERLY DISREGARD DAMNABLE LETTER. I LIED. CANT LIVE WITHOUT YOU."

This time, however, Chuck was deeply hurt. It took several more letters, phone calls, and a visit from him to New York to patch up that quarrel. They agreed to start "all over again," and soon their letters were more than ever filled with passionate longing for each other. In an attempt to avert future misunderstandings, Marjorie warned Chuck, "Sweetheart mine, you musn't interpret a *mood* as a permanent state of mind."

Some weeks later Marjorie told him that she had an opportunity to go to Russia to work for the government for two years. When he told her to go ahead if that was what she wanted, she was furious. She had not seriously considered going, and her motive in telling him about it was to enjoy having him blow up and tell her to stay home. "If you knew how I *yearned* to be told to act sensible—how I *yearn* to be bossed . . .," she told him. "You ought to have been up in the air! You know as well as I do, there would be nothing in the world more absurd, as well as dangerous, for me to do, than to prance off to Russia!" In retaliation for his coolness, she spent the rest of her letter describing a "wonderful" (underlined three times) double date she had gone on with a man she had known at Wisconsin, who was now an *officer* in the navy.

From time to time Chuck retaliated by mentioning some girl he met at camp. Marjorie responded with obviously false cheerfulness, telling him he certainly deserved female companionship to break the monotony of camp life. When she went to dinner or a show with some old college friend, she always told him in great detail about the evening, and he usually reacted with a satisfying jealous outburst.

But the theme of the majority of their letters was the delight, comfort, and strength they found in each other's love. In one letter Marjorie told him she had been thinking it was a shame they did not enjoy their times together more, since they loved each other "so terribly much." She decided it was largely her fault for taking their affairs so seriously "in spite of my usually good sense of humor." They were both moody, she reminded him, and at the least little reverse, inclined to go "down, down, down." In the future, she urged, they must "toss life up, and laugh, and watch it glitter in the sunshine."

Two minor operations and an "abdominal difficulty" had made her nervous with a tendency to burst into tears. Now that these problems were over, she felt sure their future would be such a "gloriously, jolly existence" that nothing would bother them. Chuck responded to her soaring mood by promising they would be so happy together, they would teach God to remodel his heaven. Actually, the stomach pains Marjorie suffered continued to recur occasionally and may have been the forerunners of the more acute attacks of later years, which were finally diagnosed as diverticulosis.

By early November of 1918, peace seemed near enough for them to think seriously of being married. Occasionally in a tired or lonesome mood, Marjorie pictured them living in a bungalow with a big lawn. She saw herself in the kitchen preparing a dinner of "baked sweet potatoes, thick steak, mayonnaise on lettuce, and chocolate cake." And then, after a ride in their low-slung roadster, coming back to a roaring wood fire, with one huge armchair for them to cuddle in and watch the flames.

But more often her dreams were for a life "adventuresome and marvelous." She thought they might go overseas as a husband-and-wife team working for the Red Cross in the postwar reconstruction effort. "Doesn't that appeal to you like everything?" she asked Chuck.

If we could only make enough to pay our expenses, it would be worth it by a long shot. We could write a couple of books,

*and lots of articles & when we come home the papers &
magazines would gobble us up—if we'd written anything worth
while. Golly, wouldn't that be slick? And we'd have goats'
milk, and peasants, and fur coats if we went to Russia—and
oh, jiminy, it would be great. . . . And we'd run around in ox-
carts, and maybe go to England during the summer, & tramp
along the English lanes like gypsies—Oh Chuck! I HON-
ESTLY would start TOMORROW if it were possible. I mean
it—I'm CRAZY to do it.*

"Think how fond we'd be of each other among foreigners," she said.
"Why not do something fascinating while we're young and peppy?"
She hadn't forgotten their dream bungalow. That and "babies and
comfort and quiet" could come later. "And we could have our can-
dlelight and big chair *wherever* we were!" Lest he should think the
idea was just one of her passing fancies, she added, "It's not just a
mood—I *want* it."

Underlying her enthusiasm for going abroad was the fear that
they would end up in Rochester, staying with Chuck's parents. The
Rawlingses had already invited them, with the implication that in
the future they in turn would look forward to living "with Charles
and Marjorie." Almost frantically Marjorie begged Chuck not to
accept his father's offer of a "good proposition" in Rochester. Even
though she knew his parents were "good and kind and fine," she
was sure Rochester was bound to lead to an unbearable humdrum
domesticity for her.

"We're not like average, normal humans," she told him. "We've
got to be out, where things are moving and we can catch some of
the enchantment and swing of life. . . ."

Early in December Chuck was released from the army and returned
to Rochester. Marjorie worried that he was under the influence of
his parents at this crucial time when he must decide about his
future—and hers. And yet when he described a quarrel he had with
his parents, Marjorie wrote him a long lecture, scolding him for his
treatment of them. Even though they might be "unreasonable" she
told him, they were only acting out of love for him. She admonished

him to be pleasant and kind to them, remembering what he owed them.

"My dear," she warned, "if you're going to be a success at anything, you've got to hold that nasty tongue of yours, and the devil behind it." Their future troubled her. "Tell me," she said, "are you ever going to swear at your Skinney? I'll pull an awful boner some day sure as sin—and what are you going to do?" She described to him how she had fought her own private devil of intense dislike for a superior at the Y.W.C.A. and finally turned their relationship into a pleasant, if not a close, one. She fought not to hate the woman because, "I hate so hard and so completely when I do give up to it," she said prophetically.

Chuck took her lecture to heart, admitting he had been a "cad" and a "horrid wretch" and promising to treat his parents with loving kindness in the future. The trains between Rochester and New York carried their daily letters, and once when Marjorie failed to receive one on schedule, she wrote in a panic to Mrs. Rawlings, begging her to wire if Chuck were ill. Her panic was caused, she explained, by a psychic experience in which she had a strong feeling that something terrible was happening to Chuck or to her brother, Arthur. She and Mrs. Rawlings had discussed the fact that they both were subject to these experiences because of their "supersensitive" feelings. In this case, her feelings proved groundless as Chuck had merely procrastinated in writing.

The exploration of the unconscious fascinated and frightened Marjorie. She had turned down a job in a psychoanalyst's office for fear that listening to people exposing their souls would have a morbid effect on her and "spoil" her happiness as a "normal, wholesome" human being. The main temptation of the job had been that it would be, she felt, a rich source of material for her writing. She also had a great interest in dreams, and often felt as if Chuck came to her in the night during her sleep. "You were with me all last night," she wrote him. In another letter she begged, "Come to me again, dear, as you did last night."

Plans were made for Marjorie to go to Rochester for Christmas, and her holiday there was happy. The Rawlingses made every effort to please her. Chuck and his mother had made an elegant plum pudding from an old family recipe brought over from England by their ancestors. Chuck's younger brothers, Jimmy and Wray, made her feel welcome. She and Jimmy especially formed a warm, teasing brother-sister relationship. "Daddy" Rawlings, as usual treated her like a daughter.

Although the Rawlingses and Arthur enthusiastically supported her engagement to Chuck, Ida Kinnan still did not. Marjorie was determined to win her mother over "subtly and gradually without arguing" until she was at least willing for them to marry. As part of this strategy she suggested to Chuck that he send Ida a small pot plant "preferable a purple or red cyclamen" with a "tiny little note *very* kind and tactful" for Christmas.

When Chuck received a job offer as an assistant to the overseas advertising manager of a large export firm in New York City, Marjorie encouraged him to take it. "I can *feel* that you'd go big in it," she told him. "You'd get your literary material too—the sea, trade, ships—a *man's* subjects." She promised to study Italian and Spanish with him if he should be assigned to an overseas branch of the company. And she agreed to be married as soon as "We both *know* you're in your permanent line, will always be happy in it, and are showing that you'll make good."

Chuck took a room near Marjorie on Morningside Drive and settled into the job. Their financial situation looked bright. Even though Marjorie's job would gradually be phased out, she planned to stay with it as long as it lasted, and then she would do free-lance writing. Failure to find a job with a publishing house or to sell any of her poems, and only a few of her stories, had not destroyed her faith in her talent as a writer.

Marjorie's year as a young career woman in New York City had at times been "forlorn" and "lonesome." But it had also been exciting and fulfilling. Having lived with her mother all during her college years, it was her first chance to prove that she could manage her life on her own. She had defied her mother not only by choosing to remain in New York, but also by continuing her engagement to Charles Rawlings.

They had so much in common and were so physically in love

that it was easy to dismiss their violent ragings at each other as lovers' quarrels caused by raw nerves, discouragement, weariness, or irritability with outside events. They also blamed the hurtful things they said and wrote to each other on the frustration of being separated when they longed to be together. Marjorie's desire to be "cuddled" and to cry on his shoulder in her moods of depression or discouragement seems to have effectively blinded them both to the fact that she was much the more strong-minded and tougher of the two.

On April 15, 1919, Chuck sat down to write Ida Kinnan that he planned to marry her daughter the first week in May. He assured her he was no longer the "worthless chap" who used to sit on her divan in Madison. Describing his position with the export firm, he said, "There is not one slightest possibility of anything else but success." He told his future mother-in-law that Marjorie loved her more deeply than either of them realized "or you would not hurt each other so." Awkwardly but sincerely he wrote, "[B]ecause you are her mother something she loves I must love it too. I am not going to break your heart!"

CHAPTER · 3

Marjorie Kinnan Rawlings

The spring of 1919 was an exciting time to be in New York City. The arriving troop transports, their decks packed solid with men, were greeted by the mayor's special committee, headed by the dapper young secretary, Grover Whalen. At the Public Library on Fifth Avenue there was a shrine of pylons and palms called the Court of the Heroic Dead. The returning troops marched in victory parades up the flag-hung avenue and through a huge temporary triumphal arch erected at Madison Square, while confetti and ticker tape rained down on them and the bands played "There's a Long, Long Trail." The atmosphere was saturated with emotion.

But for Marjorie and Chuck their own quiet marriage before a judge was the most stirring event of the season. The wedding, which took place in New York City early in May, ended the agony of separation and physical frustration.

In 1919 cosmetics were still suspect and women wore their hair and their skirts long. Marjorie, aware that she looked her best in informal attire such as kimonos, adopted these for at-home wear, but she was never sloppy. In his love letters to her Chuck often mentioned her physical attractions. Like Rossetti, whom he enjoyed reading, Chuck was a "hands" admirer, and he frequently referred to Marjorie's small, white hands. He adored her soft skin and the feminine aspect of her nature that made her want to curl up against his shoulder and to surprise him with his favorite dishes.

To her dismay, Marjorie found that having watched her grandmother and her mother with fascination while they cooked had not taught her the subtleties of the art, especially those connected with timing and measurement. Although she had a few specialties such as mayonnaise which she did well, her everyday meals left a great deal to be desired. Years later, tracing her steps to becoming an expert cook, she laughingly recalled that after visiting the newlyweds in New York, Mother Rawlings sent her the Fanny Farmer cookbook even before she wrote her bread-and-butter letter.

When Marjorie's Y.W.C.A. job ended, she turned her energy to writing short stories and poems but still had no luck selling them. Later, she would be thankful that these slick, overwritten stories had not seen the light of day in publications and so could not return to haunt her. But at the time her inability to sell her work was deeply discouraging. She picked up a little income by helping to write three Boy Scout manuals. When the export company for which Chuck was working as a publicity agent folded, it was a devastating blow, and they had to decide quickly on some means of making a living. With hundreds of returning soldiers lined up for any available jobs in New York, it was not a promising hunting ground. Marjorie was as set as ever against living in Rochester, so when friends in Louisville, Kentucky, told them of openings for reporters on the Louisville *Courier-Journal*, they packed up their typewriters and books and headed south.

On Breckenridge and Third streets in Louisville they found a small apartment in an old-fashioned building next to a gas station. On frigid mornings they scurried across bare, cold floors and huddled over gas grates to keep from freezing, and they suffered claustrophobia in the tiny bathtub. But a few years later, passing through Louisville on a trip, Chuck looked up at the light in the bedroom window of their old apartment and tears filled his eyes at the thought of strangers occupying their "sanctum." He told Marjorie, "The bit of me that I left there, embracing the bit of you, shrieked in agony as I rolled past." And he quoted from the *Rubaiyat*:

> *The lion and the lizard keep the courts*
> *Where Jamshied gloried and drank deep.*

For two years Chuck worked as a reporter and Marjorie worked as a feature writer for the *Courier-Journal*. Her typing skill improved, although she always typed with two fingers on each hand, and she became adept at composing on the typewriter. She learned to write without wasting words and to drop superfluous adjectives and adverbs. Later, she credited her newspaper experience with teaching her more about writing than she had learned in all her composition classes.

"Live Women in Live Louisville" was the title of a series of stories she did for the *Courier-Journal* Sunday magazine. Among the women she interviewed and featured were the chief probation officer for Jefferson County; the only woman state bacteriologist in the United States; and the cashier for one of the South's largest manufacturing concerns.

The closest friends of the young couple were Lois Clark Hardy, a sorority sister at Wisconsin, and her husband Ed, who was beginning to make a good living in the manufacturing business. One of the activities the two couples enjoyed was going together to the Kentucky Derby in May. Like many of their newspaper friends, Marjorie and Chuck flouted prohibition and indulged in drinking as often as their desires or their budget allowed. Both also became heavy smokers.

In addition to her newspaper work, Marjorie wrote advertising copy for the Stewart Dry Goods Company of Louisville. But after almost two years, it became apparent that their journalistic work in Louisville had little future. They reluctantly concluded that the move had led to a dead end. Chuck's father was urging him to take a selling job with his shoe factory, dangling prospects of huge commissions that would allow them to become financially independent in a few years. It seemed the only thing for practical romantics to do.

By January 1922, they were back in Rochester, living with the Rawlingses at first and then in a small house of their own. Chuck became a traveling shoe salesman, and left in the middle of January for a month-long selling trip. Marjorie took a vacation to visit her mother in Madison and relatives in various towns. Since her marriage, Marjorie had dutifully written weekly letters to her mother, putting the best face on their financial problems and omitting mention of any marital ones. During the war, she had joined forces with Ida to dissuade Arthur from joining the British forces in Canada to get around the age limit of the U. S. military. From college he wrote Marjorie confidential letters describing the girls he was "fussing" with, his problems in keeping up his grades (because of too many extracurricular activities), and his disillusionment with his fellow Phi Psiers, who often came in "drunk to the gills."

Returning to Wisconsin, Marjorie found that her mother was making a satisfactory new life for herself, having accepted a position as hostess and chaperon at the Theta sorority house. The young women students were fond of her and kept her room filled with flowers, presenting her with corsages when she hosted their dinners. Ida apparently enjoyed her role, dressing in pretty gowns for afternoon and evening affairs and sporting a lorgnette to aid her increasing nearsightedness.

One of Marjorie's stops on this trip was at the Traphagen farm in Michigan. The farm was now owned by her Aunt Ethel Riggs, but the food was still bountiful and fresh and delicious. Following a breakfast of buckwheat pancakes, sausage, and fried cakes, Marjorie asked to be allowed to turn the cream separator herself. After she had gathered a pail of golden, thick cream, she insisted on washing the separator—all fifty "becreamed" parts.

One day, hurrying to a dining room window to watch the antics of a cat on the lawn, she fell headlong through a trap door into the cellar. Turning a complete somersault, she tumbled down the steps, landing in a sitting position, but crashing her head against the stone wall. "By every right," she told Chuck, "I should have broken, first, my neck, and then every other bone in my body." She escaped, however, with a large lump on her head, skinned knees and elbows, bruises, and a gash in one leg. During her lifetime, she suffered many potentially fatal accidents such as this one and miraculously lived to make the incident into a good story.

Returning to Rochester, Marjorie could not find a market for her short stories, no matter how hard she worked on them. To help their finances, she again tried newspaper work. In the 1920s Rochester had a tight-knit social hierarchy. It had numerous churches and banks, a boxing coliseum, and several theaters where Broadway shows sometimes tried out and famous artists performed. It also had five newspapers. By the fall of 1922, Marjorie was writing feature articles for the Rochester *Evening Journal* and the Rochester *American* under her own by-line. Although they were written in the slick, often flippant popular journalistic style of the day, her articles were full of human interest and enlivened with telling quotes and anecdotes.

From time to time, she was assigned interviews with visiting celebrities. After an interview with Herma Menth, a beautiful Viennese pianist, Marjorie wrote an article that had as its theme Menth's views on American men. The glamorous concert artist found them less ready with compliments and "blandishments" than European men, but she admired them for being more sincere, more steadfast in their love, and less demanding of their women. Marjorie concluded the article with her own advice to American women to continue with their men as usual: "neglecting them a bit, scolding them more and—loving them most of all."

In an interview with Lou Tellegen, a matinée idol, who was recently divorced from opera singer Geraldine Farrar, Marjorie confided to her readers that she had discovered the key to the break-up of their "perfect" marriage. Tellegen was touchy on the subject of the divorce and refused to discuss it with her, but by indirect questioning Marjorie got him to exclaim passionately, "Women are spoiled!" This, she reported, was probably the explanation of the "ruined fairy tale."

In a feature article Marjorie described the Mechanics Institute of Rochester, which offered women training in many arts and crafts, including woodworking, painting, weaving, pottery making, and cooking. She spent the most space describing the cooking classes. "How far cookery ranks above the other fine arts!" she exclaimed. "How more important a perfect pie than a perfect poem!" A husband might forgive a flirtation, she exclaimed, but never poor food.

These opinions cannot, of course, be swallowed whole, nor did she probably intend them to be, given her devotion to the art of writing. She did develop into a brilliant cook and hostess, but she never developed a liking for the drudgery of preparing three meals a day on a regular basis. She knew, however, that many of the women in her reading audience were more adept at and interested in cookery than in writing poetry, and she slanted her material accordingly.

She went to the Rochester jail to interview a runaway sixteen-year-old girl, who had been found living in a rooming house with her lover. Although Marjorie called her "a little tramp on the trail of Romance," she showed sympathy for the misguided girl, whose father was to take her back to the safety of her home in the little village of Tonawanda.

In interviews with young women students from Wellesley and Mt. Holyoke colleges, Marjorie asked their opinions about the furor over their schools' ban on women smoking and wearing knickers. All of the interviewees sided virtuously with the authorities, agreeing that laxness in behavior led to laxness in morals. Remembering the sensation she had caused at Wisconsin by wearing red bloomers to play practice, Marjorie concluded that the war had made young women more blasé but also more serious. "Young girls do not have the spontaneity of former days," she concluded.

To Chuck she wrote that she felt very far removed in time from the college girls she talked with. But she found hope for women in the avowed young flappers at the local high school. In an article about them, she defined a flapper as "any personable female of the younger generation who is obviously enjoying herself."

Occasionally Marjorie's feature stories made the front page of the Rochester Sunday *American*. Later Marjorie would refer to herself as having been a "Hearst sob sister," but it was an experience she was glad she hadn't missed. "You learn a lot when you must put down what people said and how they acted in great crises in their lives. And it teaches you objectivity." But she also knew it was a "scrappy" kind of writing. And the pressure to produce copy to meet deadlines bothered her. She always hated to be hurried in her writing as she was a meticulous polisher and revisionist. Her success as a journalist did not make up for the pain and frustration of receiving only a constant stream of rejection slips for her short stories and poems.

During the four years that Chuck traveled around the South and

East trying with decreasing success to sell shoes, Marjorie wrote to him faithfully, so he would always find her cheerful letters waiting at his next stop.

At first Chuck's letters were optimistic about his prospects. He expected to make money quickly and was sure he would get a large order "in the next town." Each of them was hypersensitive and each was adept at pricking the other's tenderest spots with words like daggers, and the difficulties and disappointments of the months of financial uncertainty often set their nerves on edge. But the physical attraction was still strong.

In a letter in which he referred to the suffering they caused each other, Chuck added, "But I guess we are well-mated at that. Our fault is that we love too much for every day daily food. He pictured her sitting at the breakfast table in her long silk robe, and told her, "I would give my soul to have you wrapped up tight in my arms."

Apparently she sometimes told him her dreams, and on one occasion he responded: "Oh-h-h-h you made my mouth water with your story of your dream. I have been so eternally busy and so wrapped up in this hectic job that I have neglected dreaming of your spare parts, but your letter suddenly sent the blood all around in me with a mad surge. . . . God in his heaven only knows how I adore you, Dearest Marjorie."

The newspaper business was an irregular one that often required late night hours. All kinds of people worked on the papers—some of them young, attractive, and bright. Meeting deadlines was demanding and often the journalists relieved the tension of their work with after-hour drinks and talk fests when the paper had been put to bed. Chuck knew that Marjorie was appealing to men, and there are flashes of jealousy in his letters. In one he mentions "Burt," a reporter whom he could have "killed" for his "damned sugary smirking" at Marjorie.

A more serious affair was her relationship with Harry Grey, the managing editor of the Hearst paper. Grey was a brilliant man, and Marjorie enjoyed long, intimate talks with him. They became good friends, whether or not he went "over the keep off the grass sign" as Chuck accused him of doing. At times Chuck was driven to distraction, imagining them together during his long absences. Her letters to him during this time have not survived, but apparently she explained her relationship with Grey in a way that partially at least satisfied Chuck. He swore that he trusted her completely, and in the next sentence told her he would go on loving her "no matter what happened between them." "I am sappy with love," he said.

In 1923 Chuck's father died, and Marjorie showed a sympathy and tenderness toward Mrs. Rawlings that endeared her to her mother-in-law. Year's later Mrs. Rawlings said that at the time of her husband's death, Marjorie, although only "a green girl," had been the one who offered her the most comfort and understanding.

Toward the end of the year Marjorie suffered an even more personal loss when her mother died at the age of fifty-five. Ida had gone to the family farm for the Christmas holidays and become ill quite suddenly, possibly from a stroke. Whatever the cause, in a few days she was dead. One of Ida Traphagen Kinnan's sisters-in-law described her as a "strong, serious type," and in her meticulous housekeeping, in her determination to give her children a good education after she was widowed, and in her ambition for her talented daughter, the description seems apt. With the patronizing attitude of a worldly-wise college man, Arthur, referring to their mother's rigid standards, called her "poor mother," but he added, "she is good—*so good*, Peaches," in a letter to Marjorie.

Marjorie, too, appreciated her mother's goodness and her desire to give them the best possible start in life. But she was distressed when that desire curtailed her freedom and conflicted with her own strong determination to make her own choices. Some literary critics have argued that the stern, inflexible, humorless Ma Baxter in *The Yearling* was derived from the puritannical Ida Kinnan, but although she traced the prototypes of many of her characters, Marjorie was silent on this one.

The small inheritance that came to Marjorie from her mother's estate was put away as a nest egg. As Chuck's sales trips were becoming less and less rewarding, they agreed that he should quit the business and join Marjorie as a journalist in Rochester. Good looking, personable, and outgoing, he made many friends in the newspaper business, and he was often given assignments dealing with yachting and sailing on the nearby Lake Ontario. In addition he covered other gentlemanly sports events for the *Times-Union*.

When Rochester newspaperman Henry W. Clune started a magazine called *5 O'Clock*, he hired two promising young journalists, George S. Brooks and Marjorie Kinnan Rawlings, to be his main reporters. He later admitted he paid them a "shamefully low salary." George Brooks eventually moved to New York, where he wrote short stories that were published in *Liberty, Saturday Evening Post* and *Collier's* and became an editor of *McClure's* magazine.

Clune appreciated Marjorie's cleverness and talent, but not her potential. *5 O'Clock* was a sophisticated magazine covering music, art, theater, and books, with a section of chitchat that bore a resemblance to the *New Yorker's* "Talk of the Town." Under the elegant pseudonym Lady Alicia Thwaite, Marjorie wrote caricatures of the boxing and wrestling at the Hippodrome and of the shows at the burlesque house. Her spoofs were some of the best writing that appeared in the magazine, which lasted for about a year.

On the front page for May 24, 1926, the *Times-Union* announced that it was beginning an experiment. Under the title "Songs of the Housewife," Marjorie Kinnan Rawlings would reveal the "romance of housework." In her verses she would sing of the everyday life of the housewife. "Does the housewife want to be glorified?" the paper asked. If so, they were invited to send postcards expressing their opinions. Apparently they did, for the verses, which ran for almost two years, were syndicated by United Features and ran in fifty newspapers. The poems were light and cheerful, often with a sentimental or humorous twist. When Marjorie invited her readers to send in suggestions, they did and she tailored the poems to fit the subjects they requested.

Eventually these slight verses covered everything from the joys of cooking to the satisfaction and frustration of such housekeeping chores as making beds, darning socks, washing pots and pans, dusting, cleaning the attic, and polishing silver. Many were about people: mothers, babies and children, relatives, friends, guests, neighbors. Some were about things: rocking chairs, old brooms, old clocks, and pets. Others dealt with feelings: jealousy, love, memories, and nostalgia, or revealed flashes of insight. A typical poem ran on August 14, 1926:

Washing on the Line

I've studied all my neighbors
From their washings on the line.
Their linens, socks and shirts have been
Often a tell-tale sign!

The fashionable Miss Spenser
Wears many a torn chemise.
Our high-toned doctor's underwear
Needs patching at the knees!

As I hung out my wash today,
I noticed that my sheets
Were ragged and that Tommy's pants
Were sadly minus seats.

It dawned on me in horror—
As for washings on the line,
While I've been studying my neighbors',
Neighbors have studied mine!

Later Marjorie acknowledged that writing "Songs" was a potboiler activity. With characteristic humor, she said she avoided one kind of prostitution by practicing another. Nevertheless, she labored diligently over her daily verse, and many housewives wrote to say that they identified with the sentiments expressed in them.

The success of "Songs of a Housewife" and of some of her newspaper feature stories was pleasing but entirely inadequate to satisfy Marjorie's wish to achieve recognition as a writer. Her short stories and serious poetry continued to garner only rejection slips. Both she and Chuck seemed to be stalemated in their careers, and the strain was reflected in their marriage. Quarreling and making up became increasingly a pattern in their lives.

A vacation was suggested and since Chuck's brothers, Jimmy and Wray, were working in Florida, Marjorie and Chuck planned a sea trip to visit them. In March of 1928, their Clyde Line steamer sailed from New York down the East Coast and into the mouth of the St. Johns River.

At Jacksonville they were met by Zelma Cason, a brusque but friendly little woman, who took them to a hotel on the banks of the river. Wray and Jimmy came to meet them and to show them the area. They soon found that the north central interior of Florida was nothing like the famed Florida Gold Coast with its well-heeled tourists and languid beachcombers. Island Grove, where the brothers had a filling station and dabbled in real estate, was on the upper edge of the citrus-growing country. As they drove across the peninsula, Marjorie noticed the native Cracker men hunting, fishing, and cultivating small farms and the deeply tanned women washing outdoors in iron kettles over open pinewood fires and sweeping their cabins with homemade brooms. The term "cracker" was not pejorative but was in use throughout Florida (and parts of Georgia) to denote the rural white natives of English or Scottish ancestry.

During the next few days, the three brothers and Marjorie visited the scrub area, fished for bass on the lakes, and took a boat trip on the meandering Oklawaha River. Here they saw the sparkling fountains arising from underground limestone springs as described by early American naturalist William Bartram in his classic *Travels*. Bartram's description became the basis for Samuel Taylor Coleridge's sacred river Alph in *Kubla Khan* (even if an opium dream did help inspire his use of it)—a fact that delighted Marjorie. At the time the Rawlingses explored it, before it became commercialized and vulgarized, they could see why another poet, Sidney Lanier, called it "the sweetest water-lane in the world, a lane which runs for more than a hundred and fifty miles of pure delight betwixt hedgerows of oaks and cypresses and palms and bays and magnolias and mosses and manifold vine-growths, a lane clean to travel along . . . ."

The half-wild remoteness and mystery of the Scrub fascinated Marjorie as did the simplicity of the people's daily lives. She and Chuck were charmed by the natural beauty of the area, the rivers and the lakes with floating islands, the tall palms and great live oaks dripping with Spanish moss, and the fragrant orange groves.

"Let's sell everything and move South!" she said to him. "How we could write!" He agreed, and before they returned to Rochester, they asked Jimmy and Wray to look for a place for them where they could grow citrus fruit for a living while they tried to market their writing.

On July 9, Wray wrote suggesting they buy the Armstrong place in Cross Creek. "It has drawbacks galore," he told them, "but most of them can be improved." The property included seventy-four acres, a shabby eight-room farmhouse, a four-room tenant house, a two-story barn, some thirty-three hundred orange trees, plus eight hundred pecan trees and a number of grapefruit and tangerine trees. The price was $9,000.

Chuck and Marjorie agreed this was the opportunity they had been waiting for. She used the money from her share of her mother's estate, which originally came from the sale of her father's Maryland farm, to make a payment of $7,400. The balance of the mortgage was to be paid off at $500 a year. By November 1928, Chuck and Marjorie had quit their newspaper jobs, sold their Rochester possessions, said goodbye to their friends, and moved to the tiny hamlet of Cross Creek, Florida.

The village of Cross Creek takes its name from a creek that crosses between and connects two large lakes named Orange and Lochloosa. After she had lived in Cross Creek for over a dozen years, Marjorie wrote a semiautobiographical book about the area and its people. She titled the second chapter "For This is an Enchanted Land." For her the enchantment never wore off from the first moment she saw it and fell under the spell of its timeless, natural beauty. After a quarter-century of city life, she had found a place to satisfy a hunger to live close to the land that had gone unfed since childhood. With "mingled delight and terror" she recognized the old grove and faded farmhouse at once as the "home" to which she was committed irrevocably, whatever joy or sorrow might result from that commitment. When her Aunt Madelaine, her father's sister, heard about the move, she lamented, "You have in you that fatal drop of Pearce blood, clamoring for change and adventure, and above all, for a farm. I never knew a Pearce who didn't secretly long for a farm." Marjorie responded that she saw no reason to deny so fundamental an urge, even if it meant ruin, as her aunt feared. "It is more important to live the life one wishes to live, and to go down with it if necessary, quite contentedly, than to live more profitably but less happily," she maintained.

Although she felt drawn to the Cross Creek area by an "ancient and secret magic," Marjorie had no illusions that it was a perfect paradise. Her vision was clear. She saw the simple grace of line of the low, rambling nineteenth-century farmhouse, which was actually three separate buildings joined together. But she also saw its gray dinginess, its ugly tin roof, the inadequate rough porch, and the bare yard dotted with sandspurs. Inside, the battleship gray walls, "muddy ochre" floors, and fireplaces walled over with tin cried out to be redone. And the grove, too, had suffered neglect and needed immediate attention.

Jimmy and Wray joined Marjorie and Chuck in working the grove and in fixing up the place, which they named "Los Hermanos" (the brothers). Included in the sale were two cows, two mules, 150 chicken coops, two chicken brooders, a decrepit Ford truck, a planter, a reaper, cultivators, sweeps, and various other farm implements. The new tenants set to work to improve grounds and grove. While the men mended fences, planted a vegetable garden, milked the cows, and tended the grove, Marjorie cooked three big meals a day on the wood-burning stove, washed clothes in an iron pot, cleaned the house, and planted flowers and vines. There was no water heater, but she was grateful to have a water faucet in the kitchen, since many of her neighbors did not. Completing the facilities were an outside tin stall shower with an icy spray and a primitive outdoor privy with a screen door. Marjorie longed to paint the house and redo its interior, but first they needed to establish an income.

Making a profitable citrus crop proved more expensive than they had expected. Their small supply of cash dwindled rapidly as they replaced worn-out equipment and machinery and bought seeds, fertilizer, spray, feed for animals, and groceries. At times the weather played havoc with their crop. Storms, freezes, and droughts cut into their profits. It became evident that the grove would not soon, if ever, support four adults; and before two years had passed, Wray and Jimmy left to find other work.

Amid all their physical activity, Chuck and Marjorie had not forgotten their commitment to write. Chuck explored the sponge-fishing industry at Tarpon Springs near Tampa, making trips there to do his research among the Greek fishermen. At times he lived among them and sailed with them, and on one occasion he brought back some of their recipes to Marjorie.

From the time of their arrival, Marjorie took notes on the country and the people. With typical energy she set out to learn the name of every unfamiliar tree, shrub, flower, bird, and creature in her new environment. She studied the people closely, finding them "elemental folk" with a vital quality lacking in more civilized types. She filled notebooks with examples of their phrasing and unusual speech mannerisms.

The observations she made on her detailed study of the birds in her area illustrate how deep and thorough her research was. In addition to studying their nesting, mating, and feeding habits, she learned the variations of their calls. And she practiced identifying them by their flight patterns without being close enough to see them clearly. In one journal she noted that "a hawk flaps its wings up and down like a child playing bird"; "doves seem wind driven"; "flickers push, coast and swoop, like a child on a scooter"; "ducks churn ahead like engines"; and "coots take off like sea planes." "Red birds in swift flight fly head downward, fluttering"; "vultures soar on air currents"; and "hummingbirds make an arc, swinging on invisible light threads."

Her notebooks are filled with descriptions of daybreaks and sunsets, of the work connected with the grove, including frantic efforts to save the orange crop from sudden freezes and the deadly fruit fly. She did not fail to include the daily torments of mosquitoes, ants, chiggers, poison ivy, and sandspurs. But most of all she recorded the picturesque life of the people in her immediate vicinity and of those she discovered living a little farther away in the area called the Scrub.

One bright fall morning she set out on horseback with Zelma Cason, who had been appointed to take the census in the back-country sections of Alachua County. After doing the counting along Orange Lake, they crossed over the River Styx into deeply shadowed hammock and then into cypress swamp. She thought to herself, "It is not given to many to cross the Styx and live to tell it," and she found the area "darkly beautiful." Near a turpentine still they counted a dense population of blacks. Zelma joked and sympathized with them, recommending cures, promising to send medicines, seeds, and quilt scraps to various individuals. During the several days it took to cover the area, Zelma told Marjorie the history of the different families and a great deal about the wild life of the region, so that when the census taking was finished, Marjorie felt she would never again be a stranger in the area.

In 1930, a little over a year after moving to Cross Creek, Marjorie sent a group of sketches of her new friends and neighbors to an editor at *Scribner's Magazine*. She called them "Cracker Chidlings." This editor had made a kind comment on one of her rejected slick stories, and now she wrote that she hoped he would be interested in this new material, which seemed to her to "transcend fiction." She told him modestly, "I am only too sure that you won't want anything as—well, raw—as these true sketches of the Cracker folk in the still pioneer heart of Florida."

On March 11 she received a letter from Alfred Dashiell, who had taken over the editorship at the magazine. He offered her $150 for the sketches and asked for biographical information. Marjorie was delighted to have her material accepted by *Scribner's* and sent the information Dashiell asked for. But she told him that her past years had become unimportant to her. "They are a shadow, against the satisfying substance that is our life in the heart of the Florida hammock," she said.

CHAPTER 4

This Enchanted Land

"Cracker Chidlings" appeared in the February 1931 issue of *Scribner's Magazine,* with the subtitle "Real Tales from the Florida Interior." A humorous comment on the ill will between Georgia and Florida Crackers introduced the sketches. Marjorie claimed they have a common ancestor in the "vanished driver of oxen, who cracked yards of rawhide whip over his beasts and so came by his name." The vignettes included descriptions of social get-togethers, the life of a moonshiner, the rough jokes played on strangers by the natives of the area, the beauty of the untamed land, and the food, such as squirrel pilau.

Her sketches were taken from real life and in some cases she used real names. She underwent an appendectomy just about the time "Cracker Chidlings" appeared. As she lay recuperating in the farmhouse at Cross Creek, the mother of a young man whom Marjorie had painted in an uncomplimentary light stalked up and down the road outside the house, threatening to come in and give Marjorie a horsewhipping. Zelma Cason came to the rescue and acted as an intermediary. When Marjorie was on her feet again, Zelma took her to meet the family, and after Marjorie had apologized to the mother, they became friends.

Some other Floridians, especially those connected with the tourist industry, were outraged by Marjorie's revelations of the Crackers, warts and all. The editor of the Ocala *Evening Star* labeled the sketches "Literary Chitterlings" and blasted them as "libel against the citizens of Florida." Calling them "crude and unsympathetic," he declared that she hadn't described typical Crackers, and added that the descriptions of chiggers, mosquitoes, and freezes were unnecessary. He also criticized the author's use of dialect and questioned her sources.

In a scathing reply that ran to several pages, Marjorie gave the editor a lesson in etymology to prove her accurate use of dialect. She informed him that her sketches were so true, she had softened, not colored them. In denying the red bugs and mosquitoes, he simply showed his ignorance of the backwoods, she declared. He was the unsympathetic one, she claimed, for to her the people she described were "all that is delightful." She concluded by saying, "I have only begun my re-creation of these people" and told him she planned to do further prowling through the piney woods and shadowy hammocks, "where, alas, my dear sir, I am never likely to meet you."

Although Marjorie claimed she had been determined to give up writing if "Cracker Chidlings" was not accepted for publication, this is a doubtful assertion. For one thing, she admitted to having an "incurable" writer's itch, and for another, she was so stimulated by her new surroundings that she was "boiling over" with ideas for short stories and novels. She developed one of her ideas into a long short story, or novelette, which she at first called "High Winds" but later changed to "Jacob's Ladder." It is a sensitively told story of a simple, rabbity Cracker couple named Mart and Florry. They are buffeted about by hurricanes and other natural disasters and by cruel and greedy humans, but sustained by their love for each other.

Like most of her stories, it has a factual background and a blend of real and imaginary characters. She was inspired first by a place. One day on the road near Cross Creek village she saw a great spreading live oak tree and saw indications that someone had lived there, such as a rough table, a rusty pot, and a clothesline. The villagers told her that a very young man and woman had lived under the tree for one summer and then with the coming of cold weather had gone away with sacks over their shoulders.

In the tenant house that came with Marjorie's property lived a reclusive young couple. The man, Tim, worked in her grove for a small wage, but his passion was for trapping and selling hides of wild animals. Thinking they could use a little extra income and knowing she herself needed the help, Marjorie asked Tim one day if his wife would do her washing for her. He angrily spat tobacco juice and gave her a lesson in Cracker ethics: "A white woman don't ask another white woman to do her washin' for her, nor to carry her slops. 'Course in time o' sickness or trouble or sich as that a woman does ary thing she can for another and they's no talk o' pay." Soon thereafter, Tim announced abruptly that they were leaving, saying, "I ain't made for this kind of work." When Marjorie asked where they would go and what they would do, he answered vaguely that they could live in the woods. "Us'll make out," he told her. The memory of Tim and the small, tawny woman with soft, honey-colored hair and voice like a wood thrush who was his wife haunted Marjorie. They became Mart and Florry in "Jacob's Ladder."

When Marjorie sent her manuscript in to *Scribner's* under the title "High Winds," it was passed up to the chief editor, Maxwell Perkins, to read. He wrote her that it was excellent, but asked if she would consider making certain revisions. He suggested the title be changed, as "High Winds," had recently been used by another author. He also wanted Florry to be made more of an individual, instead of a representative of the Florida Cracker. His main suggestion had to do with the ending of the story. One of the chief virtues of the story, he said, was that she treated the Crackers sympathetically and made the reader see them in that light, but at the end of the manuscript a change in the point of view shattered this feeling as the couple was seen through the eyes of a Yankee, who viewed them as miserable white trash.

Perkins also wished for a happier ending. "Might not these two people in some way find a permanent resting place?" he asked. As for the technique, he pointed to places where the author "intruded" to tell things that could better be shown by the action and speech of the characters. Marjorie gratefully accepted his suggestions and sent back three possible endings. Perkins chose the one he thought the strongest and again suggested strengthening the human interest in the characters. His suggestions were acute and to the point, but they were always cushioned by such phrases as "if you agree," "perhaps," "it might be better to," and by the use of the editorial "*we* think." His credo was that a book belonged to its author. "We must not persuade you against your convictions," he told Marjorie.

He was quick to recognize her talent and potential, and she was quick to recognize the astuteness of his constructive criticism. From this time on, she was his protégé and he was her mentor, and in a short time he also became her friend and at times her comforter. Maxwell Perkins was the editor of Thomas Wolfe, Ernest Hemingway, F. Scott Fitzgerald, John Galsworthy, Taylor Caldwell, and Ring Lardner, among other notable writers. But his basic philosophy that the chief duty of an editor is to help writers "realize themselves" was never more clearly and happily revealed than in his relationship with Marjorie Kinnan Rawlings.

After the revisions were made, "Jacob's Ladder" was published in the April 1931 issue of *Scribner's Magazine*. The check for $700 in payment for it was joyfully received at Cross Creek.

During the summer of 1930, Marjorie had stayed at home to work on "Jacob's Ladder" while Chuck went north to cover yacht races on assignment from his old Rochester paper. She felt herself enclosed in a silent, stifling hot world of beauty with violence lurking in the shadows. Following the sudden appearance of a black man inside the yard after she had stripped for her shower, she sent word to the several black families across the creek that she was likely to shoot anyone taking her by surprise. Thereafter, she reported, they "shouted fearfully . . . from the farthest gate of the plantation."

Nature, too, provided excitement. One day the Widow Slater, a neighbor, who milked for the Rawlingses in return for pasture for her own cow, reported seeing a rattlesnake in the field. Marjorie joined her in hunting it, hoping to find it before it found them or a cow. Unsuccessful, they were left with the nervous dread that it might turn up another day.

Dread of stepping on a snake was the worst fear in visiting the shower or the outhouse after dusk. But close encounters with lizards, toads, and teacup-size spiders, which seemed harmless and even friendly by day, were scary after dark. Therefore, when the check for "Jacob's Ladder" arrived, Marjorie quickly designated it for an indoor bathroom before the money could dwindle away in paying off notes or in buying fertilizer and groceries. The lavatory and a tub with crooked legs were bought secondhand, but the toilet was ordered new from Sears, Roebuck. The bathroom was formally opened with a party to which the neighbors were invited. The bathtub held ice and soda, a tray of glasses sat across the lavatory, and a bouquet of roses sprouted from the toilet bowl.

Like her "Cracker Chidlings," "Jacob's Ladder" was sniped at by some Florida editors and reviewers. Max Perkins sympathized: "Anything written about a given region, even in a tone of highest compliment, is always objected to. We might have warned you." Other critics, however, including the book review editor of the Miami *Herald*, gave her encouragement, praising her mastery of the Florida back country dialect, her evocation of the fury of a hurricane, and the misery of unrelenting drought. Others commended her use of sensory appeal, her "limpid" prose, and her "unfailing, concealed artistry." Marjorie herself told Max Perkins that she knew the story was "overwritten," but she added she could do better work if he would be patient with her. And she wrote to Alfred Dashiell, the editor of *Scribner's Magazine*, that with the inevitable exceptions, "the Florida elite" were now opening doors to her instead of slamming them. After the Woman's Club of Ocala and the mayor gave her their official and personal approval, she was constantly being approached by people who wanted to give her some "marvelous Cracker material." When some of her new friends wanted to be funny, they presented her publicly with a box of snuff.

Her environment provided new discoveries and new excitement almost daily. Along with her letter she mailed Dashiell a small alligator hide and the skin of a rattlesnake that Chuck had shot in their garden. Eager as she was to collect information for short stories and books, she soon realized that she could not change the unhurried pace of life among her Cracker friends, nor could she rush them. "I have more than one manuscript waiting for information to come out casually," she told him.

Her natural, down-to-earth friendliness made it easy for her to talk to people. After buying gas at the Absteins' filling station and shopping at the grocery store or William (Old Boss) Brice's mercantile business in Island Grove, she would sit on the steps for a while to talk with whoever came by. In brief casual encounters with her neighbors or informal visits with them in their homes or in hers she picked up stories about their childhoods, what food they ate and how they got it, their names for the local birds and plants, what they did for work and for play, and how they felt about themselves and the land. And always as she talked with her new neighbors—the Brices, the Glissons, the Townsends, the Basses—her sharp ears were picking up the nuances of their speech and her sharp eyes were taking in the details of their dress and mannerisms.

For everyday life at the Creek, she happily shed her sophisticated city clothes to wear the simple, loose fitting housedresses that were standard wear for the Cracker women. For hunting or fishing trips or forays into the hammock, she wore jeans, or jodphurs and boots and, if she expected to be in the sun for a long time, a hat made of palmetto fronds.

Undoubtedly, part of her appeal to the natives of Cross Creek was her sincere interest in them and her frank eagerness to learn from them everything they could teach her, from how to prepare their native dishes to how to hunt and fish. According to Chet Crosby, who became Marjorie's grove manager and who taught her a great deal about hunting and fishing, she became a "good fisherman" and a "pretty good hunter." A few years later, when her love of animals overcame her enjoyment of the sport of hunting, she still loved to go along with the huntsmen for the pleasure of the company and the enjoyment she got from being outdoors.

When white newcomers moved into the creek, they were sized up by the black residents, who then decided whom to assign to them as help. In *Cross Creek* Marjorie uses the elderly black woman, Martha Mickins, as a unifying element and gives her more importance than she actually had in the community. Nevertheless, Martha and her large brood were a constant presence and sometimes an irritation in Marjorie's life at Cross Creek. Martha, always neatly dressed with a large handkerchief tied around her head, had limited cooking and cleaning skills, but her spirit was willing. When Marjorie was between housekeepers, as often happened, Martha was faithfully there to "take up the slack," as she put it. Martha and her various offspring often entertained Marjorie and her guests with spirituals sung to an intricate accompaniment of syncopated foot patting and hand clapping. Her favorite, and Marjorie's, was "Come, Mary, Toll the Bell."

Marjorie could no more keep from getting involved with the family problems of her household and grove workers than she could keep from breathing. She paid for their operations and their doctor bills, helped them out when they had brushes with the law, drove them to distant villages to see kinfolk, and eventually became involved in fighting for the civil rights of her black helpers.

'Geechee, a one-eyed, fierce-looking black girl from the Ogeechee River area, appeared one day as Marjorie was typing away on her screen porch. Belligerently, 'Geechee announced that she had come to work for Marjorie, and that she would kill herself if she didn't give satisfaction. Half afraid of being murdered by the wild-eyed young woman, Marjorie took her on trial. Never had she found anyone who cleaned her house so thoroughly, cared so much for her comfort, or tried so hard to please in every way. Before long Marjorie was attached to 'Geechee and dependent on her, but as usual she found herself serving 'Geechee's needs, too. At 'Geechee's tearful insistence, Marjorie arranged to have Leroy, 'Geechee's "man," released from prison by promising to give him work. Leroy, however, proved to be shiftless and demanding and had to be dismissed. 'Geechee chose to stay with Marjorie rather than to leave with Leroy, but she soon began drinking heavily and uncontrollably. Sadly Marjorie and 'Geechee agreed that they must part. Once a year 'Geechee returned to visit, but she could not quit drinking, and they both realized the situation was irremediable.

When Max Perkins wrote to assure Marjorie that he was greatly interested in her future work and asked if there was any chance that she would write a full-length novel, she replied that she was "vibrating with material like a hive of bees in swarm." She had not one but four novels and a number of short narratives in mind.

To gather material for one of the short pieces, she drove over to the Suwannee River valley to uncover information on a man named

William E. Bell, a railroad building foreman, who had died a dozen years earlier. From stories she had heard about Bill Bell she concluded he was a legend in the making on the order of Mike Fink and John Henry. Everything about Bell was gargantuan—his size, his appetite, his strength, his voice, and his personality.

Making her headquarters in Trenton, the town Bell had built, Marjorie roved up and down the Suwannee, talking to the oldtimers who had known Lord Bill, as he was commonly called. On the stoops of feed and seed stores; in the back of general stores; in banks; on a pine Cracker porch; leaning on a split-rail fence around a watermelon field; in the glaring sun on a sandy road with mules and automobiles going around them, she talked to the people who remembered Lord Bill. She caught their delight in telling of this man who worked hard, played hard, drank hard, and fought hard;—and who was implacable to his enemies and sometimes embarrassingly generous to his friends and to strangers he chose to help.

In her sketch, Marjorie described Lord Bill as being about the size of "two Teddy Roosevelts" and looking a lot like him without the whiskers. Bill's 300 to 325 pounds were hard, except for an inch or two of fat on his big paunch. His voice, "deep as thunder and rich as flat-woods honey," struck terror into those who feared they had displeased him, and when he opened up and let it out it was like a "bull romping out of a pen."

Comparing him to Henry VIII, she called him the "king of two counties," who ruled their industries, their people, and their courts. She recorded the rowdy jokes he played indiscriminately on his friends, his black workers, and local lawmen; his feats of strength, his prodigious appetite; his love of fighting and hunting; and his capacity to wear out relays of men as he worked all day and played all night. Lord Bill was part owner of a palatial riverboat, and the stories she collected often ended with the refrain:

> *He went up and down the Suwannee River in a floatin' palace, straddlin' the stern and shuckin' hisself oysters. He ate them all the way up from the Gulf of Mexico, three or four crocus sacks of oysters.*

Convinced she had discovered a myth in the making, Marjorie worked on the narrative during the late spring of 1931 and submitted it to the *Scribner's* fiction contest for that year. "Lord Bill of the Suwannee River" was turned down by *Scribner's*, so she sent it to an editor of the *Atlantic Monthly*. It came back with a brief note saying that while they found it pleasant reading, the editors thought it "rather a pity that you haven't told a genuine story instead of piecing together these scraps of legend." Too busy with other writing projects for revisions, Marjorie put the manuscript away. Thirty years later, it was discovered and edited by Dr. Gorden E. Bigelow, a professor at the University of Florida, and published in the June 1963 issue of the *Southern Folklore Quarterly*, a decade after Marjorie's death. In Trenton in 1961, Dr. Bigelow found few people who had heard of Lord Bill. Therefore it seems that Marjorie's recording of the legends about him has preserved a colorful bit of frontier history that might otherwise have disappeared without a trace.

Growing oranges, trapping, fishing, and sometimes moonshining provided the livelihood for most of the Crackers in the Cross Creek area. Instead of playing cops and robbers, their children played fishermen and game wardens, with the last one chosen having to be the game warden. Some time after the turn of the century, large fishing companies that had discovered the richness of the Cross Creek lakes came from cities like Jacksonville to sweep the lakes with wide nets. The indignant Crackers went to their legislators and had it made illegal to seine or trap on the lakes, with the unwritten understanding that the law didn't apply to the local residents.

As transportation improved, sports fishermen from Gainesville and other places were attracted to the area, especially to Orange Lake. The state decided to enforce the law against seining and hired local game wardens. The Crackers had their own unwritten laws to protect the fishing. One was that no seine could have a sweep of more than seventy-five yards. Also no one could use a seine with a deep-water pocket take-up; the fishermen had to stand on shore or in shallow water to pick up the net. This way they couldn't ruin the lake for others.

The state law said the warden could take a seine anywhere he found it, even in the woods. Cracker law designated someone as the master of the seine, and only he could decide when to pull. It was a great honor for a boy to be allowed to serve as watchman for the seiners and to be the runner who went around whispering through screen doors, "We're gonna pull tonight."

Anytime the warden spotted the seiners and gave chase, there were numerous plans for eluding him. The rules were clear—the Creek's, not Tallahassee's, rules. If the game warden touched you, tagged you, you were fairly caught and must appear in court to answer his charges. The next morning after a chase the Crackers met at the bridge (the social center of the Creek), scratched, skinned, and mosquito-chewed from running through the woods and swamps, to tell and retell their adventures. If the local game warden, a man they had known all their lives, came up, he would say, "I understand there was a little hell of a chase on B____ Island last night." The Crackers responded, "Is that right?" and shook their heads as they played out the ritual.

Trapping was basic to the Cracker's lives. Here, again, they set their own limits and territorial rules, which had little to do with state laws, but a great deal to do with their understanding of natural laws and human needs. Before hunting season began, they would meet at the bridge and decide what the bag limit would be. In a bad year, with dry weather, they might decide not to shoot quail that season or to shoot over the coveys and break them up so the quail would pair off the next year. In a good year, when one kind of creature was overpopulated, their limits were apt to exceed those set by the government.

As Marjorie came to understand the Cracker's viewpoint, she also came to sympathize with it. In a number of her stories and novels, her Crackers do things that are wrong according to the law but right according to their own code. Moonshining was an even more dangerous way to eke out a living than illegal trapping or seining. One spring Marjorie visited the federal court at Gainsville, when the docket consisted mostly of Cracker moonshine cases. Her sympathies were entirely with the 'shiners. She told Samuel Crichton, a Scribner editor, that she despised the "rat-faced, whining-voiced" agents who testified "unctuously," and the "well-fed, detached" judge, who laughed at his own jokes and refused to give the impoverished Crackers a second chance.

One case in particular touched her. Jim, the defendant, admitted to having made and sold some moonshine. When his crops failed, he had turned to making corn liquor to get cash to feed his family. Marjorie saw Jim and his wife as an "elderly Mart and Florry," with seven clean, quiet, undernourished children. Even though Jim promised not to make moonshine again, the judge fined him $100. With no chance of raising the money, Jim would have to work out the fine on the county work gang at a dollar a day. For one hundred days, Marjorie wrote, "The woman will plough their small patch of corn, the children will weed sweet potatoes by hand, and they will have less to eat than ever." She added, "And they say *I* malign the Crackers in my descriptions. Do, Jesus!" (An expression she had picked up from Martha Mickens.)

One of her short stories about moonshining appeared in the *Scribner's Magazine* for December 1931. It concerns a young moonshiner named Tim, who by pluck and perseverence outwits the revenuers lying in wait for him. Tim tells his own story in authentic Cracker dialogue with self-deprecating humor. Called "A Plum Clare Conscience," the story enhanced the growing reputation Marjorie was earning as a regional writer.

A second story she was working on at about the same time was based on a personal experience. Beans were among the garden vegetables she and Chuck grew to supplement their income, but making a successful bean crop depended on luck and a willingness to gamble. If the beans were planted early, a late spring frost could kill them. If they were planted late, the market might be glutted and prices at rock bottom by the time they were ready to harvest. In the spring of 1931, they had planted their beans early. When a late frost was forecast, they desperately covered each of the young bean plants one by one with sand. After the cold passed and the sun warmed the earth, they fearfully scraped away the sand. The plants emerged a little yellowed and wilted, but soon recovered from their warm burial. All the other bean crops in the area were destroyed by the freeze, and the Rawlingses got a high price on the produce market. This true incident, plus one connected with the sudden closing of a bank (a common event in the early thirties), formed the main story line of "A Crop of Beans," which was bought by *Scribner's Magazine*.

"Jacob's Ladder" and her short stories had caught the attention of editors in several publishing houses, and from some of them Marjorie received tentative inquiries about her next work. Scribners advised her it was time to get an agent to represent her foreign, serial, and movie rights. At their suggestion she selected the firm of Brandt and Brandt to represent her, and Carl and Carol Brandt, the owners, soon became her trusted friends.

In order to gather material for her first full-length novel, Marjorie made arrangements to board with the Fiddia Family in the Big Scrub country. Arriving in late August of 1931, she remained for two and a half months with the family, which consisted of a tiny wiry old woman named Piety and her long, lanky son, Leonard, a moonshiner. Living in their house on a high bluff above the Oklawaha River, she immersed herself in the life of the scrub country. Helping Piety with her chores, Marjorie washed heavy quilts by stomping them in wash tubs and then boiling them in the same tubs over fatwood fires. She made lye soap from wood ashes and grease and brooms from sage. Under a mosquito net, she slept as the Fiddias did on one sheet covered by a light or a heavy quilt, according to the weather. She scrubbed floors with corn shuck brushes and dried them by shuffling over them barefooted on cloths.

She helped keep the family in squirrel meat, and she did all the illegal things with the men of the Scrub, including stalking deer with a light at night, out of season; paddling the boat while Leonard dynamited mullet; and shooting limpkin (a kind of crane). She told Max Perkins, "If you haven't eaten roast limpkin, you just haven't eaten, but you can go to county, state, and federal jails for shooting them." But she defended her new friends, who killed only the game they needed for food, by comparing their hunting with the wasteful and unnecessary killing done by licensed hunters for sport.

Marjorie also learned a great deal more about the technique of making moonshine, which was to be an important element in her novel. A week before she had arrived at the Fiddia house, a cousin of Leonard's had betrayed him to federal agents, who smashed and burned his still. She sat in on a discussion by a group of 'shiners and their friends as to what should be done to the traitor. "They are closing in on him," she told Perkins, "and some day he will simply disappear." This incident, too, would become a part of the plot of her book.

Her willingness to enter wholeheartedly into their lives won the confidence of the families she met in the Scrub. In addition to the Fiddias, she became particularly close to a family named Long. Cal Long, whose family had been pioneers in the Big Scrub in the 1870s, proved to be a valuable source of information about the early days in the Scrub, and in the future she would give him credit for furnishing her with much material for *The Yearling*.

She found it so easy to live these people's lives with them that she told Perkins, "I am in some danger of losing all sophistication and perspective." She was surprised to find how precarious and literally hand-to-mouth their living was; and yet, though they lived on the edge of starvation and danger, she found a zest, a sense of humor, and an alertness to beauty that delighted her. Determined to capture the essence of their lives in her book, she sat under her mosquito netting, night after night, filling her notebooks by the light of a kerosene lamp.

When Marjorie returned to Cross Creek in mid-October, her notebooks were crammed with "voluminous notes of the intimate type, for which the most prolific imagination is no substitute," she told Perkins. She set about immediately transcribing them into a novel.

CHAPTER 5

An End and a Beginning

Although Marjorie liked to start with a title and "work around it," and often did with her short stories, she usually had to struggle to find the right titles for her novels. She considered calling her first book *The Scrub* or *The Big Scrub*, but was afraid of the word's football connotations to people who lived outside Florida. She finally settled on *South Moon Under*, a phrase she had learned from the people of the Scrub, who were conscious at all times of the position of the sun and the moon, the stars, and the wind. It was important to them to know that deer, fish, and other creatures stirred and fed "on the moon"—at moon rise; at south-moon-over, when the moon was at its zenith; at moon down; and at south-moon-under, when the moon was directly under the earth. Max Perkins enthusiastically endorsed her choice.

As the book evolved, the two main characters became based on the Fiddias. Piety Jacklin, like her namesake, grows up to be a wispy ninety-pound woman who can plow a field, hunt, or fish for the family's supper, fell a tree, or kill a rattlesnake. The adoration that Piety as a child feels for her father clearly echoes Marjorie's feelings for her own father. Lant Jacklin, Piety's son, is based on the gangling, self-sufficient Leonard Fiddia, and he, too, is a child of the Scrub. He knows and understands it and the surrounding country and the river and its ways as well as any human can. He is an expert woodsman and naturalist who, as conditions dictate, makes his living tracking, trapping, fishing, 'gatoring, hunting, logging, and making moonshine.

Like Thomas Hardy, Marjorie considered place so important that it almost becomes a character in her novels. In fact, she had to constantly prune and cut back her descriptions of Florida background in her books to keep it from taking over. She defined the actual scrub area of Florida for Max Perkins as the entire area bounded on the west and north by the Oklawaha River and on the east by the St. Johns River and Lake George. The setting of *South Moon Under* is the northern portion of the Scrub, lying between the crossroads town of Eureka and the junction of the Oklawaha and the St. Johns. The area, she told him, is covered with scrub pine (also called sand pine and southern spruce), scrub oak, a little blackjack oak, and low bushes. The hammock fringe, lying in a thin strip between river and scrub, she described as being composed of live oak, magnolia, sweet gum, ironwood, several kinds of bay, holly, ash, dogwood, hickory, and cabbage palms (palmettos). The swamp at the foot of the hammock contained dense stands of cypress, palmetto, and ash intertwined with briers and rattan. Low, marshy places, wet, grass-filled, and boggy, are called prairies, and islands are pine islands—sections of slash pines or long-leaf yellow pine.

Prowling this region with Leonard Fiddia, Cal Long, and other natives, Marjorie learned the names of the plants and trees and their uses and their dangers. She knew which wood made good axe handles and which did not, and she learned that the red cypress gum that blistered her skin was thought to be a cancer cure by the local people.

Once, hunting with a small group in the Scrub, she got separated from the others. Surprised to find she felt no panic, she sat down on a log. For the first time she experienced "the palpability of silence." Such a sense of peace settled over her that when she heard the signal shots of her friends who were searching for her, she was reluctant to answer. This mystic experience confirmed her belief that the danger and vast silence of the wilderness area must have an effect upon the people who lived close to it. In *South Moon Under* there are several occasions when characters get lost in the Scrub.

The Oklawaha River, which ran swift and deep and was from fifty to three hundred feet wide, was a transportation route for the people of the region. Marjorie learned from Leonard to know it and its creeks and tributaries well. In *South Moon Under*, the descriptions of the river trips that Lant makes, rafting cypress logs to the Palatka market, have the realism and richness of detail of Mark Twain's river descriptions.

Marjorie's experiences with the wild life in the Scrub are woven into the story. From her own observations, she described hunting for alligators and skinning them; deer hunts and butchering; fishing for bait and for large-mouth bass; trapping and finding skunks, possums, weasels, and otters in the traps. And she included the unpleasant experience of finding the toes and fur of coons that had chewed their way free from the traps. She also used her feeling of chagrin when she accidently killed a mother squirrel with breasts full of milk and her sorrow in thinking of the bright eyes of the baby squirrels who would be peering eagerly from their nest, awaiting the return of the mother.

Marjorie's descriptions of making moonshine, building a fence, fire fighting, logging, and cane grinding are filled with such accurate details that they can be used as guides for performing these activities. She was scrupulous in her use of historical detail so that in the forty-five years covered by the action of the story, the types of transportation, the ways of cooking, and the kinds of guns used, change to fit the time. And she incorporated into the action the folklore and superstitions of the people, such as turning a hat inside out to stop the noise of a screech owl, and planting crops and killing hogs "on the moon."

She made good use of recent as well as distant events that were told to her. One of these occurred when a stranger moved into the cattle area across the river from the Scrub and fenced in his land. This was perfectly legal, but it was not in accord with the Cracker practice of fencing in crops and letting cattle range freely as they needed to do in order to find sufficient food and water. When the stranger ignored the requests and then the warnings of the local cattlemen, they banded together, took the offender into the woods, and gave him a harsh beating. After a similar incident in *South Moon Under*, one of her characters expresses the Cracker philosophy: "They's things beyond the law is right and wrong, accordin' to how many folks they he'ps or harms."

One night Marjorie had gone by rowboat with Piety Fiddia to visit an old woman who was dying. The woman described her spells of semiconsciousness, telling them, "I go off into the twilight; into some lonesome-looking place." These are the exact words Piety Jacklin speaks in the deathbed scene in the book.

By the middle of August 1932, Marjorie had completed a draft of the book, and she decided to deliver it personally to her agent and publisher in New York. Chuck had gone to Lake Ontario to cover the yacht races for a Canadian paper, so she got an excursion boat to New York, planning to return to Florida with him by water. She stayed with her Aunt Wilmer Kinnan, a teacher in New Rochelle, and went into New York to leave copies of her manuscript with Carl Brandt and with Max Perkins in his cluttered office on the fifth floor over Scribner's elegant bookstore on Fifth Avenue. She left no record of these meetings, but apparently the personal encounters only reinforced her warm relationship with her editor and agents.

Then she joined Chuck in Canada for three days. Chuck was in a good mood, doing the thing he loved, mixing with the yachting crowd, and they had a pleasant time. It would be the last good time they would have together.

After Max Perkins had read Marjorie's manuscript, he wrote that he found it "highly interesting." He pointed out, however, that she had let her eagerness to use the masses of material she had collected cause her to create more of an episodic "social chronicle" than a novel. In an eight-page letter he made specific suggestions for weaving the episodes together and for arousing reader interest and expectation by intensifying the relationships of the main characters. He especially wanted Kezzy, who supplies the love interest and adds to the rivalry between Lant and his treacherous cousin Cleve, to appear earlier in the story. Perkins called the fence-raising scene that opens the book "a classic," but suggested she let it be seen through Piety's eyes rather than through the author's. He praised the river material as being as "good as Huckleberry Finn," but urged her to tell it directly and specifically, instead of generalizing about it.

Chapter by chapter he made suggestions for strengthening the story line and for increasing the readers' interest in the characters. He praised the ending as "splendid" and told her, "I have great hopes for the book." Marjorie responded enthusiastically to his suggestions. "I am astonished at how far I went out of my way to be random and rambling," she told him. "The direct narrative form throughout is so patently required. . . ." She was eager to rewrite along the lines he suggested; but, perhaps remembering her childhood stories, she half-humorously said that the only hard thing he asked of her was to give up the wolf in the story. Always sensitive to his authors' wishes, Perkins took her seriously and suggested ways in which the wolf *could* be used in the action. In the end, however, Marjorie put the wolf material aside. Several years later she would use the material effectively in *The Yearling*.

She began work on the revisions at once, sending them in installments to Perkins, but she was alarmed when he began turning the chapters over to the printer after only a brief look at them. He soothed her by telling her they could look at it closely and judge how it read better in the galley proofs. He did not tell her until later that his reason for hurrying the book along was that he secretly hoped it would be chosen as a Book-of-the-Month Club selection.

As she worked on the revisions, Chuck read some of the chapters. On several occasions Marjorie had told Max Perkins that she trusted Chuck's critical judgment. Now Chuck said, "I'm going to make a suggestion that will infuriate you . . . take out all your profanity. If you do this, you automatically open up a wide and continuous market for the book among boys. . . ." He was right about the effect of his suggestion. Caustically, Marjorie replied that if she followed his suggestion, the book could be the first of a series titled, "The Rover Boys in Florida." After being calmed with "copious draughts of native rye," she listened while Chuck explained that what he meant was that it was a shame that a book with so much woods and river lore should be cut off from the young audience to whom *Treasure Island, Huckleberry Finn*, and some of Kipling appealed, simply because of "unnecessary" profanity.

Marjorie submitted the suggestion to Perkins, telling him, "In spite of your betrayal of me by handing over the manuscript to the printer without being sure that it contained no atrocities, I trust you implicitly as an artist and a critic, and I shall accept your judgment in the matter without further question."

Perkins replied, "The truth is that words which are objected to have a suggestive power for the reader which is quite other than they have to those who use them. But most of your words are not of that character." He told her he felt Hemingway had sacrificed thousands of sales by his gratuitous use of profanity, adding, "I do not think he need have done it." He did not feel there was much language in *South Moon Under* that would hurt its popular appeal. He pointed that it would be unnatural for Lant, after struggling repeatedly to roll a huge dead alligator into his boat, to say through his tears of frustration anything else but, "God damn you, you stinking bastard, I'll not leave go. . . ."

Perkins also told Marjorie that although some people would object to the speeches of a crazy character named Ramrod, his words would lose their point if "Jesus" were changed to "Satan." According to her story, the minister who baptizes old Ramrod in the Oklawaha River steps into a deep hole and in his panicky scrambling for the bank almost drowns Ramrod, cracking his head on a rock as he drags him out. Since that time, Ramrod has never been right in his mind and has blamed "Ol' Desus Chwist" for all his troubles. In the end, a few substitutions (especially for the many "sons of bitches") were made, but most of the language was deemed by Perkins and by her to be integral to the story.

While Marjorie worked at the revisions of *South Moon Under* galley proofs, she was running a low-grade fever and was belatedly diagnosed as having "double malaria." Nevertheless, throughout the autumn, she continued to exchange revised chapters and corrected galley proofs with Max Perkins. She sent off her final corrections with a note, "If you like the book, I shall drink a quart of Bacardi in celebration. If you don't like it, I shall drink a quart of Bacardi."

The malaria finally forced her to collapse. Her fever peaked at 105°, and throughout December she took large doses of quinine. By Christmas she was recovered enough from the malaria to go with

Chuck to spend the holiday at the hunting lodge of their Tampa surgeon friend Dr. J. C. Vinson. After four years of mostly corn liquor, they enjoyed his fine Burgundy and other wines. Back at Cross Creek they went duck hunting with friends, but Marjorie had little luck. "I'm no good at hunting anything on the wing, anyway," she admitted to Perkins.

In response, Perkins told her about going on a duck hunting trip with Ernest Hemingway in Arkansas and nearly freezing to death. Marjorie repeated the invitation she had made to him several times, to come to Cross Creek where he could enjoy hunting and fishing in more comfort. Perkins promised that if she ever considered it indispensable to consult him about a novel, he would feel he had the right to come.

About the middle of January he wrote to tell her that the Book-of-the-Month Club had chosen *South Moon Under* as its dual March offering along with George Bernard Shaw's *Adventures of a Black Girl in Her Search for God*. As Perkins pointed out, this was a fortunate advertising break for the book in a time when advertising budgets at publishing houses were pinched by the Depression. Ironically, in another way it turned out to be an unfortunate break. To meet the Book-of-the-Month Club date, Scribners delayed offering the book to the public, so that it actually made its appearance on the very day in 1933 when President Roosevelt ordered all banks closed for a holiday. They could not have found a worse moment in the century to bring out her first novel, Perkins later told Marjorie. But Marjorie was delighted with the Book-of-the-Month selection, and told Perkins, "You are taking the most beautiful care of me." And she found it "rather amusing" to bring out her first book on the day "the financial system of the country goes to pot!"

Surprised to find that the publicity man at Scribners apparently didn't know the difference between crocodiles and alligators, she informed him that crocodiles existed only in the extreme southern portion of Florida and were quite distinct from the alligators common to most Florida waterways. She also verified for the doubting Thomases at Scribners that a thirty-foot alligator had been caught on the Oklawaha.

Now the book was out of her hands, she half-dreaded its publication. Lamenting that it fell short of the artistry she had struggled to achieve, she said, "It's like being caught half-dressed." Waves of depression overwhelmed her, and she wondered if she would ever write again. She tried to find mental rest by prowling around Florida, spending some time on the St. Augustine beaches. Her acute emotional distress was not simply the postpartum blues felt by many writers after the labor and delivery of a book. Her marriage with Chuck was in the final stages of breaking up.

The excitement and diversion of the move to Florida had only delayed what now began to seem inevitable. Publicly, both Chuck and Marjorie were careful not to criticize or blame each other. In interviews or autobiographical sketches, Marjorie always spoke of their parting as "amicable," and each of them praised the other's work to outsiders. Privately, and to their relatives and intimate friends, each accused the other of being impossible to live with. Marjorie could not understand why Chuck could not recover from her volatile moods as quickly as she did, and she could not tolerate his increasingly hypercritical attitude.

One of Marjorie's most admirable qualities was her complete freedom from professional jealousy. She wrote many warm, impulsive letters of praise to authors whose work she liked. Since before their marriage, she constantly praised Chuck's writing, always urging him to do more. His articles about sponge fishing and yachting appeared in such reputable magazines as the *Saturday Evening Post*, the *Atlantic Monthly*, and *Adventure*. When he made his first sale to the "Boston Bastards" (the *Atlantic Monthly*), they had a big celebration.

However, when Marjorie's Florida writings began to bring her recognition, Chuck found it hard to bear. His criticism of her writing and of her personally became increasingly harsh. During a showdown in March of 1933, he told her he realized he had always had an inferiority complex as far as she was concerned. Trying to explain their break-up to Bee McNeil, Marjorie said they had never been happy for very long at a time, although they had been very much in love and had similar tastes and backgrounds. She admitted, "I don't question that my independence, my very love of the fight of life, all my character, were too harsh to bring out the best in him." For years she had thought if she could be a gentler and more patient wife, it would solve their problems, but, she told Bee, she had finally come to realize that changing her behavior would not change his immaturity. This immaturity, she decided, was the root of their difficulties:

> *You will remember that rather ingratiating shyness and self-deprecation. He never got over it. He never, in a way, matured. He kept a high school boy's philosophy and psychology to the end. That might have been rather touching if it had taken a touching or appealing form. But with me, he was completely the bully. I took constant abuse. And because I loved him so, and just couldn't admit, even to myself, that he was an utterly impossible person to live with, I kept on year after year kidding myself, thinking that if this was changed, or that was changed, he would be all right and we would be happy.*

"He kept his good looks, charm, delightful personality (when he felt like it), brains and so on," she told Bee, "but with a queer something to spoil them all." These attributes and the remembrance of their early love held her long after "I really in my secret heart hated him." As she increasingly became his scapegoat for everything that went wrong with his work or in their lives, she awoke each morning dreading the first ugly remark. During the last winter they were together, Marjorie told Bee, Chuck tried to convince her she was going crazy. Ida Tarrant, Chuck's great-aunt by marriage, happened to be visiting them and "almost tore him down," threatening to make his life hell if she ever caught him at such a vicious thing again.

Although she hated the idea of a divorce, by the spring of 1933, Marjorie was so miserable she decided her only choice was between separation and suicide. One day when she was particularly depressed, Chuck asked her if she wanted him to leave, and she said yes.

She felt an immediate sense of relief, but also one of doubt, wondering if she had made the right decision. The good reviews and fan mail for *South Moon Under* that began coming in failed to rouse her spirits. In an effort to escape the restlessness and depression that enveloped her, she agreed to make a river trip with Dr. Vinson's wife, Dessie Smith Vinson. Dessie, whom Marjorie described to Perkins as "an amazingly capable sportswoman," was as forthright and adventure-loving as Marjorie herself. Although she was some ten years younger than Marjorie, she was her mentor in many ways and always called her "young un."

The two women planned to go down the St. Johns River (which flows from south to north) from its source, ominously named Lake Hellenblazes, for several hundred miles in an eighteen-foot rowboat with an outboard motor. Their way lay for at least one hundred miles through forsaken marsh country dotted with palm islands. They were warned many times over of the danger of getting lost in false channels. "All this strenuous out-door stuff is new to me since coming to Florida," Marjorie told Perkins, adding that her chief claim to capability in such matters lay only in being "game for anything." Perkins wished her luck and expressed some anxiety about the trip, as she no doubt intended him to do. Citing the dangers to him, she quoted the motto of a Cracker friend, "No fool, no fun."

The trip did have its moments of danger and of extreme discomfort, but these were more than compensated for by moments of pure delight and by the satisfaction of making a trip that caused river men to shake their heads—and to express envy. Dessie did the steering and hunting, and Marjorie handled the navigating and the cooking. They were occasionally lost, but Marjorie was pleased with herself for learning to find the river channels by observing the movement of the floating hyacinths that covered it. She also took pride in her ability to whip up a tasty meal out of whatever Dessie or nature provided. In her all-purpose Dutch oven, she roasted wild duck, simmered swamp cabbage with white bacon, and baked cornbread. And over hot coals she broiled shad, shad roe, and other fish.

On the last day of the trip, Dessie insisted Marjorie shoot turtles along the Oklawaha River, nearly all day. As a result Marjorie injured her right thumb, which became badly infected. She hastened to assure friends who might think she was a "wanton murderer" that the shooting of the turtles was not just for target practice, although she did need that. But the fact was that the turtles were the worst enemies of fish life in the river. The natives used to think the alligators were, but now they knew that the alligators kept down the turtles. And since so many of the alligators had been killed off, the turtles had multiplied dangerously.

After she returned to Cross Creek, Marjorie wrote an article describing the trip, which was published as "Hyacinth Drift" in *Scribner's Magazine* and later as a separate chapter in *Cross Creek*. In the last paragraph, she speaks of her homecoming. "The creek was home. Oleanders were sweet past bearing, and my own shabby fields, weed-tangled, were newly dear. I knew, for a moment, that the only nightmare is the masochistic human mind." She was, almost certainly, referring to Chuck.

A pile of correspondence awaited Marjorie at Cross Creek. Some of it concerned a mix-up over the foreign rights to *South Moon Under*, which occurred when both Scribners and Brandt and Brandt sent copies of the book to literary agents in England. Max Perkins took the blame for the misunderstanding upon his own shoulders, although Marjorie was inclined at first to blame Charles Scribner. Perkins wrote to her on his own personal stationery, begging her *not* to blame Mr. Scribner, whom he described as "almost quixotically honest." Perkins was anxious for her to meet Mr. Scribner and see for herself what an honest and sincere person he was.

Marjorie, still euphoric from the river trip, wrote a rather flippant answer. This was followed the next day by an apology, in case she had hurt his feelings, and a quotation from Robert Louis Stevenson:

> *Down life's great cathedral aisle*
> *I love to scamper, love to race;*
> *To swing by my irreverent tail*
> *All over the most sacred place.*

The problem was smoothed out; the English agents were pacified, and *South Moon Under* was published in England by Faber and Faber that same spring. And before long Marjorie was counting Charles Scribner as one of her good friends.

She found the reviews of *South Moon Under* both gratifying and exasperating. Most of them praised her writing highly. The New York *Times* said "it glows with the breath of life" and called it "a living document," but the reviewer described Piety as a "blind and toothless hag" and referred to the setting as "a remote and repellent region of stunted trees, rattlesnakes, and 'gators." The New York *Herald Tribune* spoke of the novel as being rich in emotion and understanding, but defined the characters as "members of the sub-species of the human race called Florida Crackers." Marjorie told Max Perkins she felt like a Judas for having delivered the Crackers into the hands of the Philistine critics. He and she agreed that the English and Scottish reviewers showed more insight. The Aberdeen *Press* found her Crackers "spirited and virile pioneers," and the Oxford *Times* called them "rugged settlers" who struggled against great odds. She was especially pleased that the London *Times Literary Supplement* emphasized the cosmic pattern she had used in the book, an element that American reviewers tended to overlook.

Fan mail was a problem. Her experience with the responses to "Jacob's Ladder" and to her short stories had convinced her that it was almost impossible to hit the right note. If she answered with too much warmth, she found herself involved in correspondence with strangers, which was impossible to keep up. If she sounded too cool, she was marked as being "high-hat." Her solution was to answer only those that interested her. One of these was the president of the National Association of Audubon Societies. Having grown up in the Florida piney woods, he wrote that he had read the book through twice with great delight and satisfaction at her familiarity with the Cracker, his point of view, his language, and his daily life.

Another enjoyable correspondence grew out of a fan letter from novelist Robert Chambers, who called *South Moon Under* "a work of art." And the playwright Sidney Howard equated her novel with Kipling's *Jungle Book*, adding that no novel in a long time had given him so much pleasure and happiness. Another long-lasting friendship resulted from her correspondence with Florida writer and conservationist Marjory Stoneham Douglas, who urged Marjorie to visit her in her thatched roof cottage in Coral Gables. She was gratified to hear from old college friends like her *Lit* co-editor Ernest Meyer, who marveled at her understanding of the Crackers and her lyric description of the region. He had a hard time reconciling the author of *South Moon Under* with the popular college girl, who went to picnics in silk stockings and high heels. Arthur C. Nielsen, who had founded the A. C. Nielsen Rating Company, wrote that he felt a special elation at her success. He confessed that he had made many poor selections in the field of business, but back in 1917 he had placed a heavy bet "mentally" that she would reach the top.

The reaction that Marjorie enjoyed most was that of Leonard Fiddia, the model for Lant, the protagonist in the novel. Before the book was published, she had read a large part of it to Leonard, asking if he would be upset by her protrayal in the book. He told her, "Good Lord, no, that don't hurt nobody." But he did tell a mutual friend, "It's a good thing she didn't tell no more'n she did about my huntin'—she'd of had the game warden on my neck shore." He seemed unconcerned about the danger from the revenue agent, perhaps because his new still was well-hidden.

When Marjorie brought the Fiddias a copy of the book, "suitably and gratefully" inscribed, Leonard told her, "You done a damn good job, for a Yankee." His relatives and friends tormented him to lend them the book, but he refused at first to lend it to his Uncle Zeke to take home because he told Marjorie he was afraid his uncle's wife would tear up the book or burn it. Astonished, she asked why his aunt might do such a thing. "Well," Leonard said, "She's one o' them Christian-hearted sons o' bitches, and peculiar as Hell, to boot. You got right smart o' cussin' in the book, and she might be scairt her boy Lester'd learn to cuss by it. Now Lester kin out-cuss the book right now—but his Mammy don't know it."

Marjorie was pleased that Leonard treasured his copy of "The Book," as he called it, so it surprised her to see it one day sitting on his table, swollen about three times as thick as it should be, showing signs of having been left out in the rain. Leonard told her he had finally lent the book to his Uncle Zeke, who had hidden it under some bushes to keep his wife from seeing it. "Come up a storm and it just caught hell," he said. When Marjorie asked Leonard if he would like another copy, he said, "If it don't disfurnish you none." When she brought the new book out to him, she asked if he would like her to autograph it. He said, "What's that?" and when she answered, "Sign my name," he replied, "Hell, that don't benefit nobody."

When Marjorie described Leonard's reaction to the book to Perkins, he thought it would make interesting reading in the publicity for the book and asked her about using it. To protect her friends, she warned him against making public mention of her connection with any particular family in the scrub, since it was conceivable that "one of them 'Christian-hearted sons of bitches' would raise a great row about moonshining in Marion County being so common and public that a Yankee writer could make a book about it." She did, however, use the story, disguising the identities, as an ice-breaking introduction in many of her lectures.

CHAPTER · 6

Divorce

In the 1930s publishing houses tried to avoid giving advances against royalties to their writers; and in any case, Marjorie never liked to take money in advance for her writing because she felt it put her under a kind of pressure to produce and complete her projects that she did not like. When Chuck left in March of 1933, they divided everything they owned jointly. The combination of a poor orange crop and low prices had been a heavy blow, and by mid-April her cash supply was almost exhausted. She wrote to ask Perkins when she could expect to receive a royalty check.

Her contract with Scribners for *South Moon Under* called for a 10 percent royalty on the first 3,000 copies sold, and 15 percent thereafter. The book was on the New York *Herald Tribune*'s best seller list by the middle of April and was advertised as selling sixty thousand copies in sixty days. But since it retailed for only two dollars, it took a lot of sales to amount to much in royalties. Marjorie had to bite her tongue when friends in Ocala proudly told her they were on the library's waiting list for the book or were waiting to borrow it from a friend. "Do they think I'm an orchid that can live on air?" she complained to Perkins. He sent her a check for $1,000, for which she thanked him, but asked for more information about the money coming to her. She had long overdue notes, a car that was falling to pieces, and a roof that leaked.

"Is a writer supposed to be kept in mystical ignorance like a child waiting for Santa Claus? What will be the total figure and total cash settlement?" she asked. She needed to make long-range plans about whether to use her small cash reserve. Perkins explained that the Book-of-the-Month Club paid a flat rate of $8,000, which was divided equally between author and publisher. He sent her her $4,000 share, telling her to let him know if she needed more money.

South Moon Under was a contender for the French Prix Femina Americana award for 1933. When it lost out in the final competition, Marjorie told Perkins, "Prizes are relative, don't matter, All that does is coming as close as the limitations allow to re-creating the thing that stirs me." She mentioned coming to New York, and Perkins invited her to attend a dinner for authors sponsored by his Alma Mater, Princeton. She decided not to go to New York at that time, telling Perkins, "After your threats about the dinner, I can't say I'm sorry. Can you imagine anything more revolting than a large room crawling with authors?"

After finishing a number of short pieces, she was thinking seriously about her next novel, which she at first called *Hamaca*, the Spanish word for the hammock area that was to be its setting. Her main character was to be a young Englishman who was exiled by his family to Florida with a remittance. She planned to contrast his loathing for the savage aspects of the hammock area with the serene acceptance and love of its wild beauty by the Crackers. "It goes without saying that you are indispensable to my plans for another novel," she told Perkins. He did not discourage her from doing this book, but on June 1 he wrote a sentence that teased her imagination. "I want to talk to you about another possible plan for you in connection with writing."

Marjorie wrote back that the only possible plan she could imagine his having for her would be to do a textbook for Scribner's educational department on "The Principle and Practice of Moonshine Liquor." And, of course, she baited him into telling her immediately what he had in mind:

I was simply going to suggest that you do a book about a child in the scrub, which would be designed for what we have come to call younger readers. You remember your husband spoke of how excellent parts of South Moon Under *were for boys. It was true. If you wrote about a child's life, either a girl or a boy, or both, it would certainly be a fine publication.*

It need not interfere with the novel she was working on, but could be incubating in her mind, he told her. Her first reaction was one of "sheer distress," but on second thought she was intrigued. Recalling her success as a child in telling spellbinding stories to her young peers, she told Perkins, "We'll certainly have to talk about it."

In the meantime she struggled with her second novel. As always her research was painstaking. The time of the book was to be in the heyday of the orange industry from 1890 to 1895, before the disastrous freeze of 1895, and during the five years following it. She traveled around the state searching out the remnants of English colonists who had experienced the devastation of the big freeze. She took notes of their recollections, and some of them put her in touch with English relatives who could help with background material there.

Now that her royalty checks were coming in, she decided to go to England to look over several shires in order to choose the area from which her remittance man would have come. She hoped also that a change of scenery would lift her spirits and give her a clearer perspective on the breakup of her marriage. She planned to spend all of August and the first week or two of September in England, with a stopover in New York to consult with Max Perkins about her "young readers" book.

Arriving in London, she rented an Austin and toured the countryside, staying in quaint old country inns. One night in Hampshire she stayed at a place run by a hideous pugilist and overrun with cats. Generally, she found the English people kind and friendly under their outer crust of reserve. "If you sit quietly at table and don't speak and don't spill things, all of a sudden someone passes you the toast and accepts you," she told a friend. She reported to him and to other acquaintances that she had a "grand" summer, but she confided to Bee McNeil that she was in such despair and torment that she might as well have been in jail. Apparently, however, she found one new friend who brightened some of her days and to whom she confided her black feelings. They went fishing together, and it may have been he who traveled with her to show her some of the shires. After she left, he wrote telling her he missed her and longed to hear her voice again. He signed his letter, "Yours ever and more unsaid, Bertie."

En route home on the S. S. *Minnewaska*, Marjorie wrote to Ernest Meyer, expressing her discontent. She avoided mentioning the pending divorce, but told him that although she had found a measure of success in her writing, peace and security still eluded her, and she was overcome with *Weltschmerz* (literally "world pain" or sadness over the evils of the world).

Ironically, while she was in this despairing mood, two of her best comic stories were lifting the spirits of thousands of readers. "Alligators" appeared in the *Saturday Evening Post* on September 23, 1933. At Marjorie's insistence the credit line read "by Marjorie Kinnan Rawlings with Fred Tompkins." Tompkins, her neighbor and friend, had taken her on a number of 'gator hunts and he had supplied most of the anecdotes in the story. Nowhere in her writing is Marjorie's mastery of the Cracker dialect better illustrated. In between the opening paragraph:

> *Bless Katy, I don't know nothing about alligators. You belong to talk to some of them real old-timey Florida 'gator hunters that has messed up with 'em deliberate. I don't never mess up with no alligator. If so chance me and one meets, it's just because he comes up with me—I don't never try to come up with him. There ain't never been but once when me and a alligator met more than accidental.*

and the closing one:

> *You see how come it to happen. 'Twasn't nothing in the world but the banana brandy. I didn't have no intention of riding no alligator. I ain't the man you belong to talk to at all. You*

*go talk to some of them fellers that has hunted alligators. I
just naturally don't know nothing about them.*

the narrator spins a number of wildly exaggerated alligator yarns.
They involve such characters as Br'er Cresey, who hates a varmint
or a snake or a 'gator the most of any man; Rance Deese, who can
grunt alligators out of their holes, and Nub-footed Turner, who had
his foot bit off by a 'gator.

When she received a check for several hundred dollars from the
Post in payment for the story, she went to Fred Tompkins's home
to pay him the half she had promised him. Tompkins was away, and
his wife refused to take the money, saying it was too much. Marjorie
reminded her that Fred had supplied most of the material. "I know,
honey," Mrs. Tompkins answered, "but tellin' is one thing and composing is another." Marjorie was impressed by the woman's insight,
and she later used this incident to illustrate the difference between
fact and fiction to the creative writing classes she taught at the University of Florida. It showed, she told them, how the artist must
transfer the facts he works with by using his imagination and creative
skill.

"Benny and the Bird Dogs," which appeared in *Scribner's Magazine* in October, was the first of Marjorie's comic stories told by
Quincey Dover, a philosophical Cracker woman, who weighs almost
three hundred pounds. The Cracker vernacular drips from her tongue
like melted butter. Quincey describes Uncle Benny (for whom Fred
Tompkins was the prototype) as a "comical-appearing somebody":

> *He's small and quick and he don't move—he prances. He has
> a small bald suntanned head with a rim of white hair around
> the back of it. Where the hair ends at the sides of his head,
> it sticks straight up over his ears in two little white tufts like
> goat horns. He's got bright blue eyes that look at you quick
> and wicked, the way a goat looks. That's exactly what he
> looks and acts like—a mischievous little old billy-goat.*

Uncle Benny, who calls his wife "Old Hen," because she constantly clucks at him, is notorious for playing the fool, which usually involves playing tricks on somebody. He has seven bird dogs that go with him everywhere in the back seat of his old Model-T Ford. The dogs sit in seven rocking chairs on his front porch when he lights long enough, but mostly Benny and the bird dogs swoop around the country in the Model-T like "a bull bat after a mosquito." At the end of the story Benny pulls such an outrageous swindle that the Old Hen is permanently stifled, or as Quincey says: "She was hornswoggled." The story was immensely popular, and the readers begged for more Quincey Dover tales. Marjorie had created a truly great comic character, and her comic stories were favorably compared by critics with those of Mark Twain and Ring Lardner.

Back home, after her trip to England, Marjorie was still in such a distressed mental condition that she couldn't settle down to work. She was undecided whether to continue to work on *Hamaca* or to start the juvenile book Perkins had suggested to her. She decided to accept an invitation to visit Cal Long and his family in the heart of the Big Scrub. The Longs were having increasing difficulty eking out a living as the deer and foxes were eating their crops before they were ready to gather, and since their area was now a forest preserve, they were not allowed to kill these animals. When Marjorie asked what she should bring, Mrs. Long cheerfully answered, "Something to eat."

Cal Long was full of stories his pioneering ancestors had told him and of his own memories of growing up in the Scrub. He told Marjorie about a pet deer he had had as a boy, a deer that grew to yearling size and was able to jump any fence. When the deer repeatedly jumped the fence and ruined the corn crop, which was the livelihood of the humans and the beasts belonging to the family, Cal's father ordered him to take the deer out in the woods and shoot it. He did as his father ordered, but he told Marjorie, "All my life it's hurted me." She returned to Cross Creek with her notebooks and her memory filled with Cal's stories.

After receiving a letter from Whitney Darrow, vice president of business affairs at Scribners, mentioning the "boy's book," Marjorie wrote to Perkins for clarification of the term. Did he expect her to write a children's book or one that adults would read as well as young people, she wanted to know. Perkins replied that they should not get into a "tangle" over it. "I am thinking," he told her, "about a book about a boy, but his age is not important." He associated the book with *Kim, David Crockett's Memoirs, Huckleberry Finn,* and *Hoosier Schoolboy*. These books were primarily for boys but were the favorites of many men, he pointed out, adding, "And the best part of a man is a boy." What he had in mind was a book about a boy and the life of the Scrub with river trips, hunting, dogs, guns, and the companionship of simple people. "It is all simple. Don't let anything make it complicated to you," he urged.

"Do you realize how calmly you sat up there in your office and announced that you were expecting a boy's *classic* of me?" Marjorie demanded. She could toss off a potboiler boy's book in a hurry, she told him, but she needed time to accumulate more material slowly for a really decent boy's book. She decided to go ahead and finish *Hamaca* while she collected the material.

In October she had a new cypress cedar roof put on her house and some other necessary repairs made. One day in her absence, Moe Sikes, the carpenter, took it on himself to panel her living room closet. When she returned, she found he had completely sealed up the ten gallons of liquor she had been aging in the attic. Not wanting it advertised that she had that much liquor on hand, she had to think up some fancy reasons to get him to cut a hatch large enough to get her kegs through.

On November 10, 1933, she received official notice that her divorce decree was granted. The next day she wrote Chuck, who was at Key West, "You're free as the wind, big boy, and I hope you make the most of it." She told him the local news, asked where he wanted his odds and ends sent, and wished him good luck with his writing. Chuck's mother wrote Marjorie that the news of the divorce shook her terribly. "My heart cries and cries for you," she said. "[Y]ou have your own place in my heart and always you shall have it."

To Max Perkins Marjorie wrote that the divorce ended a fourteen-year struggle to adjust herself to a "most interesting but difficult—impossible—personality." "I'm not riotously happy," she said, "but I feel a terrific relief. I can wake up in the morning conscious of the sunshine, and thinking, 'How wonderful. Nobody is going to give me hell today.' " One of the last things Chuck had said to Marjorie before he left for good was, "Of course you realize you have no friends. Nobody likes you."

As if to belie his words, some Ocala friends drove to Cross Creek to cheer Marjorie up the night the divorce became final. They were Marjorie's lawyer, Frank Greene, and his wife Dorothy, and they brought along the brand new manager of the Marion Hotel in Ocala, Norton Baskin. Norton, who had only arrived in Ocala three days earlier, knew few people in the area and was willing to go along, although he asked, "Who in the hell is Marjorie Rawlings?" He soon found out, and reported to his friends that he was "bowled over" by her at their first meeting, which turned out to be quite convivial.

Norton Baskin was eminently suited for his profession, as he loved people and social activities. From Union Springs, Alabama, he had worked briefly on a newspaper in Palm Beach, but most of his training had been in hotel management. The classes he had attended in public relations had only added to his natural courtly southern manners and his innate instinct to pay chivalrous attention to women. An omnivorous reader, he was also an excellent storyteller and had a wit that more than matched Marjorie's. At the time they met, he was thirty-three and looked about eighteen. Marjorie was thirty-seven and looked thirty-seven. The age difference never bothered him, but later in their relationship, she would sometimes say to him, "For God's sake, don't look so young!"

At the time of their meeting, Marjorie was painfully aware that charm could be deceiving, and she had no intention of putting herself in a position to be betrayed again by a charming veneer. She was quite willing, however, to match drinking ability and wits with her personable new acquaintance. She had saved a newspaper clipping for her friend, Dorothy Greene, who, as president of the St. Agnes Guild of the Episcopal church of Ocala, had recently helped arrange a benefit bridge luncheon at the Marion Hotel. The clipping reported that the new manager, Norton Baskin, had wheeled around a cart, passing water at each of the forty tables. Gleefully reading the report aloud, Marjorie asked, "How in the world did you manage that?"

Solemnly Norton replied, "You've got to save up."

The exchange set the tone for their relationship for the next couple of years, during which Norton usually came to Cross Creek in the company of two or three other people. Asked her opinion of him a short time after their first meeting, Marjorie conceded he was nice enough but added he impressed her as "one of those damn personality boys."

Marjorie sometimes said that if she had to choose between people and trees, she would choose trees. However, left on her own at Cross Creek, she found that she needed human companionship to overcome the desolation that at times engulfed her. She went on hunting and fishing trips, and she found pleasure in entertaining and in being entertained by friends from Ocala, Gainesville, Tampa, and Jacksonville. Of necessity and by preference, she served the fresh fruits and vegetables from her garden and orchard, her own dairy products, chickens and ducks, ham and bacon, and the crab, fish, and other seafood of the area. Her growing reputation as an excellent cook and hostess gave her great satisfaction. She especially enjoyed the company and praise of men, and their admiration and interest helped to heal the wounds inflicted by Chuck's scathing criticism.

One reason Marjorie got along well with her neighbors was that she quickly learned their values, including the code of barter and exchange. She used Old Boss Brice's mules for her occasional light plowing, and he used her truck to haul his vegetable crops to the station. Neighbors picked up her pecans in exchange for enough of the crop to last them through the winter. One of the fishermen sometimes borrowed cash and then supplied her with fish. They never sat down and calculated their accounts, but she felt the scales were always tipped in her favor.

On a few occasions, however, her sense of right and wrong and that of her Cracker neighbors came into conflict. After repeated invasions of her prized fluffy-ruffle petunias by a neighbor's pigs, she shot the "red-bristled fiend" who was obviously the leader of the intruders. Then she took the slain pig to a butcher and had him dressed, wiring Norton in Ocala, BRING TEN OR TWELVE SATURDAY NIGHT FOR WHOLE ROAST PIG BARBECUE. The roast pork was delicious, the meat as white as the skimmed milk and petunia roots on which the pig had been nurtured. Afterward she read aloud Charles Lamb's essay on "Roast Pig."

The next day when Mr. Martin, the owner of the pig, arrived for a confrontation, she readily admitted to having shot and eaten it. "In a way, I had a right to shoot it, because it was an outlaw," she told him. "In another way, the right is on your side, because in a no-fence county you have the right to turn your stock loose. But I'll pay for it very gladly. Oh, Mr. Martin, I did so enjoy shooting that pig." Eventually she replaced the pig with another of equal value, and Mr. Martin offered to take her out on Orange Lake to the best duck stand there because he figured "a quick shot like you" would enjoy duck hunting.

Her break with Tom Glisson was of longer duration. When the first of her three beloved pointers was killed by strychnine poison, she at first blamed Tom, whose dislike of female dogs was well known. After a year of unpleasant relations, she and Tom had a talk during which he convinced her of his innocence, and they became good friends. At least this is the way she told the story in *Cross Creek*. Years later, when Tom himself died of accidental poisoning, Marjorie's mystic sense was stirred, and she felt a little frightened. She wrote a friend: "[A]lthough Tom and I became true friends later, I have never satisfied myself that it was not he who poisoned my dog. Nemesis? Accident? How lives are tangled together."

In January, she accepted the invitation of Ross Allen, a young Florida herpetologist, to go on a rattlesnake hunt. Like many people, she had come to Florida with an irrational horror of any kind of snake. During her study of the wild life of the state, she learned that there were three poisonous reptiles in her area: rattlesnakes, cottonmouth moccasins, and coral snakes. With characteristic courage, she decided to confront her fears head on. The hunting ground was Big Prairie (in the northwest corner of the Everglades), a desolate cattle country west of Lake Okeechobee. Here she and Ross were joined by a big Cracker named Will. The first day of the hunt, watching the men catch the snakes and drop them live into crocus sacks before emptying them into a wire cage, she couldn't eat because of the fear that churned in her stomach. That night, after Ross taught her to catch harmless water snakes with her bare hands, she came to see them as living, breathing things with a mortality like her own. She gained more confidence as the men taught her the habits of rattlesnakes: that they tried to avoid encounters with humans; that they would not strike an immobile object; that their aim was inaccurate; and that they had limited vision.

Her new knowledge was soon put to test. Leaning over to pick a white violet, she discovered a rattlesnake under it. Two days earlier she would have fainted on top of the snake or fled. But now, fortified with her new knowledge, she laid her stout stick with its L-shaped steel prong just back of the snake's head and called to Ross: "I've got one!" He strolled over and said, "Well, pick it up." As she had watched him do, she released the prong and slipped it under the middle of the body and lifted the snake. She managed to carry it to the nearby truck, and while Ross held open the top of the cage, she reached up the six feet to drop the snake into the box.

The rattlesnake slipped off the prong onto Ross's feet. Standing dead still, he told her to pick it up again. She did and again dropped it. As it slithered over his boots, Ross suggested she pick it up with her hand just behind the blunt head, but she much preferred to use the stick. When she dropped it the third time, she gasped, "I'm just not man enough to keep this up any longer." He laughed and lifting the snake with his hand dropped it into the cage. She found herself actually wanting the hunt to go on another day, for she believed that by then she would have been able to bring herself to pick up a snake with her own hand. Back at the Creek she felt relief that she had fought and conquered a haunting fear. She could now consider reptiles with tolerance and interest, if not with affection. She even enjoyed the presence of a friendly king snake that lived in a hole by her front gate and draped himself on her fence post to watch for rats, mice, and frogs. At shedding time, he seemed pleased to have her scratch his back. She did not, however, welcome snakes into her house, and twice dispatched cottonmouth moccasins that tried to take up residence in her bathroom.

Being on her own meant learning to cope with many things in addition to snakes. The six thousand dollars she earned in 1933 for *South Moon Under* disappeared with alarming speed. Two thousand dollars had gone to Chuck, representing their joint income on the sale of their Rochester house. Another thousand went to pay old bills. The trip to England cost more than she had expected it to—a total of about eight hundred dollars. And after tucking away $1,000 in a savings bond, she paid five hundred dollars for a new car, plus her trade-in. The remainder of the money paid for the new cypress shingle roof, painting the house, having a new tenant house built (the only way she could keep help) and having a porte cochere added to the side of the house for the car. She also bought a hundred dollars' worth of young orange trees for her grove and fertilizer for the whole grove. She was eager to do well with the grove, especially as Chuck had predicted "dire disaster" if she tried to manage it on her own. Taxes, mortgage payments, and interest ate up the income from her short stories sales as well as the small grove profits.

In later years she often told interviewers that she was down to a box of Uneeda biscuits and a can of tomato soup when a $500 check arrived, the first prize in the O. Henry Memorial Short Story contest, for her long short story "Gal Young 'Un." In the same anthology were short stories by Conrad Aiken, Erskine Caldwell, and F. Scott Fitzgerald. Pearl Buck won the second prize ($250) for her short story "The Frill."

"Gal Young 'Un," which had first been published in two parts in June and July 1932 in *Harper's*, concerns a lonely middle-aged widow who marries a callous bootlegger. After using most of her life savings to set up a still and to buy a flashy new car, the man arrogantly brings home a pitiful young prostitute, who is little more than a child. When the story was eventually made into a movie, audiences became so outraged at the man's self-serving meanness that they cheered and clapped when the widow finally sets fire to the still and the car and drives the man off by shooting a rifle at his feet. Victor Nuñez, the independent film maker who made "Gal Young 'Un," won acclaim for his artistic treatment of the story. Marjorie, however, was never pleased with the story, considering it more of a potboiler than an artistic creation on her part. Taking the prize for it was like "committing murder," she told Max Perkins.

Marjorie had hoped to make two trips in the early spring of 1934. She was eager to visit her brother Arthur, who was living in Seattle; and she also wanted to make a trip to Cincinnati to visit Ida Tarrant. Reluctantly, she decided she could afford neither the time nor the money for the trips. Writing to tell her adopted aunt of her disappointment, Marjorie told her, "It is always you I think of on Mother's Day, because you have done more for me and meant more to me and been closer than anyone but my own mother." She reassured Aunt Ida that she had nice men and women friends and that she was enjoying life more than she had since she was a girl in college. "Everyone says I look like a different person and 10 years younger," she told her. In fact, she said, her problem was finding time to work as her social opportunities steadily increased.

She was beginning to feel desperate about her lack of progress on the new novel and her inability to concentrate on it. Struggling to get into the book, she wrote six different beginnings. She asked Perkins to be patient with her "as always." He consoled her, telling her that all good writers struggled with their writing and especially with beginnings. Finally, after she realized that the book should start in Florida rather than in England, she was able to get past the opening and into the story. As she worked with it, she talked the book over with her friend, Carl Bohnenberger, a librarian in Jacksonville, and afterward felt this was a mistake as talking about the book drained rather than filled her creative reservoir.

Sitting on the front porch that she had had screened, with her typewriter set on the large round table with a palm trunk base that Chuck had made for playing poker, she plodded away. She set herself to average a steady thousand words a day and sometimes managed as many as three thousand.

In February she met novelist and professor Robert Herrick at a dinner in Winter Park. Finding him enthusiastic about *South Moon Under*, she told him of her struggles with the new book. He offered to consult with her about it. Tempted by this offer, she asked Max Perkins's advice. Perkins wrote in alarm that it made him "very anxious" to hear she was considering Herrick as an intimate adviser on her book. He pointed out that Herrick's novels, although fine, belonged to a "time long ago." Perkins thought Herrick an exceptional person, but feared he had fixed ideas which would harm Marjorie's writing. Perkins assured her that she underrated her abilities and that she could and should do the book by herself. Marjorie answered that she would have felt a sense of betraying Perkins if she worked deeply with anyone else "because you have more to give than anyone else could possibly have." She continued to correspond with Herrick and to exchange books and opinions on many topics with him, but she did not seek his further advice on the book. He tried, unsuccessfully, to persuade his brother-in-law, who was on the Pulitzer Prize committee, that the award should go to *South Moon Under*.

When Marjorie had about ten thousand words done on her new novel, she sent them to Perkins, asking for his general opinion of the way the story was going. Although he was wrestling day and night with Thomas Wolfe over *Time and the River*, Perkins took time out to read the chapters. He wired Marjorie enthusiastically and then wrote her an encouraging letter. "I really had a pleasant morning reading it and could have gone on reading a manuscript that quality all day," he told her. He particularly liked her Cracker couple, Luke and his sister Allie, and the anticipation she created in the reader over the impending arrival of the Englishman Tordell.

Perkins told her of his struggle with Tom Wolfe and his book within a book, and Marjorie, in turn, gave her editor sympathy and advice, "I pity you with Tom Wolfe's gorgeous bedlam. As I see it, he *must* discipline himself. Please don't spare the blue-pencil, as far as he will stand for it without shooting you on sight. He repeats and repeats, and says in four magnificent ways, what could have been said more magnificently in any one. His own sonorousness betrays him. If you would only give him Hemingway's restraint!"

F. Scott Fitzgerald's *Tender is the Night* was published while Marjorie was working on her novel. She told Perkins that she felt Fitzgerald had filled the contract she was setting for herself—to write a book "disturbing, bitter and beautiful," adding:

> *I am totally unable to analyze the almost over-powering effect that some of his passages create—some of them about quite trivial people and dealing with trivial situations. There is something terrifying about it when it happens, and the closest I can come to understanding it is to think that he does, successfully at such times, what I want to do—that is, visualizes people not in their immediate setting, from the human point*

*of view—but in time and space—almost, you might say with
the divine detachment.*

At the end of July Marjorie sent Perkins another section of the book
and an outline of the rest of it. This time she asked for specific and
detailed criticism. She wanted the book to be intense and disturbing,
with a bitter and beautiful emotional quality. "I want drama and
emotional excitement, and a shade in the wrong direction will produce melodrama and tommy rot," she told him. Perkins pointed out
some "false notes" in the story. She thanked him for his guidance,
telling him she had complete confidence in his ability to show her
what was wrong and what to do about it. "Don't spare me," she
told him. "You know I don't mind work . . . anything to get it
right." And she threatened, "I will bring a live rattlesnake and drop
it on your desk if you are ever polite about my stuff and I catch you
at it."

In a letter that was also a progress report, she again invited him
to visit Cross Creek. Realizing that his old fashioned sense of propriety might make him hesitate to stay with a single woman, she
offered to ask someone else to stay, too, or he could stay in the
hunting lodge of her friend, Dr. Vinson. She urged him to bring
Hemingway, if possible. Hemingway could get tight "on the 5-gallon
keg of good rye that has lain in a charred keg for over a year in an
attic that must hit 140 degrees at times, or he can run around Cross
Creek, naked, or anything that amuses him," she told Perkins. She
had recently read *A Farewell to Arms*, and in arguing with Robert
Herrick about it had realized that Herrick's "personality is infinitely
beyond his literary gifts," as he had seen Hemingway's book as only
a love story until she had pointed out the deeper symbolism and
undercurrents of meaning in it.

Another of Marjorie's short stories, "The Pardon," appeared in
the August 1934 issue of *Scribner's Magzine*. It tells the story of a
man named Joe, who kills another in self-defense but is convicted
and sentenced to life imprisonment. After seven years he is unex-
pectedly released through a pardon by the new governor who reviews
the case. Joe returns home to find a neighbor has been keeping up

his place and supporting his wife and their two children. He also finds a new child, a four-year-old boy in the house. Slowly Joe comes to realize and accept the reasons for his wife's betrayal of her marriage vows and to empathize with the child. At the conclusion of the story, he comforts the boy, who is having a nightmare. "Poor little bastard," Joe says, "I reckon you wasn't much wanted."

When Max Perkins received a complete draft of Marjorie's novel, still called *Hamaca*, in the fall, he took it home with him to read over a weekend. He thought the first 250 pages were magnificent, but he had suggestions to make about the last third of the book, which he considered marred by romantic and melodramatic elements.

He liked the portrayal of Luke and Allie, the Cracker brother and sister. Allie, like Florry in "Jacob's Ladder," was based on the shy, fragile Cracker woman who had lived briefly in Marjorie's tenant house. Her treatment of other characters, including Tordell, the Englishman, Perkins found less realistic. He liked Camilla, a spirited, independent young woman who carries a flask filled with mint juleps as she rides around overseeing her enormous orange grove, but felt she needed work to be made to seem more realistic. He suggested doing away with the invalid husband whom Camilla has hidden away in her house. He liked the doctor, who is an important character, but thought the doctor's son, who is insane, to be a character "out of a melodrama."

Perkins warmly praised her overall accomplishment, and as usual told her she must be the judge of whether or not his criticisms were valid. "It is your book and must be as you want it."

Marjorie was so stirred by his long, thoughtful letter that she stayed home from a deer hunt to answer it. Once again he had clarified her vision. She had known there were problems but couldn't figure out what they were. He had shown her. She told him:

> *I do hope you don't mind my saying again what a prodigious genius I feel you have for getting inside a writer's mind and judging absolutely from the inside; for making the incoherent, coherent. Frankly, I could not endure the thought of having to get along without your help, and I hope no circumstance ever deprives me of it. . . . I have put up a stiff fight against*

despair of one sort or another—the feeling you give me of
accomplishment is like firm ground under my feet after strug-
gling in quick sand.

By mid-December Marjorie still did not have a title she liked for
the book. She sent Perkins a list of titles including: *The Grove, Sweet*
Oranges, Sour Oranges, The Intruder, and *The Betrayal.* At the
bottom of her list was *Golden Apples,* which was the title Perkins
preferred, and the one they finally agreed on. It refers to the golden
apples in mythology, which some said were oranges, and to the
Florida orange groves that are important to the plot of the book.

Brandt and Brandt sold the serialization rights of *Golden Apples*
to *Cosmopolitan* magazine, and although Marjorie thought serialization "somewhat cheapening," she was glad to have the extra income. It proved especially providential as her orange crop had been
partially destroyed by an untimely hard December freeze that year.

Scribners gave her a contract for *Golden Apples* for 15 percent of
royalties from the start—their highest rate. They planned a July
publication date. Serialization in the April through July issues of
Cosmopolitan meant that Marjorie had to revise the manuscript into
four installment-length segments and cut it from 130,000 words to
80,000. When someone at *Cosmopolitan* suggested that she modify
Camilla's personality, Marjorie wrote to Perkins: "Damned if I'll
make Camilla noble. I like pitiful people and loving people and hard
people and people who have any elements of strength and put up a
fight, but nobility turns my stomach." She also told him she would
lose all her friends and readers among sporting men if she turned
out something "old women in rocking chairs think is 'too sweet.' "

Early in January 1935 she was in bed for a week with bronchitis
and "just missed pneumonia." Then in February she fell from a horse.
At first she thought she only had muscular injuries, but the pain kept
getting worse. She went to Tampa for X-rays, which showed a chip
of a cervical vertebra and a fracture of the skull. She had to wear a
neck brace, which she thought made her look like Joan of Arc. She
was not permitted to use a typewriter again until almost the end of
April. Fortunately she had finished the third installment for *Cos-*
mopolitan before the accident. She was able to write in her large,

sprawling longhand, and she and Perkins worked back and forth on last-minute revisions.

When she saw the maimed story as it appeared in serial form in *Cosmopolitan*, she regretted the sale to a magazine. She wrote the last installment grimly "one word at a time" with set teeth and hypnotic concentration. "The worst has happened," she lamented to Perkins. "One of my virgin aunts wrote me that it was "just dear." The thought of other people reading it in that form made her feel ill. She conceded it would probably be popular but worried that it had little literary value. When her *Cosmopolitan* editors called the book "great literature," she snorted, "How can they be so unperceptive!"

While she was unable to use the typewriter or to do anything much physically, she turned to writing poetry. She sent some of it to Robert Herrick, who had moved to St. Thomas, where he was serving as the secretary to the government. Herrick liked one poem especially, "Having Left Cities Behind Me," and suggested she send it somewhere for publication. The theme of this poem is that having turned away from cities with their "strange gregarious huddling of men by stones," her memories of them fuse together in the fire of her detestation. Her memories of her life in these human-made complexes are all of things irrelevant to cities: rain and wind, moons setting and suns rising, and wild ducks flying southward. *Scribner's Magazine* liked the poem also and bought it for publication in their October 1935 issue. Perkins expressed the hope that she would send them more poetry.

As the galley proofs of *Golden Apples* were being printed, he looked again at the whole structure of the book and found that the last part still had romantic and melodramatic qualities that were not compatible with the realism of the earlier parts, even though Marjorie had made many changes in the manuscript. Her best writing, Perkins told her, had its roots in direct observation, in presenting people and things the way they are. "Mighty few people can truly do that. You can and you ought not to diverge from it," he told her. He suggested they could work together to revise the proofs chapter by chapter.

Marjorie felt both relief and despair over Perkins's comments. She, too, saw the "unreality" in parts of the novel but couldn't think how to correct them. Throughout June a series of telegrams and letters flew back and forth between them as they struggled to iron out the rough spots in the proofs of *Golden Apples*. At one point Marjorie cried out in frustration in a telegram: "CAN'T THINK ANY FUR-THER WITHOUT YOU. YOU THINK!" Too soon the book publication date was upon them, and they could revise no more. Neither was satisfied, but at least their long agony over the novel was ended.

CHAPTER · 7

"Dear Max"

Marjorie's writing and occasional speaking engagements brought her an ever-widening circle of friends in Florida. She came to know a number of people at the University of Florida, including the president, Dr. John J. Tigert and his family, and Dr. Clifford Lyons, head of the English faculty and his family. She also became friendly with Major Otto F. Lange, professor of military science and his wife, who was deaf, and his children. Otto Lange and Marjorie went on a number of hunting and fishing trips together and often he came to her house afterward for drinks, her good cooking, and good talk. He was well-read, articulate, fond of the outdoors, and knowledgeable about trees, plants, rivers, birds, and animal life. He filled a lonely void in Marjorie's life, and their friendship gradually deepened into affection. His letters to her were addressed to "Dearest Diana." In one he told her, "What a joy and relief those days together are to me. Hope you get as much pleasure and happiness out of them." Although Marjorie admitted to a close friend that he was one man with whom she "felt the magic," there was no question in either of their minds of his leaving his handicapped wife and his children. Evidently Marjorie confided her pleasure and her frustration in the relationship to Robert Herrick. He warned her to guard her "tempestuous heart" against too deep an involvment with a lover "who has a divided soul and who is merely assuaging his thirst at a gushing fountain." Herrick urged, "Do not give 'all' to this lover. No man who offers a woman what he offers you—a divided life and devotion should expect or get more than that."

Herrick's advice was no doubt tempered by his own feelings for Marjorie, whom he found appealing both intellectually and physically. He visited her two or three times at Cross Creek and urged her to visit him at St. Thomas. In spite of his advanced age and increasing ill health he expressed his desire for Marjorie in several letters. But their relationship remained platonic, although their letters remained warm, intimate, and affectionate until his death in 1938.

Finally in August 1935 Marjorie was able to make the long-anticipated trip to Seattle to visit Arthur. Since their father's death, Peaches and Artie, as they called each other, had been very close; and after their mother died, Marjorie's role was more maternal than ever toward her handsome, willful younger brother. She was the one to whom he turned for advice and to whom he confided his never-ending problems with money and women. After college he worked briefly for various companies, but was never satisfied working for other people nor in being away from the sea. In Seattle he had bought a power cruiser for tourist sightseeing trips into Alaska and for fishing expeditions. In 1925, Arthur had married a California girl, and they had two children, Marjorie and Barbara. In 1931 he was divorced in May and married again in June. He had been urging Marjorie to visit since her own divorce, promising her a trip up the Inland Passage to Alaska and intensive hunting and fishing.

Leaving her important papers and her car keys with Otto Lange, Marjorie took a train heading west. En route to Seattle, she stopped off in Hollywood for a week long visit with her friend Bee, who had married William McNeil, and was living in a canyon in the Santa Monica Mountains. Like Marjorie, Bee kept pets that became a part of her family and spent considerable time and energy planning and maintaining a large variety of flowers in her yard. She was teaching and writing plays for her students to perform. Several of her plays were published by Baker's Plays (now Samuel French) and received considerable success. One of them, *Elmer*, was polled as the most-used school one-act play in the country.

Sam Wright, a fraternity brother of Arthur's, lived down the street from the McNeils, and the four of them drove in Bee's small convertible to hear concerts at the Hollywood Bowl and to Laguna Beach. They celebrated Marjorie's thirty-ninth birthday on August 8 at the Coconut Grove. One day Bee and Marjorie drove down to San Juan Capistrano. Marjorie had gone to the Baptist church in Washington, D. C., as she grew up, and although she rejected formalized religion in college, she had gone to a Congregational church in Madison to "do her praying." Despite the fact that at times she half-seriously categorically expressed a strong dislike for all preachers, she frequently read the Bible, savoring the drama and the beauty of the language of the King James version. The music, incense, ritual, and architectural beauty of cathedrals had great appeal for her. Touched by these sensory attractions and by the aura of history and legend enveloping the old mission, she told Bee, "I could so easily be a Catholic."

It was a relief for Marjorie to be able to discuss with Bee the disaster of her marriage. She summed up the fourteen years: "The first five years I cried; the next five years I fought; the last four years I didn't give a damn." Trying to explain why she had stayed with Chuck so long, Marjorie acknowledged that she had been willing to exchange "a week's worth of cruelty for a good turn of phrase." Marriage to a man who could say of a balmy summer night, "violins are singing in me" had seemed worth trying to salvage, even when her reason told her it was hopeless. Once while Marjorie was driving Bee's car, she was unloading on her sympathetic friend the difficulties and frustrations of being single again. When they narrowly missed running into a streetcar, Marjorie said, "You see, that's what my life has been like recently!"

Marjorie and Bee had no trouble reviving the happy companionship and easy laughter they had shared as college students. When both had been skinny students, they had worried about covering up the deep "cisterns" in the regions of their collar bones. Now Marjorie complained to Bee that she had developed a "positively pompous behind," and Bee told Marjorie that her idea of controlling her weight was to eat what she pleased and pay a lot for her corsets.

On August 12 Marjorie was met by Arthur in Seattle. His first wife and children were living in the same neighborhood as Arthur and his second wife, a situation Marjorie found a bit strained. But she enjoyed immensely the trip on his cruiser up the Inland Waterway. The two-thousand-mile round trip fascinated her so much that she began immediately to plan a novel set in Alaska. She told Perkins "that dark and forbidding and mountainous country offers a setting for the theme of betrayal." She took detailed notes of the scenery and wildlife for a short article to be called "Tidal Highway." And before she left the area, she had a whole set of characters in mind for an Alaskan novel. Writing Perkins about her intended theme for the book she said, "Human treachery is the most appalling thing. You have to learn to expect to be betrayed. Yet you must learn never to betray." She added that she was thinking seriously of returning to Alaska for a year or two to write this book, but other projects intervened, and the idea died.

The reviews of *Golden Apples* had begun to appear during Marjorie's absence. She was surprised at the generosity of most of the reviewers, although *Time* called it "dull melodrama." She was also amused at the way the critics contradicted each other: what one liked, another condemned. Always her own severest critic, she called the book "interesting trash, not literature."

She had told her editor that she would call him "Max" if he liked her second book, and from that time on their letters were on a first name basis. Now she told him, "You should have bullied me and shamed me further. I can do better than that and you know it." She blamed the flawed quality of the book on the pressure of producing the serial version, and wished she could take the novel and rework the last half of it. She saw, too late, that it should have been Luke's story instead of being Tordell's. But she accepted full responsibility for having let "personal ambition" drive her to accept the *Cosmopolitan* offer, even though she had badly needed the money at the time. In spite of the fact that some readers liked *Golden Apples* better than *South Moon Under*, she told Max, "You and I know in our hearts it isn't right."

What upset her most was that all the American reviewers missed the one point she had wanted to get across: the struggle of a man against a natural background. When one English reader wrote to say he found this struggle with the environment the crux of the story, she rejoiced. She told Max not to bother to send her any more reviews. "They were kinder than I should have been. I'm not in the least interested. They said nothing I didn't know." Even though the book held a place on best-seller lists for two months, Marjorie knew better than to equate that kind of popularity with literary value. Nevertheless, she scolded Scribners for not promoting *Golden Apples* by advertising it as vigorously as she thought they should for the Christmas trade.

Max Perkins frequently sent his writers books he thought would be helpful or interesting to them. In November he sent Marjorie a copy of Tom Wolfe's new book of stories, *From Death to Morning.* She wrote a few lines of criticism that Max thought were "acute" and important enough to show to Wolfe:

> As a writer who has always had to fight overwriting, it seems to me that his fault as an artist lies in indulging himself in the deliciousness of piling word on word, phrase on phrase, rhythm on rhythm. Used judiciously, his cumulative effect is prodigious, of course. Over-done, it is like too much poetry, or too much symphony music, or too much passion—cloying; surfeiting. I have often been tempted to write him, but being entirely inferior as an artist, it would be presumptuous, so I have never done so.

Wolfe took her criticism well, Max reported, adding that he thought and devoutly hoped it had made its mark on the verbose author.

As for her own writing, Marjorie felt at loose ends. She worked on the Alaskan article, "Tidal Highways," but finally discarded it because she felt it had turned out to be "stilted and valueless." She lacked enthusiasm for the boy's book, feeling that the material she had for it was "too thin." She was more interested for the moment in continuing to collect notes and ideas for a nonfiction book of sketches, narratives, and essays about Cross Creek. The notion for doing this kind of book had grown since her first success with "Cracker

Chidlings." She told Max that she hoped to capture the quality of life that made her "cling so desperately and against great odds to this place." She decided to "putter along" through the winter with short pieces, but after the first of the year, she promised Max to "take the veil" again and do some serious writing. With Robert Herrick's warm encouragement, she was continuing to work on her poetry.

As usual, the fall season was filled with hunting and camping trips, often with her friend Dessie Vinson. She also went duck hunting with Major Lange, and she had the whole Lange family at Cross Creek for an elaborate Thanksgiving dinner.

In early December she returned to visit Pat's Island, the pine "island" in the heart of the lower Scrub where she had stayed with the Cal Long family. Long had since died and his widow had moved from the house, which was rapidly decaying. But Marjorie still found the location "one of the strangest and most beautiful places I have ever seen." She realized that this was the setting she wanted for the boy's book. There was a large sinkhole near the place, and she asked Max what he thought of "The Sink-Hole" as the title of the book. By January of 1936 she was thinking of the boy's book as a novelette of about fifty thousand words. "It will be a story *about* a boy—a brief and tragic idyll of boyhood. I think it cannot help but be very beautiful," she told Max.

During the winter, spring, and on into the summer, many different types of distractions kept her from beginning work on a third book. The work of the orange grove went on, and the crop had been good enough so she was able to send oranges to Max Perkins and other friends for Christmas. She told Aunt Ida that she had half a dozen parties and dances to go to during the holidays. In late January she had one of her large sows butchered and she made scrapple while Martha Mickens made lard. During that month the Hardys from Louisville came to visit, and she and Lois enjoyed having Martha serve them their breakfast in bed, a custom Marjorie dearly loved.

In February Phil May, her friend and lawyer from Jacksonville, brought his friend the poet Wallace Stevens to dinner at Cross Creek. Having been warned that Stevens was on a strict diet, Marjorie prepared a special cut of lean beef for him, plus green salad and fruit.

For the rest of the company she prepared ham baked in sherry and other rich dishes, and she was annoyed when the poet renounced his beef in favor of the ham and other dishes, as his diet was only for reducing purposes. On his bread-and-butter note she scribbled: "From Wallace Stevens who spent an evening at Cross Creek being disagreeable and obstreperous. Got drunk, read his poems with deliberate stupidity. Held out his arms to me and said, 'Come, my Love.' " She did, however, appreciate his artistry and sometimes used his poetry to illustrate points in her creative writing lectures.

During another dinner party at Cross Creek, Phil May suggested an idea for a book to Marjorie. Aside from those that came from Max, she usually resisted other people's ideas as to what she should write about, but Phil fired her imagination with his description of Zephaniah Kingsley, an early nineteenth-century Florida planter, who married a black woman. Marjorie became interested enough to begin doing research toward a book on Kingsley.

Toward the end of March, Marjorie again entertained the Langes at Cross Creek, along with the major's mother, who was visiting from Minneapolis. "It was mighty fine of you to give my mother such a happy time. She is bubbling over with good spirits and happy memories," Otto Lange told her. Their relationship continued its rocky path. In one letter he summed up his opinion of her as "a fine woman, courageous beyond the courage of even the average man, wonderfully keen of mind, warm-hearted, generous, at bottom gentle, truly sweet and good and tolerant and broad-minded." But her letters to him he described as being "vitriolic, acid and cutting." He concluded that her opinion of him was that he was "a compound of a bounder, a cad, a liar and one totally lacking any of the qualities of a man, not to mention a gentleman." And yet he knew she had, in spite of this lack of respect, a "real affection" for him. Her abusive letters were often followed by others asking him to forgive her. Evidently their relationship caused her emotional distress, as she felt drawn to him even while her conscience created a wracking sense of guilt because she did not end it.

In June Marjorie accepted an invitation from a New York friend, Mrs. Oliver Grinnell, to visit Bimini on her yacht. Mrs. Grinnell was a former president of the Salt Water Anglers of America, who sometimes wrote articles about fishing, and worked with people like Zane Grey and Ernest Hemingway on conservation. While Marjorie was in Bimini, Hemingway visited Mrs. Grinnell's yacht. Having heard tales in Bimini of his going around knocking people down, Marjorie was surprised to find him a "most lovable, nervous and sensitive person." Although she had been afraid he might announce loudly that he never accepted introductions to female novelists, Marjorie reported to Max that Hemingway took her hand "in a big gentle paw and remarked that he was a great admirer" of her work. To her hostess's chagrin, he talked more of literature than of fishing during the visit. The day before she left Bimini, Hemingway battled almost seven hours with a 514-pound tuna and then got "gloriously" drunk as the pilot of the *Pilar* brought it back to harbor. Marjorie's last impression of the dynamic author was of his standing alone on the dock where his giant tuna was hanging—using it as a large punching bag.

In a letter to Max, Marjorie attempted to analyze Hemingway. "He is so vast, so virile, he does not need to go around punching people." She thought the key to understanding the man lay in seeing the conflict between the sporting life he played at and the literary life he worked at. The life on the water with its excitement, she herself had found to be a self-contained entity. "When you are a part of it, nothing else seems valid." Yet at times she felt a great guilt in her enjoyment of it. "You feel clean and natural with the sporting people," she said, "they lave your soul." But on leaving them, she was overcome with the knowledge that she was worlds away from them. They enjoyed life hugely, but they were not sensitive to it. She thought that Hemingway was afraid of the reaction of these people to his "lifting . . . the curtain that veils the beauty that should be exposed only to reverent eyes." That was why, she thought, that as in *Death in the Afternoon*, after a beautiful, sensitive passage, he immediately "turns it off with a flippant comment, or a deliberate obscenity." His sporting friends would roar with delight at the obscenity while not understanding the beauty.

Marjorie's imagination was captured by the loveliness of the island, with the incredible changing colors of the surrounding waters, by the oddities of the whites, and by the extreme poverty of the blacks.

'Bimini caught at my throat the way the scrub does," she told Max. As it had been with Alaska, her reaction was to want to do a book using this intriguing setting. Unless somebody really good, like Hemingway, wrote about the area, she wanted to come back to Bimini to live a while and write about it. "There is a stirring novel there. I can see its outlines and most of its people, very plainly," she said.

After she read "The Snows of Kilimanjaro" in the August issue of *Esquire*, she wrote a letter of praise to Hemingway and invited him to some to Cross Creek to visit and to hunt, urging him to bring along his family and also Max Perkins. She mentioned to Hemingway some of the ideas she had expressed to Max about the difficulties caused by his being a sportsman *and* an artist, and her impression that the sporting people were "blunted" in their appreciation of beauty. Hemingway replied that he would like to come to Cross Creek sometime to hunt turkeys or other birds. He told her he had fished and hunted since he was old enough to carry a cane pole and a single-barreled shotgun for the "great inner pleasure" it gave him. He got the same pleasure from writing:

> *only it is a goddamned sight harder to do and if I did nothing else (no fish, no shoot, no drink) would probably go nuts doing it with the difficulty, the times in between when you can't do it, the always being short of what you want to do, and the rest of it . . .*

He agreed with her about the sporting crowd. "The women who fish seriously are the worthiest but dullest bitches alive. 90 per cent of the men the same with a tendency toward old maidism." But, he said, he still enjoyed them and got an "awful lot of fun and excitement" out of his life on Bimini. He was, at the time of writing this letter, in Montana working "like hell" on a manuscript (later published as *To Have and Have Not*).

In July Marjorie went to North Carolina to give a talk at the Blowing Rock School of English run by Rollins College. While there she met the author James Still, becoming friendly with him during a climb up Grandfather Mountain, a peak of some 5,900 feet. They kept in touch, and Still had a dulcimer made for her in Kentucky.

Although she never learned to play it, she wrote a poem about it titled, "To an Unplayed Dulcimer."

At Blowing Rock she also met Herschel Brickell, an editor, journalist, and book reviewer. He admired her writing, and she was impressed with his intellect. "Contact with a spirit and personality such as his doesn't come often" she told Max. For a time she subscribed to the New York *Post*, in order to read Brickell's book reviews.

She told Brickell a little about her plan for a boy's book set in the Florida Scrub, and he encouraged her strongly to make it a full-length novel. She was tempted to go to New York to talk with Max about the novel but instead went reluctantly home. She had met Barney Dillard, a pioneer Cracker, and been taken into his confidence, so now she planned a visit of a week or two with the Dillard family, who lived in the Scrub. She told Max that Barney Dillard was a famous " 'bad man,' but honorable and respected and at one time prosperous." He took her hunting and fishing and on at least two bear hunts. Some of Barney's fifteen children were suspicious of Marjorie, thinking she was going to make money by writing up their father's life. So one morning when one of the most resentful sons heard the old pioneer describing for her the various plants and herbs used in the old-time medicines of the area, he asked, "She writing up sich as that?" in surprise.

The father answered, "That's just the kind of thing she's writing. She's not like you sorry, no-account things. She's interested in the old days and the old ways. Why, I never heard a woman cuss like she cussed this morning when we went to Juniper Springs and she found the government had cleaned out the Springs and put up picnic tables." The son said, "Well, I'll be dogged," and when Marjorie left he sheepishly gave her a handsome ram's horn as a gift.

As Marjorie's mass of material grew, so did her enthusiasm for the book. She told Max she was going "perfectly delirious with delight" in her material and with the characters that were taking shape in her mind, and she sketched one of them for him:

Wait until you see Grandma Hutto. A little impudent, infidel, sharp-spoken thing with gold circle earrings and Spanish or

Minorcan blood who scandalizes the staid residents of the scrub and who tells the boy wise and impudent things. She doesn't want to go to Heaven because they live on milk and honey, and she likes a piece of fried mullet now and again. She likes music made from a harp and a bass violin and an octave flute, and she couldn't get along listening to just a harp. . . .

[O]h Max, the stuff is going to be grand. . . . You and I are going to love the book if nobody else in the world reads it. I am very happy and confident about it as it forms. None of the fear and torment of "Golden Apples." Then the following book will be hell again. [The Kingsley book]

She again urged Max to come to Cross Creek. "I think I shall burst sometimes at your not coming to Florida and letting me show you some of the places I shall use for background." She told her editor that she had decided the story must be all told through the boy's eyes, and she had decided to make him twelve, as she didn't want the problems of puberty to complicate things. This also meant that the time period had to be short, not more than two years at most. She was feeling happier than in a long time, and feelings of desolation didn't strike nearly so often.

Marjorie and Ida Tarrant had decided it would be a good idea for Aunt Ida, who was living alone in Cincinnati, to move to Ocala to be nearer Marjorie. Consequently, during the hot weeks of August, Marjorie spent days combing the residential sections of Ocala to try to locate an apartment for Ida. She wrote her long detailed accounts of the possibilities, including the building structures, heating facilities, neighborhood surroundings of the apartment buildings, convenience to groceries and other stores, and a list of rent comparisons compiled from her investigations of different sections of the city.

Among other news Marjorie wrote Aunt Ida that she had acquired two new pets—a baby raccoon named Racket and a pedigreed pointer puppy named Pat. She also told her that Chuck was marrying again, a twenty-six-year-old woman (Chuck was forty-one), who had worked as a journalist in Rochester. Chuck's mother had written to Marjorie, hoping she would try to stop the marriage, telling her "It's you I want." Marjorie answered her former mother-in-law as gently as she could "because a son is a son," but declined to do anything to interfere, for as she told Aunt Ida, the wedding was a burden off her mind. Marjorie wrote to Max that it was a relief to her to know that Chuck was "taken care of," as she never wanted anything at the expense of anyone else—"even peace."

In September Marjorie had another bout with malaria. When Dr. Vinson found that she had an enlarged spleen and was running a daily fever, he put her on quinine and advised her to get away from the sticky heat and mosquitoes for a few weeks. Through friends for fifteen dollars a month, she found a small cabin in the mountains near Banner Elk, North Carolina, equipped with handmade furniture, electric lights, and a fireplace. Taking her well-worn copy of Proust and her pointer Pat for company, she planned to work hard on the boy's book as she regained her health in the mountain air.

The invigorating air and beautiful mountain scenery renewed her energy, and she felt she had found the right place to regain her strength and to make a good start on the new novel. She frequently walked down to the country hotel for dinner, finding the food there good and inexpensive. From the local people she bought fresh vegetables and ducks at a quarter apiece. On her long walks with Pat she made friends with her neighbors, whom she found poor but self-supporting and kind-hearted. A woman with two crippled children insisted on giving her flowers when she learned how much Marjorie loved them. Another gave her apple jelly because she was a stranger, and another brought her cottage cheese for which she would take no pay. Marjorie tried to find ways to return the favors without offending the pride of the independent farmers, and she often took little gifts to the crippled children. "The courage of such unfortunate people should shame complaining people who have everything but courage," she wrote Ida.

One thing that kept her from being completely contented in her mountain retreat was the fact that Aunt Ida was moving to Ocala in her absence. Before she became ill with malaria, Marjorie had expected to be there to help with the move, and although she had tried to make arrangements to smooth Ida's move and had generously paid her first month's rent and other expenses, everything seemed to go wrong at the last minute. The apartment wasn't ready, the furniture didn't arrive when expected, and the electricity wasn't turned on—among other problems. Marjorie felt she had failed her friend, after encouraging her to make the move, and was sick at heart about it. Marjorie's Florida friends did their best to come to the rescue. Phil May met Ida in Jacksonville, and Norton Baskin entertained her in Ocala while the apartment was being readied. Promising to "make it up" to her, Marjorie stifled her impulse to pack up and return to Florida immediately.

Max Perkins sent Marjorie books to read for relaxation, and he suggested that, if it were possible, she visit Scott Fitzgerald, who was staying at the elegant Victorian Inn in Asheville, eighty-five miles from Banner Elk. Fitzgerald was recovering from a broken clavicle and dislocated shoulder, which he had received while doing a fancy dive to impress some debutantes, and he was also supposed to be drying out after too much drinking. Max was concerned about Fitzgerald's mental state following a series of confessional articles published earlier that year in *Esquire*, called "Crack Up," "Pasting it Together," and "Handle with Care," in which the author revealed his feelings of despair and discussed his inability to write. On September 25 the New York *Post* published an article called "The Other Side of Paradise," describing Fitzgerald as a defeated has-been, and *Time* magazine picked up the story the next week. Hemingway had not helped improve Fitzgerald's morale when he referred to him as "ruined" in "The Snows of Kilimanjaro."

Max told Marjorie his object in asking her to visit Fitzgerald was that he thought she could make him feel better and restore his courage "because you do seem to have that power." Marjorie replied that she thought the *Post* article cruel. She could understand how Fitzgerald's state of mind "creeps over one when one's personal background is unstable or unsatisfying or empty." She herself had fought it. She realized that Fitzgerald had indulged himself by wallowing in self-pity, and she thought "the world is too much with him," but she felt sorry for anyone who could find no comfort in the earth and hills and wind and stars. She sincerely admired *The Great Gatsby* and felt that Fitzgerald was as fine a social historian as Thackeray, but with a better literary style.

She wrote to Fitzgerald inviting him to go with her to Pisgah Forest to visit a pottery, where she wanted to have some dishes made. He declined to go to Pisgah Forest, but spoke of his admiration for *South Moon Under* and some of her short stories and expressed a desire to meet her if she could stop to see him on her way to the pottery. He described himself as an invalid, and she suggested they meet for a chat in the early afternoon, adding that she didn't mind if he didn't feel like getting up. "Good God, I've seen men in bed before," she told him.

Fitzgerald invited her to lunch and ordered up a bottle of sherry followed by generous quantities of port, much to the distress of his nurse. Exactly the same age, forty, the two writers found such pleasure in each other's company that they "talked their heads off" for almost five hours. They took turns pacing the floor as they covered everything from the wretched journalist who wrote the *Post* article to Hemingway to the problems of writing, to suicide and finally to their expectations of life. Their difference on this subject, Marjorie told Max, was that she always expected the crest of the wave to have a consequent and inevitable trough, but when she was at the bottom of the trough, she knew there would be another up-turn sooner or later. Fitzgerald, on the other hand, expected the crest to last indefinitely. However, she reassured Max, "I am firmly convinced that the man is all right. He has thrown himself on the floor and shrieked himself black in the face and pounded his heels—as lots of us do in one way or another—but when it's over, he'll go back to his building blocks again." From experience, she understood the feeling of cosmic despair that had overwhelmed him and knew what a "devilish job" it was to get out from under it.

Marjorie told Max that it might shame Fitzgerald to visit some of the mountain families with her, and particularly to meet the twelve-year-old boy from the nearby Grandfather Orphanage, who came every day to cut wood for her fireplace. The stamina and honesty of the child impressed her deeply. She described him to Aunt Ida as a "brave but lonely little fellow—a real little man." The boy brought her flowers from the orphanage grounds, played with Pat, and gradually spent more and more time visiting with her. She referred to him as "my dear little orphan" and began to think seriously of taking him home with her until she discovered that he had a mother who paid for him to board at the orphanage.

Out of this situation she wrote a short story called "A Mother in Mannville." It involved a woman like herself who becomes attached to an orphan boy like the one who visited her. Her agents, Brandt and Brandt, sold the story to the *Saturday Evening Post* for one of their December issues.

By the first week in November the weather in the mountains of North Carolina had turned bitter cold and Marjorie returned to Cross Creek. She found things there disorganized, the house and yard in "complete confusion," and the grove neglected. She had to hire a new house woman and five new grove workers and spend valuable time getting things back in order. "I get so tired of carrying such a complete responsibility, but my place here offers the only security that is at all tangible, so I cling to it," she told Max.

When she finally achieved tranquillity, she sat down to report to him on her progress on the novel. She was pleased with the work she had accomplished during her stay in North Carolina, and the rich material tempted her forward. But she was concerned that there be a clear understanding with Scribners that the book never be labeled a "juvenile" in any of its advertising. She intended only that it should be so "simple and elemental and full of natural stuff" that it would naturally appeal to boys as well as to adults. She felt that the title was important, but as usual had difficulty coming up with the right one. Among her suggestions were: *The Flutter Mill, The Yearling, The Fawn, Juniper Creek,* and *Juniper Island.* She thought *The Flutter Mill* would be intriguing, but Max disagreed. Even though the words in themselves had appeal, he told her, few people would know what they described until they read the opening chapter. He thought *The Fawn* a bit too poetic but liked *Yearling.* Marjorie thought that a bit stark, and they finally agreed on *The Yearling,* with its dual symbolism of the boy in the story and his pet deer.

Four and a half months
(The University of Florida, Department of Rare Books and Manuscripts)

Twenty months
(Courtesy Jean Kinnan Peterson, Phoenix, Arizona)

Four years   (The University of Florida, Department of Rare Books and Manuscripts)

Arthur Frank Kinnan,
Marjorie's father
(Courtesy Jean Kinnan Peterson, Phoenix, Arizona)

Ida May Traphagen Kinnan,
Marjorie's mother
(Courtesy Jean Kinnan Peterson, Phoenix, Arizona)

Arthur H. Kinnan,
Marjorie's brother
(Courtesy Jean Kinnan Peterson, Phoenix, Arizona)

Marjorie at University of Wisconsin; picture in yearbook as one of selected "Representative Women"   (The University of Florida, Department of Rare Books and Manuscripts)

Gertrude Johnson,
Marjorie's speech teacher
and drama coach at the
University of Wisconsin
(Courtesy Beatrice H. McNeil,
Los Angeles, California)

Marjorie and Bee
in "Lima Beans"
costumes,
University of Wisconsin
(Courtesy Beatrice H. McNeil,
Los Angeles)

*Marjorie with Charles
Rawlings, about 1919*
(The University of Florida,
Department of Rare Books and
Manuscripts)

*Marjorie as Pierrot
in a Union Vodvil
performance
as a junior at the
University of Wisconsin*
(The University of Florida,
Department of Rare Books
and Manuscripts)

Marjorie Kinnan, early 1920's
(Courtesy Beatrice H.McNeil, Los Angeles, California)

CHAPTER 8

The Yearling

*T*he November 1936 issue of *Scribner's Magazine* carried a story by Marjorie called "Varmints." It was another Quincey Dover tale, and one that Marjorie always referred to as "the mule story." The mule in the story was based on one called Old Joe, a faithful worker at Cross Creek in spite of certain peculiarities, including a platonic friendship with a couple of Jersey cows. The story concerns two Crackers, Jim and Luty, who jointly own a tobacco-chewing, rum-drinking, stump-sucking mule. The men are as stubborn as the mule. In her inimitable way Quincey describes Jim as "shingle-butted and hollar-chested and a mouth like a sewed-up buttonhole and light blue eyes as mean as the Book of Job." Luty is depicted by Quincey in combination with a description of the mule: "He looked like Luty more'n most persons could of done. Pot-bellied and low-coupled and big-eyed and easy-going and biggety, too. And chewing his tobacco and looking at you sideways, I'll swear."

For thirty years Quincey tries to stop the feuding between Jim and Luty. As she says, "There's no woman in the state of Florida has got more patience with the varmint in a man than me. It's in his blood, just like a woman has got a little snake and a mite of cat. A man's borned varminty and he dies varminty. . . ." But when the mule finally dies in the middle of her sweet potato field and each man obstinately refuses to remove the carcass, her patience is "plumb wore out," and she has them posted as "varmints" in the local paper. Readers received the story enthusiastically, and Max frequently urged her to do more Quincey Dover stories with the idea of publishing a separate collection of them. She liked the idea and agreed to write more but only got around to doing one more that was successful enough to publish.

"When anything is bursting to be done, interruptions make you seethe," Marjorie wrote to Scott Fitzgerald. But late in the fall of 1936, she had two visits that delighted her, although they stopped her writing completely for several weeks. The first was a visit from her good friends, the Hardys and their children, who were driven from their Louisville home by the devasting floods there. The second and even more welcome visit was by Arthur, who arrived in Cross Creek about Thanksgiving time. In her letters, Marjorie invariably described him as "my beloved brother," and he called her "the only perfect woman." He stayed until New Year's Day, and Marjorie had her happiest Christmas of many years. They had splendid duck hunting and feasted on their booty. Actually it was Arthur who bagged the ducks, while Marjorie went along for the pleasure of being with him in the outdoors. She did arrange for an ideal setup, with herself and Arthur behind blinds in small boats and a man in a motor boat to circle and keep the ducks in motion. They also enjoyed quail hunting, Marjorie's favorite kind of hunting as they were a quarry she could hit. When it was time for Arthur to leave, she told Max she would be quite desolate without him. "We are devoted to each other, and it seems silly for us to be separated by a diagonal line across the continent." Yet both had ties to keep them in their respective parts of the country.

After Arthur left, she was plagued with domestic problems that brought her to the point of "exploding with frustration." There was so much work that *had* to be done, and when she was without reliable help, she could get no writing done. She didn't mind feeding chickens, milking the cow, caring for dozens of baby chicks, ducks, and turkeys, or even driving the truck on grove work, but she chafed at the time involved—at least six hours of hard work, aside from the grove work. And by the time the work was done, it had drained her energy. "My nervous energy burns fiercely about so long and then the current just stops," she told Max. When she finally did get a satisfactory housekeeper, the woman became ill and Marjorie felt obligated to take her to the doctor and to nurse her. There was also Aunt Ida, now in Ocala, with whom Marjorie felt obligated to spend time.

In March she finally was able to write Max that she was back at work on *The Yearling*. She was making drastic revisions in it and finding it terribly slow going. "I have to visualize, to feel, with great clarity, every moment, allowing no looseness, no unawareness, in order to show the boy's world through the sensitive medium of adolescent being. . . . I still think it may be something beautiful and moving." Max was encouraging and eager to see chapters, even in the rough. Marjorie sent him a chart that showed the events covered in the one year that she had decided would be the time frame for the book. She promised to have it done by the end of August or mid-September or "you will publish the fragmentary manuscript posthumously." There were "gorgeous" characters in it, she told him. "They not only breathe, but bellow. . . . God, if I can only get down what I sense and see."

She was determined not to let anything spoil the artistry of this book. When Carl Brandt pressed her to send him some of the manuscript to show to *Cosmopolitan* for possible serialization, she wired back that it was unsuitable for them. Telling him that it was about a twelve-year-old boy and had no love interest, she added, desperate to convince him it was not suitable for *Cosmopolitan* to serialize, ALL WOMEN CHARACTERS PAST MENOPAUSE. The village telegraph operator pushed his spectacles down on his nose and began to count the words ". . . 48 . . . 49—now this word here . . ." She thought, "Of course, Damn the Western Union." The man continued, "This word here, menopause. Is that all one word?"

In spite of her determination that *The Yearling* not be serialized by *Cosmopolitan*, Marjorie admitted to Max that if the *Saturday Evening Post* offered a large enough sum, she would be tempted to let them serialize the story, although it was "too damn good for them." In making this confession, she compared herself to Mrs. Simpson, who, Marjorie said, was perfectly happy with Ernest Simpson until the Prince of Wales "made improper proposals."

When Max expressed dismay that Ernest Hemingway was going off to Spain to become a correspondent in the civil war there, Marjorie replied, "It is one of those inevitable things, and death for him, or no, is somehow right. I only hope for myself that if I ever become too firmly entrenched in a meaningless safety that something as fatal and as luminous will drag me out."

"I am one of your duties, Max, and you really must write me at least every couple of weeks," she told him. "Sometimes a letter from you is the only thing that bucks me up." She poured out to him the torment of writing "when the inner compulsion fails and the writer questions everything: the ultimate value of their work and its immediate quality." Almost none of her friends could understand, and human relations constantly impinged. She complained that people accepted "I have no help" as a legitimate reason for staying home, but did not understand the agony of wanting to work and being interrupted. This was more true of her friends living outside Cross Creek than it was of her neighbors, who had learned to walk past without greeting her when they heard the clackety-clack of the typewriter on her screened porch or even when they saw her walking down the road late in the evenings sunk in thought.

Despite everything, she had a good part of *The Yearling* manuscript finished by the first of June. She sent the chapters to Max, telling him, "I don't know if it is stupid or no good. Need your opinion." Then she drove up to New York with her friend Mrs. Grinnell, for an extended visit at the Bayshore, Long Island, estate of the Grinnells. She planned to consult with Max on the manuscript and to do some rewriting there with the help of his suggestions as well as have a vacation. The drive from Florida through the Carolinas was beautiful. Marjorie described to Aunt Ida the profusion of mountain laurel, wild azalea, roses, daisies, and rhododendron. She felt refreshed and when they arrived on Long Island, she thought the Grinnell estate "too lovely to be true," with its huge old-fashioned house and acres of grounds and gardens. Mrs. Grinnell was a warm, gracious hostess and a good companion who liked to laugh as much as Marjorie did. The fresh seafood, Long Island vegetables, and other good food pleased

Marjorie, although she had begun to worry about her weight.

A long wire from Norton Baskin informing her that Aunt Ida was fine and that everything at Cross Creek, including the livestock, was in good shape, put her mind at ease about domestic matters, and she turned her attention to having a good work and play time.

Tom Wolfe was in New York, and one evening Max Perkins got his two authors together for drinks and dinner. It turned out to be a very long evening indeed. They began with drinks at Chatham Walk. At nine-thirty they ate a steak dinner, which was followed by more drinks. At midnight they went to a Chinese restaurant where Wolfe ate another full meal. It was here that Marjorie unfortunately brought up the subject of suicide, intending merely to discuss it as an abstraction. Wolfe decided she was urging him to commit the act, and glaring at Max, he belligerantly refused, "even to satisfy my publishers!" At three a.m. they went down to the Fulton Street fish market for oysters on the half shell. At four Wolfe was plowing his way in a drizzling rain among the vegetables in the wholesale market with Max and Marjorie following "like pieces broken off a meteor in transit." When Wolfe finally agreed to call it a night at four-thirty, it was too late for Marjorie to go out to Long Island to Mrs. Grinnell's. Max Perkins took her home with him and had to explain her the next morning to his wife and daughters. Meanwhile Wolfe called Mrs. Grinnell to tell her not to worry about Marjorie because she was spending the night with Max Perkins. Marjorie suggested to Max that he call his memoirs "The Perils of an Editor; or Days and Nights with the Authors."

When Max sent Marjorie an autographed copy of Wolfe's *Story of a Novel*, which she found "unbearable" for its honesty, its fierceness, and its beauty of expression, the book reminded her of the great part Max played in harnessing Wolfe's explosive talent. "When all of us are done for, the chances are that literary history will find you the greatest," she told Max. "Certainly the wisest of us all."

In spite of the fact that Tom Wolfe, Ernest Hemingway, and Scott Fitzgerald were all in New York at the same time and about to give Max a "nervous breakdown," the editor found time to talk with Marjorie about *The Yearling* and to look at a handful of poems she brought to him. Of the poems, he particularly liked "Mountain Rain" and "From the Faithless to the Unfaithful." The latter, about the suicide of a woman who has been betrayed by her lovers and in her turn has betrayed them, Max felt expressed "utterly sincere feelings," but he felt it a theme that had been too much written about. "Mountain Rain" is a lyric description of the writer's seduction by the "arrogant hemlocks lifting gentle, dripping hands" and the "tear-washed rhododendrons and the wet-lipped mist" of the mountain area so that she found herself being "faithless" to the lowlands. Max called it "beautiful," and it was bought by *Scribner's Magazine* for their July 1938 issue.

Max had some helpful criticism to make on her manuscript of *The Yearling*, and when she read it over in her room on Long Island, she sent him a note asking, "Why didn't you tell me how *sappy The Yearling* was? It has a saccharine stupidity of style and movement. On reading it over I thought it hopeless, and I'd just have to drop it in Mrs. Grinnell's private canal where her gardener dumps the too-full blown roses." She decided to rewrite the manuscript from the first chapter on. Her expectation that she would be able to do a great deal of work during her visit proved overly optimistic. She had a lovely room overlooking a broad lawn full of flowers and birds and a fine view of the bay and Fire Island, but Mrs. Grinnell had many friends and a busy social life that constantly drew Marjorie away from her work.

She was grateful for her friend's hospitality and glad to repay it a little by taking her and Charles Scribner to lunch at the Ritz. Describing the luncheon to Aunt Ida, Marjorie said that when they got into the limousine dolled up in their best, with Mrs. Grinnell wearing a "fistful of diamonds," and Mrs. Grinnell said to the chauffeur "To the Ritz," she thought "Do, Jesus!" Later that same afternoon, she had Max Perkins and Ernest Meyer to cocktails at Chatham Walk to meet Mrs. Grinnell.

Finally, the last week in July, Marjorie started back to Florida by train, with a stopover in Washington, D. C., to visit friends. One of the people she saw there was Robert Herrick, who was on a mission to try to persuade the Congress to give the Virgin Islands money for immigration.

Back home, Marjorie found everything in good order. The Langes were leaving Gainesville to move to Ft. Benjamin Harrison, Indiana, where the major had been assigned to an important command post. He spent one more night with her at Cross Creek and there was a tearful farewell. They made plans for her to visit the Langes in Maryland after she finished her work on *The Yearling*. Lange gave her his beloved pointer, Steve, and a sundial which she had placed beside her front gate. The engraving on it quoted Browning: "Grow old along with me! The best is yet to be."

In late summer, Mrs. Grinnell sent Marjorie newspaper clippings describing the celebrated fracas between critic Max Eastman and Ernest Hemingway in Max Perkin's office. Marjorie sent her sympathy to her editor. The honors, she declared, went to Eastman as Hemingway had definitely proved Eastman's contention that the author lacked confidence in his manhood. She was referring to a review, "Bull in the Afternoon," in which Eastman compared Hemingway's literary style to "wearing false hair on the chest." Hemingway had sworn to get even and seized his opportunity when he ran into Eastman by chance in Perkin's office. No serious injuries resulted from the pushing match that ensued, but a great deal of publicity was generated. Later, when Max wrote to Marjorie praising Hemingway's play, *The Fifth Column*, she replied that Hemingway seemed to be maturing, adding, "If someone could only wash out his mouth with soap, now, he might become the truly adult artist he should be. If he only knew the real he-men who object to his little-boy dirtiness."

Work on *The Yearling* went forward slowly but steadily. She refused most social invitations, telling her friends she was not fit human company. After working until five-thirty or six, she forced herself to take a four-mile walk at the end of the day. "Between punishing my thin brain and my fat body, I have nothing left by sunset but a swell set of cuss words," she told Edith Tigert. She was so exhausted, she often went to bed by seven. When she passed the length of between 100,000 and 120,000 words that she had planned for the book, and still was not near the end, Max told her not to worry about it. Cutting could be done later, and he assured her that she had one reader "who will not object, however long it may be."

She knew what she wanted to say and where she was going with the book, but "getting it out" still took a prodigious effort. Finally she reached the last chapters, which were "pure pleasure" to write as they gave her the chance to say what she had set out to say. By mid-October she had finished and was editing the manuscript. At times, she told Max, it was like "walking on quicksand." She asked him to pray for her sanity, and told him she had come within a breath of throwing the whole thing in the fire one day. The first of December she sent the manuscript to Max by express, warning him to watch for any taint of sentimentality, which she called "sappiness." If some word or phrase made him feel uncomfortable "it is that," she told him.

In November Marjorie had torn herself away from her work to fulfill an obligation she had made to give two lectures to creative writing classes at the University of Florida. In the first one she told the students some of the important things she had learned about writing through personal experience. She warned them to beware of "a fatal fluency" and described her own ability to string words together glibly without realizing that she was only creating meaningless confusion. She talked about the importance of careful research, and the necessity of self-discipline. "You must deliberately don the hair shirt and put peas in your shoes," she told them, and described the only completely joyous moment in a writer's existence as the moment of initial inspiration. The dream must be dreamed, she said, but then its intangible loveliness must be made so tangible that critics' teeth will find actual substance to tear into. Comparing the artist's initial inspiration to Wordsworth's emotion remembered in tranquillity, she said:

> The memory of the joy is there, the hope sustains you all the way through, but ladies and gentlemen, don't let anyone talk of the delightful light life of the author. The moment you put down your title, or, if you write without a title, your first line, you're in for a job of carpenter-work, of brick-laying, of roof-covering, of intricate plumbing.

Her second lecture was titled "Fact and Fiction." Although she disliked making formal speeches of any kind, she had a spellbinding way of talking intimately with audiences and constantly delighted them with personal anecdotes and with her frankness. Word spread of her ability as a speaker, and for the second lecture many of the university professors and outside visitors filled the front rows of the auditorium. Annoyed by the distance these intruders put between her and the students she had come to talk to, she walked down from the stage past the first few rows, and delivered her talk facing the students with her back to the dignitaries.

The ideas she presented in this lecture were ones she was to use over and over in her future speaking engagements. "Fact is fiction, and fiction is fact," she said, pointing out that Galsworthy, who used a huge number of characters, said that he never invented a character in his life. Although everything in life and in living is source material for the writer, he must take his initial inspiration and fertilize it with the creative germ, according to his own response to people and situations, she told the would-be writers. A writer is dealing with dynamite when he deals with facts, she told the audience. "Facts are unreliable and treacherous . . . facts let you down." She used examples from Wolfe, Hemingway, and from her own writing to illustrate her point that facts alone are empty, valueless, inartistic, and dangerous until a writer gives artistic unity to them. "A fact is a page of writing in a dark room; you have to turn the light on to read it," she said. And that light is the imagination of the creative artist. She closed the lecture with a quotation from Wallace Stevens, in which he uses the blue guitar as a symbol of imagination. His theme is that imagination is the only reality, and he expressed the idea Marjorie wanted to leave with the beginning writers:

> But play you must
> A tune beyond us, yet ourselves.
> A tune upon the blue guitar
> Of things exactly as they are.

Max reported to Marjorie on December 13 that he had read *The Yearling* with "constantly growing interest." He thought the beginning with the boy Jody and his parents on the island was perfect, "as good as can be." The father, Penny Baxter, Max thought especially good. Penny's real life antecedent, the father of her friend Cal

Long, had been transmuted into a character who also had many of the qualities of Marjorie's own father, and, as she often said, he became the spokesman of her philosophy. In writing the book, she had had a hard time keeping Penny from becoming more important than Jody at times. Many of the facts that Cal Long and Barney Dillard had told her are woven into the events of the story and especially into the adventures of Jody.

Although the mother in *The Yearling* bears some of the traits Marjorie at times ascribed to her own mother, Ma Baxter is a distinct person whose bitter personality has been shaped by the hard circumstances of her life and by the loss of all of her children except Jody.

The Forrester family in the novel are not farmers like the Baxters, but live almost entirely by hunting, fishing, horsetrading, moonshining, and running cattle and hogs. Four miles from Pat's Island Marjorie had met a family named Sullivan, who lived in much the same way. The touching character, little Fodderwing Forrester, was inspired by two young boys who lived in Cross Creek: J. T. Glisson, the son of Marjorie's neighbor and friend Tom Glisson, and Rodney Slater, the son of the Widow Slater. In *Cross Creek* Marjorie would describe J. T.:

> *J. T. was a tragic little cripple when I first knew him. I would see him hobbling down the road on his crooked legs, with the luminous expression on his face that seems so peculiar to those we call "the afflicted."*

And in the same book she says that Rodney Slater had club feet and twisted legs and tortured back but he also had a gift for foretelling the weather "with a strange accuracy," and he always had some small pet, a squirrel or chameleon or perhaps a chicken hurt and crippled like himself. In *The Yearling* little Fodderwing, crippled in body and so different from his burly brothers, has a mystic communion with nature and always has a number of small animals he is caring for.

Max, as usual, had specific suggestions to make about the story. He detected a trace of "theatricality or romanticism" in the description of the first trip that Penny and Jody make to visit the Forresters

and wanted her to show some of the meanness of character in the
Forrester men that is later so important to the plot. He thought
Grandma Hutto "first rate," but did not think her sailor son, Oliver,
realistic enough. These two characters are evidently wholly fictional,
except that Marjorie's love of the "fight of life" can be seen in Grandma
Hutto. Max thought all her descriptions of nature and hunting "superb." None of his suggestions required any major revision.

Marjorie was greatly relieved at his reaction to the manuscript.
She wrote to him on December 29 that she must have some money
within a week, although she hated to take an advance. But the profits
she had expected to make from her grove had been canceled by an
early cold spell. Even while her orange crop was being ruined, the
artist in her saw beauty and drama in the situation. She wrote Max
a lyric account of trying to save the crop:

> *I fired my young grove two nights in succession. It was very*
> *beautiful. There was a fat-wood bonfire in the center of each*
> *square, that is, one fire to each four trees. The light from the*
> *fat pine is a rich orange, and the grove seemed to be full of*
> *bivouac fires, as regular as a geometric design. They illumi-*
> *nated the sky to a Prussian blue, with the palm tops against*
> *it. Facing away from the fires, the light gave my low rambling*
> *house, the orange trees and palms around it, a flat silver-gold*
> *wash, most theatrical. The cold sky was absolutely sequined*
> *with stars. It was so beautiful that it was almost worth what*
> *it cost me.*

She told Max that for the next two nights she was ready to fire, but
by four in the morning knew she did not have to. She was up with
her crew of nine men for the four nights, keeping them in food and
coffee and liquor. The young grove was saved, but the mature oranges
were damaged and just before Christmas the inspectors condemned
carloads of fruit, including some of hers. This incident was added to
the growing pile of material she was collecting toward her proposed
chronicle of Cross Creek.

Explaining to Max her urgent need for an advance, she told him
that in addition to notes of eight hundred dollars she had to meet,

there were unexpected expenses. When a transient worker split his foot on an axe while working for her, she was afraid he might bleed to death if they waited to get him into a charity hospital. Consequently, she took him to her own doctor for surgery, X-rays, and dressings and paid the bills herself. That sort of thing did not bother her, she explained, as she increasingly had the feeling that "nothing tangible belongs to us." She had supported with work and assistance several of her neighbors, all summer and fall, and it seemed to her that it "doesn't make a scrap of difference whether the few hundred dollars involved are in my pocket or theirs."

By the last week in January, Marjorie was working on the galley proofs of *The Yearling*, going over them with a "cold eye," trying to eliminate any flaccid quality, trying to "stiffen" her descriptions. She was pleased that Edward Shenton, who had illustrated Hemingway's *Green Hills of Africa*, was to do the headpieces for the chapters, but she was concerned about the cover. She had not liked the jackets on *South Moon Under* and *Golden Apples*. She suggested that *The Yearling* jacket show Jody and his deer side by side, with the boy's arm across the deer's neck, "the two looking out with the same expression of big-eyed wonder," with perhaps a stylized magnolia tree behind them. She considered it important that the cover reveal the meaning of the title, which otherwise was subject to misinterpretation before the book was read. She worried that the drawings of the vegetation might not be accurate as the vegetation of the Scrub is "like nothing anywhere," and she had taken great pains to be accurate about physical details.

When she received copies of the Shenton drawings, she found their quality exquisite, but had a few quibbles about his portrayal of the characters. Jody was a little too dainty for her conception and the sink hole wasn't right. But she admitted that "Rembrandt or Corot" could not have done it to please her completely without having seen the country. The deer, somehow, didn't look like a Florida deer since the ears and tail weren't right. On the whole, though, she thought that Shenton had captured the spiritual and emotional quality of the book and the feeling of the Florida country.

Robert Frost and his family were in Gainesville for the winter, and Marjorie was introduced to them by some of the University of Florida faculty. After spending a day in Frost's company, Marjorie wrote Max that she had formed what she hoped was a "real friendship" with him. It did prove to be a lasting friendship, and whenever Frost came to lecture at the university, they got together either in Gainesville or at Cross Creek. They also corresponded and on at least one occasion he visited her at her house in Van Hornesville, New York. Several times he tried unsuccessfully to get her to take part in the Breadloaf Writer's Conferences in Vermont and to visit his farm there.

One of the things Marjorie discussed with Frost at their first meeting was Tom Wolfe's defection from Scribners to Harpers for a large advance. Both Marjorie and Robert Frost took it as a menacing sign for Wolfe, and Marjorie wrote indignantly to Max, "And after all Wolfe owes you. . . . No advance could make up for losing you as an editor and critic. His artistic future certainly hangs in a perilous balance."

Marjorie entered the new year with a sense of lightness at having completed her third book—but not with complete satisfaction. For although she had "sweat blood" over *The Yearling*, trying to "make the intangible tangible, to pick emotion out of the air and make it true for others is both the blessing and the curse of the writer," she told Max, "for the thing between book covers is never as beautiful as the thing he imagined."

As he worked on the final proofs, preparing them for publication, Max Perkins increasingly fell under the spell of Marjorie's book. The war in Europe and the threat it posed to the United States preyed on his mind. Toward the end of January 1938, he wrote to her:

> *I'll tell you what* The Yearling *has done for me. You know how much there is to worry about when one goes to bed these nights. But my mind often goes to* The Yearling—*the country, people, and the hunts—and then all is good and happy. Now that's a test of how good a book is.*

CHAPTER · 9

An American Classic

When the editors at the *Saturday Evening Post* reluctantly decided not to take *The Yearling* for serialization, Marjorie was relieved. The money would have been welcome, but she hated the idea of butchering the story for publication in installments. She and Max were of course delighted when the Book-of-the-Month Club chose it as their April selection. Accordingly, Scribners set April 1 as the official date of publication.

She agreed to read from her new novel for the "Animated Magazine" at Rollins College in February and asked Max his opinion as to what she should read. He suggested she read the chapter in which Penny and Jody visit the Forresters and Penny swaps a sorry hunting dog for a good gun. Although she felt as if she were putting on a vaudeville performance, her reading pleased the audience of five thousand. She also accepted an invitation to speak to the Florida Historical Association on her use of historical material. She felt obligated to accept this invitation, she told Max, as she expected to use the society "ruthlessly," in gathering material for her book on Zephaniah Kingsley. She also acknowledged to him that the prospect of doing that book both tempted and terrified her.

Max Perkins and his wife, Louise, planned a literary tea for Marjorie to coincide with the publication of *The Yearling*, and the Book-of-the-Month Club editors had arranged for her to give a radio talk about the book, for which she was to receive an additional fee. So at the end of March she took the train for New York. At the tea she met such interesting people as Edward Shenton, her illustrator, and Malvina Hoffman, the sculptor, with whom she began a lasting friendship carried on mostly by correspondence but punctuated with occasional visits in New York and at Cross Creek.

On her way back home, Marjorie stopped in Louisville to visit friends, including the Hardys. She also visited the Langes at Ft. Benjamin Harrison in Indiana. After she left, Otto Lange wrote that he had walked alone counting the call of the whippoorwill—257 times—and each call reminded him of her. He was full of praise for *The Yearling*, telling her it reflected her character, which was essentially good, gentle, and sweet in spite of her occasional "hell-roaring." He told her he was saturated with thoughts of her and his homesickness for her was perpetual. He concluded, "[W]ell, dearest Diana, my loving you is your fault and you can't help it."

Although she had had a wonderful time on the trip, Marjorie told Max, it was "heavenly" to be home again. Something in her was increasingly restless on streets and within walls. A tempting invitation from her brother Arthur was awaiting her. He asked if she could come to Alaska for several months to go with him to take colored films to be used for publicizing his guided hunting and fishing expeditions. Although the idea appealed to her greatly, she decided she could not afford to go. The bean crop, which she owned on shares with the man who worked it, was a total loss for lack of rain, and she had accepted a teaching engagement at the University of Florida for the summer session.

On May 20, however, she wrote an indignant letter to the dean of the College of Arts and Sciences at the university rejecting the offer to teach there. She told him that she was "profoundly shocked" to learn that the salaries for summer school teachers were scaled down according to the enrollment. She informed him that because of her personal friendship with Dr. John Tigert and Dr. Clifford Lyons, she had lectured at the college for a fraction of what she would have asked elsewhere. Her indignation was not for herself, but for other teachers, who needed the "honorable guarantee of fixed salaries." She caustically suggested that President Roosevelt might use such an arrangement to balance the national budget.

Dr. Tigert himself answered her letter, telling her that she should not have been sent a copy of the regulation letter about the prorated salaries of summer school teachers. He assured her she would be paid the full fee or honorarium promised and begged her to reconsider for the sake of the students, who gained "tremendous inspiration" from her lectures. In reply, she assured the president that the money paid her was not the main issue. Her protest was being made on behalf of other summer school teachers, who might not be in a position to refuse the "dubious" arrangement. Therefore, she wanted her withdrawal to stand and to become a matter of record with the hope that in the future teachers at the University of Florida would be protected against this unreasonable policy. In conclusion, she assured him of her friendly feelings for all of the faculty of the university and for himself.

The Yearling received an abundance of rave reviews.

One Florida reviewer said she would give ten years of her life to have written the book. The *Saturday Review of Literature* said, "Mrs. Rawlings has written a wise and moving book informed with a love of all living kind." The Philadelphia *Inquirer* called it "truly American and deeply human." William Soskin in the New York *Herald Tribune* maintained, "With Tom Sawyer and Huckleberry Finn well in mind it is quite possible to maintain that Jody Baxter . . . is the most charming boy in the entire national gallery." William Lyon Phelps called it "tremendously interesting and wholly charming." *Time* said that the book "stands a good chance, when adults have finished with it, of finding a permanent place in adolescent libraries." Others found it a "leisurely, beautifully composed record of a year's living" and a book with the same "irresistible appeal" as *The Swiss Family Robinson*.

The warm praise of reviewers for the book she had once been tempted to chunk into Mrs. Grinnell's canal was gratifying, but among all the comments there were a few less agreeable to Marjorie. Clifton Fadiman in the *New Yorker* advised his readers to "Take note of

The Yearling by Marjorie Kinnan Rawlings, who writes the kind of regional novel that makes sense." The word "regional" always made Marjorie's blood boil. She thought it was a misleading and limiting term that ignored the fact that a writer uses his art to transform his regional material into something universal. She appreciated the closing sentences of the laudatory review by Edith Walton in the New York *Times*: "*The Yearling*—and this is the best tribute one can pay it—is nothing so narrowly limited as a 'local-color' novel. Rather, it recasts with unusual beauty the old, timeless story of youth's growth to maturity." Likewise, the *North American Review* thought the label "regionalist" obscured the major import of her work. Calling her "a new classicist," the *Review* compared her work to that of Willa Cather and Edith Wharton (both of whom Marjorie admired).

Edward Weeks, editor of the *Atlantic Monthly*, called *The Yearling* the "best and most endearing" book of the year and the London *Times* said the book was "bound to please everybody," a statement that seemed valid as praise for the book continued to pour in. Marjorie's meticulous care with the details of her descriptions of the country, the animals, and the hunting episodes was rewarded. She wrote Max on May 14 that her secret fear that old-guard hunters and woodsmen would find flaws had been allayed. One old hunter told a friend, who had passed it on to Marjorie, that the book made him so hungry for the Scrub that he was ready to throw over his job and get back to it. And Hubert Lyman Clark, the curator of the Museum of Comparative Zoology in Cambridge, Massachusetts, wrote to thank her for writing the book. He marveled at her ability to depict a boy's mind and emotions so perfectly. He was equally amazed at the accuracy of her natural history. Birds and snakes, he told her, had been his lifelong hobbies, and not once in reading *The Yearling* did he detect a careless or an inaccurate statement. "Your description of animal, bird life, scenery and the boy's reaction to them are simply delightful."

She did not accept criticism of her nature lore by those who did not know what they were talking about. She was tempted to jump on Lewis Gannett for questioning her "*provable*" nature incidents in his otherwise generous review, she told Max. But she had grown wise in dealing with critics, for she added she didn't think a writer ever got anywhere with any sort of protest "no matter how right he is."

Max told Marjorie he had never known a book to be so universally liked, and the sales figures bore him out. Fourteen days after publication *The Yearling* was on most lists of best sellers. It quickly moved upward and reached the top of the lists, where it remained for ninety-three weeks. During the first two months, sixty thousand copies were sold and during the first year, the total reached two hundred and forty thousand.

Fan letters began to trickle in soon after publication and gradually became a flood. The letters, often written in bursts of spontaneous gratitude for the pleasure the book had brought the reader, continued even after Marjorie's death, fifteen years later. Strangers wanted to tell her what had touched them most in the book. For some it was the prayer that Penny says over the grave of little Fodderwing. For others it was the poignant scene at the end of the book when Jody returns home after trying to run away from the reality of the death of his beloved pet and the feeling that his father had betrayed him. The writers endorsed the message of the book that is delivered by Penny when he tells his son:

> *Ever' man wants life to be a fine thing, and a easy. 'Tis fine, boy, powerful fine, but 'tain't easy. Life knocks a man down and he gits up and it knocks him down again. . . . What's he to do then? What's he to do when he gits knocked down? Why, take it for his share and go on.*

Other readers wrote that they treasured the book for its nature lore, its humor, its poetic quality, the cadence and accuracy of the dialogue, and for individual reasons. One woman, who had two suitors, reported that she had each of them read *The Yearling*. One responded to it warmly, while the other was indifferent to its quality. She married the one who liked it.

Most touching of all to her were the letters that came from children, and especially those from boys. From Pennsylvania a thirteen-year-old named Frank wrote that he had always thought his father liked his two sisters best. Reading *The Yearling* had made him realize that they had always paid more attention to their father than he had. Seeing how Jody worked for his father and "made over him," had opened Frank's eyes, and he told Marjorie he thought that his reading her book "will start a better love between my father and I." "I will always remember *The Yearling*," he promised.

Marjorie wrote to Frank that she was deeply touched by his letter and encouraged him to show his father that he loved him. Grown people can be very shy, she said. "Parents often do not feel sure of their children's love and hesitate to make friendly advances to them. So they respond more easily to children who do make it plain to them."

It was especially good to hear from old college friends like Esther Forbes, who told Marjorie that she had finished *The Yearling* late at night in a flood of tears. She hastened to add that she liked to cry over books and enumerated some of the things that pleased her most, including the "rhythmic flow of the language" and the humor of such passages as the one in which Mr. Forrester praises his boys because they have never cussed their Pappy and Mammy at the table. A newer friend, Marjory Stoneham Douglas, called *The Yearling* "so lovely, so finely felt, so beautifully unified and sustained." And from Kentucky, James Still wrote, "Few of us write a book people love. Surely this is one of them."

Marjorie's share of the Book-of-the-Month Club sale was $5,000, and as a major best seller the book's royalties began to mount up. In addition, Carl Brandt sold the movie rights for *The Yearling* to Metro-Goldwyn-Mayer for $30,000. It was evident from the almost universal praise by critics and the enthusiastic letters from readers that the sales would continue to be excellent. For the first time in her life Marjorie had to be concerned about receiving too much income in one year. Otto Lange gave her advice on the subject, suggesting she hold on to her mortgage, and her Aunt Wilmer sent advice telling her to pay off her mortgage first thing. More helpfully, Max Perkins worked with the Scribners business department to devise a plan so the income could be spread out and not all be taxed the first year.

The first week in June, Marjorie had a severe flare-up of diverticulitis. When her appendix was removed in 1931, it had proved to be perfectly healthy. Her problem was belatedly diagnosed as chronic diverticulosis. This condition, in which small pouches along the border of the colon become filled with foreign matter, may give rise to irritation, inflammation, and abscess and can lead to excruciating pain. Massive hemorrhage is a danger. Diverticulosis is common in populations, like those in the western world, where a low-roughage diet is usual. As Marjorie grew older, her chronic diverticulosis caused severe inflammation (diverticulitis) with distressing frequency. During this attack Dr. Vinson, her surgeon in Tampa, took a series of X-rays and advised an operation to remove a section of the lower intestine. The immediate danger, she told Max, was of a peritonitis that might get out of control. The ultimate danger, her doctors warned, would be of a malignancy. The operation had a 30 percent success rate, and she had no doubt that her life was at stake. But with bravado she wrote her editor and friend: "If I should die, it would not matter. . . . I have lived so full and rich a life, with so much more than my share of everything, that I feel indebted to life, instead of life's still being indebted to me." In case the operation was not successful, she told him that her brother was her heir and her executor, and that her close friend Norton Baskin would have charge of her affairs if she was in for a long siege of recuperation. She did not notify Arthur of the impending operation as he was just leaving for his Alaskan trip to make the colored films, but she did wire Otto Lange about her condition.

Norton Baskin was in Alabama on family business, but Cecil Bryant telephoned him about Marjorie's condition. Norton returned to Florida immediately and, with some difficulty, persuaded Marjorie she should have a second opinion. Consequently, he, Cecil, and Bob Camp took Marjorie to Riverside Hospital in Jacksonville where Dr. T. Z. Cason and two collegues agreed that an operation in her case should be a last resort. They put her on a rigid diet and sent her home, assuring her that if she had had the operation, she most likely would by that time be "cavorting with the angels." Marjorie informed Norton, Cecil, and Bob that since they had "undoubtedly" saved her life, in the future whenever she was bored, she would feel free to wire any of them anywhere, saying, "Having a rotten time and it's your fault. Come and do something about it."

Before she became ill, Marjorie had planned to join Mrs. Grinnell in Bimini for a fishing vacation. As soon as she was able to travel, she made the trip and spent the first week in July with her friend, fishing in all kinds of weather. She returned to Cross Creek feeling passive and lethargic. The heat and a lingering weakness made her want to do nothing but lie on the daybed on her screened porch. From there she could see the redbirds that came to the feeder baskets in her crepe myrtle and to the bird bath, and watch the little West Indian ground doves that walked up and down the front path with bobbing steps.

For a dime, some of the little black boys in the neighborhood would pull armfuls of Egyptian lotus blossoms from a nearby marsh. She described them to Max as a cross between a magnolia and a water lily, with long stems and pale yellow blossoms that spread wider and wider until the huge petals dropped with a sound "like a large bird fluttering in a tree." And she told him she was content simply to lie on her couch watching the blossoms fall.

Magazines were "tormenting" her for stories and articles and she hated it. She balked against coercion and could not and would not write to order, she insisted. The immediate writing project that interested her was the dramatization of *South Moon Under*, a project that had been proposed to her. Recalling that she had written plays in college with some success, she told Sam Byrd, the actor, to come to lunch and they would discuss the project, which he was promoting. Marjorie served the actor blackbird pie (since she didn't know at that time that the taking of red-winged blackbirds was forbidden by federal law) and they made plans for a dramatic version of her first novel. However, she never got off to a satisfactory start on the script, and other writing plus bouts of ill health interfered with her concentration on it. She finally abandoned the idea completely.

With Marjorie's approval, Scribners was planning to publish an anthology of her short stories, and Max suggested that she begin editing some of them and perhaps even write another Quincey Dover story or two for it. She made excuses of needing to gather more material and of not feeling up to it. Also, she told him that a writer cannot go ahead with new work until he is free from the old. As long as one book was in the news and being talked about so that everywhere she went, questions were asked and comments made and letters coming in every mail about it, she did not feel free. She also agreed with novelist Ellen Glasgow's comment in her *Prefaces* that a writer had to wait for the well of the subconscious to fill after working with sustained creative energy. "Or maybe I'm only rationalizing," Marjorie admitted.

Actually she was still suffering from the prolonged bout with her troublesome diverticulosis and running a constant low fever. Toward the end of July she went back to Riverside Hospital for ten days of rest and treatment that included a rigid diet. She chafed against leading a methodical life as her doctors ordered, remembering what she had said in *Golden Apples*: "only endlessness is torture." Charles Scribner and Max Perkins sent her books and Max sent her tidbits about *The Yearling* that he thought would amuse her. He told her that Bing Crosby had talked about the book on the radio, and that a "great" sports writer named Joe Williams had discussed the hunting and fishing episodes from it in his column. Max also enclosed a clipping that said, "Who cares who is going to play Scarlett in *Gone With the Wind*? What we want to know is who is going to play Penny and Jody in . . . the lovely fable, *The Yearling*."

While she was in the hospital feeling depressed and a little sorry for herself, the person she most wanted to see was Norton Baskin. Over the past two years he had become the one she turned to for practical assistance, for comfort in her low moods, and for affection. Although she sometimes still said to him, "Don't give me that damned hotel smile," she had come to know she could rely on him. His ability to see the ridiculous side of life matched her own. She signed her occasional ribald notes to him, "Dora Rolley." (Dora was the name of her valuable but evil-tempered Jersey cow.) But even more important than his ability to make her laugh was the fact that he made her feel she had someone to turn to who cared deeply for her, for in spite of her vaunted independence she needed this kind of relationship. Although Norton had proposed marriage several times she was afraid of making a more permanent commitment.

During the late summer, Max's letters had mentioned that Tom Wolfe was seriously ill. After Wolfe died of tuberculosis of the brain on September 15, a few weeks short of his thirty-eighth birthday,

Max sent Marjorie a copy of the last letter that Wolfe had written him from his sick bed. Marjorie told her editor:

> *I have grieved for you ever since I heard of Tom's death. I grieve, too, for the certain loss of the work he would un-questionably have done, for his very touching letter to you shows a chastening and mellowing of that great, half-mad, diffusive ego. . . . I know how glad you must be that you never withdrew your personal goodness from Tom, even when others were bitter for you.*

In October she went to Kentucky to continue her recuperation on a visit to the Hardys. On the way back she stopped in Atlanta where she met John and Margaret Mitchell Marsh. Marjorie and Margaret Mitchell enjoyed each other immensely. Their backgrounds had many similarities: each had a strong, dominant mother and fathers who were patent attorneys; each had developed her story-telling abilities early in life; each had made a first marriage to a charming, immature man; each loved acting and had been involved in theatricals; each had had journalistic experience on newspapers. Their personalities, too, were similar: both were subject to fits of dejection and uncertainty about their creative powers; both loved jokes and tall tales; both had a bawdy streak; both could drink heavily and both at times flouted convention and society. Both of them were popular with men and both of them suffered from frequent illnesses and accidents.

Soon after the meeting, Margaret wrote to Marjorie that her brief visit was the most pleasant thing that had happened to the Marshes in a long time. "We knew we would meet you some time and we knew we would like you. It's seldom we have had that feeling about people but we liked you so very much . . .," she said. Marjorie told a friend that Margaret Mitchell had so much personality she "threw off sparks."

The Marshes expressed disbelief that Marjorie was really a business woman who ran an orange grove and a farm, but when Marjorie urged them to visit Cross Creek, Margaret replied that the squawks of mallard ducks and the bleats of a bull calf would sound like "Angelic music" to a couple who had endured for two years the repetition of the question: "Now tell me confidentially, who do you want to play Scarlett?" However, the Mitchells did not get to come to Cross Creek for Christmas as they felt they had to stay in Atlanta to take care of business connected with the issuance of the low-priced edition of *Gone With the Wind*. Marjorie's usual Christmas gifts to friends and relatives outside of Cross Creek were the produce of her groves and Florida jellies and preserves. When the Mitchells received a crate of oranges, kumquats, and tangerines they were convinced that Marjorie was a business woman and found the fruit "as excellent in its way as your writings."

During the Christmas holidays Chuck Rawlings stopped by to see Marjorie, somewhat to her dismay. He seemed unchanged physically, except that his face was becoming lined. He was accompanied only by his dog and did not mention his second wife; but he told Marjorie he had spent the summer with his mother in Rochester. She did not encourage him to stay and felt relieved when he left.

The thing Marjorie enjoyed most about having money was that it enabled her to indulge her impulse to give generously to others. She delighted in fixing boxes at Christmas for each of the Cross Creek families and for a number in the outlying area. Each box was filled with gifts carefully chosen to fit the recipients. For the children there were toys, clothes, candy; and for the adults there were turkeys, hams, fruitcakes, fruit, nuts, liquor, plants, and so on. Out of tactfulness and a wish not to appear to be putting on a "Lady Bountiful" act, she often delivered her gifts when she knew the families were temporarily away from home. On January 21, she asked Max Perkins to send $4,500 out of royalties due her in February to Arthur either by certified or cashier's check as a "loan." Her brother was buying a new boat for his tourist business and she was making what proved to be a contribution toward its purchase. Although she had only a poor return on her 1938 orange crop, the income from *The Yearling* was taking care of her nicely. As a matter of fact, sales were expanding rapidly in Europe, where rights had been sold in England, Norway, Sweden, Denmark, Poland, Finland, Germany, and Italy.

The New Year started off with a domestic crisis. Marjorie was at Daytona Beach for a few days visit when the Gainesville sheriff called to tell her that Sampson, her grove manager, had been shot, and wanting to know if she would guarantee his hospital bills. At the time, one of Martha Mickens's daughters, Adrenna, was working as Marjorie's housekeeper and had tried for months to trap a husband, largely so they would have a man on the place. When Adrenna found Sampson, Marjorie paid for their wedding, even though she had reasonable doubts about the legality of Adrenna's divorces from her previous husbands. From the start, there was bad feeling between Sampson and another of Martha's sons-in-law named Henry Fountain. It was Henry who fired three loads of No. 5 shot into Sampson from a distance of a few yards. For a long time, it was touch and go as to whether Sampson would survive; but he did and Marjorie paid all the hospital bills and drove him back and forth to the doctor as long as he needed medical attention.

Although she and everybody else in Cross Creek liked Henry much better than they did Sampson, Marjorie tried to see justice was done by forcing a trial for Henry. A clever Gainesville lawyer, Sigsbee Scruggs, defended Henry and the judge took the position of the prosecuting attorney. Marjorie lost her bid for justice as Henry was released for "lack of evidence," but peace was restored at the Creek, and she realized the importance of this. In a few years she would have the opportunity to know Mr. Scuggs much better when she used him as her own lawyer. In the meantime, she kept careful notes of the drama and its cast of characters for future use in her projected Cross Creek chronicle.

Marjorie refused an invitation from Irita Van Doren, editor of the New York *Herald Tribune* book review department, to speak at the spring Book and Authors Luncheon in New York. She wanted to settle down to work for two or three months and public speaking and public attention were too disrupting, she told Max. She also refused many other offers to speak or to write or to be interviewed, but there were some she felt obligated to accept. In January she was elected a member of the National Institute of Arts and Letters. And toward the end of February she went to Rollins College to receive an honorary degree.

Scribners was planning a new edition of *The Yearling* with illustrations by N. C. Wyeth. Marjorie was delighted that Wyeth wanted to come to look over the country and agreed to take him over the territory herself. Wyeth was enchanted with the vast wilderness of the Scrub. He watched alligators, caught a glimpse of a bear and heard the scream of a panther. Twenty-one-year-old Andrew Wyeth was with his father and spent his time doing water colors. Marjorie was impressed with his work, which he did directly from the landscape, without sketching. She particularly liked a painting he did of a marsh scene near her place. She asked him if his work was for sale and young Andrew said it was and that he usually got from $100 to $150 for his paintings. The only person Marjorie was stingy with was herself, and her Scottish blood rebelled against paying that much for an hour's work by "a boy." She later realized that was an "asinine" way to judge art and deeply regretted her thriftiness.

Another visitor was her English publisher's son, a man named Evans, who spent a six-day vacation with her. When Max accused her of putting out a "flower-strewn welcome mat" for a foreign publisher, she tartly reminded him that she had often begged *him* to come for "6 or 60 days."

In between visitors and engagements, Marjorie was researching material for her book about Kingsley, the early Florida planter and slave trader who married an African princess. Her main theme, she told Max, would be conflict between the world of the imagination and the world of reality. But she worried about the underlying theme of miscegenation in the book. Max encouraged her and gave her suggestions for working out some of the difficulties she foresaw. Phil May enthusiastically helped her locate information and planned a trip to Haiti to search for material there on Kingsley's family.

One day in early March Marjorie noted in her journal that she had a sense of well-being when farm matters were going well. From her kitchen window she could see forty biddies busily feeding from a trough. The ducks, which wandered at will, were calling for feed to be put in the safety of their pen. The heavy, fragrant orange bloom was setting well because of abundant rainfall. The redbirds were busy at the bath and in the feed baskets. She could hear milk hissing in the pail, and Pat was toting a palmetto fan across the yard intent on some plan of his own. She kept careful notes of the birds in her area from the tall white egret, who regularly came to her gate for crumbs to the rare Cape May warbler she spotted near the house. One day she watched a bald eagle fly to its nest, observing that it didn't fly direct but made a broad circle and lit on a branch a couple of feet from the nest and surveyed the territory. Her notebooks and her mind were becoming crammed with this kind of information and with memos about people and things in her neighborhood that would *have* to be used in her writing before long.

Marjorie sometimes told interviewers that she took more pride in her cooking than in her writing and professed to being more sensitive to criticism of it. One of the groups she entertained, the Juniper Club, was composed of Louisville businessmen who owned a large hunting preserve that she had visited in the Ocala scrub on the west shore of Lake George. She had come to know the club members through Ed Hardy, the husband of her old friend Lois Clark Hardy. Marjorie's cooking skills had advanced far since the steak and potato meals that were the height of her culinary ambition in the early days of her marriage to Chuck. For this group, a typical menu was:

> *Quail on toast*
> *Romaine with dressing*
> *Sautéed frogs' legs*
> *Stuffed potatoes*
> *Asparagus with hollandaise sauce*
> *Biscuits*
> *Kumquat jelly*
> *Tangerine sherbet in orange cups*

Martinis, fine wines, and strong coffee rounded out the meal. They heartily responded to her hospitality, and she thoroughly enjoyed their praise. She enjoyed writing about food as well as preparing it, and the February 1939 issue of *Vogue* carried her article "I Sing While I Cook." In it she said:

> *Writing is my profession, my exaltation and my torture. I write as an introvert, attempting to turn an intangible loveliness into a tangible conception. But I cook as an extrovert,*

*singing at the top of my lungs, in ecstasy and the certainty of
fulfillment.*

She quoted Adrenna, who told her, "I sho' loves to see you cut loose
in the kitchen." Claiming that she played to the gourmet, never to
the gourmand, she described desirable guests at Cross Creek as those
who after two or three cocktails, "sit down with well-bred greediness
to my careless and carefree table. . . ." She lyrically described her
Crab à la Newburg, Cross Creek, her favorite dish. The source of
the crabs was a stream in the scrub area formed by springs bubbling
from subterranean depths. There, she claimed, are found the largest,
sweetest blue crabs, whose cooked meat is "white as the breast of a
Virgin and as tender." The flaked morsels she then sautéed, allowing
them to absorb butter "as flowers absorb the sun." After adding
lemon juice, salt, a dash of cloves, a fainter dash of nutmeg, and
wisps of red pepper, she poured in, slowly, devilish Dora's cream,
thick and golden, and simmered slowly. Three beaten eggs and enough
dry sherry to thin the simmering mixture to a "shade" beyond the
original thickness of the cream, plus two-thirds of a tablespoon of
cognac completed the dish. She advised serving it on toast points,
garnished with parsley, in a red-hot serving dish.

In the article she described the evening when Racket, her tame
raccoon, grew instantly to manhood by imbibing an Alexander cocktail left unguarded by an unwitting guest. He slept it off on her bed,
and then, joining the group for dinner in the dining room, fell growl-
ing on a pair of frogs' legs tossed him by an alarmed guest whose
leg he tried to climb. Before the meal was over, Racket had eaten six
pairs of frogs' legs in all.

When the Juniper Club learned that Marjorie was planning a trip
to Louisville in the spring of 1939, they insisted she be their guest
at a dinner there. The trip was timed so she could attend the Derby
at Churchill Downs with the Langes. It was a combination pleasure
and business trip that included a lecture at Ohio State University in
Columbus, Ohio, a visit to the Langes at Ft. Benjamin Harrison, and
a few days with the Hardys in Louisville. Aunt Ida Tarrant drove
with her as far as Cincinnati to visit friends there.

While Marjorie was at the Gibson Hotel in Cincinnati, she read in the papers the announcement that she had won the Pulitzer Prize for the best novel of 1938. Other winners for the year were Carl Van Doren for his biography of Benjamin Franklin and Robert E. Sherwood for his play *Abe Lincoln in Illinois.* As was her way with events of great importance in her life, she took the news with outward casualness. Writing to Norton, she said she was glad for Scribners' sake because "Publishers get an awful kick out of those things." She really had had as much luck as she felt she deserved with one book and hated to think how blue the unsuccessful candidates were feeling when she "wouldn't have minded particularly" losing. She told Norman Berg, an Atlanta friend, who was a sales representative in the Southeast for Macmillan, that it was impossible not to take a certain pleasure in the Pulitzer, but that it was impossible for her to take "any of those things too much to heart." The competition had not been great, she pointed out, and wondered how *The Yearling* would have fared if it had come out the same year as *The Grapes of Wrath.* In spite of her disclaimer, the competition in 1938 was not negligible, for it included Kenneth Roberts' *Northwest Passage*, Louis Bromfield's *The Rains Came*, Esther Forbes's *The General's Lady*, and Sinclair Lewis's *The Prodigal Parents.*

After her lecture in Columbus, Ohio, a newspaper reporter asked if she planned to travel over the country and become "the darling of the book shops." Marjorie answered, "Hell, no, I'm going back to Cross Creek where people don't give a damn." Back home, when she tried to explain to Martha Mickens what all the fuss was about and about winning the Pulitzer, Martha responded that it was a fine thing because she doubted that anyone else at the Creek had ever done it.

Others, however, did not take the news so calmly. Again letters of congratulations and praise poured in from strangers and from old and new friends. John and Margaret Mitchell Marsh, who had won the Pulitzer two years earlier, sent a telegram of CONGRATULA-TIONS, APPLAUSE AND LOUD EXCLAMATIONS OF PLEA-SURE. James Still told Marjorie he danced a jig of delight when he heard the news, and Bee McNeil wrote that she was bursting with pride. Fredric March wired: THERE YOU ARE WINNING PRIZES FOR WRITING ABOUT A DEER AND HERE I AM TRYING TO

ACT LIKE ONE. And Ernest Meyer wrote a column of tribute in the New York *Post*. An English teacher from Marjorie's high school days wrote to tell her former student that she had seen the promise in her, and W. E. Leonard, her professor at the University of Wisconsin, told her that he had never forgotten her, adding that none of his old students in the art of serious fiction had made him as proud as she had.

Particularly pleasing to Marjorie was the praise of Ellen Glasgow, whose *Prefaces* she admired. Glasgow said, "Few books have ever moved me more deeply than *The Yearling*. . . . It is a perfect kind of thing with the accent of inevitability that tempts me to use the word 'genius.' " She asked Marjorie to stop and visit her when she came through Richmond. Charles Scribner wrote to tell Marjorie she got what she deserved. The book, he said, had taken on a life of its own, and it would be a hundred times harder to make *The Yearling* stop selling than to make it sell more. Max wrote that it ought to be a great pleasure to her to have written such a book—"one that must become an American classic." He told her that Scribners planned a Pulitzer Prize edition of *The Yearling*, which would be elegantly bound in heavy linen crash with a line drawing of a palmetto stamped on the ecru cover and a dust jacket featuring a colored painting by N. C. Wyeth, showing Baxter's Island with Jody, Penny, Ma Baxter, and Flag, Jody's deer, in the picture.

The *Saturday Review* ran a cover story on Marjorie and requests for public appearances proliferated. She agreed to do a reading of "Varmints" in the Union Auditorium at the University of Florida on May 20. She delighted the capacity audience with her reading of the Quincey Dover story and then answered questions. When asked if she had any plans for improving the economic conditions of the people about whom she wrote, she snapped, "They don't need any improving. They are happy as they are." Any change imposed by others, she went on to explain more mildly, might upset their present harmony and happiness.

Marjorie's relationship with her neighbors was very different from her relationship to the professors, doctors, lawyers, and others from Gainesville and Ocala with whom she exchanged dinner and party invitations. As she explained in *Cross Creek*, she lived "within screaming distance" of her nearest neighbors, the Glissons and the Brices. With them, and with the other families in the Cross Creek area, she was on friendly terms, often visiting on porches and in kitchens, helping with such chores as stringing new fences, or in times of sickness or other trouble. "Each of us," she said, "knows the foibles of the others and the strength and the weaknesses, and who can be counted on for what." Probably one of her greatest satisfactions in living at the Creek was that the inhabitants had great respect for each others' privacy and yet were extremely clannish and supportive of each other when there was a menace from outsiders or from the weather or any other cause. Before many years had passed, she would find this quality of sticking up for their "own" to be of great value.

On June 20, the Marion Chamber of Commerce gave a testimonial dinner for the woman some of them had excoriated a few years earlier for her portrayal of the Crackers in "Cracker Chidlings" and "Jacob's Ladder." The dinner was at the Hotel Marion in Ocala. The Ocala *Banner* reported that the two hundred people attending included "local yokels, local sophisticates, local swells, local plains, plus some of the scrub people." The last included the Fiddias and Barney Dillard. Marjorie, wearing a chiffon gown in shades of orchid and an orchid corsage, told the audience that she would not make a formal speech but would simply talk to them about her writing. She said she would avoid cussing for "Aunt Ida's benefit," but the *Banner* reported that she did cuss "a little." For an hour Marjorie charmed the guests with anecdotes and stories of her life, beginning with her childish attempts to write and her father's influence on her love of nature. Then she told them of her experiences, humorous and poignant, since moving to Florida. She spoke as well as she wrote, the paper reported, and the audience would have been willing to listen "to plenty more." Her hosts presented her with a set of carved wooden figures of the characters in *The Yearling*. It was a gift she cherished and kept on display in her living room at Cross Creek.

That same month, some three months after its publication, the New York *Post* began serializing *The Yearling*, and although sales on books in general were down because of war scares, orders for Marjorie's best seller continued to pour into Scribners. Papers and magazines constantly beseeched her for interviews. Their questions became tiresomely repetitious. Over and over she told different questioners that her only formula for success was hard work. One of the interviewers' favorite questions was how she would use the $1000 Pulitzer Prize cash award. With a gleam in her eye, she liked to tell them that she planned to plow it under in her orange grove; that is, use it to buy fertilizer.

Marjorie's self-deprecating humor was one of the qualities that made her speeches so entertaining. She liked to tell audiences that just after she had been awarded the Pulitzer Prize for *The Yearling*, and was sure the whole world was aware of it, she was introduced at a party as "Marjorie Rawlings, the writer." The woman said, "Indeed! And have you published anything?"

On another occasion, Marjorie related, while *The Yearling* was being filmed, a middle-aged former southern belle flounced up to her at a cocktail party and said, "If I was just ten years younger, honey, I'd be right out there in Hollywood this minute, playing Scarlett in your book."

CHAPTER 10

Riding
the Crest

On May 9, 1939, Max Perkins had written to discourage Marjorie from undertaking long lecture engagements, as he felt they put too much strain on her physically and drained her creative energy. He suggested she might write a book about the region of Florida she lived in as it was at present. It could be a book of description and incident that would "put the place and the life and the beauty and all before a reader," and she could include many of the anecdotes that she had from time to time told him. Marjorie replied that his suggestion was "uncanny," as she had already decided to do just such a nonfiction book about Cross Creek as soon as she finished the two or three new stories for the anthology; but she had not yet mentioned it to him because she was afraid he would be dubious about such a project. At this time the Kingsley book was put aside and never again resurrected.

Before the publication of *The Yearling*, Marjorie's main interruption, as she worked on her screened porch at Cross Creek, had been to watch birds. But after she won the Pulitzer Prize, carloads of tourists managed to find her out-of-the-way place, and even if they only sat and gawked, her concentration was broken. Papers and magazines continued to beg her for interviews, and reporters managed to track her down even though she didn't have a telephone. Sometimes they used the fact of her not having a phone as an excuse simply to drop in on her. Finally, in July, she rented a cottage at Crescent Beach on the ocean, not far from St. Augustine, as a retreat.

The cottage came with a daily manservant, and she took along her pointer Pat for company. They enjoyed daily swims and long walks together. She got permission to crab off a private dock on the river. Tying a chunk of ripe raw beef on a heavy string, she let it hang down until it reached the river bottom. When she felt a tug on it, she eased it up gently until the crab was almost on the water surface and dipped under it with a net. It was not easy to manage alone, and several times she nearly fell off the dock. But she persisted and relished her catches boiled and served with fresh mayonnaise. She also enjoyed gathering donax, small clams, on the beach, fishing with Edith and Verle Pope, friends from St. Augustine, and sometimes playing bridge and having dinner with them.

On a canopied terrace overlooking the Atlantic, she caught up with her back correspondence and worked on her stories. But she missed Norton, who could not get over to Crescent Beach as frequently as he had been able to come to Cross Creek. On her trip in May she had written him, "Darling, I miss you painfully. I'm not going to ever leave you again. Well, hardly ever. . . . I despise being away from you." When he did not take what she considered a perfectly good opportunity to come over to the beach cottage, she was terribly upset. "I can't begin to tell you what a cruel thing that was for you not to come to see me Saturday when you could," she told him. In a long letter she analyzed their courtship and accused him of not wanting marriage (even though he had suggested it repeatedly) as much as she did. She told him that she was not concerned with the legal or social or ethical aspect of marriage. "It is just that I am convinced that the greatest good can be had of life when a man and a woman who love each other and are happy in each other's company, live it together."

She admitted that she needed more solitude and more privacy than most women but assured him she could get all she wanted of being alone in the course of a day. "I loathe living alone," she said. She did not want the "usual" kind of marriage where the "poor man and woman are handcuffed together, neither able to move an inch without the other." She realized the difficulty of their living together, since she could not live the "hotel life" required by his profession. She admitted that their relationship, "romantic and charming" as it was, did not satisfy her, but told him she loved him too much and appreciated too much the large measure of happiness they did have to be able to break it off.

A few weeks later, after he had spent some time with her at the cottage, she wrote in a completely different mood, telling him that her "mental kinks were straightened out again" and thanking him for his patience with her. "I insist that I'm good for you. And I know you're good for me," she said. His bathing suit, radio, and the two reading lights over the bed they shared, made her homesick for him. "I don't know why, but this seems more your place than Cross Creek," she decided. The cottage seemed to be an ideal retreat, and she began negotiating to purchase it as a second home.

As her relationship with Norton deepened, Marjorie's mood swings, with their alternation of accusations of indifference followed by apologetic protestations, were similar to those during her courting days with Chuck. But Norton, unlike Chuck, refused to fight back. His usual reaction, when her temper flared, was to leave her alone until the flame sputtered out, and her equanimity and sense of humor were restored.

By mid-August she had finished the first drafts of four stories and planned to finish revising them by the first of October. Just as she began her editing, she started having acute intestinal pains. After trying unsuccessfully to calm it with diet and rest, she went to the Riverside Hospital in Jacksonville. X-rays showed one area of her colon to be "in rags and tatters, with one diverticulum so thin-walled that puncture seemed a matter of hours," she wrote Max. She wasn't upset or worried about her condition, she told him, "just mad as hell!"

In spite of her editor's advice, she made plans to give lectures that fall in Louisville, Chicago, and New York. When they learned of her illness, the Hardys suggested she consult a well-known physician named Rankin on her stopover in Louisville, and she agreed to do so. After getting her four stories in the mail to Brandt and Brandt, she left for Louisville on October 1. Mark Ethridge, the managing editor of the Louisville *Courier-Journal*, and an old friend, was the one who had engaged Marjorie to speak there and he arranged a royal welcome with a corsage and a large box of flowers.

Under the auspices of the Kentuckiana Institute, she spoke at the Woman's Club to an overflow audience that lined the walls. She told the audience the story of her writing career and got in a few digs at the use of the word "regionalism." If people really are "as quaint as all get out," write them up for *National Geographic*, but don't write a novel about them unless they have a larger meaning than just quaintness, she said. Some of her lecture was taken from the "Fact and Fiction" talks she had made at the University of Florida. The press stories stressed the warmth, informality, and humor of her presentation. The next day Marjorie had her consultation with Dr. Rankin. He told her she did not need an operation and had nothing "particularly" to fear, but he warned that her condition would probably not get any better. His only prescription was to try to avoid acute attacks by leading a prudent life—meaning moderation in food and drink, and ample rest and exercise. Marjorie spent a week with the Hardys and had a grand time. The day before she left for Chicago, she was the honored guest at a buffet luncheon for sixty-five people given by Lois Hardy.

By contrast with the warmth of her visit in Louisville, Marjorie found Chicago cold and lonely. She spoke at Mendel Hall at the University of Chicago. The hall was full, but the icy breath that lifted from it was like the air from a "super-size Norge refrigerator," Marjorie wrote Mark Ethridge. After making a few formal remarks, she thought, "Why, you poor frozen bastards, you've had the living hell educated out of you." Tossing away her notes, she "swapped the bread of information for hyacinths for the soul, and went to town." When she concluded her informal talk, the students refused to leave, and she had to tell them anecdote after anecdote about her experiences in Florida until she was forced to say she wasn't going to tell them any more stories and they might as well go home. "The poor devils hadn't been talked to by a human being since Robert Herrick's day," she said. After the lecture, she went back to the Balinese Room at the Blackstone Hotel where she was staying and got tight all by herself and charged it to the entertainment fund of the University of Chicago. She was to meet Norton in Montgomery, Alabama, to visit some of his family, and wired him LEFT LOUISVILLE WITH REGRET. LEAVING CHICAGO WITH JOY AND RELIEF. When Norton met her at the Montgomery train station, he said, "But where are the twins, Joy and Relief? And what have you done with poor little Regret?"

When Marjorie received the Wyeth illustrations for the new edition of *The Yearling*, she was impressed by the artist's backgrounds, animals, and action but thought Ma Baxter looked like a Pennsylvania Dutch farm woman. Max agreed with her but felt that Wyeth had caught the color and glamour of the Scrub and a quality of magic that would make adolescents, in particular, pore over the pictures. Wyeth's daughter, Anne, wrote to Marjorie that the spirit of *The Yearling* was "all around us this year." She thought her father's pictures for the book some of his best work and reported that he was getting supreme enjoyment out of doing them. When Marjorie was sent 850 sheets to sign for the special limited edition of the Wyeth *Yearling*, she dutifully signed her long name in her sprawling handwriting to 849 of them. It was a frightfully boring chore, and on the 850th sheet, she signed "Dora Rolley Dooflickit." When Wyeth discovered it, he wrote under it, "I always suspected she did." Confessing the practical joke to Max, Marjorie said, "Scold me if you must—I am Dora Rolley at just the wrong moments and I can't help it." She wrote to Wyeth to thank him for the effort he had put into his illustrations. He was touched by her generous praise and answered that since she particularly liked the illustration of the dance of the cranes, he would make her a present of it. He did, and it hung over her living room fireplace at Cross Creek until her death, when it went to Julia Scribner Bigham, as directed by Marjorie's will.

In November Marjorie was off on another lecture trip. She took the train to New York, where for five dollars a day she had a room on the eighteenth floor of the Hotel St. Moritz on Central Park. From her room she had a grand view straight up the park, where she could see ducks and the moon shining on the pond. But she wrote Norton that without him there to share the view, she had rather be looking at the ducks and the moon at Cross Creek. "I lay on my bed and watched the lights come on over Central Park and wished for you," she told him.

On November 25, she spoke at the annual luncheon of the National Council of Teachers of English, held at the Hotel Pennsylvania. Her topic was "Regional Literature of the South." When she got up to speak, she handed her manuscript to the secretary of the organization and told her the council could publish her formal remarks. Then she told the two thousand cheering English teachers that she preferred to talk with them informally. Without using any notes she related to them her life in Florida and discussed her writing experiences. She had a great deal to say about the Crackers and their speech. The inveterate profanity of the men, she showed was merely a mannerism, hardly to be called irreverent or offensive. "In manners and human dealings they are naive and loyal and courageous," she told the teachers.

In her formal paper, which was published in *College English* for February 1940, she expressed her dislike for the term "regional" when it was connected with literature. "Regionalism written on purpose is perhaps as spurious a form of literary expression as ever reaches print. It is not even a decent bastard, for back of illegitimacy is usually a simple, if ill-timed honesty." Simply to hold up the speech and customs of the people of a certain area for the gaze of the curious, she said, is a betrayal of the people of that region. Regional literature she defined as something quite different. Using Thomas Hardy and Ellen Glasgow as outstanding examples of writers of regional literature, she explained that to use a background that is loved and deeply understood so that it becomes an inextricable part of the work, like colors of a painting or the dye of the wool of a tapestry, is to create a work of art. Her implication was that only in this context would she accept the term "regionalism" in connection with her own writing.

She had a few days to enjoy herself between this lecture and the one scheduled at Columbia University—and she did. One evening she went to the annual Christmas punch-tasting festival of the Wine and Food Tasting Society at the Sherry Netherland Hotel. She started out discreetly sipping, and then encountered Pierre of Pierre's

Hotel and settled down to steady tasting. Then she went to Malvina Hoffman's studio for dinner with cocktails, wine with dinner, and drinks afterward. One Sunday she spent at the estate of Charles Scribner and got to know his wife, Vera, and his two children, Charles Junior and Julia. Charles Scribner was already her good friend, and the other family member she truly came to love was young Julia, whose independent spirit and determination to know all she could of life appealed to Marjorie.

Marjorie shopped in New York and for her Columbia lecture bought a black crepe dinner dress, and she was pleased to find, at a discount, a black velvet gown by Schiaparelli. She watched a rehearsal of Paul Robeson in *John Henry*, and at the instigation of Sam Byrd, she made a small investment in the play. Although the "angels" of this production were asked for more contributions, it eventually failed for lack of sufficient funding. On this trip Marjorie had the time and money to indulge her love of the stage. She went by herself to see *Hellzapoppin'* and was so disgusted with it that she walked out at intermission, even though she had paid $3.30 for her seat. She told Norton that she would have paid another $3.30 not to be compelled to go back, as she thought it was the "tackiest kind of burlesque, not even enjoyably dirty, and as un-funny as possible." But she found *Yokel Boy* and *Too Many Girls* delightful comedies, and although she thought Gertrude Lawrence was "coy" in *Skylark*, she "adored" Katharine Hepburn in *The Philadelphia Story*. Marjorie told Bee that from her second row seat she could see that Hepburn got so worked up at one point that she was crying real tears. Marjorie thought *The Man Who Came to Dinner* a perfect riot and was "mad" about Paul Muni in *Key Largo*. She reported that she alternately shrieked with laughter and wept bitterly at William Saroyan's *Time of Your Life*, which was her favorite of all the plays she saw.

Another play she enjoyed immensely was *The Little Foxes*, which Wilmer Kinnan, her schoolteacher-aunt, took her to see. But an entire Sunday spent with Aunt Wilmer, Marjorie described to Norton as "awful." First they went to a "big, new thought" church and then to a vegetarian health food restaurant, where she ate baked potato and undercooked broccoli. After that, Aunt Wilmer took her to one of a series of lectures she was attending. This one, on the "Rejuvenation of the Face," Marjorie described as the "damnedest *medicine show*" she had ever seen perpetrated. The audience of the "most incredible hags" were all promised miracles if they bought the capillary cleansers, wrinkle removers, and other chemical "trash." Aunt Wilmer disapproved of Marjorie's drinking and smoking and lectured her on violating the laws of health. She told Marjorie that she planned to study jujitsu and thought Marjorie should too, because when a woman knew it, a man "simply could not get a grip on her." Marjorie reported to Norton that she told her aunt in that case, she didn't want to know even the first principle.

While Marjorie was in New York, one of her short stories, which Carl Brandt had sold to the *Saturday Evening Post*, appeared in the magazine's November 25 issue. "Cocks Must Crow," probably the most popular of the Quincey Dover stories, tells of the time Quincey's man, Will, is involved in cockfighting. As usual, Marjorie had done careful research, attending cockfights often enough to know exactly how they were run, the kind of game fowl used, and the sort of people who engaged in this activity. As the editors of the *Post* were preparing the story for publication, they questioned Quincey's saying she boiled up hotter than "a Presbyterian hell." Marjorie wrote in the margin "fix the fires of hell to suit the Post's religion." They did and it came out "a sinner's hell."

Quincey was entirely imaginary but so real to Marjorie that she "could smell her." "She is, of course, *me*," Marjorie told a friend, "if I had been born in the Florida backwoods and weighed nearly three hundred pounds." In "Varmints," when Quincey is teased about her weight, she says, "You can't shock my modesty that-a-way. I can out-eat ary one of you and get enjoyment ten to your one." In "Cocks Must Crow" Quincey expresses a number of her author's beliefs about the relationship between men and women. When they are "fresh-married," Quincey says to Will, "You're soft-acting, Will Dover, but you got a will as hard as a gopher shell." And Will answers, "You ain't fooling me none, neither. You got a tongue as sharp as a new cane knife, but you heart's as big as your behind, and soft as summer butter. And that's why I love you, Quincey Dover." Quincey knows, "Ary woman could get along with a man like that." Over the years she becomes a kind of town oracle in Oak

Bluff, mainly because of her common sense and her understanding of human nature. Part of her philosophy is:

> *Man-nature is man-nature, and a woman'a a fool to interfere.*
> *A man worth his salt can't be helt to heel like a bird dog.*
> *Give him his head. Leave him run. If he knows he ain't running*
> *under a check-rein, the devil hisself can't get him to run more'n*
> *about so far away from his regular rations. Men is the most*
> *regular creatures on earth. All they need is to know they can*
> *run if they want to. That satisfies them.*

Quincey readily admits that Will is right about her sharp tongue, but she doesn't want to change it because there are times she needs it. For example, when she gets ready to bless out the Widow Tippett, who she thinks is fooling around with her Will, Quincey prays, "O Lord, give my tongue a long reach." Then she relates with satisfaction, "I looked at her. I takened my tongue and I flicked it, like a man flicking a fishing rod. I takened it like a casting line and I laid it down right where I wanted it."

In another passage of self-analysis she describes her tender heart— and that of her creator:

> *I can't help being tormented when ary living thing, man, woman*
> *or dog, be hungry. I can't help feeling all tore up when another*
> *grieves. And when a old tabby cat has got no place to birth*
> *her kittens, or some poor soul in the woods is fool enough to*
> *be bringing another young un into the world, and not a piece*
> *of cloth to wrap it in, and a blessing if it was stillborn, why*
> *I got to light in and fix a bed for that tabby cat or that fool*
> *woman.*

At just about the same time this story appeared, Marjorie was writing from New York to Aunt Ida, back in Florida:

> *[M]uch of the pleasure I would otherwise get from the city is*
> *upset for me by running into obviously poor and unhappy*
> *people, and when I pass them in my fur coat, with my stomach*

full of expensive food and drink, and my purse full of money,
it seems to me that it is wrong for anyone to have either an
under-*share or an* over-*share of comfort and security. An old,*
old woman selling 5¢ bunches of lavender outside the theatre
last night—not right.

One of the ways Marjorie was enjoying her new affluence was in
buying furniture in New York for her new beach cottage. Cross Creek
was furnished with plain, old-fashioned comfortable furniture, but
she wanted the cottage to be bright and modern and to reflect the
colors of the sky and sand and ocean. For the living room she chose
pickled pine furniture: a davenport and love seat upholstered in shades
of aqua and two large, deep armless chairs in soft coral. She bought
a cotton chenille rug in a lavender that was almost a gray. For her
large bedroom, looking out on the ocean, which was paneled in a
dull green and dusty rose, she purchased a chaise longue covered in
dusty rose with huge white magnolia blooms. The guest bedroom
had twin beds, for which she chose covers of marine-blue and white.
And for the dining table she bought aqua glassware and Swedish
modern dishes in soft gray.

On December 15, 1939, at the invitation of Margaret Mitchell,
Marjorie and Norton took the train to Atlanta to see the premiere
of *Gone With the Wind*. She found Vivien Leigh to be the perfect
Scarlett and thought the Technicolor lovely but felt the picture lacked
the magic of the book. Some heavy partying with friends had preceded
their viewing of the film and may have clouded her perception, for
several years later when she saw it again, she thought better of it.

Following the premiere, she returned to Cross Creek to a series of
Christmas festivities and a duck hunt on the last day of the season.
After sitting frozen in a duck blind from six A.M. to one P.M. in a
cold, drizzly rain, she came down with the flu. As soon as she felt
better, she completed the revisions of her short stories for the anthology and sent them off to Max. Then she went to bed with a
relapse. While she was ill she received a note from Spencer Tracy,
who had been selected to play Penny Baxter in the movie version of
The Yearling. He thanked her for the inscribed copy of the book she
had sent him and told her it was the most beautiful story he had

ever read. He promised to make every effort "to do your Penny some small justice and not too much harm." The director, Victor Fleming, wrote to tell her not to let herself be pestered by mothers who wanted their sons to be Jody or by people who had a pet deer that would be "perfect" for the picture. He advised her to send all requests for interviews and so forth on to the studio where they would receive proper attention.

The winter social season continued busy. At the Popes Marjorie met James Branch Cabell, the novelist and essayist, whose satirical work she had long admired. They enjoyed a spirited conversation about the relative intelligence of men and women until Cabell's wife, Priscilla, who did not care for such abstract discussion, dragged him away. Cabell promised they would continue their talk, and they did—in person and through letters for the rest of Marjorie's life. From his home in Virginia, Cabell sent her a copy of a pamphlet he had written about Ellen Glasgow, who was his aunt. Cabell also told Marjorie that he was "heels over head" in love with Quincey Dover.

Marjorie had long admired Ellen Glasgow, a Virginia novelist whose realistic writings about the South and about the relationships between men and women had brought her fame when she was past fifty. *Barren Ground* and *The Sheltered Life* are considered by many critics to be her best works.

Chuck Rawlings gravitated back to the Tarpon Springs area again to spend the winter. He sent a message through a mutual friend asking if he could visit Marjorie. She reluctantly said yes and found that having shed his second wife, he was obviously prepared to make a serious bid for them to get back together. She quickly discouraged him. With a slight exaggeration of the time, she wrote Max, "I think fifteen years of sheer sadism are enough to take." Although the visit upset her less than she was afraid it would, she was glad when it was over.

The Brandts sold "The Enemy," one of Marjorie's new short stories intended for the anthology, to the *Saturday Evening Post*. In this tale, she takes the opposite side than she had taken in *South Moon Under* on the quarrel between the Crackers who let their cattle roam on an open range and cattlemen who moved into an area and fenced in the land. While she was working on the story, Max made suggestions about ways she could strengthen its emotional impact. She gratefully used his ideas and "The Enemy" appeared in the January 20, 1940, issue of the *Post*.

An omnivorous and eclectic reader, Marjorie often discovered new writers before they became widely known. She was an early fan of Anaïs Nin and tried her own hand at using the surrealistic and psychoanalytic elements found in Nin. It may be that since Marjorie was such an admirer of Proust, and critics have compared Nin's writings to those of Proust, she was influenced by this likeness. At any rate, the same month "The Enemy" appeared in the *Post*, an entirely different kind of story by Marjorie, "The Pelican's Shadow," appeared in the *New Yorker*. Marjorie told her editor at the *New Yorker* that she had an "evilly good time" doing the characterization of Dr. Tifton, an affected, completely self-centered man married to a much younger wife. In the story the pelican and the shadow it casts as it flaps along the shore come to symbolize for the frustrated wife the qualities of her husband, whom the pelican resembles. "He [the pelican] was neatly gray, objectionably neat for a creature with such greedy habits. His round head, lifted to a peak, was sunk against his heavy shoulders. His round gray eye looked down below him, a little behind him, with a cold, pleased, superior expression. His long, thin mouth was unbearably smug, with the expression of a partial smile." Marjorie accepted the editor's changes with good grace, except for the substitution of "punctilious" for "meticulous." She told the editor that she was "very sensitive to the connotations of words," and that to her the implication in "punctilious" was one of formality, while the implication in "meticulous" was of precisely the finicky fussiness that she meant Dr. Tifton to have. "Do concede me my 'meticulous,' " she requested. And they did. This story, she decided, was "too vicious" to appear in the anthology she and Max were working on.

Her fourth new short story appeared in the February 3, 1940, issue of *Collier's*. More on the order of her previous short stories, it is the sympathetic story of a huge black man whose size frightens people and keeps him from winning jobs, a wife, or even friends. He is shot by another black man in an incident similar to the one in which Marjorie's grove man, Henry Fountain, shot her newly hired worker Sampson. Like Sampson, the big black man in the story has gentle hands that carefully nurture tender plants and flowers, and she had originally called it "Black Bat's Hands." On publication, however, the title was changed to "In the Heart." It drew a number of enthusiastic letters from readers and became a story that colleges liked to use, in an abridged form, in declamation contests.

On February 25, Charles Scribner and his wife delivered Julia Scribner to Cross Creek on their way to Miami. Marjorie entertained them with a fancy dinner to which she also invited the Tigerts and the Lyons. She asked Norton to come and bring along a quart of French vermouth and two quarts of choice rye. She cautioned him to be on his best behavior in such august company, and to keep his mouth shut until he was spoken to. But Norton, having opened one of the bottles of rye to sustain him on the drive, had a couple of martinis and was not willing to wait to be spoken to. He became the life of the party, entertaining them with his endless supply of jokes and anecdotes. The next day Marjorie told him, "You were very cute and funny, but I just didn't want you to get any cuter or any funnier."

Instead of returning to New York with her parents as previously planned, Julia was having such a good time she stayed with Marjorie for two weeks, enjoying hunting, fishing, and exploring the countryside. Cecil Bryant, Bob Camp, and Norton helped entertain her and became her good friends also. On Julia's last day at Cross Creek, as Marjorie and Julia were driving into Gainesville, they had a freak accident. A runaway mule crashed into Marjorie's car, crushing the hood and shattering the windshield. The mule was killed; Julia received slight bruises and scratches; but Marjorie was unhurt. The next day, Julia was to take the train home, so Marjorie towed the car into Ocala in the farm truck with Julia sitting in the car steering it.

This friendship with Marjorie, just as she was coming into adulthood and struggling to find her identity, was tremendously important to Julia, a girl in an almost dynastic family. As a child she was a tomboy who tried to join the Boy Scouts under the name of Julius. Beyond her boarding school training, she had educated herself in the areas of art, music, and literature by study and wide reading. Both she and Marjorie were proud of what they knew and had learned. "How happy I was with you. How much I miss you. How lonely I am when I see something I'd like to talk with you about or something I think you'd enjoy. But most of all how proud I am of your friendship," Julia wrote. A few weeks later Marjorie sent Julia a Beethoven album for her birthday, and Julia called it the most "unexpected and nicest" gift she had ever had.

In a letter to Norman Berg, Marjorie described Julia as "one of the grandest youngsters I've ever known."

From time to time throughout her life Marjorie referred to her childless state with a tinge of regret. But it was always a son she wished for, not a daughter. At Cross Creek, in the mountains of North Carolina, and eventually at Van Hornesville, New York, there was usually some neighborhood boy she especially befriended, and once she told a friend, "There's always some damned little boy to break your heart."

Norman and Marjorie had developed a strange sort of flinty friendship from which sparks often flew, but now she consoled him on his recent divorce. "I know only too well not only the hell you've been through, but the hell you're in for . . . we who are idealists read into others the qualities that we long to find. Then when the truth hits we have a fresh sense of betrayal and frustration."

In March of 1940 the short story anthology was published. Marjorie had at first called it *When the Whippoorwill Calls*, but Carl Brandt suggested omitting "Calls," and this was done, making the title more suggestive. The selections included in *When the Whippoorwill* were chosen jointly by Max Perkins and Marjorie. It contains all of her Florida short stories except the *New Yorker* story, "The Pelican's Shadow," and the *Collier's* story, "In the Heart." At first Max had wanted to include "Cracker Chidlings," but Marjorie objected. She felt they were more journalistic than literary, and she was well aware that of all her writings, "Chidlings" was most subject to being labeled "regional." Even though he was very fond of "Hyacinth Drift," Max reluctantly vetoed it because he thought they should not include any nonfiction.

The reviews of *When the Whippoorwill* were almost unanimously good. The New York *Sun* said the stories are "vitalized by that knowledge of human hearts" and called it a "must" volume for read-aloud shelves. The *Atlantic Monthly* said, "the stories are as good reporting of life in the United States as we have today. She is one of he two or three *sui generis* story tellers we have, and we'd better hank God for her." The Boston *Herald* reviewer said that if there were a Pulitzer award for short story collections, this would win it. He also declared that Marjorie Kinnan Rawlings was the equal of O. Henry, Edgar Allan Poe, Jack London, Ernest Hemingway, and Edith Wharton as a short story writer. The New York *Herald Tribune* found *When the Whippoorwill* far above the average of the usual collection of stories, pointing out that "side by side with supremely comic yarns, there are stories with the same tender and moving quality that so distinguished *The Yearling*." In his *New Yorker* review, Clifton Fadiman said that Marjorie Rawlings and Mark Twain shared the gift of double vision: "the ability to keep one eye on a local patch of earth and the other on human beings in general."

When Charles Scribner sent Marjorie a handsome royalty check in the spring, he joked with her that besides himself, at least two other men at Scribners were in love with her—Max Perkins and Whitney Darrow, the vice president in charge of business. But, Scribner told her, he was the one she should care for most as he never criticized her writing as Perkins did or told her sad stories about sales being down as Darrow did. Instead, he just sent her fat checks. At forty-four, Marjorie had no trouble charming men. Victor Fleming made a visit to Florida to look over the layout for *The Yearling*. He was entertained at Cross Creek and taken over the Scrub by Marjorie. After he returned to California, he read the rest of her books and then wrote to tell her he had fallen in love with them and with her.

While in New York, Marjorie had been offered a lucrative lecture tour, which would include three weeks in the spring and three in the fall. Bernice Baumgarten, who handled foreign rights for Brandt and Brandt, added her opposition to that of Max Perkins, telling Marjorie, "It takes writers months to get over these things." Marjorie agreed and turned down the long tours, but she did accept a shorter one for twelve days in the spring. Her speaking engagements were scheduled for Shreveport, Nashville, Chattanooga, and Tallahassee. By April 2, when she had to set out on the trip, she was sorry she had made the commitment. She was weary from entertaining, although she enjoyed her company, and she hated to leave Cross

Creek in the spring with her orange grove in full bloom, her choice flowers coming into their glory, and her two perverse cows giving buckets of rich milk daily.

Although she always performed well, speaking engagements put her under a nervous strain, and she badly wanted Norton to come with her, but he had obligations connected with his hotel business that took him to south Florida at the same time as her trip. From Miami he wrote her a ten-page letter and assured her he would have written more except that he had used up all of the hotel's large and small sheets of stationery and was afraid the toilet paper would not hold up under his scratchy pen. "You are sweet and dear to me. I mean—I love you," his letter ended. Marjorie enjoyed the trip more than she expected to as it took her through some lovely southern scenery and everywhere flowers were at their peak of beauty. In New Orleans she prowled the antique shops and bought some English Sheffield serving dishes, "much too nice for the way I live at the creek or cottage," she told Norton. Although the drive in the dark from Baton Rouge to Natchez was "a bitch," she was fascinated by the antebellum charm of Natchez that she had experienced only in books. She was warmly received by large audiences, who were delighted when her story telling ran away from her formal speech.

Back in Florida, she began another round of entertaining. Two guests she particularly enjoyed were Walter and Bernice Kenyon Gilkyson, whom Max had wanted her to meet. Walter was a novelist and Bernice a poet and an editor at Scribners. Marjorie had them to Sunday dinner and for a long afternoon visit. She invited Thornton Wilder, the novelist and playwright, to lunch and felt he and she seemed to "begin talking where we had left off." She admitted to Max that Thornton's brilliant mind made her feel "positively illiterate."

At Cross Creek she was continually bothered by the tourists who "just wanted to see" where she lived. Margaret Mitchell wrote in sympathy, telling Marjorie that she was sure they were the same ones who "just wanted to get a peek" at Margaret. This kind of tourist, Margaret felt, was not interested in their work and would just as soon have been viewing the Dionne quintuplets or a "two-headed baby in a bottle of alcohol." To escape the interruptions and the humidity, Marjorie retreated in May to work at her cottage on Crescent Beach. She had the terrace screened in to make it more comfortable. She and Pat again took long walks and swims and enjoyed each other's company. Her domestic peace was upset when Adrenna eloped with a man Marjorie felt sure was only after her small savings. As usual, Old Martha was there to take up the slack. However, although Martha was a "great spiritual satisfaction," she couldn't make a decent cup of coffee or a tidy bed. Marjorie was not a fanatical housekeeper, but she needed clean surroundings and a sense of things running smoothly in order to work well.

A quarrel with Norton also upset Marjorie. On June 14, she wrote to him explaining that her "ugliness" (that is, her blasts of anger and cutting remarks) meant nothing, but that for him to answer back in kind was devastating to her. She accused him of not needing her or wanting to be with her as much as she needed and wanted him. "It's possible," she told him, "that I'm asking of a man that he act as a buffer for me against the strange despair that hits me and that I can't seem to lick. Only I've hoped that a man I could care for would be glad to help me." She called him the "sweetest, kindest, most generous person I've almost ever known," but suggested that he not come to the cottage and that they not see each other for a while. Of course, he *did* come to the cottage at the first possible moment and assured her of his love and concern. The truth was that her emotional dependency on him was deepening, and she was desperately afraid of being hurt again and had to keep on testing the strength of his feelings for her.

There were larger spheres of worry, too, beyond the immediate and personal, during the summer of 1940. Earlier in the war, Marjorie had written Max:

I have always had a cosmic awareness. I am conscious most of the time of the universe of which we are a small part. But only lately have I become aware of the moment's earthly turmoil. I hate it. It seems as though the whole plunge into ruin were a tangible cohesion of evil superimposed on the reasonable and kind and peace-loving individual. Each of us asks

only to breathe without pain, to love and be loved, to work
for the daily bread, without interference.

Now Marjorie told Max that the war intruded on her daily work. As she tried to record for her Cross Creek chronicle the simple everyday things of life in her neighborhood, sometimes what she was doing seemed an exercise in futility measured against what was happening in Europe. She knew, however, that in the long run, it was the things she was trying to record and not empires that are timeless. But she told Max, "I am more depressed than I can tell you."

In July of 1940, Norman Berg asked for the use of Marjorie's beach cottage for a ten-day honeymoon with his new bride, Julie. Reluctantly Marjorie moved back to Cross Creek to work, because she felt it would be "too cruel" to refuse. But she wrote Charles Scribner that when she thought of the ocean breezes and the ease with which she could be working on top of her sand dune, she couldn't help hoping they got "sunburned and divorced."

CHAPTER · 11

Coming into Harbor

*D*uring the summer of 1940, a series of articles entitled "Why I Am an American" was published in various syndicated newspapers. Marjorie was one of the well-known artists and performers asked to contribute. Her true feeling was that democracy was actually a failure because the very individualism entailed made for chaos. Above all, she thought that individual and national and racial greed and selfishness made the outlook for democracy "entirely hopeless." She didn't express this pessimistic view in the article but emphasized her belief that Americans really believe, whether they practice it or not, in a basic kindliness, and consideration for the rights of the individual. It was time, she said, to be concerned with the responsibilities and obligations of the individual.

She herself had learned from her father to take her responsibilities as a citizen seriously. She followed local and national politics and voted conscientiously. In the summer of 1940 she listened to the Republican National Convention on the radio, and as an ardent supporter of Wendell L. Willkie, sent telegrams to the chairmen of the Florida and the Wisconsin delegations, urging them to cast their votes for Willkie. She was thrilled when these delegates did switch their votes to Willkie. Marjorie told Aunt Ida she would vote for Willkie over any candidate except Roosevelt—and might even vote for him anyway, as he would balance "Republican practicality with Democratic progressiveness."

By the end of the first week in August, she had two hundred pages of a first draft of her Cross Creek book done. She offered to send some chapters to Max with the provision that he not show them to "Charlie or anyone." It was all tentative, she told her editor, for she was most unhappy about the style.

In mid-August Bee McNeil came to visit for a week. Marjorie met her in Jacksonville and took her first to the cottage and sightseeing around St. Augustine. When the driver of their buggy laid on too hard with his whip, Marjorie scolded him roundly for mistreating his animal. Then she took Bee to Cross Creek and to Ocala to meet Aunt Ida and Norton, but her pleasure in the visit was marred by a flare-up of diverticulitis, which was probably aggravated by the fact that she was deathly afraid of its spoiling Bee's visit. In a letter to Gertrude Johnson, Marjorie called Bee "a queen of the earth," and said, "it makes you feel good to know there are a few people like that, doesn't it?"

At the end of August, Julia Scribner arrived for a three-week visit. They had agreed that Marjorie would continue to work during the visit, but the agreement was soon broken. One weekend Bob Camp, Cecil Bryant, and Norton came over to the cottage to play. Then Marjorie and Julia went to Silver Glen for a picnic with the trio and spent the night in Ocala at the Marion Hotel before going on to Cross Creek. After a few days they went back to the cottage, which Julia called "Crawlings-by-the-Sea" because of the numerous spiders that tried to take up residence there. Edith and Verle Pope entertained them in St. Augustine, and the Norman Bergs stopped by for dinner and to spend an evening.

One evening when Norton and Marjorie were entertaining Julia at Marineland, Marjorie saw Ernest Hemingway with a woman across the room. She sent him a note, "Are you Ernest Hemingway? Marjorie Rawlings." His answer came back, "If you're Marjorie Rawlings, I'm Ernest Hemingway." They got together for drinks and Ernest introduced Martha Gellhorn, a writer, soon to be his third wife. The couple came back to Marjorie's cottage and stayed until very late into the night drinking and talking.

After Julia left, Marjorie told Norton she felt as if her own child had gone. They kept in close contact through frequent letters. Marjorie told Bee that she put Julia in the rare class of her close women friends, which numbered only two ahead of her—"you and Lois Hardy." Marjorie and Julia shared a sense of the ridiculous, a loathing for hypocrisy and pretense, and high-strung nervous systems. Julia's emotional stress was expressed in sudden vicious headaches. Both women felt free to be completely themselves in each other's company. They enjoyed long walks and long talks and also long silences, sitting at opposite ends of the couch, devouring books and absentmindedly scratching Pat's head as he moved contentedly from one to the other.

Marjorie sent her sample chapters of *Cross Creek* (for once, there was no problem with a title) to Max "most unhappily," for they fell so far short of what she was trying to achieve. He sent her an encouraging note, telling her the material was splendid for "just such a book as I think you could do better than anyone." He promised detailed suggestions when he had studied the manuscript. On September 20, he wrote a long letter in which he tried to put his finger on the problem spots in her material. The book must give the neighborhood and its characters so there would be a kind of completeness, he said. The material for this effect was there or implied, but was not sufficiently developed. He compared the desirable structure of the book to a single piece of string with knots in it. The knots would be the episodes, each connected with the others by incidents and by the talk of her blacks. "No one does negroes so sympathetically and so well, themselves and their talk." He suggested that some of the characters recur a good many times in the book so the reader would look forward to seeing them again, and he pointed out specific characters and how they could be used in both episodes and incidents. He suggested she use parts of her "Cracker Chidlings" and "that most lovely of descriptions, 'Hyacinth Drift.'" He thought a division of the material into a seasonal pattern—spring, summer, autumn, and winter—might give the book a better shape. In the end, as usual, he told her to use her own judgment and apologized if he had "said too much."

There are very few "true writers," he told her. They varied widely but shared one trait: when they began a big piece of work they had vastly less confidence than those who just follow the trade of writing and who always knew where they were going and went there like businessmen. "Those we publish to keep the business going because the real ones are so few," he said. The only thing she lacked at the moment, he assured her, was confidence. He was alarmed because she had commented that she sometimes felt she should be using her writing talent on the "issues of the day." "What you want to say comes through in your writing," he told her and begged, "Don't let anything tempt you into the lists of controversy."

In October Marjorie made a trip by train to Madison, Wisconsin, to give a lecture for the benefit of the Alumni Scholarship Fund. It seemed little enough to do for one's own college, she told Max. She traveled at her own expense and stayed in two rooms at the Union, overlooking the lake on whose shores oak and maple trees were in full autumn foliage. Marjorie's return to her hometown as a celebrity was triumphant. More than two hundred and fifty alumni attended the banquet in her honor that preceded her lecture. As usual, she was in such a state of nerves that she was unable to eat a bite and only drank a little black coffee. The new theater in the Union was packed for her lecture. Wearing a gown of heavy white brocade with a tailored jacket and an orchid corsage, she faced the audience without a note or a stand between her and them. Later she admitted that she was never so scared in her life as before and during the first part of her lecture. She could see Gertrude Johnson sitting on an aisle seat, patting her foot, and suddenly Marjorie felt as if she were a student again. "Oh, God, here I go," she thought. But after the first few minutes when the audience laughed at the right times and she felt in rapport with them, it was all right. The Wisconsin *State Journal* reported that she thoroughly delighted her listeners "with a bit of unrepressed and colorful Florida cracker language, an infectious smile, some priceless anecdotes, and just the right amount of serious message." Her lecture was billed as her familiar "Fact and Fiction" speech, but as always she shaped it to suit her audience. She spoke for over an hour, and the dean of men told her, "Lady, you simply wowed that crowd!" The lecture netted $750 for the scholarship fund.

Members of the *Badger* board gave a luncheon for Marjorie, and she was guest of honor at a large tea and at a dinner given by her sorority. She asked Gertrude Johnson to have a private lunch with her in her rooms, so they could have a good visit. She talked to Gertrude's classes, telling tales on her former teacher and mimicking her mannerisms, to the delight of the students. And one night she went to Johnson's home for dinner. While in Wisconsin, Marjorie was introduced to other local V.I.P.'s, including Sinclair Lewis, John Steuart Curry, and Frank Lloyd Wright. When Marjorie said that Wright was "embarrassingly pleased with himself," Curry called it a masterpiece of description and asked permission to quote it.

From Madison Marjorie made a quick trip to New York to confer with Max about *Cross Creek* and with Charles Scribner and Whitney Darrow about a low-priced edition of *The Yearling*, and about the feasibility of including it in their Illustrated Classics series.

Back home in Cross Creek Marjorie was approached by a friend to use her speaking ability in another worthy cause. After nine years of treatments at the Shriners Crippled Children's Hospital in Greenville, South Carolina, J. T. (Jake) Glisson's congenital leg deformity was corrected and he had become a normal, healthy teenager with a love for fishing and hunting and a dislike for spending too much time doing school homework. He often visited with his neighbor, Marjorie Rawlings, who treated him as an equal and showed a warm interest in what he was doing and in what was going on in his life. Undoubtedly, J. T.'s imaginative and enterprising qualities attracted Marjorie to him, and one day he made a request that as a friend and neighbor she couldn't refuse. He was having trouble with English, and his teacher at the high school in Hawthorne had agreed that if J. T. could get Marjorie Rawlings to speak to his English class, he would get a passing grade. The teacher, of course, knew of Marjorie's celebrity status and never dreamed that she would take time to come to their tiny hamlet for a talk to a high school class. But Marjorie, whose code was never to let a friend down no matter what the cost, did come to the school and, after securing the assurance of the principal and the teacher that J. T. would get a passing grade in English, addressed the whole school in assembly.

After she settled down to struggle with her *Cross Creek* manuscript again, Marjorie finally got the introduction to suit her, but tore up half a dozen beginnings of the narrative part. The time element baffled her. On November 25, she wrote Max in a "furious" mood. An unprecedented November freeze had killed her young grove, in spite of the great efforts she and her workers had made in firing it. She hated looking at the brown damaged trees, not because of the money lost, but because something that had been beautiful and satisfying was now hideous and depressing. "Don't mind my sputtering," she told Max. "I have learned that I always feel this way when I'm working something out, but God it is *torment*." She asked him to send her everything to read that he could, as she read about a book a night.

Max answered soothingly that he knew the difficulties of shaping her material were great and an inevitable part of the process of writing a good book. He offered to read any part of the book in any condition she cared to send it. And he sent her the reading material she requested. Among the books he sent was *For Whom the Bell Tolls*. She was so enthusiastic about it that she wrote Hemingway a letter of warm praise. Martha Gellhorn Hemingway answered for them both. She told Marjorie that Hemingway was extremely pleased by her praise and mentioned the good memories they had of their evening with her and Norton, promising that they would again "burst" in on her when they came to Florida.

The news of Scott Fitzgerald's death on December 21 saddened Marjorie. His life was more tragic than his death, she wrote Max. His tragedy, she thought, was in having a spectacular success too early and in valuing the wrong things in living. "It is difficult enough to be happy when one takes satisfaction from the simple and infallible things, but it is an R.S.V.P. invitation to disaster to depend on the quicksands of the treacherous things that to him represented the 'gloria mundi.' "

A bright spot that fall was the acquisition of a well-educated, efficient housekeeper at last. Idella Parker could cook, liked to prepare for company, didn't drink or entertain boyfriends, and was cheerful and understanding of Marjorie's need for quiet and peace for her work. It was especially a blessing to have her when Mrs. Grinnell and other friends came to visit during the holiday season.

When her tax attorney told her she owed another $1,000 in taxes for 1940, she was not dismayed. Money was to spend for necessary things like a new farm truck, to use for gifts, to lend to friends and relatives, and to buy things to please her mind and spirit. If there was money left over after some savings were put aside, she spent it on herself. When she found her expenses were more than she had expected for 1940, she canceled the purchase of some Audubon prints for which she had been negotiating. She sometimes said of herself that she was "careless" with money, but actually she checked her royalty statements carefully and argued forcefully with Scribners and Brandt and Brandt if she thought they had not allowed her everything she was entitled to. Her "carelessness" was only in the truest sense of the word: she *really* cared less for money than for nature or friendship or other pleasures, and she often refused lucrative writing and speaking opportunities that she thought would be downgrading of her artistic integrity. Like other famous people, she was besieged with requests for donations and support for all kinds of organizations. She listed a few for Max: "China's Children, Exiled Writers, Committee for aiding the Allies, Committee for Keeping us out of War, Hoover's Committee to Feed Europe, Somebody's else's Committee to block such feeding." She sent checks to a few of the petitioners and threw away the rest.

The February 22, 1941, issue of the *New Yorker* carried Marjorie's short story "Jessamine Springs." The protagonist is a lonely and alienated itinerant preacher. He is unaware that it is his own personality that isolates him and is dismayed to find that even in a rented bathing suit, he is easily recognizable as a preacher. Although Marjorie read the Bible constantly and was deeply sensitive to religious feelings, she had abandoned formal worship in early adulthood, and she often expressed an antipathy for ministers. Nevertheless, in "Jessamine Springs," even though the preacher's character comes through as timid and ridiculous, he is revealed as a pathetic and vulnerable human.

In January, Martha Gellhorn Hemingway wrote to ask if Marjorie would be willing to do a favor for Eleanor Roosevelt. She explained that every year in March Mrs. Roosevelt and Miss Malvina (Tommy) Thompson, her secretary, and two other friends went off on a vacation. They liked Florida and the sea and looked forward to being warm and swimming. The only requisite was privacy so Mrs. Roosevelt could have rest and quiet and a little time away from people. Martha had suggested Marjorie's beach cottage as a lovely retreat and wanted to know if she would be willing to rent it to the president's wife, whom Martha called "the best person in this country."

Marjorie immediately offered either the beach cottage or her farm at Cross Creek, or both, with maid service for as long as Mrs. Roosevelt and her friends liked, and refused to consider any rent at all. Mrs. Roosevelt herself wrote to thank Marjorie and to say they would like to stay at the beach cottage for the last two weeks in March. However, a few weeks later she wrote again to say that her friends had decided they preferred to go to the same place they had stayed the previous year. She invited Marjorie to come visit them while they were in Florida. Marjorie, of course, did not accept this opportunity, as she knew the vacation was intended as an escape from visitors for the first lady.

As a result of this exchange, Marjorie received an invitation to spend the night of April 1 at the White House during her visit to Washington to attend the Women's Press Club dinner. Going by train, she was disappointed that spring was late that year, and she saw only a few daffodils in Virginia. She was therefore doubly glad that she had decided to surprise the ladies of the Press Club with a bit of her own Florida spring. Before she left Cross Creek, she had carefully picked and packed in ice and water a huge mass of orange blossoms. To her dismay, the blossoms turned brown and fell off their stems by the time she reached Washington, and she had to discard them. To make matters worse, Hedda Hopper had packed California orange blossoms in a coffin, for which she reserved two seats on her airplane, and arrived with her spring offering in perfect condition. Marjorie made a humorous story out of the incident in talking with reporters and was quoted in news stories as saying, "Hedda outsmarted me. I sat and sulked while she distributed her orange blossoms to the ladies."

In addition to the banquet there were cocktail parties, teas, and luncheons honoring the invited guests. Besides Marjorie, they included Margaret Mitchell, Clare Boothe Luce, Mary Martin, Eve Curie, Mrs. Nelson Rockefeller, Ilka Chase, Lily Daché, Dr. Margaret Mead, and Wendell Willkie's wife, Edith, who sat next to Marjorie at the banquet and who turned out to be a sorority sister. Marjorie also enjoyed seeing old friends like Sigrid Arne, a journalist and an old girlfriend of Jim Rawlings, and the Ernest Meyers, with whom she partied until two a.m., long after their other guests had left.

At the White House she was ushered into the Lincoln Bedroom, which she told Norton was somewhat larger than his hotel dining room. She was awed at the thought of sleeping in Lincoln's bed. "Do you suppose he might possibly have liked *The Yearling?*" she wondered and described her quarters to Norton:

> *The vast room is comfortably shabby, and the draperies are almost a duplicate of my English material that is on my davenport—and there is dust on the marble-topped center table—so I feel almost at home.*

After the Meyer's party, she rolled up to the White House in a taxi at three in the morning and woke up in the Lincoln bed with a terrific hangover. Early that morning Mrs. Roosevelt took a plane for New York, and when the door closed on her cheerful voice and easy laughter, Marjorie began to feel like an orphan. She called Miss Thompson, Mrs. Roosevelt's jolly secretary, and told her she had never felt so lonesome in her life. Miss Thompson and Mrs. Edith Helm, the social secretary, came to Marjorie's room and made her feel so welcome she was persuaded to stay over in the White House an extra two days.

Remembering Ellen Glasgow's long-standing invitation to visit her when traveling through Richmond, Marjorie wrote a note to the novelist asking if she might stop to pay her "profound respects" on her way back to Florida. Glasgow sent a special delivery letter to Marjorie welcoming the visit, even though she had been seriously ill and was allowed only one visitor each day. The two writers found they had much in common in their backgrounds and in their emotional sensitivity. Both strongly resented being tagged as "regional" writers. And they each had sharp antennae for detecting hyprocrisy and deplored social injustice, although they both understood human nature too well to have illusions about social reform. After the visit, James Cabell reported to Marjorie that she had scored "a tremendous hit" with his aunt. "She informs me that you both figuratively let down your hair and babbled out your past to each other without any authorial embellishments," he wrote, adding, "Wish I could have been privileged to sit by and listen."

The trip was a good one with many pleasant memories, but Marjorie arrived back in Florida with her energy and resources depleted. She wired Norton from Jacksonville: PLEASE MEET 10:49 WITH MONEY FOR THE PORTER. AM BROKE.

Offers came in frequently that would have meant fairly quick and easy money, but Marjorie usually resisted doing any kind of writing that she felt was below her high standard for herself. Whenever she was seduced by such opportunities, she invariably regretted it. When Brandt and Brandt passed along a request from the *Reader's Digest* to do articles for their "Most Unforgettable Character" and "Profit by My Experience" departments, she was tempted by their lucrative rates to comply. Reporting to Carl Brandt, Marjorie told him she had actually written "stuff" the *Digest* might accept, but it made her want to "woops" and she couldn't send it to him. "I cannot, or rather will not do the tripe they want," she told him. Unless she or Brandt and Brandt were facing starvation she vowed never to try to write for the *Digest* again.

She returned to her struggle with *Cross Creek*, and when the writing did go well, she feared she was falling into her old habit of writing too glibly and creating a superficial narrative style that was almost journalistic. She knew what she wanted artistically, "The sense of knowing a particular place and people with a deep, almost Proustian deepness and intimacy and revelation, with my own deep feeling about things back of it." She told Max that she had to project herself painfully and slowly into years and scenes and feelings that she had actually forgotten and had to re-create. She refused to discuss illustrations or any publishing matters concerning the book. It could only be done right, no matter how long it took, she told her editor. "If it is right, it will be good and if it is not right, it will not be worth publishing." As usual, Max comforted and encouraged her, telling her that good writers always struggled with their material and reminding her that in such a book as she was attempting she need not be strictly bound by fact so long as she gave poetic truth. "But you know all that. . . ." And she did. In her lecture at Madison she had said, "Facts go through the emotions and philosophies of the writer and filter through into a new form, a better form than the original facts." But it was easier to know than to do.

With the arrival of hot weather, she moved over to the beach cottage, planning to stay there and work until the manuscript was finished. In May she interrupted her work long enough to write a preface for an educational edition of *The Yearling*. She also signed contracts for it to be published in Spanish in South America. Another distraction was the arrival of a Hollywood caravan to begin the shooting of *The Yearling*. The director, Victor Fleming, was nervous and dissatisfied with the location and with his actors. Gene Eckman, the boy playing Jody, seemed charming to Marjorie, although he was a little delicate for her conception. Anne Revere, the Ma Baxter, Marjorie thought was too stern for her character. But after she got to know her, they became very fond of each other. Spencer Tracy, playing Penny Baxter, had rushed through the making of *Dr. Jekell and Mr. Hyde* to come to Florida, but now he seemed bored, morose, and unhappy about the bugs and heat, and rumor was that he was drinking heavily.

In one important scene in the movie, a bear was supposed to be chased and cornered by Penny's dogs, but the trained dogs that had been shipped in from California were unable to corner the bear and chaos reigned on the set. Watching the action, Marjorie said to Jake Glisson, who was with her, "Those are city dogs!"

Jake agreed, "Yep—sure look like city dogs to me." Marjorie offered to get some Creek dogs and the next day delivered three wiry, smelly dogs with coats that hadn't been washed within recent memory. But the Florida dogs knew what to do when they saw a bear, and in one take they chased the bear and cornered him.

There was talk in Cross Creek about the internal dissension among the movie makers and about labor trouble, which was confirmed when the whole crew suddenly left for California after spending half a million dollars and shooting only a few scenes. Word got back to Florida that Victor Fleming was being replaced by King Vidor and that Spencer Tracy, Anne Revere, and Gene Eckman were out. Then came word that the picture was being shelved—whether temporarily or permanently nobody knew. Margaret Mitchell, whom Marjorie kept informed about the movie makers' antics, was amused and sympathetic, although not reassuring. She warned Marjorie that the film makers could ruin her beautiful classic, and told her not to be surprised if the Marx Brothers wound up playing the Forrester clan. But, at least, Margaret told Marjorie, she should be thankful that she was not as deeply involved in the movie process as Margaret Mitchell had been when *Gone With the Wind* was filmed.

The June 1941 issue of *Woman's Home Companion* carried a short story by Marjorie titled "The Provider." It is the story of Joe, a fireman on a train who provides coal for a poor family he notices on his weekly run. When the father of the family dies, Joe feels that he is obligated to provide for the widow and her child. He is fired for a coal shortage, and goes to visit the family to tell them he will find a way to help them. When he reaches the house, he finds them gone, and at the end of the story he is setting out to search for them.

In July Marjorie was back in the hospital with an attack of diverticulitis. A certain nervous tension in her inevitably built up under concentrated mental work, she told Max, and it had a fatal effect on her "mixed-up and inadequate insides." She had expected to have to go to bed at the end of a book, but begrudged the time in the middle of it. After two weeks of rest and careful attention to her diet, she felt much better.

On the night of July 18, she had such a vivid dream about Ellen Glasgow that she felt compelled to write and tell her about it the next day. In the dream Ellen came to live with Marjorie, who was away when she arrived. Upon her return, Marjorie found Ellen outside in the bitter cold, cutting away ice from the roadway and piling it in geometric patterns. She was alarmed, remembering that Ellen had heart trouble and led her inside the house (a mansion in the dream) and brought her a cup of hot coffee. "You had on blue silk gloves, and I laid my hand over yours, and was amazed, for my own hand is small, to have yours fit inside mine, much smaller." Ellen chose her room and suggested draperies to supplement a valance, which was of red chintz, and she showed Marjorie a sample of a heavy red brocade of the same shade. Marjorie told Ellen that from then on she would take care of her and that she must not do strenuous things, such as cutting ice in the roadway. James Cabell came into the room at that point in the dream and asked what the two of them were up to. After relating the dream, Marjorie expressed her admiration of Ellen, "You as a person have the vitality, the wit and the irony of your work, but I was not prepared to find you so warm and so beautiful. . . ."

After telling Ellen about her struggle with her manuscript and about having put herself in the hospital for a week because of the emotional turmoil it created in her, she said, "It wouldn't seem necessary to tie oneself into knots to get out a few ideas, but while I *feel* at the drop of a hat, thinking is terribly hard work for me!" She told Ellen she was about to send a first draft of the manuscript to Max Perkins, and hoped he could straighten it out with some of his "marvelous suggestions." Ellen answered Marjorie's letter at once, saying, "I cannot tell you how much your letter meant to me and still means." She called the dream "extraordinary," and "singular," for she had felt herself drifting in an "icy vacuum" since finishing her last book. She treasured the warmth of the dream scene where Marjorie took care of her and told her, "Ever since you came to see me—so strong and warm and vital, I have felt very near to you and you have had your own chosen place in my life, just as I had in the house of your dreams." She understood Marjorie's struggle with her material and the slow agony that follows an author's first "rush of impulse" to bring a book into the world.

Finally, near the middle of September, Marjorie sent Max her *Cross Creek* manuscript with a long list of questions she wanted him to answer about it. She reminded him that she did not want it to be an autobiography of her past thirteen years, but an objective story of her personal reaction to the Creek, "its natural aspects and its people." She wanted to avoid any mention of Chuck, and so had only spoken in passing of the three brothers for whom the pattern proved within a year not the right one. She wanted Max's opinion as to whether this observation seemed valid and not offensive to the three brothers. She told her editor that she had used true names in practically every instance, but had tried not to put in things that would hurt anyone's feelings. "These people are my friends and neighbors, and I would not be unkind for anything." Also there was the possible libel danger to think of, and she wanted to know what Max thought about this possibility. She asked him to check for places in which she was too preachy, too flippant, or too seemingly boastful in mentioning her own writing and the kindnesses she had done for her neighbors.

Upon receipt of the manuscript, Max wired: THINK CROSS CREEK WILL MAKE VERY FINE AND UNUSUAL BOOK. REVISION NOT DIFFICULT BUT NEEDS SOME DAYS STUDY. WILL WRITE FULLY.

Marjorie felt a wonderful sense of relief upon receiving the wire. No one knew better than she that it was a *"queer"* book," she told him, but if she could get it right, she hoped its effect on readers would be to take them into a totally strange world, and that they would feel a certain delight and enchantment in the strangeness.

Cross Creek might be queer, but it was lovely and human, Max replied. He called it a rare book, and said it was a great pleasure to read such a book in such times. Its whole quality and the implied philosophy in it made one feel better, he told her, adding that it was a book that would stand all by itself, "as the finest books do." He thought her use of Martha as the thread to hold the narrative together was good, but reminded her that it was herself as narrator who really bound the book together. He suggested omitting a few sententious paragraphs, but assured her she was never in the least egoistic. Chapter by chapter, paragraph by paragraph, he made suggestions for minor revisions and deletions. One omission he suggested concerned the chapter dealing with the evolution of her plumbing facilities from an outhouse to indoor bathrooms. He was afraid it might offend some of her devoted fans. But although Marjorie accepted almost all of his other suggestions, she decided to leave this chapter in.

As to the libel question, he doubted there was any real danger, because of the character of the people. He didn't think any of the people in the book would bring a suit but told her she must be the one to judge. He called the chapter about Zelma Cason and the census taking "grand," and urged Marjorie to use Zelma more in the book. The irony of this request was to haunt author and editor before many months had passed.

Toward the end of September Marjorie helped Aunt Ida move from Ocala to St. Augustine. When Ida had decided to make the move, Marjorie was again the one who found the place for her to live, helped her learn her way around the town, lined up potential friends Aunt Ida's own age, and helped her pack and move. By the end of the month, Marjorie was glad to escape to New York. There were several reasons for the trip. Although she and Max communicated quite well by mail (and perhaps even better than in person because of his increasing deafness), still she found a satisfaction in talking over a manuscript face to face with him. Her second reason for the trip was to have a complete medical checkup at the Harkness Pavilion of Columbia-Presbyterian Hospital. After that she and Julia Scribner were planning a "ramble" to see the autumn foliage.

At the Harkness Pavilion, she had a spacious room on the twelfth floor looking out over the Hudson River and the Palisades. The food was good and the nurses pleasant. Best of all, she felt lucky to have as her diagnostician Dr. Dana Atchley, a psychiatric diagnostician who tried to evaluate the possible mental and emotional problems underlying the more physical ailments. She and the psychiatrist had excellent rapport from the beginning. He laughed at her, she wrote Norton. "Such humiliation to find out you're just funny, not even queer." Dr. Atchley, who she discovered was the physician and intimate friend of John P. Marquand and Stephen Benét, knew that "you don't get books out of contented cows," she added.

Shortly before she left for New York she had had another quarrel with Norton and had written him a letter accusing him of hating her for "having fits." She told him she was ashamed of her emotional outbursts but exercised as much control as she could and that when she boiled over, she simply could not help it. "My temperament is what it is, volatile and high strung—my virtues, if any, come from exactly the same temperament as my faults. . . . I couldn't write books, I couldn't have a warm, emotional nature, if I were a placid pond." Dr. Atchley told her that her rages had nothing to do with Norton.

When she told the doctor of her dilemma in loving Norton and wanting to marry him but not wanting to give up her way of life at the Creek, he suggested that Norton was exactly what she needed, and the rest could be worked out. "So," she told Norton, "I'm giving you the chance either to run like everything or to propose to me!"

Although the verdict on her health was the usual one that nothing could be done for her physically except what she could do for herself by easing up on nervous tension, she felt rested and refreshed when she left the hospital. She liked Dr. Atchley's metaphor that her engine was too big for her chassis. On October 7, she wired Norton: THERE ARE OTHER BUMS THAN THE DODGERS. SEE NO REASON FOR RETURNING AT ALL. NO MESSAGE FROM ANYBODY. DORA. Several long, affectionate letters from him and a beautiful bouquet of huge yellow chrysanthemums cheered her immensely. On October 14 she sent him a birthday greeting telegram: HAPPY BIRTHDAY TO MY BULL FROM YOUR EVERLOVING PSY-CHOANALYZED DORA.

A week's drive through Vermont and New Hampshire with Julia completed her rest cure. Afraid that Norton would think she had let an outsider influence her decision to marry him, she wrote again to tell him that he must decide what he wanted to do. Dr. Atchley had told her she was looking for a will-o'-the wisp that was right in her own back yard, so in reply to her letter, Norton wired: I AIN'T RUNNIN'. WILLY WISP.

Just before she left New York for Florida, Marjorie wrote him:

> Am setting out on the noon train, very, very happy to be heading back, and toward you. Will reach Gainesville at 10:40 tomorrow, Wednesday morning and have wired Idella to meet me there. We'll come over to the cottage Saturday morning —and you'll never have anybody in your life more glad to see you than I'll be. . . . Last warning I won't even be facetious about it—when you ask me, the answer is the right one. . . . I love you very, very much and my labyrinth is coming out on a good, straight lovely road.

The marriage was a simple one performed by a county judge in the courthouse at St. Augustine, on October 27, 1941. Only Edith Pope and Ida Tarrant were in attendance. On her wedding day Marjorie wrote Max Perkins that she was "terribly happy" about her marriage. He replied, "Anything that makes you happy, makes me happy. . . . I'm sure I shall like anyone who loves you and should have much in common with him too. All good fortune to you both."

Margaret Mitchell sent them her good wishes for their happiness, adding, "It seemed to me when I saw you together that you belonged together." And James Cabell, with his usual impudence, told Marjorie that marrying Norton was a remarkably intelligent action on her part.

The honeymoon was brief—a quick trip to Miami and a few days' visit with Marjory Stoneham Douglas—for Norton was frantically trying to ready a new hotel, for which he would be the owner-manager, to open for the holiday season in St. Augustine. And Marjorie was desperately trying to finish the revision of *Cross Creek*.

The eight years following her divorce from Chuck had been filled with grove work, her writing, casual friends, and occasional emotional entanglements; but these things had never been enough to satisfy her. During those years, Norton had increasingly become the stabilizing element in her life, but she knew that their marriage was something of a gamble. "Long independence, and above all, the peculiar mental independence of the creative worker, is not the best of bases for a successful marriage," Marjorie admitted to Ellen Glasgow, but she added:

> The circumstances are such that I feel the odds are in its favor. The man too is accustomed to independence. And his nature is so generous, so tolerant and so tender, and we care for each other in so deep and quiet a way, that being with him is like coming into harbor after long storms.

CHAPTER 12

Cross Creek Chronicle

Norton's elegant new hotel, the Castle Warden, located in St. Augustine near Matanzas Bay, had been the palatial showplace home of William Warden. It contained twenty-five sleeping rooms with baths, marble staircases, an English ash-paneled dining room, and large sun porches. After decorating it throughout in 1890s style, Norton decided to do the Baskins' top-floor apartment in strictly modern decor. This apartment, which was created from seven cell-like servants' rooms, had a view of the bay and the ocean as well as of the large grounds filled with huge live oaks and magnolias. Although the formal opening of the hotel was set for January, the Castle Warden opened its doors for business on December 7, 1941. The news of its opening was of course drowned in the outcry following the shock of Pearl Harbor and the entrance of the United States into World War II.

The pall cast by this event was increased for Marjorie by a personal tragedy. Her pointer, Pat, was run over and killed at the Creek on Christmas Eve. She and Idella wept on each other's shoulders, for to them both, as Idella said, "He wasn't a dog. He was somebody."

Edward Shenton, the illustrator for *Cross Creek*, made a visit to

Florida so Marjorie could show him the country described in the book. Shenton afterward wrote a brief biographical sketch of Marjorie for the *Reader's Digest*. In it he told of spending a day exploring the Big Hammock and returning to Cross Creek to sit by a fatwood fire, enjoying good food and good conversation. He was impressed by Marjorie's "uncanny" ear for the native dialect, and he mentioned her infectious laugh. Comparing her humor to Mark Twain's, he called her "a mixture of simplicity and sophistication."

Soon after her marriage Marjorie mailed Max the first half of her *Cross Creek* revisions, suggesting he get them into galley proof while she completed revising the remaining chapters. Then, as usual, they could work together on the galleys and page proofs. Rereading the manuscript, Max Perkins was again struck with the "terrible old libel fear that besets a publisher." He worried over derogatory comments about the judge and lawyer in her description of the shooting of Sampson by Henry Fountain. He realized that a good many other people were technically libeled in the book but didn't think there was much risk that any of them would think to bring suit, or would do it if it were suggested to them. He asked Marjorie about the blacks, and she assured him they were all "positively" all right, but she requested that he satisfy himself "completely" about the whites involved in her episodes. Assuring him that "Old Boss [Brice], the Glissons, the Bernie Basses, Snow, and Zelma [Cason]" were "perfectly all right," she added that the Townsends and George Fairbanks would never sue for libel. She could easily fix the statements about the lawyer and the judge. The only one she had any concern about was Mr. Martin, whose pig she shot for repeated offences, including tearing up her prize fluffy ruffle petunias. She decided to approach the problem head-on and took the chapter to read to Mr. Martin for his reaction. He told her it was quite all right with him, accepted the bucket of pecans she brought him and offered to share fish and frogs' legs with her the next time he caught any. And so Marjorie and Max relaxed in the belief that the specter of libel had been laid to rest.

On January 14, Max wrote to Marjorie that the Book-of-the-Month Club was taking *Cross Creek* as a dual selection with John Steinbeck's short novel *The Moon Is Down*. "Now three out of four of your books have been taken by BOMC, and I don't believe that has happened to anyone else," the editor gloated. With her customary striving for perfection, Marjorie worked with him up to the last moment to make sure everything about the book was as right as they could make it. She pointed out that Shenton's drawing of a magnolia tree was too spindly and described how it should look. In another picture the artist had drawn a boy holding water lettuce, when it should have been a lotus. She sketched a lotus blossom so the picture could be corrected. She looked again at the last paragraph of the book and reworked it so it would begin with the question: "Who owns Cross Creek?" and end with the statement: "Cross Creek belongs to the wind and the rain, to the sun and the seasons, to the cosmic secrecy of seed, and beyond all, to time."

On January 25 the Castle Warden opened formally with an elegant cocktail party. Amid lavish floral arrangements, Marjorie and Norton received the guests in the second-floor lobby area. Most of St. Augustine's old-time society families came to see the transformation that had been wrought in the handsome gray stone building, and the cream of the regular Old Guard tourists were there also. The Baskins' apartment atop the hotel was not due to be finished until sometime in March. Marjorie had stationery printed with the heading: "Mrs. Norton Baskin, Castle Warden, St. Augustine, Florida." From then on she insisted on being Mrs. Norton Baskin in her social and private life.

When the Baskins' apartment atop Castle Warden was completed, Hamilton Basso, the novelist, called it the "Queen's Tower." Although she tried to settle down to work there, Marjorie found it difficult. There were hordes of tourists in San Augustine, and many of them tried to include seeing a famous author as part of their trip. Sometimes, thanks to Norton's wit, the tables were turned. One afternoon a little woman scuttled into the lobby of the Castle Warden and asked Norton in a rather furtive way if she might have tea. She went into the dining room and gave her order and then scurried back into the lobby to ask Norton, "Will I see Mrs. Rawlings?" When he told her that Mrs. Rawlings was away, she sighed and said, "Oh, dear, then I won't have tea."

"Very well, Madam," Norton answered gravely. "It's just as well.

Mrs. Rawlings only comes with the blue plate dinner."

Marjorie told Max, "My husband is so completely lovely a person, and it grieves me to see him grieved when I simply have to clear out and go back to the Creek."

Because of the Baskins' unusual living arrangements, which seemed more unorthodox in the 1940s than they would today, rumors spread from time to time that they were separated or separating. When friends wrote to ask if the tales were true, Marjorie was always indignant that anyone would start such stories. "Husbands like Norton don't grow on trees (wives like me, MOST fortunately, don't either)," she told Norman Berg, who had heard such a rumor. Love and mutual respect helped to keep the marriage intact in spite of long physical separations. Throughout the twelve years of their marriage, Norton also kept his independence, pursuing his work as the owner-manager of the Castle Warden and then as the manager of the Marineland restaurants. "Norton would get away from me over my dead body, and he feels the same way about me," Marjorie told Norman. But it was soon clear to both of them that Marjorie would not be able to work at the Castle Warden.

In addition to Cross Creek, she used the ocean cottage as a retreat, but it was not as pleasant as it had been before the war. Passes were necessary to travel the ocean road that led to the cottage, and at night blackout shades had to be drawn tightly. Convoys went by, bombers droned overhead, and big ocean tankers could be seen sliding along close to the shore to evade submarines. Except for the military traffic, the beach was lonely and deserted, and sometimes when Marjorie was there alone, the thought of saboteurs landing on the isolated beach was vivid. "I have the *best scheme* for trapping spies here and hope some land," she told Carl Brandt. But she didn't reveal her plan, even to Norton. Both of them took their turns as fire wardens and aircraft spotters, and twice submarines were spotted from the post where they did duty; but the subs had disappeared by the time planes could reach the spot.

The publication date for *Cross Creek* was March 16, and on that date a luncheon was given in Marjorie's honor by the St. Augustine branch of the National League of American Pen Women and the Florida Historical Society. It was held in the second-floor lounge of the Castle Warden and was a grand affair. Lace tablecloths covered the tables and roses in bubble bowls and vases were placed along their length. The "all-Florida" menu included grapefruit halves, deviled crab, local vegetables, individual lemon cream pies, and watermelon and grapefruit preserves. James Branch Cabell introduced Marjorie, who read excerpts from *Cross Creek*. Edward Shenton's original sketches for the book were displayed around the room on easels.

Cross Creek received immediate critical acclaim. A number of reviewers dubbed Marjorie a "female Thoreau." *Time* called the book a prose poem, praising Marjorie's "reminiscent, unhurried, humorous account of how she discovered and took possession of a new United States literary landscape in Florida." The Omaha *World Herald* suggested that people should read *Cross Creek* in an anguished world for its quietness and dignity and decency. The Hartford *Times* said it was a lovely book with an appealing record of hard work and adaptation to difficulty and danger, a piece of writing deftly proportioned, "graphic and lyric without sentimentality." The New York *Times* characterized the book's narrator as a generous, impulsive woman who encompassed hot enmities and long loyalties and placed her chief value on integrity. The reviewer pointed out that her style, like her mood, was always suited to her material and concluded, "She catches the community of land and people in the strength and mirth and loveliness of her book."

The *New Yorker* maintained that the chapter titled "A Pig Is Paid For," which described the shooting of Mr. Martin's pig, proved beyond doubt that "Mrs. Rawlings is one of the funniest writers now operating in the United States." The reviewer drew from his reading of the book an accurate, if incomplete, picture of Marjorie's character. He stated that the central fact about her was that she was a "mystic" with a pawky and tender humor and listed as important qualities her sharp, almost New Englandish eye for character; sturdy common sense; highly agreeable Rabelaisian vein; deeply-rooted love of earth; and the sense of herself as sort of "worshipping tenant that gives to all her tales and people their quality."

Cross Creek quickly rose to the top of the best seller lists and remained there for many months. It was also popular in England.

As always the sweetest praise to Marjorie was that which came from friends whose opinions she valued. Dr. Dana Atchley wrote that he was glad he hadn't read *Cross Creek* before she came to the Harkness Pavilion, or he would have felt self-conscious in discussing her problems in an advisory role. "The warm, tender, human, sound philosophy that runs through the narrator's relationships with Cross Creek people, leaves me brim full of admiration," he told her. And Ellen Glasgow wrote that the writing was like a "luminous web which captures and holds some vital essence of a particular place and moment of time." Thornton Wilder told her he greatly admired the book and warned that he planned to steal from it.

Marcia Davenport also sent her congratulations. The daughter of Alma Gluck, well-known American opera singer, Marcia Davenport became an internationally famous author of such works as *Mozart, East Side, West Side,* and *The Valley of Decision.* As was the case with many of Marjorie's friendships with literary people, it was Max Perkins who had introduced them. Before they actually met, he had sent Marjorie and Marcia each other's books and they had come to appreciate the other's work. Both women were strong-minded, tough-talking at times, sensitive, and lovers of animals. As often as they could they visited each other in New York or at Cross Creek.

Marjorie received a few vicious letters, some anonymous, calling her a low, evil woman for writing about the disgusting sex relations of animals. But she told Max they didn't bother her as they were plainly from the "peculiar kind of Puritan who, himself or herself, has the dirtiest kind of mind." The vast majority of her letters, she reported, were "simply beautiful," and several were from ministers who used bits of the book as texts for sermons.

The British novelist A. J. Cronin wrote from Blue Hill, Maine, where he had retreated from the war, that the book had enchanted and infuriated him. Only a varmint could fail to be enthralled by her lovely description of the Florida country, he wrote. He had never been to Florida, but her description of "magnolias and moccasins, petunias and passion fruit," and her mastery of the local idiom bowled him over. What infuriated him was her chapter on food, "Our Daily Bread." He could not believe that she could be a gourmet cook, living in the middle of a swamp, and yet her description of the Florida dishes she whipped up with the help of Dora the cow set him to drooling for crab à la creme and broiled alligator steak. He invited her to come to see them when she came East, promising to serve her the local "dry beans and stinking fish cakes."

Marjorie answered him in kind, sent him some of her recipes, and invited him to come and visit Castle Warden. When he found out she was living in "fashionable St. Augustine," Cronin accused her of letting her husband's cook fix the dishes she described and pictured her lying languidly on a Louis Seize couch in a lounging robe, dictating into a machine. "You are unmasked, Mme. de Pompadour," he told her. This exchange was the beginning of a prolific correspondence in which each tried to outdo the other in dry Scots humor. Sometimes their letters included serious discussions of literary matters and world affairs.

Excerpts from *Cross Creek* ran in the March and April issues of the *Atlantic Monthly*, and *Reader's Digest* printed a shortened version of it. Again, Marjorie could respond to only a small fraction of the requests for interviews and articles that inundated her. She did write one short piece for the July issue of *Vogue*, based on memories of her Grandmother and Grandfather Traphagen. The title, "Fanny—You Fool," was based on her grandfather's usual response to his wife's frequent practical jokes.

The special armed forces edition of *Cross Creek* brought Marjorie many letters from servicemen. One soldier said, "You are writing about the simple things for which we in the Army are fighting." And an aviator wrote from Cairo that, although space in his duffel bag was at a premium when he left for Egypt, he felt he had to take *Cross Creek* along because it was something valuable that he wanted to hang on to. The New York *World-Telegram* carried the story of a signalman on the S.S. *Lexington* who ran to his locker to get his copy of *Cross Creek* before abandoning the sinking ship. He climbed down a rope into a lifeboat and was later picked up by a small destroyer. *Cross Creek* was the only book aboard the destroyer and was read constantly for the next few weeks. Touched by the response from servicemen to her books, Marjorie asked Max to find out how many libraries there were for soldiers and sailors as she wanted to send copies of her books to all of them.

Many readers besides A. J. Cronin responded enthusiastically to the chapter in *Cross Creek* called "Our Daily Bread." It begins with Marjorie's experiences as a child in her mother and grandmother's kitchens. Then she describes her early attempts at cooking as a young bride. The main part of the chapter deals with her experiences with the native foods she found in Florida. The dishes range from simple to complicated and include everything from cornpone and white bacon to pilau and the crab Newburg, which she considered her *pièce de résistance*. Her unabashed pride in her culinary skill and her confession that she was a slave to any guest who praised her cooking charmed her readers. A number of them urged her to do a whole book on cooking.

When she broached the idea to Max, he thought it an excellent one. He suggested there be an introduction and quite a bit of narrative in and around the recipes. Marjorie eagerly set to work, and for once found the creative process almost pure pleasure—except for the heat in the kitchen while testing recipes—and the extra pounds she put on. Norton helped, writing down measurements and timing for the dishes as she put them together. Their friend Robert Camp did the drawings for the book, and the whole project went surprisingly fast. Since Marjorie considered cooking a form of art, she was not bothered when her Aunt Wilmer wrote, "I just don't know what to think about your writing a *cook book*. Somehow it doesn't seem at all *classical* or *literary*."

The only hassle in putting the book together came over the arrangement of the material and the naming of the chapters. The title of the introduction, "To Our Bodies' Good," comes from the grace Marjorie's father used to say: "Receive our thanks, our Heavenly Father, for these mercies. Bless them to our bodies' good, for Thy name's sake. Amen." The introduction is followed by a section on soups and includes two Greek soup recipes that Chuck brought her from Tarpon Springs, some soups created by the chef at Castle Warden, and such Florida specialities as cooter soup and crab soup.

The introduction to the hot breads section includes the fact that A. J. Cronin called her "a plump imposter" and her motto, "It is better to be plump than to live on baker's bread." Her mother's and Idella's biscuits, various kinds of cornbreads, including doughnut-shaped hush puppies, and an ice box roll recipe from "my friend Zelma, the census taker," are included in this section.

Among the vegetable recipes are some for four different ways to fix swamp cabbage and one for "Poke Weed, Cross Creek." The Florida sea food section includes ten crab recipes, six for shrimp dishes, and others for Florida lobster or crawfish and frogs' legs. The game and meat section contains such exotic recipes as "Coot Surprise," "Bear Steak," "Jugged Rabbit," "Alligator-tail Steak," "Blackbird Pie," "Pilaus," and "Smother-Fried Quail, Dove, Rabbit, or Squirrel." The salad section includes Ida Kinnan's special "Sunday Night Fruit Salad." Marjorie was especially proud of her marmalades and jellies and included a good number of recipes for them.

By far the longest section is the one for desserts, which is understandable given Marjorie's sweet tooth. Her grandmother Traphagen's sugar and molasses cookie recipes are included as is her own famous "Utterly Deadly Southern Pecan Pie." For the timid she also included "My Reasonable Pecan Pie." Among the thirteen ice cream and sherbet recipes is one for mango ice cream and one for "Dora's Ice Cream." Since so many of the recipes call for Dora's cream or butter, a friend suggested she give away a Jersey cow with every book. The recipes are interspersed with lighthearted anecdotes about the sources of the recipes or about her experiences in serving them to her guests. Many are about Dora, the cantankerous provider of superb sweet cream and butter. One anecdote tells of a comment Edith Pope made when Marjorie's pointer, Pat, was killed. "I'm so glad it didn't happen before you were married," Edith told Norton. "You can more or less take Pat's place." "Yes," Norton answered gravely, "I just hope nothing happens to Dora." Marjorie checked with Max on the propriety of including this anecdote, and he thought it too good to leave out.

Cross Creek Cookery contains menus for camp dinners as well as menus for regular breakfast, lunch, and dinner. And these, too, Marjorie enjoyed testing. She told Max that she had tried out her "Wild Mallard Duck Dinner" on several friends at the cottage. The meal began with iced honeydew melon with lime juice, followed by roast wild duck, wild rice, carrot soufflé, fresh lima bean croquettes, whole small braised white onions, tiny cornmeal muffins, kumquat jelly, celery hearts, and fresh mango ice cream. The guests pronounced the meal truly delicious, and she had had a "heavenly time" cooking it, she reported.

Marjorie worked hard on the manuscript for the cookbook through the spring and early summer, as Scribners planned to publish it in time for the Christmas trade.

After she and Max had worked through the galley and page proofs of *Cross Creek Cookery*, Marjorie set out on a trip to fulfill another writing obligation. She planned to travel for two weeks with members of the U. S. Forest Service, covering nearly five thousand miles through the Southeast to gather material for an article on American forests. The idea for the article was sparked by her comments on trees in *Cross Creek*. A member of the Forest Service had written her agents about her doing the article and the *Saturday Evening Post* had expressed interest in publishing it. Julia Scribner accompanied her on the trip, which went from the forests along the Florida Gulf Coast to the coastal forests of Alabama, Mississippi, Louisiana, Georgia, and South Carolina. Although she tried hard to use her journalistic skills to make the article interesting as well as having it bring home the message of the urgent need to conserve trees as a great national resource, she was never able to get it to suit the editors of the *Post*. When Brandt and Brandt sent her the *Post*'s editors' suggestions for revisions, she fired off a curt telegram: CERTAINLY NOT.

Finally the article was sold to *Collier's* and appeared on May 8, 1943. Marjorie's message in the article, which was titled "Trees for Tomorrow," was that American forests are not infinite. The war demands for wood she called the "final tragic note" following the fact that the use of lumber had been much greater than its annual growth for many years. She showed the impact of the devastation on the countryside, on towns, and on people. She combined interviews with lumber experts and with simple people whose livelihood had disappeared with the disappearance of the forests in their environment. She pointed out the solutions to the relentless destruction of an essential natural resource: scientific tree farming and controlled cutting. She called on the Congress to pass laws promoting these practices, and she condemned the "powerful and selfish" interests lined up against such laws.

The reality of the war was increasingly brought home to the Baskins. Gas rationing required careful planning of trips to Cross Creek, as its remoteness meant periods of being marooned there for Marjorie if she ran low on gas coupons. Norton had added a cocktail bar at the Castle Warden, and it became a favorite place for military officers in the area to gather. Food rationing involved complicated planning in order to have enough meat and sugar to prepare meals for guests. Marjorie put about 80 percent of her 1942 income into war bonds, and on December 2 made an appearance on behalf of the war effort, her second. She and her friend and illustrator Robert Camp appeared at a benefit "Gala Community War Chest Luncheon" held in the George Washington Hotel in Jacksonville. Phil May, her friend and attorney, was there to introduce her to the audience. Many friends, like Otto Lange, now a general, and James Still, who was in Africa, wrote Marjorie of their war experiences. And her growing correspondence with servicemen and with people like the novelist Sigrid Undset, whose life was dedicated to war work, also gave her an inside view of the progress of the war in different areas of the world.

Sigrid Undset, who had been president of the Norwegian Author's Guild for six years, told Marjorie that every week she learned of more of her country's authors who were in concentration camps in Norway, Germany, or Poland. "My relatives starve and freeze and walk in and out of prisons, but nobody gives in," she told Marjorie proudly. Gestapo officials were occupying her house in Lillehammer, and the thought of the Nazi flag flying from her flagpole made her ill. Sigrid spent her time in New York speaking at rallies, giving radio talks, and writing articles as requested by her government in exile. She also helped war refugees and worked to expose "rowers," that is, quislings who were trying to "row ashore" after being associated with Nazis. They published lists of new members of "that boating club," she told Marjorie.

Both *The Yearling* and *Cross Creek* were published in armed forces editions and by the end of 1942 had been translated into thirteen foreign languages: German, Swedish, Danish, Italian, Polish, French, Norwegian, Finnish, Czech, Hungarian, Spanish, Japanese (a pirated edition), and Dutch. Earlier Margaret Mitchell had written to tell Marjorie that the same Dutch firm that had pirated *Gone With the*

Wind, and which she was suing in Dutch courts, had announced they would publish *The Yearling*. Marjorie wrote to the Dutch publisher, telling them she had Dutch blood from both sides of her family and had always considered the Dutch the "soul of honor." She pointed out how uncertain a writer's income was and told them she couldn't believe they had meant to cheat her out of her rightful royalties. The Dutch firm replied that the situation was the fault of the United States for refusing to subscribe to the International Geneva Convention protecting authors and artists. They sent her a check for $100 and their beautifully illustrated copy of *The Yearling*. Marjorie learned that from then on they advertised the book as being written by a "Dutch Pulitzer Prize Winning Author."

Reviewers and readers liked *Cross Creek Cookery*. Even A. J. Cronin, who had predicted it would be a "compendium of horrors" about alligator and rattlesnake dishes, admitted it was a "grand" cookbook. It sold well and a number of articles appeared in popular magazines about Marjorie's cooking skills. One, titled "Marjorie Rawlings Hunts for Her Supper," appeared in the *Saturday Evening Post* for January 30, 1943. It showed pictures of Marjorie gigging frogs (catching them with a pronged spear), hunting for a proper palm tree for swamp cabbage, receiving a live alligator from her neighbor Bernie Bass, catching crabs, and posing with a large turtle she had caught. Marjorie herself wrote two spin-off articles from the cookbook. "Cross Creek Breakfasts" appeared in *Woman's Home Companion* for November 1942 and "Sweet Talk, Honey," in the December issue of *Vogue*. A Missouri food company wrote to ask Marjorie to send them two quart jars of swamp cabbage (hearts of palm) for testing and suggested it might mean new industry for her part of the country. She sent them a scathing reply:

> *In answer to your suggestion that we cooperate in putting swamp cabbage or hearts of palm on the commercial market in large quantities, I wish to state that I personally shall shoot dead . . . with my Winchester 38-40 rifle, any individual or group, incorporated or unincorporated, that starts such commercialization.*

> *As I said in* Cross Creek *and* Cross Creek Cookery, *taking the heart of the palm means the death of the tree. I take one rarely. If the product were commercialized . . . there would be no more palm trees in Florida and Florida without palms would be as God-forsaken as Missouri.*

In early January 1943, Arthur Kinnan wrote from Alaska in alarm to Norton Baskin. Arthur had just received a card from a friend saying, "Very sorry to hear about your sister." Since Marjorie usually let him know of her catastrophes after she was sure of recovering from them, he was "concerned as hell." As Arthur and the world soon learned, the friend's reference was to a suit for libel that Zelma Cason filed against Marjorie for $100,000 damages, because of passages in *Cross Creek* that Zelma claimed had caused her severe pain and humiliation. Marjorie had been aware of Zelma's displeasure over the way she was portrayed in the book but had thought she had got over her ill feelings. Soon after the book was published, Marjorie had taken Zelma a copy signed, "To my friend Zelma, with love." Zelma, who had already read the book, came to the door and said, "Well, you made a hussy out of me and a lady out of a hussy" (meaning Dessie Vinson). Marjorie was so dismayed to find that Zelma had taken offense that she burst into tears. The meeting ended with their embracing tenderly, and Marjorie thought Zelma had forgiven her the encroachment on her feelings. So the suit came as a nasty shock.

The Baskins' first inkling of Zelma's intentions came from a report by Aunt Ida of a conversation she had with Zelma late in the summer of 1942. Ida and Zelma were together in Zelma's car when Ida, noticing a number of large books in the back seat, said, "You must be going to do some reading."

Zelma replied, "Those are law books. I'm going to sue that niece of yours."

"Why, what for?" Ida asked.

"Why, slander. What she said about me in that book was slander."

"I thought slander was something about your character. She simply said that you swore and used profane language and that is nothing against your character. You do swear, don't you?"

Zelma didn't answer the question but said, "Well, I'll sue her and get some of her easy money and I'm going to sue Norton, too. She isn't going to make her money over to him and get away with it."

The Baskins consulted their friend and attorney Phil May, who did not think Zelma would actually bring suit. When she did, early in January 1943, he was surprised. From Marjorie's standpoint and that of himself and of Scribners, he thought it would be decidedly better to "litigate all over the lot with her," but he promised to make the point to T. Z. Cason, Zelma's brother and Marjorie's former physician, that the case was not only hopeless from Zelma's standpoint, but if aggressively prosecuted would result to her great disadvantage and have other consequences that she "would deplore." May and his colleagues reread the passages mentioning Zelma in Cross Creek and agreed that they contained nothing that "even fanatical processes of thought could find any basis for a claim of libel."

After mentioning "my friend Zelma," Marjorie had described her:

> *Zelma is an ageless spinster resembling an angry and efficient canary. She manages her orange grove and as much of the village and county as needs management or will submit to it. I cannot decide whether she should have been a man or a mother. She combines the more violent characteristics of both and those who ask for or accept her manifold ministrations think nothing of being cursed loudly at the very instant of being tenderly fed, clothed, nursed or guided through their troubles.*

In another passage Marjorie wrote, "Zelma announced profanely that high water had covered the old road she meant to take, and we were lost." And Marjorie noted further on that when her horse ran away with her and she dropped some sweet potatoes that had been given to them by one of the natives of the area, she got no sympathy from Zelma for the runaway scare, but only Zelma's "special brand of profanity for having lost the sweet potatoes." Other references to Zelma in the book portray her as understanding and sympathetic to the people of the area, knowledgeable about the country, and highly capable.

When Marjorie read Zelma's Declaration (the pleading filed by a plaintiff in Florida to initiate a lawsuit), she thought it extremely funny. "Our so-called 'defense' is infinitely simpler than I expected," she told May. She called riotous Zelma's statement that she "consciously avoided all conduct and behavior that would or might make her conspicious or warrant general public interest in or curiosity about the private and social aspects of her daily life and the normal development and manifestations of her personality," considering it came from a woman who "cusses a blue streak in front of assorted people, and in a voice so loud that she is famous for its carrying quality." Norton pointed out that Zelma contradicted herself in the declaration. She claimed on the one hand that the sketch of her was "colored and distorted and only true in part" and on the other that Marjorie "sold her personality." Only one or the other of these claims could be true.

Marjorie suggested a number of witnesses who she thought would be good to have testify for her. One was Fred Tompkins, who had told her that he always figured Zelma was *"proud"* of her cussing. Fred, who was the prototype for Benny of "Benny and the Bird Dogs" (a story that had been incorporated into many high school and college anthologies), considered it an honor to be interesting enough to be written about. Marjorie thought his attitude would make a nice contrast to illustrate the greed and unwarranted touchiness of Zelma's.

Marjorie gave Phil May bundles of her fan letters for him to look through for comments useful to prove her lack of maliciousness, and she pointed out statements from such dispassionate sources as the *Atlantic Monthly*, which called *Cross Creek* "such a friendly book." She told her lawyer she would welcome a public airing of the matter, if it were not that losing the case would harm her "poor misguided friend financially and mentally." Max Perkins wrote that he was sorry she had the worry of the lawsuit, even though he didn't think it serious. He had shown the passages in *Cross Creek* that concerned Zelma to Scribners' legal counsel, who said that if it were in New

York, it could easily be laughed out of court.

In addition to her bouts with diverticulitis, Marjorie suffered with an abnormally painful menstrual cycle. Her Florida doctors could only give her temporary relief and advised that removal of her uterus would be the only permanent cure for the problem, which made her slightly anemic and constantly tired. She postponed such a drastic cure and continued to suffer until Norton finally insisted that she go to the Columbia-Presbyterian Hospital in New York for evaluation of her condition. She took a plane for the first time to get to New York and liked the experience of flying. Charles Scribner and Julia met her at the airport and took her to her hotel, the Gotham, where Julia stayed to have dinner with her. While they were dining, Sinclair Lewis and a doctor friend of his came in and sat opposite them. After their dinner, the men joined Marjorie and Julia for about an hour of talk. "He still looks like something abandoned to the vultures in the Libyan desert, but he's so nice." Marjorie told Norton.

When the New York doctors agreed that Marjorie definitely needed to have a hysterectomy, Norton came to New York for a few days. The night before she went into the hospital they went to see *The Skin of Our Teeth*. After the show they had dinner with Fredric March and his wife, Florence Eldridge, who were starring in the play. She was pleased to find her old fellow actor unchanged except for a "thickening up," which affected her figure too.

After the operation was over and the doctors had assured Norton that she was making a fine recovery, he hurried back to Florida. It was the busy winter tourist season in St. Augustine and getting and keeping good help at the Castle Warden in wartime was difficult. Norton also checked on things at Cross Creek for Marjorie and looked after her new pointer, Moe, who had a habit of wandering off. One day while she was recuperating, Dr. Atchley brought her the news that Stephen Vincent Benét had died. Benét, who was two years younger than Marjorie, had done a profile on her for the New York *Herald Tribune* book section in February of 1941, and she had met him and his wife socially at the Atchleys. She admired Benét's poetry greatly and thought he made a serious mistake in dropping work on his epic poem "Western Star" to do war writing. His creative gift was "so priceless" that America needed the rest of "Western

Star" more than any other type of work he could have done, she felt. John Marquand was in the room next to her, and one afternoon Carl and Carol Brandt came to see him with a large jar of martinis. Marjorie was invited to join the party but virtuously refused to drink. When she was given permission to resume smoking, the taste of cigarettes was at first nasty to her, but that feeling soon passed. She was delighted to find she had lost eleven pounds after a few days in the hospital.

Julia Scribner visited frequently and lent Marjorie a radio. Marcia Davenport came to see her and brought her a frilly bed jacket. The Castle Warden employees sent Marjorie a huge box of tulips and there were gifts of books and flowers and many other visitors, but what she wanted most of all were Norton's letters. When she didn't get one every day, she threatened and cajoled him, telling him that Moe would write her every day if he could, and that she was going to make love to the nicest of her three internists, demanding "Write me—OR ELSE!!!!!!!" When she was released from the hospital, she went to Marcia Davenport's for a quiet Sunday supper with just the Wendell Willkies and Max Perkins. Then she took the train back to Cross Creek where she could recuperate away from telephones and the bustle of the tourist season.

Norton came over from St. Augustine as often as he could get away. And she had Idella to keep the house running smoothly and to give her daily backrubs and Moe, plus a newly acquired Siamese kitten named Smoky, for company and entertainment. Gas rationing had put a stop to gawking tourists and the heavenly quiet of her surroundings with only the sounds of birds flying in and out of the feed baskets and bees humming in the orange blossoms soothed her. Soon she was actively supervising the planting around the house. She felt it her patriotic duty to put in all the garden produce that her space allowed. Her largest crops, besides the oranges, were Fordhook lima beans and sweet potatoes. For her own pleasure, she had dozens of roses planted. Another obligation that she took to heart was to catch up on her correspondence with military men, which had piled up during her absence. As usual, she managed to get mixed up in Creek business. She was caught in the middle of a serious war between Old Boss Brice and Tom Glisson, she told Max, and while trying to stand for abstract justice, she was also trying to keep on good terms with both sides. "These Creek battles are the most complicated I have ever known," she said, but she was obviously enjoying the row.

In early May, Marcia and her husband, Russell Davenport, who had been Wendell Willkie's campaign manager, stopped at Cross Creek with Willkie on a Florida vacation. With Idella's help, Marjorie gave them a luncheon so "prodigious and delicious" that everyone dispersed to lie down on the nearest couch or bed and slept the afternoon away. In her memoir, *Too Strong for Fantasy*, Marcia Davenport describes Cross Creek as a "lovely, languorous, sweet-smelling place," and Marjorie herself as having a heart "as big as the Big Scrub she wrote about." Marcia perceived the contrasts in her friend: "the robust tastes and rowdy sense of humor, the bellowing love of laughter, and also the strong streak of femininity." In turn, Marjorie admired Marcia and her writing. When Max sent her *Valley of Decision*, Marjorie wrote the editor, "I have never read a more magnificent American book. It has everything. It is as exciting as *Gone With the Wind* and is a thousand times better in so many ways, one being that some of the characters are not only strong but good, good in the most profound sense."

Toward the end of May, Norton told Marjorie some news that made her feel as if she had been run over by "God's steamroller." Although he was overage for the draft at forty-one, Norton had applied for officer's training school soon after the war started. But because he did not have college training, he was not eligible, although he was well-educated through wide reading and according to Marjorie passed intelligence tests "about 40%" higher than she did. As soon as she was well over her operation, he told her that he had signed up as an ambulance driver in the American Field Service and would be leaving for overseas duty in less than two months. He could be sent anywhere the British Army was operating, as the American Field Service operated under British officers. With a little research, Marjorie learned that these outfits worked in the front lines and that in the last war their casualties were twice the ratio of regular army casualties. "I feel utterly flattened out about it, yet I respect Norton immensely for doing something he did not have to do. . . . It is the type of decision a man has to make for himself and about which a woman has nothing to say," she told Max. "I am terribly proud of you ... even while rebelling against it with every fiber," she said to Norton. Margaret Mitchell wrote that she was proud to know Norton, and James Cabell told Marjorie she was stuck with a "God damn hero."

The short period before his departure was frantically busy, arranging for the management of the hotel in his absence and getting his shots and equipment. When he was ordered to report to New York to be assigned a sailing date, Marjorie went along in order to spend every possible minute with him. Early the morning after they arrived in New York, they were waiting outside the doors of Abercrombie and Fitch, so he could buy the necessary things he hadn't been able to get in Florida. She and Norton both developed a variety of bronchial flu, and Marjorie frantically called Dr. Atchley to get a prescription by phone. She rushed to the St. Regis pharmacy to get the codeine mixture to relieve his cough and just managed to get his temperature under 100° by the time he had to report to the American Field Service headquarters on July 6.

In accordance with wartime secrecy about ship movements, he was ordered to bring his equipment with him but was not given his final sailing orders. So when he left her on that day they did not know whether he would be coming back to the hotel or whether he would be leaving immediately. The uncertainty made it a little easier to say goodbye, but Marjorie doubted that he would be back. When Norton did not return that night, she knew he had disappeared into the darkness of the war. The next day she checked into the Harkness Pavilion to get rid of the remnants of her flu and cough. As soon as she reached the hospital, she went into a severe diverticulitis attack.

CHAPTER 13

Another War

Marjorie considered the timing of the diverticulitis attack fortunate inasmuch as Dr. Atchley had been experimenting with the proper timing and dosage of belladonna and luminol to control such flare-ups, and she was able to have him work out a dosage for her. She was optimistic that in the future she would be able to get over her attacks quickly and without pain at home.

Before she returned to Florida, she went to Michigan to visit again the farm home of her Traphagen grandparents and her Aunt Ethel Riggs, who now lived there. This visit was in connection with Marjorie's next major writing project, which was beginning to work itself out in her mind. She wanted to write on a subject other than the Florida Crackers and Florida setting she had so thoroughly explored. Max Perkins had once asked her if she ever thought of using the details of her childhood. She had answered that if she did, she would use them only objectively and creatively. Now she was beginning to plan a novel with a "wonderful farm life as the background." The basic character of the protagonist would stem from her grandfather Abram Traphagen and his wife would resemble her grandmother in many ways. The other characters forming in her mind, she told Max, seemed to her to be a cross between those of Dickens and those in some of the Russian novels she had read.

Her aunt Ethel proved a rich source of information about the earlier days of the farm and also had family letters dating back to 1822, plus old ledgers and account books. Marjorie spent most of her visit poring over these family papers. She discovered that her grandfather was better educated and more articulate than she had realized, but that fact did not change her plan for the main character in the book. She also discovered that her grandfather was passionately devoted to music, but that his fanatically religious mother had not permitted him to study an instrument. The fact that he kept a violin in the hayloft and slipped off to play it by himself fitted in with her idea of portraying a frustrated artist and a man of sensitivity. Her main character was to be called Asahel Linden; the first name was that of her grandfather Kinnan and the last name she had seen on a mailbox in the country.

One of the keynotes of her book was to be the consciousness of Asahel of the "cosmic set-up." Marjorie told Max she "all but fainted" when she found a receipt among her great-grandfather's accounts for a book on astronomy, which her grandfather must have read. She ordered a copy of the book from a dealer in rare books and felt more than ever that the novel she planned to write was a "natural." Yet she knew, as she prophetically told Max, that her bones would have to "go through a duck-press to squeeze out the essence" of the thing she wanted to do.

A sense of desolation overcame her as she started toward Florida knowing that Norton would not be there. "That's one trouble with having an almost perfect husband—anything that happens is too awful," she told Max. She was delighted to find two letters from Norton waiting for her, mailed en route. His unit had sailed on a Liberty ship with quite comfortable quarters, Norton reported. "We all talk like Hemingway characters. Now and then an eight-letter word creeps in, but then you realize it is made up of two four-letter words." He told her he was by far the oldest of the unit, "but they show me no respect."

Writing a long, detailed letter filled with all the news and gossip she thought would interest him became a part of her daily ritual. She included the happenings at the Creek and at the hotel, the antics of her pets, her doings, her thoughts, and her affection for him. Occasionally he received a bawdy letter signed "Dora Rolley." Marjorie also kept up her increasingly extensive correspondence with servicemen in all parts of the world. Her letters were so warm and friendly that some of the lonely, homesick men confided in her, and she found herself giving them advice on everything from how to write for publication to how to manage their love lives. The sad aftermath of some of this correspondence came when a grieving mother or father wrote to thank her for her warm letters to their son, who had been killed in action.

When one of her G.I. correspondents asked her to send him a scale from a ten-pound bass, she answered that she hoped he was joking, for, in the same mail, she had received the kind of naive request that "drove her mad." A Kentucky woman asked Marjorie to send her the roots from a four-foot magnolia tree, a scuppernong grape vine, and some chufa plants or seeds, all nicely wrapped in damp moss. The letter writer thoughtfully added that since she was asking Marjorie to go to all that trouble, it would be all right to send the whole parcel collect.

At the other end of the scale were fan letters like the one Marjorie received in August from a woman in Wales, who had read *The Yearling* at a time when she was in a distressed, unhappy state of mind. The book had lifted her mood and made her realize the importance of paying attention "Only to the real and important things" of life. "Your mind must be a deep and beautiful place," she told Marjorie. She did not expect an answer but had written only because she wanted Marjorie to know "what undreamed happiness" *The Yearling* gave. The letter concluded, "It may make you happy to realize that all over the world, perhaps for centuries of time, it will affect people's lives."

Marjorie moved to the beach cottage with Moe and Smoky for the rest of the summer, and tried fruitlessly to get her new book under way. She walked the lonely beach by day, skirting the oil from the ships torpedoed off the coast, the burned debris, and occasionally sailor's trousers that washed ashore. Much of her creative energy went into her daily letters to Norton and those she wrote to other servicemen. She did write a thoughtful review of James Branch Cabell's new book about her beloved St. John's River. The laudatory review appeared in several newspapers, and Cabell was delighted.

About the first of September, Marjorie got the good news from Phil May that he had just received a decision from Judge John A. H. Murphree that he found no basis for Zelma Carson's lawsuit to come to trial. The first phase of the proceedings was ended, but constitutionally, May cautioned, Zelma had a right to a review of Judge Murphree's decision by the Supreme Court of Florida if she filed such a motion within sixty days of the judgment. A bill for legal services to date for $525 was enclosed with the letter.

On September 5, Marjorie had a cable from Norton announcing his arrival at his destination, "perfectly fit." From his letters she soon deduced that he was in India, where he was getting intensive instruction in motor mechanics. He reported that the courses were providing him with interesting revelations, "though others seem to have known these things all their lives." The reason that some things "run around while others jump up and down would amaze you. It did me," he told her. He had known he would miss her, but not how much, he said. Where they lived after the war did not worry him. If she wanted to move to Pat's Island, he promised to love it and not to take in boarders.

In October Marjorie moved back to her orange grove for the winter, for it seemed more like home than any other place at the time. Max wrote encouragingly about her novel, telling her it would no doubt be harder to get started right than anything else she had written. By mid-November she had done not quite two chapters, and was unhappy with what she had written. "It is stiff, it is stilted, it is cold," she told Max. She realized she was probably trying to go too fast instead of "squeezing it out word by word, as I have known I must do." A. J. Cronin sympathized. "A book is hell anytime and a start is the deepest pit."

To help pass the time, Marjorie read voraciously. She was fascinated by Flannery O'Connor and her descriptions of the pleasures of having peacocks around. So Marjorie bought three peafowl—two hens and a cock—from a Mr. McKay. Flannery's peacocks had amused their owner by coming to peer in her dining room window and by strutting around showing off their beauty. Marjorie's peafowl immediately flew up on her water tower and stayed there making raucous noises. Only at night would they come down to eat the tender plants in her garden, and with the first daylight they were back up on the water tower. Marjorie soon decided Cross Creek could do without that kind of class. After she and Chet Crosby had managed to get them into the truck, she sent Chet back to Mr. McKay's with instructions to pay him to take them back if necessary.

When Norton finished his training in motor mechanics, he was assigned at once to hazardous duty with British troops fighting the Japanese along the India-Burma frontier. He found himself driving his ambulance on mountain roads that were one-way tracks with the mountain (often with landslides on one side) and several thousand feet of sheer drop on the other. At one place the ambulance had to back up toward the precipice to get around a curve. The driving would have been dangerous under the best of conditions, but in the frequent stormy weather and under blackout conditions at night it was a hair-raising experience. Although Marjorie sent Norton a constant stream of letters, books, food, and anything she could think of to add to his comfort, on Christmas Eve he had not received a single one of his Christmas packages and had had no letters in more than a month. In a jungle full of Japanese and tigers, he and three other men had been living for days on bully beef and tea and sleeping on the ground in a small tent without lights or a seat to sit on. On Christmas Eve they went to bed on the ground and sang Christmas carols. Christmas day was better as they were invited to dinner by British officers some twenty miles away. But that afternoon he had to make an emergency run with his ambulance. "It is hard to imagine him in such surroundings and doing such work, but under that superficial gayety, there is all the staunchness and courage in the world," Marjorie told Aunt Ida.

Norton's letters often arrived looking like lace doilies after being cut up by the censors. He most frequently ran afoul of them for telling too much about his environment. But enough of the letters remained to reveal clearly the dangers and discomforts he was suffering. At one time Norton and another man had a first-aid post on top of an isolated mountain. The post was two underground rooms—one for the first-aid station and the other for living quarters. The Japanese artillery was on one side and the British on the other with their fire criss-crossing. Supplies were dropped to Norton and his companion, who did the cooking. Norton washed the dishes and wrote Marjorie, "Here I am between shot and shell and all I will get will be dishpan hands." He got more than enough excitement though when Japanese shrapnel knocked the initial off his finger ring.

The scarcity of water frequently caused misery. Norton told Marjorie he was writing one letter "sitting nastily naked" on a stretcher in his ambulance under a net because of the flies and malaria mosquitoes. In this letter he described the problems of simple existence by outlining his day for her:

Breakfast: bran nuts and klim in a cup. Left early in a.m.—made a run of 3 hours and had a wait of 10 hours before making return run. By 10 too hot to read and flies terrible. Decided to shave—used precious water from canteen and my breakfast cup.

At 11 I had tea from same cup. At 1 I mixed bully beef, soy-link sausage and beans in cup—a small mouthful seems to grow beyond coping before you can swallow.

At 4 I had more tea and a little later a vile drink made from synthetic lime concentrate. As there was no water for washing the cup you can imagine the accumulated tastes that joined the lime wash.

He had her send him a copy of *Cross Creek Cookery*, and he shared it with his comrades. They sat around reading the recipes aloud and making up imaginary menus. "It was wonderful torture," he told her.

More disturbing were letters that revealed how close he was to the front lines. In one he reported:

Japs are in the hills between here and our base and between here and the hospitals. They move at night and mine the roads

*and place mortar guns overlooking the road. Sometimes they
blow a bridge or dig a wide, deep trench across the road. They
are veritable moles and the more our side kills the more they
increase. We are about convinced they breed in their fox holes.*

Dessie Smith Vinson, who took the St. John's River trip with her,
visited Marjorie in her WAC lieutenant uniform and tried to get
Marjorie to join also. When Marjorie declined and jokingly said she
couldn't leave Idella and Moe, Dessie pointed out that Idella could
join the colored WAC and Moe could be a mascot. Other friends
tried to keep up Marjorie's spirits during the worrying days and weeks
when letters from Norton were delayed. Edith Pope, whose husband
was stationed in England, was a frequent companion both at Cross
Creek and at the beach cottage, and Julia Scribner came for a long
visit in February. A. J. Cronin wrote cheerful letters that included
dirty stories. He admitted they were not what one would expect from
the author of *Keys to the Kingdom*, but said, "You *know* me. Nice
to be understood." He advised her to "WILL" Norton to come through.
"I know you don't stand much on praying but even a sub-conscious
plea from the heart reaches those ears we don't know anything about."
Cronin also told her it was a good sign she didn't like the start she
had made on her new novel. "It's only the poofs who think they are
Shakespeare; only the Mussolinis who believe they are God." He
himself was struggling with *The Green Years* and anxious about his
two sons on active service.

Marjorie had heard that Chuck was married for the third time,
but nothing more after that. In several issues of the *Saturday Evening
Post* she read articles he had written on the war from the South
Pacific. She wrote to a mutual friend that she thought the articles
were "splendid."

Sigrid Arne, who was with the Associated Press, watched the cables
that came into the news office and kept Marjorie informed when
there was anything about Norton's outfit. In April a report was
flashed to the United States that his unit in Burma had been cut off
by the Japanese, and that the British forces were ordered to abandon
ambulances and equipment and make their way to British lines as
best they could. For two weeks she listened to every radio report,

not knowing whether Norton was dead or alive. Then she heard from him directly. He had been on leave in Kashmir, staying at a nice hotel, having a wonderful time. Ironically, shortly after he returned to duty, he *was* cut off from his outfit and in serious danger, and Marjorie knew nothing about it until it was all over. He had been one of the American Field Service men who drove his ambulance under bombardment from the Japanese stationed in the mountains above the road through to an isolated forward British post. He barely got out with his ambulance loaded to the roof and lost all his personal belongings. He wrote that he wondered "what little yellow so-and-so" was wearing the Tibetan lama's brocaded robe he had bought for Marjorie to use as an evening wrap. She told Sigrid Arne that hearing of Norton's escape made her feel as if the governor had given her a parole from the electric chair.

No sooner was this anxiety relieved than there was a tragedy at the Castle Warden. A fire caused when one of the guests fell asleep with a lighted cigarette had killed that woman and also a good friend of the Baskins' who was staying in their penthouse apartment. Marjorie had to take care of all the details for the dead friend, keep the hotel manager from going to pieces, arrange about the fire insurance, and handle all the other details. It was a nightmare, she told Max. She suffered over whether to tell Norton about the accident, but since the Associated Press was sending the story out, she was afraid he would hear of it anyway. So she wrote him all the details. She was right in being concerned about the effect of the news on Norton, for it literally made him sick.

In addition to worrying about Norton, Marjorie was also feeling anxious about Max Perkins, who had been feeling poorly. He told her that he had had a thorough physical and had been put on vitamins and limited to two cocktails a day, but that sometimes he took three over weekends. The doctors told him he was getting at least a third of his nourishment from alcohol and not eating enough. He admitted to her that he used alcohol to slow things up. "Everything moves too fast nowadays," he complained.

Max was so intrigued by the humorous anecdotes Marjorie repeated to him from Norton's letters that he suggested Norton might write up some of his war experiences. Marjorie passed the idea along to Norton with some hesitancy, for his wit flowed "as naturally as a spring bubbles," and she was afraid of making him self-conscious. He did have a story published in the India publication of the Field Service, which she felt was all right but not told with the natural vivacity of his letters to her. Then he wrote a story of an experience of his youth that Marjorie felt was "embarrassingly" bad. Consequently she wrote him that she would quit him if he came home writing stories. "I said," she told Max, "that it was hellish enough to be burdened with the delusion that *I* could write, without having him get off the boat, bringing, like a rat carrying the Bubonic plague, the delusion that *he* could write!" This message effectively squelched any ambitions Norton had of becoming a writer of tales, although he continued to be an irrepressible teller of them.

Along with such notables as Bennett Cerf, Albert Einstein, Moss Hart, Helen Hayes, Karl Menninger, and Rex Stout, Marjorie was a member of the Pledge for Peace Committee of the Writers War Board. When she was asked by the board to do a one-hundred-fifty-word sketch on a war theme close to her heart, she sent them a true story. In it she told of sitting in a diner on a train (on her way to Michigan the previous summer) and asking a soldier seated next to her, "How does the Army feel about fraternizing with Negroes?" The soldier answered with a drawl, "Well, Lady, I'm from the South myself, but all I can say is, if a man's good enough to die for his country, he's good enough to live with." The newspaper syndicate that was distributing the sketches rejected her item as being too controversial, and she was asked to submit something else. She replied that she could not possibly contribute any "starry-eyed platitudes," as the American stand on the Negro question to her invalidated the whole war, for it could not be considered a moral or spiritual crusade "when we set out merely to stop other nations from doing the very thing that we plan to keep on doing to the Negro."

In November of 1943, Marjorie had written to a friend, "I have forced myself to take the final mental leap about the Negroes. There is no question but that we must go all out for 'full equality,' meaningless though the phrase may be. Anything else is the height of hypocrisy." She never retreated from this stand and took many opportunities to reinforce it. Earlier that year she had written a letter to John Temple Graves, an editorial writer for the Jacksonville *Florida Times Union*, taking him to task for urging justice and opportunity for Negroes, while insisting on the pattern of segregation. "Don't you see, can't you see," she asked, "that segregation denies a man or woman something more important that 'justice' or 'opportunity,' and that is self-respect, freedom from being made to feel subtly inferior, from being, after all, and finally an outcast." She admitted that she had taken segregation for granted for a long time because of her preponderantly southern ancestry. But she added:

> *I can only tell you that when long soul-searching and a combination of circumstances delivered me of my last prejudices, there was an exalted sense of liberation. It was not the Negro who became free, but I. I wish and pray for your own liberation. It is almost a religious experience. No man is free as long as another is enslaved, and the slavery of the spirit is more stringent than that of the body.*

Two outstanding black women impressed Marjorie and helped remove her last vestige of prejudice. She got to know Mary McLeod Bethune when she spoke on a program honoring the black educator at Florida A & M University at Tallahassee. The two women corresponded and visited, and on one of her visits to Mrs. Bethune, Marjorie met Indira Gandhi and had several long conversations with her. Marjorie described Mary Bethune as "a marvelous woman."

The other black woman who helped Marjorie become color blind was Zora Neale Hurston, a writer and teacher. When Zora Neale had written Marjorie, praising her writing, Marjorie had invited her to come to Cross Creek to visit. She was impressed by the black woman's "ingratiating personality, brilliant mind and fundamental wisdom." They agreed wholeheartedly that both whites and blacks made a mistake in handling "the Negro problem" with kid gloves, each afraid of the other. After she read *Cross Creek*, Zora Neale wrote Marjorie: "You did a thing I like in dealing with your Negroes. You looked at them and saw them as they are instead of slobbering over them as other authors do. You have written the best thing on Negroes of any white writer who ever lived." Their friendship deepened, and when Zora Neale heard that Marjorie was working alone on her new book at Cross Creek, she wrote that if she were not working on a book of her own, she would come and be a "buffer" for Marjorie, while she was in labor. Learning that Marjorie's housekeeper, Idella, had left her to work in Harlem, Zora Neale told her that if things got too awful "give a hoot and a holler" and she would drop her own work to come help her friend. Marjorie took her up on the offer and she came and spent ten days.

In July Norton was in the hospital being treated for carbuncles and running a high fever. Since early spring he had had recurring bouts of diarrhea and stomach pains and had lost quite a bit of weight from his already slender frame. In between severe bouts of sickness, he continued to drive his ambulance, but the dysentery continued and his condition steadily deteriorated. When his year of service ended, he was lying in a hospital seriously ill with ameobic dysentery and terribly weak after having lost fifty pounds. On October 1 he wrote Marjorie that he hoped to get on the American hospital plane in a couple of weeks, but he was afraid of the shape he would be in. He might be too sick to fly, and there might be problems getting on a flight to the states, since space was difficult to obtain. In answer to Marjorie's frantic inquiries, the director general of the American Field Service confirmed that Norton Baskin was on the seriously ill list in the British General Hospital in Calcutta and might have to wait weeks to leave for the states by boat.

Marjorie reached as high as she could for help, calling Louise Sommerville, a friend of theirs from Ocala, now in Washington with her husband General Bredon Sommerville. When Marjorie told Louise, "Our boy Norton is in trouble," Louise replied, "Why don't you talk to Bredon about it." Marjorie did and General Sommerville cabled the commanding general of the China-Burma-India theater of war that he would appreciate having Norton Baskin put on the next army hospital plane leaving for the United States. The flight to Miami was excruciatingly painful for Norton as en route an abcess on his liver ruptured. When he arrived on October 29, Marjorie had gone on to New York, expecting he would be transferred at once to another plane for New York so he could enter the Harkness Pavilion. When she discovered there was a seemingly insuperable wall of protocol and red tape in getting him flown on to New York from Miami, as a private and civilian patient, she turned again to General Sommerville.

Sick as he was, Norton still managed to make a good story out of the frustrations. He told Marjorie that when a colonel at the Miami army hospital came in to tell him that he was flying up to New York the next morning, other men in adjacent beds called out, "How come?" And Norton answered coolly, "My wife called up." At 7. a.m. the nurse came in to tell him to get ready to leave and he said he hadn't been given his breakfast yet. Then one of the G.I.'s rose up in his bed and yelled, "They damn well better get him some breakfast. His wife will call up!"

Marjorie had an ambulance waiting at the airport in New York to take Norton straight to the Harkness Pavilion. She was shocked to see that he was just skin and bones, but his fever and exhaustion gradually cleared as did the amoebic dysentery with good treatment, clean surroundings, nourishing food, and Marjorie's tender care. While he was recovering she stayed at the hospital every day from eleven to nine. Friends like Julia Scribner, the Atchleys, and Hamilton Basso entertained Marjorie at dinner. She lunched with Max Perkins and found him looking bad. A. J. Cronin sent a bouquet of chrysanthemums to the hospital and invited Marjorie to have lunch "to take your lovesick mind off Norton Baskin and the amoeba." He hesitated, he told her, to take her out of her role of ministering angel but thought it would do her good to shed her wings for a brief time. *The Green Years* had just been published, and he thanked her for her "nice lies" about it.

From India, Norton had sent Marjorie some fine cashmere wool, called finger ring wool because it was light enough to be drawn through a ring. She had kept it until he returned, and now she decided to have it made up at Bonwit-Teller. Norton had paid only forty-four rupees for the material, but the seamstress gave Marjorie a receipt for $400 for it. Marjorie told her to make the dress up in a size that would fit when she was twenty pounds lighter, as she intended to lose that much. Unfortunately, she was never able to take off enough pounds and so could never wear the dress when it was finished.

After several weeks in the hospital, Norton began to gain weight and strength. He was released to return home for his long convalescence, which the doctors thought would go much faster in the warm Florida sunshine.

After getting Norton comfortably settled at Cross Creek, Marjorie sent Christmas hampers to her aunts and other relatives, and to friends like Margaret Mitchell, Sigrid Undset, and A. J. Cronin. In her letter of thanks Margaret Mitchell recommended beer to fatten Norton up. Along with the usual Florida fruits, Marjorie included pots of Dora's butter, a most welcome gift because of wartime shortages. She also let A. J. Cronin have some of the Castle Warden's red ration coupons. He wrote back gratefully that until he received the red points he had not eaten red meat for six months. As his Christmas gift he sent her an Audubon print.

In his Hogmanay (in Scotland, the last day of the year) letter, Cronin commented that Gregory Peck had been amazingly good as Francis Chisholm in the movie version of *The Keys to the Kingdom*. And he noted that Peck had been named to replace Spencer Tracy in *The Yearling*. "He is a nice boy," Cronin said of Peck, "and I feel sure he has a great future. He will give you a wonderful performance."

Soon after Christmas things at the Creek suddenly seemed to fall to pieces. Idella, Marjorie's "perfect maid," had left her again, but hog killing passed successfully with Marjorie making sausage and scrapple and Martha making lard. Then Martha showed up with a dangerously infected finger, and Marjorie sent her to the tenant house with instructions to keep the finger in hot epsom water. Martha's daughter Sissy came up to milk and wash dishes, but was suddenly called away to return to her regular employers. Having no one else to call on, Marjorie did the milking and the household work herself. Then she got a cold that went into bronchitis and had to go to bed. Martha did the milking with one good hand and Norton got the meals and did the dishes and made butter. Marjorie got worse and was worried about Norton and he was worried about her, so they packed up and went to the Marion Hotel in Ocala. There they both went to bed, had meals served in their rooms, and had the doctor make house calls on them. At last they both felt better, and with

Martha and Sissy back to help, Marjorie was glad to get away from hotel food and back to the good, fresh food at the Creek.

By February Norton was feeling well enough for them to take a trip to Alabama to see his family. And toward the end of the month he went to Winter Park with Marjorie, who was again appearing on the Rollins College "Animated Magazine." She was always much happier about her speaking engagements when Norton was able to go along for emotional support.

Although her own writing was at a temporary standstill, Marjorie kept up with the output of other writers. When John Steinbeck's *Cannery Row* was published, she wrote to tell him that she liked it. He wrote back gratefully that it was nice to hear from someone who had understood what the book was about, since the critics had attacked it as though it were "a girl who had refused to go to bed with them." Marjorie also enjoyed Hudson Strode's *Timeless Mexico* and wrote him a warm letter of praise. She did not however write to congratulate Robert Frost on his new poem, "A Masque of Reason." It was witty and engaging, she admitted, but a disappointment to her as it was "just not poetry."

When Norton agreed to go with her, Marjorie accepted a request to appear as a guest on "Information Please" for a Red Cross benefit in Atlanta. The morning after the show, along with Clifton Fadiman and John Kieran, she went at the request of the Red Cross to speak informally at a big new veterans hospital. They were asked to go through the officers' ward just to chat at beds here and there. Most of the cases were amputees, and the men in worst shape, including a young lieutenant, whose body ended a little below the hips, were the most cheerful and wise-cracking. She and Fadiman were in tears when they left, and agreed that they felt "a peculiar mixture of sickness and pride." It proved, she said, that the spirit of a man was much more important than his physical parts.

Norton gradually resumed his duties at the Castle Warden, and Marjorie moved to the Crescent Beach cottage to be nearer him. Her involvement in war work was sufficiently draining of her energy to keep her from her own writing. She wrote some publicity material for the National War Fund, and she continued to keep up with her voluminous correspondence with servicemen. From far-off corners of the world, in places like Guam, the New Hebrides, New Guinea, and Okinawa, they wrote describing their war experiences to her. One told her of watching a Japanese suicide plane attack—"the most appallingly, disgustingly, fascinating thing" he had ever seen. Some of her correspondents sent her gifts, including coconuts, an oriental fan, and Japanese table mats. J. T. (or Jake as he was now called) Glisson sent her a Japanese kimono, which she wore often.

The servicemen's letters gave her insight into all facets of the war. One who had served in both European and South Pacific theaters described the different behavior of Nazi and Japanese prisoners of war. The Japanese were docile and eager to do good work for their captors, he told her, while the Nazis remained sullen and defiant for a long time. Some of the letters related acts of courage and bravery and others told her about the uglier parts of the conflict. One described the blackmarket place in Strasbourg, France, which was in a long, narrow tunnel under railroad tracks. In this badly lighted, poorly ventilated area with open sewers running along the walls, cartons of cigarettes, cheap watches, rings, and second hand G.I. equipment was sold. Another soldier ventilated to her his disgust at the stealing of government supplies by everyone from brigadier generals to privates, who made off with everything portable from cigarettes to an entire consignment of G.I. supplies, according to their capabilities. The writer remarked bitterly that discipline was maintained. "If a private is caught he is severely punished, while a general may get a tsk-tsking accompanied with a knowing wink."

After the German surrender in May, Marjorie's friend Sigrid Undset prepared to return to Norway. Marjorie sent her a generous check, which was eventually used by Sigrid to aid several worthy causes including the Foundation for the Education of Children set up for Norwegian children orphaned by the war.

In contrast to her deep sympathy for service men who were enduring sometimes terrible and life-threatening hardships was Marjorie's anger at A. J. Cronin for what she considered his unreasonable fussiness. When Cronin had written that he and his family had taken a house on Nantucket for the summer and that food was almost unobtainable, she went to a fancy grocer in St. Augustine and had the proprietor express him a large roast beef. The beef took eight days instead of two to arrive and was in bad shape. Cronin thought he should not be billed for the beef and asked her to send less perishable things such as "quality cheese, lean bacon and tins of ox tongues." She exploded at him for his "goddamn epicurianism" and said she would pay for the beef herself. In a few days she repented of her angry letter and sent Cronin a box of fine Florida marmalades and an apology. He replied that he too had a fiery temper and had been afraid their "beautiful friendship" was ended. He insisted on paying for the beef and in turn apologized for specifying that he be sent "choice" and "prime" quality foods. The quarrel ended, and Marjorie was mollified. After thinking again of what he had told of his poverty-stricken and harassed childhood in *The Green Years*, she could understand how this background led to his attitude that he had earned his prosperity and to his intention to have the best. However, she felt "prosperity should make one humble and grateful, not *demanding.*"

In May the movie people were back in Florida to film *The Yearling*, and there was a renewed demand for interviews and news stories about Marjorie and her life in the area. She found it impossible to work in their apartment at the Castle Warden, and Norton was so busy and his help so unstable that he could not get to the cottage very often. Marjorie told a friend that she was unhappy about the situation because although Norton was the most delightful companion she had ever had, "without that companionship, it is not a perfect marriage."

Marjorie did not go to Julia Scribner's wedding in June to Thomas Bigham, an Episcopalian minister, who was a professor at the Union Theological Seminary in New York. Always the matchmaker, Marjorie had picked out another man, Lt. Bertram Cooper, a chaplain on the U.S.S. *Bountiful* as the perfect husband for Julia. She was concerned that Julia's intended might not make her high-strung, intelligent friend happy. Privately she threatened that if Bigham disappointed or failed Julia or broke her heart, she would see that "he meets his maker years ahead of schedule." She was relieved when Edith Pope, who did go to the wedding, brought back a report that Julia was "radiantly happy."

Toward the end of July Martha Mickens wrote a penciled letter asking Marjorie to come to the Creek as the lights were off, the yard needed tending, and things in general needed her attention. Among other domestic problems, the toilet would not flush properly. After Marjorie had been using the bathroom for about eighteen hours, Martha went in to clean and sifted Dutch cleanser into the toilet bowl. As she did so, a cottonmouth moccasin stuck its head up and looked at her. Leonard Fiddia happened to come by and, laughing like a hyena at their predicament, speared the snake with an ice pick and finished it off outside. A few days after she returned to work at the cottage, Idella discovered a small snake under Marjorie's bed. This one Marjorie herself killed with a poker.

In addition to her correspondence, Marjorie was still trying to get her novel under way. She had at first thought of calling it *Earth and Sky*, but now was working with the title *The Sojourner*, which proved to be the final choice. She had found it in I Chronicles 29:15:

> *For we are strangers before thee, and sojourners, as were all our fathers: our days on the earth are as a shadow, and there is none abiding.*

CHAPTER 14

My Friend Zelma

*S*uffering had not dimmed Norton's sense of humor. He complained mildly that Moe had become spoiled and usurping during his absence. "I," Norton said, "am a scion of an old Southern family, and Moe is indubitably a son of a bitch," but in her treatment of them, he thought Marjorie sometimes tended to reverse their positions. The end of the war in the Pacific in August brought relief and anxiety—about the terrible bomb that had brought the ending.

Marjorie told Max that the start she had made on *The Sojourner* was so bad that she couldn't bear for him to see it. From the frustration of not being able to get this work to suit her, she turned to writing short stories and completed several, which she sent off to Brandt and Brandt. Some of them she called "sad, ugly stories" and was not surprised when her agent had difficulty selling them. She was surprised, though, when the *Saturday Evening Post* turned down her new Quincey Dover story. It was different from the preceding Quincey Dover stories in that it did not have a happy ending, but when the *Post* editors said the story did not "ring true," Marjorie was amused for the story *was* the true story of her friend Dessie Vinson. "This only proves what I tell young writers," she wrote Max, "that the truth is artistically fallacious." In August Marjorie agreed to let Carl Brandt sell her short story "Honeycomb" to *Town and Country* magazine. She instructed her agents to place anything she sent them as she was working toward having enough stories published to make another anthology. Max had suggested they might make up a volume of her "queer stories" and another of Quincey Dover stories as soon as they had enough of each. Marjorie told Carl Brandt that she got a great satisfaction out of the short story medium and hoped to do more.

In September her short story "Black Secret" appeared in the *New Yorker*. The heart of the story is the shocking discovery to a young southern white boy that his beloved uncle has had sexual relations with a number of promiscuous black women and that he has had illegitimate children by them. Later in the fall a second story of Marjorie's, "Miriam's Houses," also appeared in the *New Yorker*. Again it was a story with a child as the protagonist and a child's naive view of the world. The narrator, looking back many years, remembers a beloved playmate, Miriam, and her fragile mother. The two children think that the cigars and men's articles that occasionally are to be seen in the house belong to Miriam's elusive father, who "travels a lot." In a sudden burst of adult understanding the narrator realizes that Miriam's mother was a prostitute and that the reason Miriam moved so many times was because her mother was evicted for not paying the rent. The story ends with the narrator saying, "My knowledge had come to me after forty years. Ah, but when had it come to Miriam?" Max Perkins told Marjorie that "Black Secret" was very moving and beautifully told, and he liked "Miriam's Houses," but he had to agree with her own verdict and that of the *Saturday Evening Post* that her latest Quincey Dover, "Donnie Get Your Gun," was not successful.

In October Marjorie wrote to Carl Brandt that she had finished nearly a quarter of *The Sojourner*, plodding along, and reading it with her teeth set on edge. One day she could not stand it and tore up all that she written into minute shreds. Immediately she felt a terrific sense of relief. When Brandt and Brandt sent her a lucrative offer from Metro-Goldwyn-Mayer for her "next" book, provided she deliver 30,000 words within twelve months, she refused because of the time stipulation. She did not want to send them any words unless she felt right about them. Her final incentive for destroying her work had been the sudden thought, "My God, how the movies would love this tripe!" She told Carl Brandt that she was sorry about the loss of money to the agency, but she intended to make a fresh start and to take as long as necessary to make it right.

She also refused an offer to do an article for *Holiday* magazine about tourist attractions in Florida, calling it a "dull set-up." She was furious with the way *Liberty* had edited her "not-too-good-at-best" short story called "The Celebration." They changed the title to "Miss Moffatt Steps Out," a title she told Carl Brandt she would not have used in her sophomore days, and they had interpolated phrases she would not have been caught dead using. She angrily told Norton she had a mind to sue them. But he said, "Don't do that, Love, you know how it feels to be sued." She asked Carl Brandt not to think harshly of her for refusing the opportunities he offered her. "I am an artist in a very small way," she told him, "but for that iota I must fight to the end." The trial she also considered as a fight for her principles. In a letter to Phil May she said:

> *I could probably have bought off Zelma for a thousand, which would have given her a moral victory, and by offering a hundred to each and every of the ten, say, other people most likely to dream of a little rake-off, could have cleared the board without these three years of annoyance and for no more than your entirely reasonable fees. But I felt I could not stop short of complete vindication where so vital a principle was at stake.*

When James Cabell wrote to say that Ellen Glasgow was in a "horrifying" condition, mentally and physically, Marjorie sent her some mangoes and a cheerful letter urging her to come to St. Augustine for the winter. Sympathizing with her melancholia and praising her work lavishly, Marjorie begged Ellen to come to the kinder climate of Florida and promised to see that she got as much attention or as much solitude as she desired. She said:

> *Please, dearest Ellen, do come to us. Do you recall my dream*

of you, in the cold, with the red curtains? I feel somehow that
I, we, can give you some warmth—and you, of course, can
always let us warm our hands at your fire.

Ellen replied that she was too weak to travel. She praised Marjorie's "great gifts" and urged her to continue with her book. Before Marjorie received this letter, Ellen Glasgow had died.

The first postwar winter season was especially festive as people tried to make up for the austerity of the past four seasons. The Baskins had a great deal of company. For some of the visiting friends, Marjorie arranged hunting expeditions and some she entertained at their beach cottage. Late in February Charlie and Vera Scribner were in Florida and Marjorie gave a "sizeable brawl," which included, besides the Scribners, the James Branch Cabells, the publisher of *Collier's* and his wife, an editor from the *Saturday Evening Post*, Edith and Verle Pope, and the Owen D. Youngs. Owen D. Young, the former president of General Electric, and his wife, Louise, had become close friends of Marjorie and Norton. The Youngs spent their winters at Washington Oaks, their estate a few miles south of the Baskins' beach cottage. A few days after this large party Marjorie was entertaining Robert Frost among other friends for Sunday dinner.

Whatever else was going on in her life, Zelma Cason's lawsuit always hung like a storm cloud over Marjorie's head. In Zelma's Declaration she had both a claim for libel and one for invasion of privacy. The lower court had dismissed both counts. In November of 1944 the Florida Supreme Court reversed the lower court's dismissal of the invasion of privacy claim. Phil May and Marjorie continued to work together to gather evidence and secure witnesses that would benefit her defense. They had a number of conferences and a great deal of correspondence, and there were meetings in Gainesville with Sigsbee Scruggs, the local lawyer who was to help May with the defense. Depositions were taken from her publisher and her agent in New York. Charles Scribner testified on the association of his publishing house with Marjorie; Whitney Darrow supplied information on the sales and distribution of her books. Maxwell Perkins testified concerning the literary value of all of Marjorie's publications and the reception accorded them by literary critics and the public generally. Henry Seidel Canby of the Book-of-the-Month Club gave the same sort of testimony as that given by Perkins. Mrs. Philip Van Doren Stern gave evidence of the popularity of the armed services editions of her works. And Carl Brandt and Bernice Baumgarten gave testimony about the foreign editions, movie, serial and magazine sales, and reception by the public of her writing. All of these depositions were taken by Edward Perkins, an attorney and brother of Max Perkins.

Just before Christmas, Marjorie had an interesting encounter with Zelma's mother, who lived in Island Grove, only a few miles from Cross Creek. In previous years, Marjorie had always given Mrs. Cason a bottle of liquor for Christmas, and Phil May agreed that there was no reason not to do so this year. A few days before Christmas on a bitter cold evening Marjorie turned in at Mrs. Cason's about eight o'clock. The old lady was ready for bed, but she greeted Marjorie warmly and suggested they go into the bathroom, as it was the only warm place in the house. Marjorie gave her the quart of festively wrapped Calvert's and produced another bottle she had brought in for them to toast the season with. Mrs. Cason got two jelly glasses and after they each poured a generous measure into their glasses, Marjorie sat on a low stool and Mrs. Cason sat on the toilet seat, while they drank and had a long chat. They got expansive and Marjorie said that her feelings for Zelma had never changed, that she would always feel the same affection and that she felt that "behind and beyond everything" Zelma still loved her, too.

As Marjorie was leaving, Mrs. Cason mentioned that her birthday came two days later, so Marjorie dashed to the car and brought her another bottle of Calvert's for a birthday present. "Make of it what you wish!" Marjorie told Phil May. But she insisted that under all circumstances, Mrs. Cason was to be protected in the trial. "She is a *genuine* friend and must not be hurt or embarrassed," Marjorie told him.

In the spring of 1946, Norton had an opportunity to take charge of the two restaurants and bar at Marineland, which had just opened and was only a few miles from the beach cottage. By the first week in March the sale of the Castle Warden property was in progress, and he was busy setting up the Marineland restaurants.

Toward the end of March two Kinnan aunts, Wilmer and Grace, both retired school teachers, came to visit. After seeing St. Augustine, they moved over to Cross Creek for a ten-day stay. Marjorie gave them the two most comfortable bedrooms with baths and slept in the tiny room in back of the living room. She did everything she could think of to make their visit enjoyable, inviting friends from the university, such as the Tigerts and Lyons and also Phil May and his wife to dinner parties. Wilmer happily gave Phil advice on handling the pending trial, and privately advised Marjorie to import one of the Scribners' lawyers to oversee the whole thing. She also had specific suggestions as to how Marjorie should conduct herself during the trial. With her usual warm hospitality Marjorie made her aunts feel completely at home and fed them many of her special dishes. She endured being called "Peaches" and exclaimed over endlessly, and Moe was patient if puzzled when Wilmer dashed in ahead of him to retrieve the fallen birds on a hunting trip. When the aunts left, Marjorie packed them such a generous lunch it lasted them for three days. They never got over praising the visit in their letters and Wilmer told her they never expected in their lives to have "so lovely a visit—in such a world of beauty." They were also enchanted by the southern charm of Norton Baskin, whom Wilmer described as "fine as silk."

The trial date was finally set for May 20. Marjorie assumed much of the responsibility of securing local witnesses and talking with them about their testimony as well as searching her mind and her records for useful information. She also wrote to various people who might contribute helpful information. And there were continuous meetings with Phil May and Sigsbee Scuggs and endless documents to fill in and worry over. Marjorie's relationships with the Casons continued to be incongruous in view of the impending trial. In March she took Mrs. Cason some fresh-killed pork. The old lady slapped her playfully on the leg and said, "Where have you been? Why haven't you been to see me?" And Marjorie had another visit with her when she picked up a mutual acquaintance a few weeks later and took her to Mrs. Cason's house.

On April 18, Marjorie wrote to Phil May that she had had an experience so "utterly weird" that she wouldn't be surprised if he threw up his hands and relinquished the "whole damn case." Her story was that after giving a talk to about two hundred wounded veterans at a convalescent hospital, she came back to the cottage to find a note from Clare, Dr. T. Z. Cason's daughter, saying that she and her little boy had walked past the cottage, and seeing the door open had come in and were sorry to miss Marjorie. They were staying with friends nearby and hoped to get a chance to see her. Marjorie, who was genuinely fond of T. Z.'s children, was also curious. So, after their supper, Norton drove Marjorie to the place where Clare was staying, and Clare invited them in for a drink, saying, "There isn't a soul here but Aunt Zelma." They went in and Marjorie apologized for her housecoat and Zelma apologized for her bare feet. Then they had a drink together and Zelma and Norton joined forces to tease Clare's little Terry into eating his supper. They discussed Cason family matters, and at one point Zelma said, "Marge, you'd be just crazy about Terry if you knew him." Marjorie answered, "Well Zelma, you remember, you and I always did prefer little boys." Zelma responded by giving her a hard and friendly poke in the ribs, saying, "Yes, Marge, we always did like little boys." Nothing was said about the trial. Zelma told Marjorie that her mother had had a sick spell, so a few days later Marjorie visited her in Island Grove and took her a bottle of gin. Mrs. Cason hid it in a cupboard, saying, "Marge, I really like gin." Marjorie responded that she did, too, especially in hot weather. "She is a cute old gal, and I see no reason why she shouldn't have her toddy," Marjorie told Phil May.

Fellow writers such as A. J. Cronin, James Cabell, and Margaret Mitchell wrote encouragement, assuring her that her cause was one they all shared and supported. And strangers wrote, telling Marjorie to keep up her courage and commenting on how much *Cross Creek* had meant to them. One woman told her, "I'm sure that no one with intelligence after reading your books would ever accuse you of malice." She went on to say that in a measure *Cross Creek* influenced both her husband and her to settle in Florida. Another fan wrote of Marjorie's portrayal of Zelma, "You painted her as a beautiful Florida wildflower and she turned out to be poison ivy."

Observing that Marjorie was getting nervous as the trial date neared, Phil May suggested that Norton take her to Louisville for a visit with their friends, the Hardys, and to attend the Kentucky Derby the first weekend in May. Although he was extremely busy with his new Marineland food concession, Norton was glad of a chance to get Marjorie away for a few days. The excitement of the Derby, a plentiful supply of mint juleps, and the soothing company of her devoted friends provided a salutary vacation from the strain of preparing for the trial. She returned to Florida determined to hold up, no matter how the trial went. "It is inevitable . . . that all this gets on my nerves, but you can count on me not to fail you, and to rise to the mark," she told Phil May. She hoped that her sincere statement of her aims and motives and attitude in writing the book would be a valuable factor in winning the lawsuit, she told her lawyer.

When Carl Brandt approached her in mid-May to ask her about doing a dog story for the movies that Lassie could star in, she brushed it aside impatiently and wired, HERE I AM BATTLING FOR THE RIGHTS OF ALL WRITERS TO FREE EXPRESSION AND YOU ARE ASKING ME TO MAKE A LITTLE BASKET FOR LASSIE.

Just before the trial began, Whitney Darrow of Scribners sent her his best wishes, and Charles Scribner, who was abroad, sent his also. Max Perkins sent a series of encouraging telegrams. MAY YOU WIN FOR US ALL, he told her.

On the opening day of the trial, a Monday, Norton drove Marjorie the fifteen miles from Cross Creek to the old red brick courthouse in Gainesville in a jeep, the only vehicle he had been able to obtain since the war. As she stepped out of the vehicle after the wind-swept ride, Marjorie said, "I know now how Marie Antoinette felt in the tumbril." The trial was styled a "drama" by some of the Florida newspapers, and that is what it became before it was over. The cast of characters was headed by circuit Judge John A. H. Murphree, the son of the second president of the University of Florida, a pipe-smoking, mild-tempered man who had to struggle at times to keep the drama from becoming a farce.

Zelma was represented by J. V. Walton, a Palatka attorney and his daughter Kate Walton, a recent graduate of the University of Florida law school. Walton, a small man, who arrived at court wearing an English safari helmet, and his daughter were of about the same size. Their associate council, E. A. Clayton, a Gainesville attorney, dressed like an ultraconservative banker. Representing Marjorie, Phil

May and Sigsbee Scruggs were a Mutt and Jeff combination, except that May was slender and Scruggs was a huge bear of a man. His middle name was "Lee," and he had been named for the captain of the battleship *Maine*, which was sunk the day after he was born, and for Robert E. Lee. He was famous for successfully representing Crackers accused of illegal fishing and moonshining in the Gainesville area.

Zelma Cason, a tiny woman, arrived in a blue-and-white polka dot dress, wearing rimless glasses and high heels. Marjorie appeared wearing a simple brown dress and white beads and a pill box hat tilted over her right eye. Her co-defendant, Norton Baskin, wore a neat, tailored business suit. The plaintiff and her lawyers sat at one end of a long table, and the defendants and their lawyers at the other, separated by only a few feet. Norton bowed politely to the lawyers as he pulled out Marjorie's chair for her. As the process of jury selection began, Zelma pulled out her knitting and began to work industriously on a blue sweater. When her ball of yarn rolled from her lap, Norton retrieved it from under the table and handed it to her; this action was to be repeated several times.

The jury panel of fifty was almost exhausted before the six-man jury and two alternates were picked and sworn in by Judge Murphree. A number of the prospective jurors were excused when they expressed disapproval of authors mentioning names of living persons in books without the consent of those persons. However, one young automobile electrical worker was accepted even though he said he thought it was all right to mention names as "no history could be written without doing it." The other five jurors included a jeweler, a hardware merchant, a carpenter, a turpentine businessman, and a wholesale candy dealer. None of them had read *Cross Creek*, and some of them had never heard of it. The turpentine man had started to read it but had never finished it, and Marjorie grinned broadly when he said he didn't consider it "literature." Judge Murphree told the jurors they were dealing with an unusual case, since not only was the charge of invasion of privacy at issue but also that of malice. If the case went against the defendant, he indicated that she might be subject to "punitive damages" if malice was found. Misleading newspaper reports led to speculation that Marjorie might be subject to a possible jail term but Judge Murphree later explained to the jurors that this was not true. The jurors were given copies of *Cross Creek* and asked to familiarize themselves with it.

The next day in the opening statements, the prosecution contended that Zelma Cason had lived a quiet life until Marjorie Rawlings had maliciously brought on her undesirable and obnoxious publicity. The defense contended that Marjorie Rawlings's description of Zelma Cason was accurate and that she wrote about Zelma only as a friend who she believed would relish the resultant publicity.

In addition to the passage in "The Census" chapter describing "my friend Zelma," as an "ageless spinster resembling an angry and efficient canary," the prosecution took exception to a passage that appeared in the chapter "Toady-frogs, Lizards, Antses, and Varmints," which said:

> My profane friend Zelma, the census taker, said, "The b___s killed the egrets for their plumage until the egrets gave out. They killed alligators for their hides until the alligators gave out. If the frogs ever give out, the sons of b_____s will starve to death.

Zelma, who at the time of the trial was a state welfare caseworker, was the first to testify on the second day of the trial. She said that she had misplaced her friendship in Marjorie, and testified that her mental and physical health had been impaired as a result of the use of her name in *Cross Creek*. Under questioning by Phil May, she insisted she was a shy, country girl, but admitted that she occasionally directed unmentionable words reflecting on their ancestry at certain individuals. She claimed not to be able to remember saying the things attributed to her in the book. "She took a lady and made a hussy out of her," Zelma said primly, with a cutting glance at Marjorie. "My own true friends," Zelma added, "will stick to me like Panther's Fertilizer 'time tried and tested.' "

Only four witnesses were called by the prosecution. One of them was the stepfather of the boy about whom Marjorie had written in "Cracker Chidlings," with the resultant upsetting of his mother. Under questioning by the defense, the man admitted that Marjorie had apologized to the mother and that the family was now friendly with her. The other three witnesses were women who testified that they had known Zelma for years and had never heard her curse, did not think she was officious, and did not consider her to have a bad temper.

By the third day of the trial, spectators overflowed the courtroom. The defense had fifty-one witnesses lined up. As one reporter put it, they included all the characters in *Cross Creek* except Dora the cow. Mercifully Marjorie's attorneys agreed not to call all their subpoened witnesses. One of the first to testify was Navy Lieutenant Bertram C. Cooper, a friend with whom Marjorie had corresponded extensively during the war and whom she had hoped Julia Scribner would marry. Cooper, who had served as a chaplain on the U. S. S. *Bountiful*, testified that he used to give the book to servicemen as a prescription for homesickness. They liked it because it was like a long letter from home, especially to boys from Florida and Georgia, he said. On cross-questioning, J. W. Walton asked Cooper, "Didn't I see you and Mrs. Rawlings embrace very affectionately when you met in the courtroom here?" And Cooper replied, "I was enthusiastically happy to see her." Explaining that he was from Savannah, Georgia, he said it would be unnatural for him to just walk up and shake hands with her.

Another defense witness, Deputy Sheriff Noel Moore, of Island Grove, described Zelma as a "rule or ruin" kind of person and said he had heard her call someone "a son of a bitch." The lawyer asked whom it was, and when Moore answered, "*I* am the son of a bitch," the audience burst into laughter. Thelma Shortridge, a postmistress and the daughter of Fred Tompkins, to whom Marjorie referred often in *Cross Creek*, admitted that she herself was profane "as much as any Floridan is." Asked by Walton what that meant, she answered, "There are several words in a small community that if you live there and serve the public, then if you don't use them, then you can't stay there." The spectators roared and while the bailiff silenced them Judge Murphree turned away to hide a smile. Kate Walton made the mistake of asking Thelma Shortridge if she objected to the characterization of her father in the book. "No Ma'am," Thelma shot back, "It was of him truly."

Dr. A. J. Hanna, professor of history at Rollins College and a good friend of Marjorie's, told the court that *Cross Creek* was a book of "tremendous importance to the State of Florida," in that it offset the blatant publicity of Florida as a tourist resort and gave a clean-cut picture of rural Florida. He told the jury he was writing a section for the new *Encyclopedia Americana* in which he cited *South Moon Under, The Yearling,* and *Cross Creek* as the most accurate and sympathetic descriptions of Florida people and "an accurate and important part of the Florida scene." Calling Marjorie Florida's most prominent writer, Dr. Hanna pointed out that she was the only Florida woman who had been given honorary degrees by three Florida institutions of higher learning: The University of Florida, The University of Tampa, and Rollins College.

Mae Dupree of Citra, a small community near Cross Creek, testified that about a year earlier she had asked Zelma how the case was getting on, and Zelma had answered, "It is not my case, it is a lawyer's case, and I don't know anything about it. They asked me if they could use my name to see whether an author could use a person's name in a book." Marjorie's friend Dessie Smith said that the portrait of her in the chapter "Hyacinth Drift" was accurate. She admitted that she often used the word "bastard" which was not uncommon in their community. Tom Glisson said that the characterization of him in the book was true and had not offended him, and that Zelma Cason's characterization also was a true picture of her.

Dr. Clifford Lyons, professor of English and literature at the University of Florida since 1936, compared Marjorie's writings to Mark Twain's. Asked what the author's description of Zelma Cason meant to him, Dr. Lyons said that it was a representation of a type of person much admired in that part of the country—a pioneer—reliant, essentially kind, ready, and efficient, a person with a heart of gold. Attorney Clayton tried to make Dr. Lyons admit that passages of *Cross Creek* were vulgar, or at least indelicate. But the most Dr. Lyons would concede was that some of the passages were "inelegant," "salty," or "racy." Several times during the debate, the laughter in the courtroom got out of hand and Judge Murphree threatened repeatedly to clear the courtroom. The listeners were particularly amused at the discussion of the chapter "The Evolution of Comfort" about Marjorie's acquisition of indoor plumbing, which she had insisted on leaving in the book. Referring to her mention of an out-house of her childhood memory in which a French verse hung, Clayton demanded, "Wouldn't you consider that vulgar?" "I don't know," Dr. Lyons replied. "I don't know how good the French was." And before the prosecution's objections could stop him, the professor managed to throw out the observation, "If all inelegant passages were deleted from the literature of the world there would be some great gaps—even in the Bible."

On the fifth day of the trial when Marjorie was scheduled to testify, the courtroom was so packed that spectators stood three deep in the balcony, lined the walls, filled the window sills, and jammed the hallways outside the room. The society editor for the Gainesville *Sun* was on hand and so was a reporter from the New York *Times*. The front rows of the courtroom were filled with many of Gainesville's prominent women, including the judge's wife. Some of them had brought their lunches for fear they would lose their places if they left for any length of time. The chauffeur of one of the women brought lunch in to one group who didn't choose to carry their own brown bags. University professors and college students sat and stood, hip to hip and shoulder to shoulder. The temperature in the unair-conditioned courtroom rose as the day went on, but nobody seemed to notice.

Dressed in a cool summer dress and a white broad-brimmed hat, Marjorie lived up to her promise to Phil May to be a model witness. She and Phil May were concerned that some people were calling the trial a contest between "a cracker and a carpetbagger," and had decided in advance to anticipate attacks on her as a Yankee invader. Under May's guidance, she told the court that she was born and brought up until college age in Washington, D. C., and in Maryland. At college in Wisconsin she was known as "the little southern girl" and she belonged all through college to the Dixie Club, composed of dyed-in-the-wool southerners. She had two great-grandmothers who had lived in Kentucky, and both had been slave owners.

She briefly summarized her life before coming to Cross Creek and outlined her writing career from her childhood scribblings to the present. In a voice verging on tears, she said, "I felt I had come home when I came to Florida. The people so charmed me I determined to write about them and, if I failed, not to write any more." She explained that two of her first sketches in "Cracker Chidlings" were the result of stories that her friend Zelma Cason had told her. She denied any malice in her descriptions of Zelma and said it had never occurred to her that Zelma would be hurt, embarrassed, or humiliated by the portrayal of her.

When one of Zelma's lawyers asked about the description of Zelma as "my profane friend," Marjorie said that cussing is a matter of style. The local brand, she explained, was "just plain country cussin'." She and Zelma were just about tied in their abilities and reputations in the matter, she observed. When Mr. Walton asked her to define profanity, she asked him for his definition. As he floundered around, Phil May jumped up and said, "Mr. Walton, what are you doing?"

Walton replied, "I'm answering her question."

Grinning, May said, "Mr. Walton, you don't have to answer her question. She has no right to ask you questions." The crowd shouted, and the judge had to cover his face with his handkerchief to hide his amusement. Zelma was not amused, however, and continued to knit during Marjorie's testimony, only occasionally glancing coldly over her rimless glasses at the figure on the witness stand. Reporters kept track of her progress on the blue sweater and noted that by the end of the fifth day it was nearing completion.

In order to establish Marjorie's lack of a sense of law and order, the offense brought up the episode of her shooting of Mr. Martin's pig. Marjorie denied there was an analogy between this incident and her writing about Zelma. "I *meant* to shoot the pig," she said. Walton read passages from *Cross Creek* concerning the mating habits of ducks and drakes and asked if she did not consider them "embarrassing." Marjorie answered that she had been assured by authorities that the circumstances, though unusual, were authentic and that she considered her account proper in a book about rural life. As Walton read other passages that had been described by witnesses as "salty" or "earthy," Marjorie gently but frequently corrected his misreading of words and phrases to the delight of the audience. Asked why she had included such passages, she said, "Perhaps you have a different conception of life and what makes up life than I do. I wrote about those things because they are a part of what happens at Cross Creek. Those things to me are a part of life."

Marjorie was still on the witness stand late Friday when court was recessed for a two-day weekend. After signing autographs and working their way through a throng of well-wishers, the Baskins retired to Cross Creek to rest and regroup and to plan with Phil May their strategy for the final act of the trial. There was no way for them to tell what the jury was thinking at this point.

On Monday Marjorie again calmly but resolutely refuted charges by the prosecution that the book was "vulgar, lewd, cruel, and lascivious." Phil May objected strenuously when the offense questioned her about her current financial status, but Judge Murphree denied the objection. There was a time out while Marjorie did some figuring on the back of an envelope and came up with the figure of $124,000 including the motion picture rights for *The Yearling*.

The courtroom listened in hushed quiet as Marjorie read several passages from *Cross Creek* to illustrate the point that her theme was a love of the land. When you love a person or a place, their faults and peculiarities do not interfere with your feeling for them, she said. "*Cross Creek* is a love story," she concluded, "of my love for the land."

Phil May was denied the right to read some of Marjorie's fan mail into the record. However, he managed to ostentatiously parade before the jury carrying bulging envelopes containing the letters and to stack them in the jury's view on the court clerk's desk. Observing this bit of theatrics, a reporter commented, "If Mrs. May raised any foolish children, Phil wasn't one of them."

Monday afternoon depositions from witnesses who could not appear in person were read into the record. One of these was from Marjorie's neighbor, Mrs. A. N. Slater, described as "the Widow Slater" in *Cross Creek*. The audience tittered as the portly Scruggs took the witness stand to read the words of the widow. Her testimony said she wasn't offended by the book and that she had heard Zelma use profane language in front of the Island Grove post office.

A deposition from Aunt Ida called Zelma a "loud speaker" and denied that Zelma lived the quiet and secluded life that she claimed to. Max Perkins's deposition called *Cross Creek* a minor classic, and

Henry Seidel Canby's deposition called it "one of the most humorous and one of the kindest books I've ever read."

Tuesday was the final day of the trial. Every nook and cranny of the courtroom was filled. During the last-minute skirmishings between the lawyers before their closing statements, an odd phenomenon was observed by reporters. By ones or by twos the ladies whom they dubbed "the blue haired set" slipped out of the courtroom and returned a few minutes later with small parcels in hand. The mystery was cleared up when it was discovered that Wilson's store, across the square from the courthouse, had received an unadvertised shipment of nylon stockings (still scarce in the postwar years), and the ladies were taking advantage of the opportunity.

During the offense's closing argument, references were made to Marjorie's coming to the South and repaying friendships with unkind words in printed pages. The objectionable passages from *Cross Creek* were again read to the jury. The prosecution lawyers emphasized the common law that an ordinary citizen cannot be held up to public gaze through the printed page. Walton's most memorable analogy was "to hold that things like this can be written because the writer is an eminent author is like holding that Joe Louis could come down here and knock down the ordinary citizen just because he is world's champion."

Phil May told the jury that this was the "first time since the invention of the printing press that an author has been forced to stand trial for a true-word picture." He emphasized the right of a writer to freedom of speech. If the jury condemned Marjorie, he said, they would be striking at the freedom of all future literature. But the man the audience had stayed to hear was the renowned Sigsbee Scruggs. As an acquaintance said of him, "There was no way anybody could spend a boring day in court if he was there."

Scruggs stood up and grinned at the jury. "I'm a cracker, too," he told them. His anecdotes of his upbringing by strait-laced parents drew frequent laughter from the crowd. He contended that *Cross Creek* would have been incomplete without the inclusion of Zelma Cason. Just as one could not describe the world at that time without describing Winston Churchill, one could not describe Island Grove without describing Miss Cason, he said. Then he proceeded to paint

Zelma not as a lady of the "crinoline and old lace" period, but as a thoroughly modern woman, who shouldn't have been offended at her description in *Cross Creek*. He admitted he still got a little shocked when he saw a woman reaching for a cigarette, but he knew "the women of today do smoke our cigarettes; they drink our liquor; they use our cuss words; they tell our dirty jokes; and even wear our pants, and in the last war they fought beside us and did a good job of it, too." In a modern day, passages in a book like the one in question must be judged by modern standards, the burly Scruggs told the jury.

Judge Murphree's charge to the jury ran over a dozen legal-size pages. He tried to define for the jurors the meaning of invasion of privacy:

> *In cases of this type frequently there arises a conflict between the right of the public to the freedom of the press on the one hand and the right of the individual to privacy on the other. Neither is absolute and in matters in which the public has a legitimate interest, the right to free expression is sometimes dominant over the individual's desire for privacy.*

He also told them that the legal meaning of the word "profanity" is that it denotes blasphemy or irreverence of God and holy things. "None of the words or expressions attributed to Miss Cason in the book *Cross Creek* are of that nature. . . ."

The trial had been an unusually lengthy one, but the decision of the jurors came with surprising speed. After twenty-eight minutes of deliberation they reached a decision. Zelma had not even returned to the courtroom, but Marjorie and Norton were in their seats when the foreman announced, "We, the jury find the defendants, Marjorie Kinnan Baskin and Norton Baskin, as her husband, not guilty. So say we all."

The spectators broke into applause and many of them crowded forward to congratulate Marjorie, who clung to Norton's arm and fought to keep the composure she had so carefully maintained during the trial.

On the way back to the grove, the Baskins stopped along the way to thank her neighbors for their support. When they reached the farmhouse, Martha Mickens had ready a pilau made of chicken and a big soft-shelled cooter, a ham, and other foods. Phil May and his wife and Sigsbee Scruggs and his wife, Clifford Lyons, and Bertram Cooper joined them for a gala celebration that lasted far into the night. Martha and some of her children sang spirituals and Bertram Cooper, who had an excellent singing voice, sang Japanese songs he had learned during the war.

The fact that immediately following the reading of the verdict, Zelma's attorneys asked for an extension of time for filing motion for a new trial seemed irrelevant.

Marjorie, about 1933
(Courtesy Beatrice H. McNeil, Los Angeles, California)

The farmhouse at Cross Creek
(The University of Florida, Department of Rare Books and Manuscripts)

Will and Martha Mickens
(The University of Florida,
Department of Rare Books and
Manuscripts)

Marjorie with Mandy,
about 1930
(Courtesy Beatrice H. McNeil,
Los Angeles, California

Maxwell Perkins,
1930's
(The University of Florida,
Department of Rare Books
and Manuscripts)

Marjorie, in her garden at Cross Creek, about 1939
(The University of Florida, Department of Rare Books and Manuscripts)

Marjorie and Margaret Mitchell at premiere party for Gone With the Wind, *1939*
(The University of Florida, Department of Rare Books and Manuscripts)

With Moe at Crescent Beach cottage, early 1940's
(The University of Florida, Department of Rare Books and Manuscripts)

*Norton Baskin
about 1940*
(The University of Florida,
Department of Rare Books and
Manuscripts)

*Norton in
World War II uniform
of ambulance driver
with American Field Service*
(Courtesy Norton Baskin, St.
Augustine, Florida)

Marjorie with her attorney, Philip May, at his home in Mandarin, Florida, about 1950
(*Courtesy Fryga Studios of Columbia, S. C. and Philip May, Jr.*)

Carl Van Vechten photograph of Marjorie, 1952
(*The University of Florida, Department of Rare Books and Manuscripts*)

*Marjorie
on the film set of
The Yearling,
at Salt Springs*
*(The University of Florida,
Department of Rare Books and
Manuscripts)*

Marjorie's tombstone, Antioch Cemetery
(The University of Florida, Department of Rare Books and Manuscripts)

Publicity photo of Marjorie, taken at her famhouse in Cross Creek
(The University of Florida, Department of Rare Books and Manuscripts)

CHAPTER 15

An Unspeakable Grief

With the ending of the three-year ordeal came an inevitable reaction that Marjorie called a "nervous let down." The cost of the lawsuit to her was great both emotionally and materially. She had no help from any source in paying any of the costs, and her only material gain from it was a flurry of sales for *Cross Creek*. The best thing that came to her from the ordeal was the knowledge that all of her Cross Creek neighbors had supported her. Some of them had been friends with both her and Zelma, and they had to make a hard decision. But Zelma, who lived in Island Grove, was not a Cross Creeker and Marjorie was, and in the end they all supported her, even though some of them were not delighted to have been put into the book themselves. Tom Glisson perhaps expressed their attitude best. When she had asked him about her using him and his real name in her book, he had said, "Marge, the people that know me, know me. People that don't know me, I don't give a damn. If you can sell that stuff and make a living, help yourself." The prosecution made a serious mistake in assuming that the Crackers would think if Zelma got money, everyone mentioned in the book would get money, and so would testify in her behalf. In the uncertain days before the trial,

Marjorie, too, had worried that other characters in the book might follow Zelma's lead, or at least might feel the way Zelma did about her portrayal of them, and if so, she would no longer be able to live at the Creek. She would have to sell her beloved farmhouse and grove. But when the trial was over and her neighbors' loyalty to her proved, she knew she was right in her opinion of them.

Many friends wired and wrote to congratulate her. Among them was James Cabell, who had dedicated his latest book, *Pirates*, to her. "Now it's over," he said, "let us consider the farcical insanity of your trial. The reports of it seem to have been invented by Lewis Carroll at his top form." And he exhorted her to get down to work. A. J. Cronin told her she had shown great courage and compared her to Queen Boadicia and the Statue of Liberty.

Publishers Weekly of June 29, 1946, carried a write-up on the trial and its outcome. The article pointed out the importance of the case to publishers as well as to authors. *Time*'s memorandum on the trial on its "People" page in the June 10, 1946, issue drew a response from Marjorie. She explained that the case might not be over, since the plaintiff had filed a motion for a new trial and said she was torn between wanting to be free of the pressures brought by the suit and wanting it to go to the highest possible court:

> *A vital principle is involved: the right of anyone to write of his or her own life, where that necessarily involves mention of other people, short, of course, of libel. If a local jury had decided against me in this, it would seem that not only would all autobiography become immediately taboo, but that freedom of the press in its wider aspects might be curtailed.*

She told the editors she hoped *Time* would follow the case to its end for the same reason—basic freedom of the press in general—that had motivated her to fight the case out "so long, so hard, so expensively."

On July 17, Judge Murphree denied Zelma's motion for a new trial, and her attorneys promptly announced their intention of taking the case back to the Florida Supreme Court.

Meantime, life went on. On August 8, 1946, friends gave a big party to celebrate Marjorie's fiftieth birthday. And there were echoes from the past. She received an anguished letter from the third Mrs. Charles Rawlings, telling her of Chuck's mental cruelty and asking whether he had been that way to her. Mrs. Rawlings III reported that Mrs. Rawlings II had pinned a note to the divorce papers saying, "I beg of you not to marry again. You are not fit to be a husband." But Chuck had explained to the third Mrs. Rawlings that it meant he was not a good provider. Marjorie answered the letter as honestly as she felt the latest wife had written to her, in spite of Norton's warning not to stick her neck out.

Like everyone who paid attention to world events, Marjorie was interested in, intrigued by, and concerned over communism. When Max sent her *I Chose Freedom* by Victor A. Kravchenko, a former Soviet official, it helped to clarify her thinking. Her scorn of those who were too materialistic had led her, like many other intellectuals, to look with interest and hope toward the humanity that seemed basic to communism in its original form. However, reading *I Chose Freedom* and talking with knowledgeable friends led her to the realization that it was quite likely true that "we are ignorant of what is going on in Russia, and of the intentions of the Soviet regime, and [of the fact that] they are utterly dangerous."

When Brandt and Brandt presented Marjorie with a proposal from the producers of the radio program "Cavalcade of America" to broadcast a half-hour adaptation from *Cross Creek*, Marjorie at first agreed. But when she saw the script they had prepared, she changed her mind. "I had every intention of behaving myself," she told Bernice Baumgarten of Brandt and Brandt, who had arranged the deal, and then all of a sudden she had thought, "You damned hypocritical fools, you're more to blame than any other kind of people for what's wrong with the world," and she loosed her fury on the producers. In the first place, she told them, the script exploited her relationship with her Cross Creek neighbors. They all listened to the radio, which to them represented the outside world, and she was afraid they would feel betrayed.

"I'm sorry you asked me my opinion of the script itself," she said:

I consider it very bad, not technically, for it is extremely well

done for your purposes, but bad just as I consider your first
program, "Passport to Freedom," bad. The idea of "selling
America and the American way of life, to Americans," must
be done well and subtly, or it is worse than valueless. Stephen
Vincent Benét, my dear friend, was one of the few who could
do this job with decency and integrity. Archibald MacLeish
did it to a degree. Of course, to my notion, I do not feel that
Americans need any "selling" to themselves. We are inclined
to be a bit too self-satisfied as it is. I feel on the contrary, that
we need to be made more aware of the discrepancy between
our theories and our facts or practices. I feel that we need, as
does every nation, to be less conscious of nationalism and
more conscious of a general humanity.

She cited dialogue in the script that was unrealistic. "Not one of the
three persons, or shall we say, type of persons, would ever think in
such terms, or bleat out such 'patriotic' comments." In the second
place she said, "thumping the American chest and crying out bla-
tantly, 'Aren't we wonderful!' is not only bad taste, but sentimen-
talizes and makes obnoxiously obvious the best of good and simple
feelings. It may come down to a matter of artistry, with which the
radio has little or no concern." She assured the producers that the
"dewy-eyed haziness" of their first program and the spuriousness of
the script of *Cross Creek* was in line with the many war movies that
made servicemen who knew the truth "go quietly out and vomit."
Needless to say, the program was not broadcast.

In the summer of 1946, MGM again approached Marjorie's agents
to get her to do a story that could star Lassie and Claude Jarman,
Jr. (the young actor who finally played Jody in *The Yearling*). This
time she was responsive. She intended to get back to work on *The
Sojourner* eventually, but at the moment tackling something lighter
and easier was appealing. Too, the movies paid good money and the
uncertainty about the final outcome of the lawsuit made her feel
financially insecure. In order to work in peace and quiet, she decided
to rent a cottage near Blowing Rock, North Carolina. Norton drove
her, along with Moe and the cat, Benny, to the mountain retreat and
helped her find a house and get settled. After he left, Idella came up

by train to look after her.

The cottage had a view of miles and miles of valley and mountain ranges. The only books she took with her were the Bible, Proust, and Henry James's *The American Scene*. Her agreement with MGM was that she adapt the story "A Mother in Mannville," which had run in the *Saturday Evening Post* some ten years earlier, for the movie. To her surprise, the work went fast and she enjoyed it, although she called it "un-artistic." When Norton came to drive her back to Florida in October, she had a finished draft of the manuscript to show him. He found it touching in places and pronounced it ready to send to her agents and also suggested it might do for a magazine serial.

Readers at both Brandt and Brandt and MGM were enthusiastic about the story, which at that point was called "A Family for Jock." But Marjorie told Bernice Baumgarten that the story could not possibly be published as a book. She had hoped it might make a nice juvenile, but writing with the film in mind, the story turned into "no more than a narrative script, and has no literary quality at all. This is not modesty, but knowledge." When the Brandts and MGM continued to be "starry-eyed" about the script as a novel, Marjorie appealed to Max Perkins for his opinion. He agreed with her that "A Family for Jock" should not be published as a book. "It is not written as you would have written it had you intended it to be a book," he told her." It wasn't in her style, but he thought it a "super movie scenario" and agreed that it might make a popular magazine serial.

The movie producers asked Marjorie to come to Hollywood at their expense to work on revisions of the script. They offered to pay Norton's expenses, too, and to give them a car and chauffeur and a hundred dollars per day for incidentals. Marjorie said, "What the hell would I spend $100 a day on?" She declined to go to Hollywood but did agree to meet the studio's representatives in New York. MGM put her up in a large apartment that they kept on a permanent basis at the Waldorf Towers. It was beautifully decorated but had no view. "If they could only tether a cow out there someplace," Marjorie told Norton, who came up to be with her during the last few days of her stay.

She told him that a constant stream of callers asked for a man named Moe, who evidently was the caretaker of the apartment. Answering one of these calls, Norton told the caller, "Hell, no, Moe didn't come. Moe is our dog, and we had to leave somebody home." That night, while A. J. Cronin was there having drinks with them, a little man opened the door and said, "Moe gave me a key." Marjorie, who had had a few drinks, went to the phone: "May I speak to a manager, or at least an assistant manager? This is Mrs. Rawlings. As you know I have this apartment. People keep coming to the door and calling for Moe. My husband is here now. He's from the South, you know—and if one more little man comes to the door asking for Moe, he's liable to shoot him." A. J. Cronin and Norton Baskin were equally goggle-eyed at the thought of Norton's shooting anyone. But there were no more seekers after Moe.

While in New York, Marjorie saw Max Perkins and discussed with him an idea they had briefly talked of before. In *Cross Creek* she had written "Someday a poet will write a sad and lovely story of a Negro child." Max told her she was the one to do the story but that she should let the idea develop in her mind as it would. Max was as interested and as concerned as ever to help her work through her ideas, but his appearance shocked her. He was more stooped and thin than when they last met, and his handsome features were drawn, his sea-blue eyes clouded. She did not realize, however, that this was to be their last meeting.

Before leaving for Florida, Marjorie also spent an enjoyable evening at Marcia Davenport's, where she enjoyed conversation with Robert Sherwood, the playwright, and Jan Masaryk, the Czech foreign minister. Marcia and Russell Davenport had divorced after fifteen years of marriage. Her relationship with Jan Masaryk had grown out of her work for Czechoslovakia after that country fell victim to Hitler. Of that relationship, she wrote, "I never imagined or foresaw that it would culminate in a personal tie so absolute as to transcend the limitations of two very faulty human beings and become, in the midst of Hell, a corner of Elysium." Marjorie's impression of Masaryk was that he had "one of the most magnificent minds and spirits" she had ever met.

In November, the attorneys for Zelma Cason filed an appeal to the Florida Supreme Court for a reversal of the Alachua County

Circuit Court decision dismissing invasion of privacy charges. And, to her surprise, Marjorie found that the year 1946, which she had expected to be a bare year financially, was one of her better ones. Scribners' royalties amounted to approximately $14,000 and she netted $5,000 on her orange grove. Her literary production, however, had been slight. She was pleased that her story "Black Secret" was chosen to be included in the O. *Henry Memorial Award Prize Stories for 1946*, but aside from writing the movie script, the only new writing she had completed was an introduction for a collection of short stories by Katherine Mansfield.

The September 14, 1946, issue of *People's Voice* newspaper carried two stories that seemed to some readers to present a paradox. One story concerned the banning of *The Yearling* from the reading list of the James Monroe High School in the Bronx because it contained passages that denigrated Negroes. A few pages farther on was a review of Margaret Halsey's book *Color Blind*, which quoted Marjorie Kinnan Rawlings as condemning the book for perpetuating the hypocritical attitude of whites who would not grant blacks full equality. Had the author changed her attitude toward Negroes, readers wanted to know. If so, one of them suggested, she should make a repudiation of her "slandering" of them in *The Yearling*.

The editors of *People's Voice* presented the readers' questions to Marjorie, adding that a number of organizations had been insisting for some time that *The Yearling* was offensive to the Negro people and should not be used in public schools. The newspaper editors offered to publish any statement Marjorie cared to make. She wrote a letter to the editors and also to the National Equal Rights headquarters defending the language in her book and especially her use of "nigger" in dialogue as being accurate for the period just after the Civil War, which was the time of her book, and pointing out that it would have been an unpardonable anachronism to have used the word "Negro" in a book of this date. Her statement, which was published in the paper, said in part:

> *I approve with all my heart the policy of laying a tabu on the use of the word "nigger," not because any word is in itself offensive, since all words are only their connotations, but*

*because those who use the word in ordinary speech or casually
in print are those who have the wrong attitude not only toward
Negroes, but toward all of life and Christian living.*

During the Christmas holidays Marjorie lent her Cross Creek house
to Marcia Davenport and Jan Masaryk for a fortnight. Before leaving
for her cottage, she prepared the farmhouse with attention to every
detail that could add to their comfort and pleasure, and she left
Martha and Will Mickens and Idella with instructions to tend to
every need of her friends. In *Too Strong for Fantasy*, Marcia Davenport wrote of that visit, "It was a time lifted out of the stream of
reality. . . . Nowhere else could there have been the gentleness and
simple beauty of that place."

The harassed foreign minister, worn and weary from his struggles
against the German invaders, quickly got on friendly terms with
Marjorie's servants, who called him "Mister John." He wandered
into the kitchen to look into Idella's pots or to watch her make the
tiny crisp biscuits that were one of her specialities. And he spent a
morning sitting on a fence railing talking with Martha. When Marjorie's tamed (wild) Mallard ducks made their rackety funny noise,
Masaryk would tip his chin in their direction and say "Dooks!"
Marcia noted that months later in Prague, listening to noisy politi-
cians he would tip his chin and silently mouth "Dooks!"

In the thank you note he left at the Creek for Marjorie, he told
her that the strain of nine "not altogether idle years, the iron curtain
of duty, my country 'tis of thee, bombs, forced landings and many
other forms of tail chasing" were lifted by her generosity and understanding. He spoke of the atmosphere of silent healing that he
had found in her home. Without going any farther afield than to
pluck a tangerine, he had found himself sensing, appreciating, and
"breathing the creations of your heart, mind and love." He was
leaving her protective friendship, he told her, to revert to the "noisy
haphazard and often filthy arena of so-called world affairs," but he
was taking with him an "indestructible residue of lovingness, safety
and not shallow gratitude."

Her neighbors at the Creek were as friendly as before the trial,
Marjorie told Norman Berg. They were not people who changed

easily. "When they accepted me, it was for better or worse," she said. Although she and her neighbors had little of what was commonly known as "social contact," they were true friends. They would do anything in the world for her and she for them, and they all knew this. One of the best things about their relationships was that they could laugh at each other. She gave Berg two examples to prove this. A woman had stopped at the fruit stand in Cross Creek run by the Williams Family to ask about Marjorie Rawlings. "She thought you were next to Jesus," Hugh Williams told Marjorie. "My God, I hope you kept your mouths shut," she answered. When the Williamses stopped laughing, Hugh said, "We let her get away in the same dreamy state in which she arrived."

On another occasion, Tom Glisson told her that an "outsider" had remarked that he heard Mrs. Rawlings did a lot of drinking. Tom told the man, "Why, yes, she's real fond of it, and she's got more sense drunk than most people, sober." Both Tom and she thought that was funny, Marjorie told Berg, and more importantly, Tom felt free to repeat it to her.

The movie of *The Yearling* was released in the winter to good reception from critics and moviegoers. On January 23 it began a long New York City run at Radio City Music Hall, and the New York *Times* praised its vitality, zest, and sensitivity. When *Time* criticized the Technicolor as too brilliant, Marjorie wrote them that the "too blue sky" and "too bright sand" were made by God and not by MGM. But she admitted to friends that only the superb, sensitive acting of Gregory Peck and Jane Wyman made them acceptable to her as Penny and Ma Baxter, for "Penny was a little runty man and Ma was big as a barn."

The book, too, continued to flourish. In 1947 Marjorie signed contracts for French, German, Japanese, Korean, Hebrew, and Polish editions. And that spring in England, the B.B.C. began broadcasting a serial version of *The Yearling* in their "School Programme."

Marjorie wrote to Max that she was eager to get back to work on something she could get her teeth into. She thought she would prefer to work on the story of the Negro child, whom she was calling Calpurnia, rather than returning to the "*terrible* chore" of the book about the spiritual and inarticulate man who derived remotely from her own grandfather. She planned to stay at least two months at Cross Creek, until she really got the child's book going. "I am a lazy, shiftless bitch, and since I despise lazy, shiftless bitches, I intend to do something about it," she told Carol Brandt. Max encouraged her to go ahead with her "sad and lovely" story of a Negro child.

As usual, Norton was understanding. He knew she couldn't run over to Marineland frequently and still get her work done, although he did tempt her by telling her that Sally Rand and her girls were performing there and using boa constrictors in their act. Marjorie told a friend, "I try to put out of my mind the picture of darling Norton going into a cold, empty cottage at night, and leaving same in the morning! Once I get my book *going*, I can work anywhere, under any conditions, and then I can write and still be a Good Wife."

On March 18, 1947, she mailed a first draft of the book to Max for his comments. They had agreed on *The Secret River* as a title. She told him she had done the story pretty much in fairy tale style but asked if he thought the child protagonist should find a real river to remove an element of fantasy. Max told her it was a story of "great charm and delicacy but that he had considerable changes to suggest. He thought the river should be real—a little and deeply concealed one—that the child Calpurnia has never seen but has heard of. He wanted to see the story more developed, with Calpurnia having more experiences, and he wanted the character of Buggy-Horse (her dog) to be kept more on the scene. He had other suggestions about keeping more strictly to the child's point of view and about the use of Negro dialect. Some of his ideas concerned the mixture of reality and fantasy, which he compared to the "wild logic of Alice in Wonderland" and acknowledged was a hard kind of writing.

Marjorie told her editor that he had given her exactly the sort of guidance she had hoped for. She explained that she had avoided any trace of Negro dialect because she wanted to give complete dignity to all the Negroes in the story, with "no Uncle Remus or Little Black Sambo sort of stuff with its humorous, often deprecatory effect." Both she and Max thought that the story might be developed into a longer book.

In April Marjorie had a car accident that she was lucky did not stop her work permanently. The road department had, without her knowing of it, oiled the gravel road at Cross Creek. In a pouring rain, she skidded in her Oldsmobile and turned over twice, ploughing up some forty feet of posts and fencing. Idella, who was with her, suffered two broken ribs, but Marjorie miraculously escaped with only bad bruises. When she called Norton to tell him of the accident, he drove over and insisted on taking her back to St. Augustine. She was thankful to be there, for the next morning she was too stiff and sore to move. One side of her face, including her eye, was such an assortment of colors that Norton came in for a lot of kidding. As usual he had an answer, "The fact that I'm alive proves I didn't lay a hand on her."

The *Saturday Evening Post*, which had bought the movie story "A Family for Jock" and changed the title to "Mountain Prelude," began running it as a serial in April. Marjorie was embarrassed. "It is even worse, from a literary standpoint, than I remembered," she lamented to Max. However, when James Cabell wrote that he was reading the story with "increasing approval" and strongly recommended its publication as a novel, she felt better about it. Fundamentally, Cabell told her, it was a "good, humorous, wistful sound uncomplete story." He did have a couple of suggestions for revisions before it became a book. However much Marjorie appreciated Cabell's comments, she had no intention of approving the publication of the story in book form.

All during the spring of 1947, the pending decision of the Florida Supreme Court on Zelma's lawsuit was a worrisome nuisance. Phil May worked diligently on his presentation of the case, and Marjorie helped in every way she could. Margaret Mitchell was concerned about the case, not only because of her friendship with Marjorie, but also because of the legal precedent involved for writers. She wrote a four-page letter to Phil May, describing her own legal problems and those of other prominent writers. She told him she worked for years to be sure she didn't use real persons or houses but still had to "fight" with letters and statements against people who claimed she had used their ancestors named Rhett or their house as Tara, Twelve Oaks, or Aunt Pitty Pat's house.

On May 28, the Florida Supreme Court reversed the judgment of the Gainesville court, in a confusing compromise three-to-four decision. Associate Justice Charles Chillingworth wrote that the lawyers had conducted "warfare by pleading." He sternly criticized the "great mass of immaterial and prejudicial" testimonials on behalf of Marjorie as a novelist, community benefactor, and as a person of integrity. He also commented that Zelma failed to show she was damaged, but the evidence had established a wrongful invasion of her privacy. The court ruled that she was, therefore, entitled to compensatory and punitive damages, and a new trial was granted with the direction that the plaintiff recover nominal damages and all costs.

Phil May told Marjorie that the practical thing to do was to reach an agreement with Zelma and her lawyers and pay her off. Marjorie told Phil that she could not possibly agree to the easy way out, and that she would stand trial again. If she should lose, she told him, he was to move "Heaven and Earth" to get the case to the United States Supreme Court. Zelma and her lawyers applied to the Florida Supreme Court for a rehearing, which was denied. In June Phil told Marjorie that the next move was also Zelma's, and they could be sure that she and her lawyers had not given up hope of yet getting a substantial portion of the $100,000.

The Owen D. Young family had become increasingly close friends to Norton and Marjorie, and when she mentioned that she was thinking of going back to North Carolina that summer to get back to work on *The Sojourner*, they offered to lend her an old Dutch house, located near their summer home in Van Hornesville, New York. Marjorie was especially pleased to accept the offer because the countryside would be similar to that in her novel. Two days before time to leave for the trip, her new Oldsmobile was delivered, and Norton drove her and Moe and Benny to New York. They reached Van Hornesville quite late at night but found the Youngs still waiting up for them and insistent that they spend the night in the Youngs' house. Then Young handed Marjorie a telegram that had arrived for her from New York City. It was from Charles Scribner, who wired to tell her that Max Perkins was dead.

Marjorie's first feeling was of "unspeakable grief" at losing Max. This was followed by a feeling of utter frustration that she had made this long trek to begin work on a book that he would never see or be able to help her with. Her impulse was to go back to Florida with

Norton, until she thought how horrified Max would have been at such an attitude. She decided to stay and work all the harder. She quickly realized the irony of the fact that the place was perfect for working. Her old house was deep in woods, above a trout stream. To the south was an open field golden with buttercups, where deer came. A wood peewee had a nest with five eggs in it on her porch. The old house had a huge fireplace and modern conveniences. Roses and daylilies bloomed in the yard, and a wild raspberry thicket promised a good harvest. She and Moe and Benny were instantly at home. She gathered wild columbine and wild forget-me-nots, and when she took a bath found her skin covered with flower petals. She wrote Norton that she felt like a nymph—"if a nymph was ever of Rubenesque proportions." She had planned to lose weight, but the Van Hornesville cream, a necessity on the wild strawberries, was an obstacle. Mrs. Young lent her a maid and once a day drove or sent over mail, milk, cream, flowers, fresh fruit, and vegetables from the Youngs' garden.

Bernice Gilkyson wrote from New Hartford, Connecticut, of her feeling of pleasure in having Marjorie as a near neighbor, and of her grief at the loss of Max, with whom she had worked for twenty-seven years. She gave Marjorie the details of Max's death from pneumonia and told of attending his funeral in a small, white New England Church of the "Christopher Wren kind" on a sunny day. The service was Episcopalian, Bernice told her, and added that Max's comment on it would have been, "It was ritual, it was good and proper and what the world liked on such an occasion."

Marjorie thanked Bernice for her comforting letter, and in turn told her friend that she often dreamed of Max and woke up in tears. In one dream she went into his office and said to him, "I have terrible news for you. Max is dead." He smiled, and she said, "But you are Max. You know better than anyone what this means to all of us." In this dream Max exhibits the calm wisdom of the dead—which in his case had also been the calm wisdom he represented to Marjorie in life. Even beyond the grave she seems to still have had faith in Max as the wise counselor whose understanding of her need to believe in herself was greater than her own. But the fact that she woke in tears from these dreams indicated her shock and grief over loss.

Marjorie assured Charles Scribner that she would not be lured away from his publishing house now that Max was gone. The integrity of the establishment, she felt sure, was safe during his lifetime and during that of his son. She sent him a draft of *The Secret River* but still felt so indecisive about it that she finally told him that it would be a good idea to let "*The Secret River* flow underground for a while." In that way, something better might come of it, she told the publisher.

Marjorie was so charmed with the Van Hornesville area that she decided to buy a little house there. It was over one hundred years old, structurally sound, but needed replastering and papering, new plumbing and electricity. The house, which cost her only $1,200, came with eight acres of good land and woods and a view that included the upper end of Otsego Lake, James Fenimore Cooper's "Glimmer Glass." The Youngs themselves had bought and fixed up some of the fine old houses in Van Hornesville and so were able to help her find workmen to redo the house. She decided to have partitions taken out to turn tiny rooms into one large studio workroom and a combination country living-dining room, and to add bathrooms and closets.

The lawyer's fee for clearing the ancient title was high, but she was intrigued to find that her house stood on part of the original General Philip Schuyler grant. When she mentioned this at an antique shop in Cooperstown and asked jokingly if they had a portrait of General Schuyler, they told her no, but dug out of their attic an American primitive portrait that had been bought many years earlier from the old Schuyler mansion near Albany. When she saw that it was of Maria Bogardus Schuyler, Marjorie was startled. She wrote to her Kinnan aunts and found that her ancestor William Borgardus had had a daughter named Maria, and so did his younger brother. Therefore, the woman in the portrait was either Marjorie's aunt or cousin greatly removed. She decided the picture should go over the old square rosewood piano that she had bought with the house.

The activity connected with buying the house and the distractions of exploring the area were a relief from her struggle with *The Sojourner*, and from her grief over Max's death. Mrs. Young was determined that Marjorie enjoy herself. "Mrs. Young is 'mothering' me like all get-out, makes me go to parties, is reducing me, and my soul is not quite my own," Marjorie told Bee McNeil. However, she reported that she felt better physically and mentally. "The climate or something has made me over," she said. On one "peculiarly happy day" she went in the morning on a long walking expedition with Young's oldest son, another woman, and six assorted children to an area with caves and a beautiful waterfall.

In August she went to Saratoga with the Youngs. The Albany *Times Union* ran a picture of Marjorie chatting with Owen D. Young in his box at the race track; the headline read "Celebrities at Saratoga." She and Young had a mutual admiration for each other. She admired his accomplishments as a businessman who had served as chairman of the board of the General Electric Company from 1922 to 1939 and organized the Radio Corporation of America in 1919; and then had distinguished himself in government service by devising the Young Plan for the settlement of Germany's World War I debts and reparations. And he admired her talent as a writer and was amused by her wit and forthright personality. It pleased him very much that she was enchanted by Van Hornesville, the town of his birth.

Marjorie gave a Labor Day picnic for all the Young family, including grandchildren, plus a few of their friends—about twenty-two in all. She prepared jellied chicken, baked a big ham, and made ice cream. She had a local woman make four pots of baked beans, a huge pan of potato salad, four dozen raised rolls, and three dozen cupcakes. It turned out to be a warm and sunny day so they could enjoy being outdoors. Although she probably didn't realize it at the time, the event was the beginning of an annual tradition. It was the kind of thing she enjoyed planning and carrying out, but it took considerable time away from her work.

She did not associate exclusively with the wealthy families in the area; she made friends with the young farming couple who owned the land adjoining hers and eventually with many of the working people of the village. She happily immersed herself in domestic details, picking her own apples, Astrachans, and making apple pie—which didn't help her diet. She also made jelly from her crab apples and jelly from purple and greengage plums. She found she needed a new well dug, and when the well-digger finally hit rock and water gushed, it was "strangely thrilling" to her.

Julia Scribner came to visit a couple of times that summer and fall. In mid-October Norton came up for a week and spent another week in New York City to shop and see some plays before returning with Marjorie to St. Augustine. Marjorie was surprised and delighted at the transformation that had taken place in the beach cottage while she was gone. Norton had added a large studio workroom with fireplace, a dining room, another bathroom and dressing room, and enlarged the kitchen and maid's quarters. She had known that he was having work done on the house but not the extent of it. She was especially pleased with the new studio and felt it would be a place where she could work well. Cross Creek, too, which she still called "this enchanted place," came in for its share of face-lifting. She ordered a new gate and cedar fence posts and began searching the area for cypress shingles for the roof.

Soon after Christmas Arthur Kinnan came for a visit. He was getting over a divorce from his second wife and feeling nervous and high strung. Marjorie took him to Cross Creek, introduced him to her hunting and fishing friends, and did her best to distract him. He was still engaged in doing charter work in Alaska with his boat. In a letter to her shortly after the visit, Arthur offered insight into their inherited Kinnan dispositions, which he said were characterized by:

> an abominable nervous restlessness that can be soothed only with a strenuous treatment of mental and physical activity, and, unfortunately an activity of our creation. We all lack an inner governor of any sort. Even our complete awareness is of little help.

His analysis was confirmed by Marjorie's own explanation to Norman Berg in an apology she wrote after he found her in a black mood:

> I go up and down, you know, like a barometer in the Caribbean. . . . What happens is that a great deal of the time I am in contact with something quite indefinable, but possibly the cosmic warmth or the cosmic vitality. As long as the strong

current flows through me, I can work, I am aware. Then suddenly the lights go out. I am lost in despair.

The one person who could pull her out of her moods was Norton. In describing his patience with her and with the animals, she told Bee that although Norton wished Moe wouldn't wake him up every morning by pushing his wet nose into his face, and wished Benny wouldn't jump from the windowsill above their bed right onto his stomach in the middle of the night, still Norton "really likes all of us."

Even Norton, however, could not dispel the feeling of despair over Max Perkin's death. Marcia Davenport, like Marjorie, had at first reacted to the news by thinking she would never write another book. But she wrote to Marjorie that such a reaction would be a denial of all that Max had done for them. "So we know we will indeed write more books," Marcia wrote, "and that they will never be the books they could have been." In her heart Marjorie knew that this was the bitter truth.

CHAPTER 16

North with the Spring

During the winter of 1947 and 1948, Marjorie remained out of touch with the "cosmic warmth" she needed for hard creative work. She blamed her nervousness on being still jittery from minor surgery she had had in the fall. At any rate, she was unable to concentrate on creative work for more than a couple of hours a day. While repairs were being made to the Cross Creek farmhouse she stayed at the Crescent Beach cottage working on short stories she had begun the previous summer. The *New Yorker* and other magazines were asking for more of her short stories, and MGM was eager for her to do more Lassie stories. She told Carl Brandt that if they offered enough, she would take time out from her book to work on one or two ideas she had along this line.

Leonard Fiddia, in charge of the repairs at Cross Creek, painted the floors, replaced the screening, put down new linoleum in the kitchen and bathrooms, and put on the new cypress roof. He finished work on the house just in time for a succession of guests. Charles and Vera Scribner came for a couple of days and the Owen D. Youngs stayed at the Creek while Young took part in the three-day inaugural ceremonies for the new president of the University of Florida.

On the morning of March 11, Idella went to the mail box to get the mail and newspapers. She glanced at the front page of the paper and ran across the yard crying, "It's Mister John! Oh, Lord, it's Mister John!" The news of Jan Masaryk's death and his picture stared up at Marjorie. Fifteen months earlier he and Marcia Davenport had been at Cross Creek for a time that Marcia had told her was the only perfect happiness she had ever had. At Cross Creek Masaryk had written a speech he made a few days later in Cleveland, pleading for the world to come to its senses before it was too late. "Oh, let us have peace!" he had concluded, repeating the word "peace" in the eight languages he spoke.

Marjorie wrote to Marcia, who was devastated by Masaryk's death, and returned some of the letters Marcia had written her, as a gesture of consolation. Marcia told Marjorie, "Your understanding is not extraordinary because I would expect it of you. It would be extraordinary to anyone else." She also told Marjorie that she was a wonderful friend who went "among less than all the fingers of one hand in the very first rank."

When Bernice and Walter Gilkyson wrote that they were not coming to Florida as they usually did in the winter, Marjorie suspected that it was because they could not afford the high winter rentals. They were both working on books, and she offered to loan them her house at Cross Creek, retreating to Crescent Beach to work. The Gilkysons were happy to accept, and during the second week in March she spent several days preparing the cottage for them, checking linens, overseeing the cleaning, and stocking the pantry and refrigerator with food. After they were settled in, Bernice wrote such ecstatic letters describing the goings on at the Creek that Marjorie jokingly warned, "I'm afraid you are spending too much time with one-eyed hens, duck eggs, and kittens to get any work done."

Like other writers, before and after her, Marjorie was ahead of her times on some of the important issues just beginning to come to the attention of the general populace. This was especially true of her feelings and actions connected with the civil rights movement. During World War II steps had been taken in correcting discrimination in defense industries and segregation in the armed forces. After the war the National Association for the Advancement of Colored People pressured the Supreme Court into its decisive *Brown* v. *Board of Education of Topeka* (Kansas) (May 17, 1954) which declared that separate public schools for blacks and whites were inherently unequal and therefore unconstitutional. But this didn't happen until after Marjorie's death. In 1948 blacks were still riding at the back of buses, being refused service at cafés, and being educated in facilities that were definitely inferior.

At a social gathering at the Youngs', Marjorie fought a verbal battle with Florida's Governor Millard F. Caldwell, Jr. over the plan for state regional colleges. Branding it a way to wiggle out of the legal requirement of that time that equal educational facilities must be provided for Negroes, she insisted vehemently that undoubtedly the colleges for the blacks would not be as good as those for the whites. Owen Young came to the governor's rescue and broke up the argument. "He's about the only person in the world who can shut me up," Marjorie told a friend. Later she asked Young, "I wasn't being actually disagreeable, was I?" He answered, "No, but you *were* being extremely insistent!"

In April Marjorie accepted an invitation to speak on writing and using folk materials at the then all-black Fisk University in Nashville. She turned back her honorarium to the Fisk University scholarship fund and paid her own expenses for the train trip. In Nashville she stayed in the home of the university president, Charles S. Johnson. This was a public gesture of support for racial integration: Johnson was the first black president of Fisk, which had always had a mixed faculty. She met many blacks with "brilliant minds" and "charming personalities" on this trip. As usual she insisted on speaking informally and welcomed opportunities to talk with the students in small gatherings.

After her return from Fisk, Marjorie went into the hospital at St. Augustine for a hemorrhoidectomy. While she was under anesthetic, the surgeon noticed some cysts on the inside of her thighs and scooped them out also. It had not occurred to her to warn him that Presbyterian Medical Center doctors had advised her that the cysts were harmless and should be left alone. After she recovered from the hemorrhoid removal, she continued to have trouble with bleeding from the excised cysts. Furious, she thought of suing the "slash happy surgeon," but remembering her own painful experience in being sued and considering that she thought the doctor really "a nice guy," she refrained.

While recovering from the surgery, Marjorie reworked her short stories. And she corresponded with Phil May about the lawsuit. They were still considering taking the case to the U. S. Supreme Court, but friends like Owen D. Young warned that it would most likely not be accepted by that body. The aunts, Arthur, and numerous friends wrote advice. Marjorie was especially pleased and amused by Zora Neale Hurston's reaction. A mutual friend told her that Zora Neale had written:

> [T]he Baskins and I are very close and warm. I consider that a triumph because the justly celebrated Marjorie K. R. does not usually take to women. I could have saved all kinds of trouble if she had let me just plain kill that poor white trash that she took up so much time with, and who paid her for it by suing her for defamation of character. Marjorie Baskin does not even know the kinds of words that it would take to defame that woman. . . . You have no idea how good and kind M.K.R. is to everybody. The folks who work for her are really in soft. She no ways deserves what she got from that trash. She as a woman is a big wood while that strumpet is not even good brush. If you hear of the tramp getting a heavy load of rock salt and fat-back in her rump, and I happen to be in Fla. at the time, you will know who loaded the shell, but you need not get confidential with the police.

In late June Marjorie made a short visit to her "yankee house" to check on the renovations. She found that the plumber, carpenter, and painter had been held up by the electrician, who had not finished the wiring. She shopped for rugs, draperies, and furniture and planned to return in August when the workmen would be finished.

Shortly before she started north, the adventurous Benny was killed by a rattlesnake. Her friends, the Clifford Lyons, who had moved to Chapel Hill, North Carolina, sent her a Siamese kitten by air. She named him Uki, and told Bernice Gilkyson that he was marvelous but she didn't love him "terribly" as she had Benny. "But I can feel the symptoms stealing over me," she admitted.

Reluctantly Marjorie had decided not to pursue the lawsuit further, and she returned to Florida to await the final verdict. On August 9, 1948, more than five and a half years after Zelma filed her lawsuit, Judge Murphree rendered the final verdict in the case: "It is considered by the court that the plaintiff recover of the defendants the sum of one dollar together with the costs in this behalf expended, now taxed in the sum of $1,050.10." Marjorie was furious at the members of the Florida Supreme Court who "took a small-range point of view." Bitterly, she wrote to "Their Honors, THE FLORIDA SUPREME COURT," telling them she contemplated continuing her autobiographical study of her life in the locale of the book. "I am wondering if it is pertinent or impertinent for me to ask Your Honors' advice as to whether it is legally permissible to write such a book of personal memoirs. If the Florida law requires that I get permission in advance from each of the individuals concerned in my life story, or to pay, or agree to pay, something to each of them, it will make an almost impossible undertaking."

Marjorie assured Phil May that no one could have done a more superb job, or kept the business on a higher plane, than he. Her only reproaches were for herself, for not fighting it through to the bitter end. But she told her lawyer, she was becoming "almost dangerously frustrated at not getting my book going." Years more of conflict might make the book impossible to do at all. "And without my writing, I am nothing." A total reckoning by Marjorie and Norton of the monetary cost of the lawsuit was around $18,000. The emotional and physical toll on Marjorie was incalculable, and may have been a factor in her early death.

The last week in August Marjorie drove to Van Hornesville with Idella and Moe and Uki. Her house was finished, and she energetically set about completing her purchase of furnishings for it, using her natural flair for decorating. Every place she lived, from the tiny room on Morningside Drive in New York to Cross Creek to the beach cottage to the Yankee house, she made uniquely her own. She enjoyed making the furnishings suit the personality of the dwelling. Cross Creek was furnished in a comfortable, country style, with her special touches such as wooden bowls over the light bulbs to create indirect lighting. The beach cottage was bright and modern. The Yankee house needed antiques to fit its age and dignity. She enjoyed shopping for Hitchcock chairs; a Hepplewhite table; Boston rockers; an antique pine spice chest; pine tavern chairs; cherry and pine chests, stands, and tables; and antique china and glassware. And she indulged her taste for first edition Audubon prints in antique frames.

When Bee McNeil came for a visit in September she was enchanted with the house. She wrote Marjorie: "As long as I live I'll never forget opening that dining room door and seeing that bright fire and the warm red of the wall paper and the table laid with the blue china for breakfast and that beautiful Moe on the floor—posing. It was absolutely perfect."

After Bee left, Marjorie had a harrowing experience with Uki. She had gone to bed to read, and when the cat didn't come in after Idella had called him repeatedly, Marjorie got up to find him. Wearing bedroom slippers, a pink satin nightgown, and a thin silk bed jacket, she went out. Uki answered her calls from far away in an anguished voice. With a dim flashlight, candles, and matches, she and Idella and Moe set out to locate the cat. He turned out to be up in a tree on the steep slope of Mt. Tom, a short distance from the house. Marjorie worked her way up to him through fallen tree trunks, rocks, and occasional wet holes. When the flickering flashlight picked Uki out, crouched in the crotch of a tree, Marjorie urged Moe up to the tree and shined the light on him. Reassured by the appearance of Moe, Uki jumped down and made his way to Marjorie. She described the trip down the slope to Norton:

Uki stayed right behind me as I struggled down again. Moe slid down ahead of us. Without much to hang on to I simply could not walk or creep down, and did most of it on my bare rear. The bedroom slippers caught in the brush, and the train of the nightgown got caught in my heels and the flash got fainter and fainter. It was eleven when we got to the field, I panting with exertion and Uki with terror.

After changing gowns, she got into bed and Uki thankfully snuggled next to her. In the morning she found that her mountain-climbing gown was muddy and torn, with blood all across the back. She felt good, though, she told Norton, to know that she could still do a difficult physical thing when necessary.

Marjorie's mental difficulty that fall was with the second Lassie story for MGM. It involved the K-9's, the World War II dogs that carried messages and medical supplies under fire and located wounded soldiers on battlefields. Her working title was *A Bad Name Dog*, and the plot involved the betrayal of a man by his dog. Carl Brandt came up to Van Hornesville to discuss the story with her. She found his suggestions helpful and agreed with his idea of submitting it to the *Saturday Evening Post* as well as to MGM. When the story was finished, both the *Post* and MGM rejected it. The Hollywood producers reported that having already made a picture about rehabilitated war dogs, they were not much interested in the subject, and also they found the characters one-dimensional. The *Post* editors said the story lacked the warmth of situation and character that they had liked so much in *Mountain Prelude* and felt the story was contrived. Marjorie shrugged off the *Post's* rejection, reminding Carl Brandt, "Well they turned down *The Yearling.* . . ."

The MGM rejection of the story they had solicited may have added to her explosive fury over their production of *Mountain Prelude*, which they retitled *Sun in the Morning*. "Everything is ruined, everything is spoiled," she told Carl in an angry letter. In her script she had had the perfect reason for the main character, a widow, to "go neurotic" when her son is killed in an impromptu airplane flight since his father had also been killed in a plane crash. The Hollywood script rewriters had the boy killed by a passing bus. The whole "Goddamned thing," Marjorie told Carl, was based on the woman's being a composer and concert pianist so that she realizes the boy's talent as a pianist. The woman's successful composition was "Mountain Prelude," based on a mountain song or ballad that the boy plays on his harmonica. "What does MGM do?????" Marjorie stormed, "They ring in Jeanette MacDonald, and have a singer instead of a composer-pianist, and the dialogue in the final script made me sick at my stomach."

But, Marjorie said, the main thing that she wanted to tell Carl was that she had wasted three years by putting aside her creative work to do *Mountain Prelude* and *A Bad Name Dog,* and she did not intend to do any more "commercial" work. She had not *"quite"* prostituted herself, she told her agent, but she had come close to it, and she asked him not to torment her about doing "salable" things.

In order to give Marjorie time to cool off after writing impulsive "mad" letters (often after having a few drinks), Norton tried to intercept them to give her a chance to write in a calmer mood. Because of their frequent separations, some of her red-hot missives got by him, and then she would sometimes follow up with a disarming letter of apology. So Carl Brandt was probably not surprised to receive another letter two days later asking his forgiveness if her "quite horrible letter" had offended him. If *A Bad Name Dog* could be made usable for the studio, she was willing to "tuck my tail between my legs and have another try at it." And she admitted that she might have been rationalizing about her procrastination on *The Sojourner.* Her conception of the novel had been constantly changing as she altered the structure, the plot, and some of the characters, but never the motif. Evidently the book was not quite ready to be born, she told Carl, for nothing can hold up a birth that is ripe for delivery.

A writing task that Marjorie considered important enough to devote some time to in 1948 was to do an article for the annual supplement to the *Book of Knowledge.* In the article titled "Writing as a Career" she apparently had her recent experiences still in mind, for she defined two kinds of writers: one, she said is composed of those who write to make a living. Calling this kind of writing a trade or a business, she compared it to bricklaying or stenography. The second kind of writer she defined as writing out of the "inner depths of his heart." This writer writes because life seems tremendously exciting, because it seems beautiful or sad, because he burns to express in words the things that he sees and feels. He writes when he is cold and hungry, although he could keep warm and well-fed in some other kind of work. He writes even when everyone tells him that his work is of no account, when magazines refuse his stories and no publisher will consider his books. "He writes because he must. It is his life."

Sometimes, Marjorie told her young readers, creative writing flows like a river, and sometimes it is like digging a deep well with a teaspoon. She answered a series of questions that were most frequently asked her by aspiring writers and gave practical advice for submitting work to publishers. A bit of serendipity for having all of this information published in a readily available form was that from then on she could refer young writers, with their endlessly repetitive questions, to it.

Beginning about the middle of September Marjorie suffered for four weeks with diverticulitis. It was the longest siege she had ever had, and Norton insisted on coming up to Van Hornesville to take her to New York to see Dr. Atchley. Then he took the animals with him and left her free to take the train back to Florida after treatment had restored her strength.

By mid-November she was back at Cross Creek working with a crew of six helpers to get the house in order for the Gilkysons, to whom she was lending it again for the whole winter and spring. They hung new curtains and planted roses and prepared for the winter garden, and Marjorie longed to stay in her old home. "All my pettishness has melted away under the old spell, and I am sick at heart at having to leave," she told Phil May. She also told him that she had been making notes for a sequel to *Cross Creek*. Many of them were sad, since there had been nearly a dozen deaths since the book was written. For this reason and perhaps because she could not write with her former spontaneity about her neighbors since the lawsuit, *Cross Creek II* remained an unfinished project.

For Christmas Marjorie sent flowers to Marcia Davenport in New York. Marcia's letters were still despondent, and she told Marjorie that the flowers were the only rift in the gloom of her Christmas. Marjorie told Carl Brandt that she did not think Marcia was grateful enough for having had her wonderful experience with Jan Masaryk. She thought, too, that he would have liked it that his death "crystallized, as nothing else could have done, almost a world-feeling, a new consciousness, of just what Communism means to the rest of us."

Norton gave her three Christmas gifts, wrapped as though for mailing. In answer to her query, "What the hell?" he said, "Love, I never know where you're going to be, so I was prepared." The package addressed to "Mrs. Norton Baskin" at St. Augustine contained a black purse to go with her silk suit. The one addressed to "Marjorie Kinnan Rawlings" at Cross Creek contained china cats for her collection; and the one addressed to "Marjorie Kinnan Rawlings Baskin" at Van Hornesville held a pair of crystal vases.

On January 1, 1949, one of the short stories that Marjorie had written the previous year appeared in the *Saturday Evening Post.* Marjorie had called it "The Snow-Apple Tree," but the *Post* editors changed the title to "The Friendship." It was a simple, straightforward story of a little boy's friendship with a policeman and what he learns about selfishness from that relationship. It was as far removed in style, tone, and theme from her subtle and sophisticated *New Yorker* stories as could be: as different in mood as William Blake's "Songs of Innocence" are from his "Songs of Experience."

Out of her desperate need after Max's death, Marjorie had turned to friends like Carl Brandt and Norman Berg (Macmillan's Southeast representative) to bounce her ideas off and to discuss her literary and sometimes her personal frustrations with. She summed up for Berg her "alibis" for not being further along on *The Sojourner*: the crushing lawsuit; Norton's being overseas so that she felt that she must write him fully, give him of herself every day in her letters; a series of operations that sapped her nervous energy; and the death of Max Perkins, which still seemed too much to be borne. One night when Norton phoned asking if she wanted to go to a movie, she said no, she was sorting out Max Perkins's letters to her from 1930 through 1947. Norton said, "I know you're having fun." She answered, "No, my heart is breaking." She had a total of 178 letters from Max.

On February 14, Norman Berg wrote to Marjorie that he was very much concerned about her. On a visit in January he had found her composed, but now she seemed nervous, worried, and fatigued again. "You can not stand much more of the mental and physical beating that you are now taking," he warned her. Although this letter didn't mention the fact that she was now drinking heavily, she knew that was what he was referring to.

"I have known for some time that I was putting myself in serious danger," she told him. "I may be fooling myself in thinking that the excessive drinking is the effect, and not the cause, of my mental and emotional disturbance—at any rate, it is probably the most definite hindrance to some sort of stability." Writing was "more of an anguish than ever." Doing the two Hollywood stories had made her hypercritical of her serious work. "I shrink back in horror from every phrase, every line, that does not go deep. Not a word satisfies me that is not pure and simple and true."

It had been ten years since the publication of *The Yearling* and seven since her last book, *Cross Creek Cookery*. Since then she had published only a few short stories and articles. Increasingly, she could do hard creative work for briefer periods. She thought a change of scene would help and planned to go to Van Hornesville in early spring and stay into late autumn. This was the beginning of a pattern in which she would spend winters in Florida and the rest of the year in Van Hornesville. The greatest hardship was the long months of separation from Norton. But it was the way she had thought their marriage would be: "separate lives and professions but with a sense of security, of oneness from having formally acknowledged our bond." Someday in the distant future, she told Norman Berg, she envisioned their having a fine, quiet time together, traveling to strange places, with the Creek as headquarters. "Please do not worry about me," she told Berg, "I go down for the count again and again, but I have a strangely tough core. . . ."

One night at a party in St. Augustine, Marjorie's alter ego, Dora Rolley, took over and put her temporarily in bad grace with James Cabell. She discovered in her coat pocket a silk stocking that she had taken in to town to try to match. On a sudden, irresistible impulse she slipped it into Cabell's coat pocket with a length hanging down. Priscilla, Cabell's wife, was amused as were the guests who watched the dignified and impeccably moral author walk around with the stocking dangling from his coat. When he finally learned of the practical joke, Cabell was not amused. The next day Marjorie wrote him a letter of apology, telling him she would be crushed to have offended him. And she offered to go in "sack cloth ashes" for as long as he wished. Cabell forgave her, and the friendship was as close as ever. Norton and Marjorie planned to entertain James Cabell with cocktails and a buffet dinner on April 14, in honor of his fiftieth book, which he dedicated to Norton, and of his seventieth birthday. But on March 28, Priscilla Cabell was taken to the hospital in St. Augustine very ill, and a few days later she died and Cabell returned to Richmond.

A news story that interested Marjorie deeply in the spring of 1949 was the Chambers-Hiss debate, for she remembered Whittaker Chambers coming to Cross Creek to interview her for a *Time* magazine story in 1942. Now he was in the public spotlight because he supplied evidence to the House Committee on Un-American Activities that eventually led a federal court to convict Alger Hiss of perjury in testifying falsely that he had not passed State Department documents to Chambers. In his testimony before the committee Chambers confessed to having been a courier for a Communist spy organization in Washington and said that Hiss had been a member of the same ring.

Marjorie recalled that after their interview at Cross Creek, she had taken him over to St. Augustine where he disappeared on Sunday morning. Later he told her he had gone to the Catholic Cathedral to pray for a friend. She wondered if the friend might not have been Alger Hiss. She admired Chambers's writing, and thought his story on Mary Anderson in *Time* one of the "loveliest and most Christian" stories she had ever seen. When *Time* ran a story saying that Chambers had blackened his own character, Marjorie wrote to the editors to pay tribute to Chambers's integrity. The editors responded that they had meant that no matter how well his friends might still think of Chambers, in the eyes of the public the exposure of his private life "does not make pleasant reading."

Early in May Marjorie drove to Van Hornesville in her Oldsmobile with Idella and her animals. She reached the Yankee house completely exhausted, but the next morning she revived when she saw the lilacs putting on their blooms, the peonies in bud, and all the other signs of spring. And she set herself to make yet another beginning on *The Sojourner*.

In June when Norton came for a long stay, she gave a party and square dance for all the men who had worked to restore her house and garden and their families—almost forty people. She and Idella swept and scrubbed the upper floor of the old hop house in the back of her property for the dance. The buffet, which was set up in the dining room, included two baked hams, jellied tongue, potato salad, hot rolls and ice cream and cake. The bar for beer and soft drinks was in the woodshed. She hired a fiddler and a guitar player and a three-hundred-pound caller. The workmen and their families took a great pride in the proper restoration of the old house. The party was a huge success, Marjorie told Norman Berg, "Thanks a great deal to Norton's charm and gayety."

After Norton left, Marjorie drove to New York and brought Julia Scribner back for a visit. Norman Berg and his wife, Julie, also came for a few days. When alone, Marjorie did her writing in the morning, always her best time, and in the afternoons she gardened and made jams and jellies from the wild currants, gooseberries, and raspberries.

In June she read in the papers of the death by stroke of her beloved Sigrid Undset. In her last letter to Sigrid, Marjorie had urged her friend to come to the Creek to write, where she could have her own working quarters and all the peace and quiet she needed. Since Sigrid's return to Norway, Marjorie had periodically sent her boxes with items still scarce in Europe, such as rice, sugar, coffee, dried fruits, canned foods, chocolate, and nylons. Sigrid was especially grateful for the good-smelling soaps Marjorie sent, as the Norwegian soap "smelled of fish oil." Marjorie told Norman Berg that Sigrid's death struck her in a different way from that of Max Perkins. "The loss is that of a great friend and a great woman."

By the end of July Marjorie had completed three chapters of *The Sojourner*. Once John Steinbeck had asked her, "Do you find that the job gets more difficult as you go on?" At this point she could have answered truly that it did. Nothing she wrote seemed good enough to her. In a letter written on July 27 to Norman Berg, she said, "Oh Norman, I have been in such anguish. I came closer to killing myself than ever before, except once, last Sunday night. I have always felt that without my writing, I was nothing. And the writing was going so badly. But I made myself wait, and now it is going better."

The topic of suicide had always fascinated Marjorie, and she avidly discussed it with other writers like Fitzgerald and Tom Wolfe. At one time she planned to have Ase Linden, her protagonist in *The Sojourner*, commit suicide but thought better of it. However, death was very much on her mind as she wrote the book, and she sent Norman Berg a copy of notes she made for the book within a period of a few days. Some of them said:

> *It is not death that kills us, but life.*
> *We are done to death by life.*
> *Life is strong stuff, some of us can bear more of it than others.*
> *It is not that death comes, but that life leaves.*
> *There are two sorts of the living dead. Life has forgotten to inform the dull bodies that it (life) is elsewhere. And there are vital bodies, full of the joy of living, with no minds, and life has forgotten to tell these bodies that it is there, in them.*
> *The timid people, saying, "Life here I am," but they are bypassed.*
> *Life, a tidal river returning to the sea ———.*

Undoubtedly, her heavy drinking bouts during this period of her life contributed to her suicidal depression. She blamed the drinking on her frustration with her work, but it seems more likely that it was a large part of the cause—and not the effect. The work went unevenly, and she was torn between exaltation when a few paragraphs seemed right and deepest despair when nothing seemed to go right. Norton, who sympathized helplessly with her agony, said she worked not in an ivory tower but in an "ivory dungeon." It was a shame, he told her, that no one has "invented a twilight-sleep for book-bearing."

After her death, Norton expressed his opinion that she used liquor as a prescription for whatever affected her: if she was sad, she needed a drink; if she was happy, she needed a drink; if her work was going well, she had a drink to celebrate; if badly, she had a drink for comfort; likewise if she was too hot or too cold or too tired. He did not believe that she was ever an alcoholic, nor did many others who knew her. However, from the early days of her marriage to Chuck, she was a heavy drinker at times. As she grew older and suffered more from depression, the drinking episodes increased in frequency.

She never learned the limits of her capacity for liquor, and sometimes the results were disastrous.

One day that summer she stopped in at the Youngs', had some drinks with them, and asked them to come home to dinner with her. As their cook had been canning all day, the invitation was welcomed. By the time Idella had a rib roast dinner ready, Marjorie had tossed off quite a few more drinks with Young. The minute they sat down at the table she realized she'd never make it through the meal. "I'm terribly sorry, you'll have to excuse me, I have to go to bed, I'm drunk," she told them. Idella told her the rest of the story the next day, for that was as much as Marjorie remembered of the evening. The silent Youngs were cutting into their beef when they heard a great thump on the bedroom floor above. They told Idella to put down the broccoli with hollandaise she was passing and run up to see to their hostess. Idella found Marjorie sitting naked on the floor. When she entered the room, Marjorie gathered her slip across her front and said, "I'm quite all right."

Idella said, "Here's your nightgown on the chair. I'll bring it."

Marjorie answered haughtily, "Thank you, I can put on my own nightgown," and she did. Idella went downstairs and informed the Youngs with equal dignity that Marjorie was "quite all right." The next day Marjorie was ashamed to face the Youngs and put some ashes and a scrap of burlap in an envelope with a note, "These are samples of my new fall costume."

In August, Marjorie was shocked to hear of the death of another friend, Margaret Mitchell, who was struck by a taxi while crossing Peachtree Street in Atlanta. The two women had had much in common, and one of the private charities they each quietly attended to was to take care of the Czech translator who had worked with *Gone With the Wind* and *The Yearling*. Each of them sent money and CARE packages to the man, who was ill with tuberculosis in a sanatorium in Switzerland.

Marjorie once told Norman Berg that he was like Max Perkins in his deep concern that her writing should be the very best she was capable of and in his willingness to act as a critic in any capacity he was capable of. And also like Max, he sent her the latest books from his publishing house (Macmillan) and discussed them with her in lengthy letters. Marjorie sometimes sent him the poems she wrote as a relief from the grinding toil of writing prose. When she showed Norman some of the pages of *The Sojourner*, and he said that the book seemed to be progressing "nicely," she fired back:

> *How dare you use such an innocuous word as "nicely"?????*
> *The book progresses obscenely, through mud and mire, at the moment, it is false, but I shall make it true in the end if it kills me, and it well may.*

She agreed, impatiently, with Norman that the book was good, but lamented that she had lost her touch. "I want to make magic," she told him. But it didn't come often enough—only one sentence, perhaps, in a whole chapter. She knew she had a "most terrific job" of rewriting ahead of her. In gratitude for Berg's encouragement and helpful suggestions, she sent him and his wife, Julie, an old upright piano for their new farm home in Dunwoody, Georgia.

Late in the summer Marjorie issued a caveat to Carl Brandt: "I am at last making reasonably satisfactory progress on my book. Just don't ask any questions, don't suggest a movie tie-in, leave me alone for another six months, like the good friend you are. . . ." Her plan was to spend the winter writing at Cross Creek. During October Marjorie worked so hard at her writing that she was on the point of collapse when Norton arrived for a visit and to drive her home. But she willingly put away her typewriter and after two carefree weeks of play, they drove back to Crescent Beach. Soon after their return, Marjorie suffered an acute intestinal attack, with her temperature at times rising to 103°. It was almost two weeks before she felt well enough to travel to Cross Creek. By contrast with the Yankee house the old farmhouse was shabby, but as always the atmosphere comforted her.

Christmas entertainments and farm activities kept Marjorie away from her writing. After hog killing at Cross Creek, she made sausage, scrapple, liver paste, and lard. Two of Marjorie's Christmas gifts were purses. Louise Young, who gave her husband a $3.98 clip-on ring on his seventy-fifth birthday, gave Marjorie an expensive silver brocade evening bag, and Norton gave her the largest alligator hide bag he could find at the Alligator Farm near St. Augustine. In St. Augustine, she and Norton frequently played bridge with the Youngs, and they went to a party to help the Youngs housewarm the new addition to their house. There were many other parties, and in one way or another, Marjorie managed not to touch her manuscript during the months of November and December.

When Leonard Fiddia's little daughter died, Marjorie went to the funeral. A few days later, she took a turkey and all the accompaniments to the Scrub and had dinner with Miss Piety and Leonard. She told Norman Berg, "I don't know what inferiority of character is involved, that I am so happy in elemental places and with elemental people. I do know that so-called 'success' is a curse."

The elements of nature also continued to delight her. She found electrical storms with lightning playing all around and thunder rolling in deep bass tones "magnificent." Her love of animals and reverence for life remained unchanged. In *Cross Creek* she had said, "We were bred of the earth before we were born of our mothers. . . . [S]omething is shrivelled in a man's heart when he turns away from it and concerns himself only with the affairs of men." Julia Scribner had introduced her to Albert Schweitzer several years earlier, and while Marjorie found him saintly and moving, she thought his reverence for life was carried to "absurd lengths." She told Norman Berg, "While I am a tormented soul, with devils in me of which Schweitzer never dreamed, I think I am closer to the truth in this respect than he."

In spite of the struggle she was having with her own writing, Marjorie found time to actively encourage and abet the writing careers of three newly made young friends. Norman Berg brought an aspiring writer, Martin Dibner, to Cross Creek to meet her. After four bad years during the war—two aboard the U.S.S. *Richmond*, an outmoded cruiser in the Aleutians, and two aboard the U.S.S. *Ticonderoga*, a new aircraft carrier that was kamikazied, he was seeking refuge in Florida. Marjorie was impressed by his intellect and talent. She offered him counsel, professional expertise, lavish encouragement, and friendship. He planned to write a trilogy based on his navy experiences, and while he worked on the first book, *The Deep Six*, she lent him the farmhouse at Cross Creek as a sanctuary for several months. A gifted painter and sculptor as well as a writer, Dibner gave her a statue titled "Madonna," which she cherished and gave a place of honor in the beach cottage.

Another protégé was Gene Baroff, who later used the name Baro. A professor in the humanities at the University of Florida, he was huge in size, a half-Russian New Yorker, whose prickly personality at first puzzled Marjorie and caused her to feel ambivalent about him. But she and Norton became friends with him, and she sent him to meet Carl Brandt and also wrote to Charles Scribner about Baro's potential as a writer.

Pearl Primus, a black professional dancer, who wanted to be a writer, was also helped substantially by Marjorie. As a child Pearl had walked from 68th to 30th streets in New York for weeks in order to save her ten-cent bus fare to buy her first book, *The Yearling*. With Marjorie's help, Pearl won a grant that enabled her to go to Africa to study the native dances. At the meeting in which she was being interviewed before receiving the grant, she was so fascinated by the author of *The Yearling* that she could hardly concentrate on the conversation. She recorded her impression:

> [M]y eyes were reading this woman—following the hand which lit too many cigarettes, noticing the little tightness about the lips, brightness of eyes—hoarse laugh broken by cough—she was a mighty ocean of inspiration and love. . . .

When Pearl wrote from Africa that she was ill with malaria, anemic, and suffering with parasites acquired from primitive living conditions, Marjorie cabled her money to enable her to get back to the States. "I don't know when a truly creative personality has stirred me so deeply," Marjorie told Berg. She planned to help Pearl write a book of her experiences and suggested to him that Macmillan might want to publish it.

CHAPTER · 17

The Ivory Dungeon

Marjorie was well aware of her constitutional inability to do things in moderation, a characteristic she shared with her brother Arthur. This trait enhanced her enjoyment of the world and was the ferment that kept her striving for perfection in her writing. Late in January of 1950 she reported to Norman Berg that she was working on *The Sojourner* with great concentration and maintaining a strict, self-set schedule, turning out at least a thousand words a day. She had not had a drink for several weeks and thought she might be through with it forever. "I neither want nor miss it," she told Berg.

A week later two crises in her life drove her back to the bottle. First Moe made the mistake of lunging at a strange country cat in the same way he playfully lunged at Uki. The cat rose up in fury, and Moe in his hasty retreat caught his leg on a barbed-wire fence and cut a terrible gash in it. Norman Berg and his father happened to be visiting, and they helped Marjorie stop the bleeding and get Moe to a veterinarian. The wound, which exposed the largest leg vein, required many stitches.

The second accident occurred when Idella's husband was badly burned while lighting a leaking gas heater. Marjorie was very concerned about Bernard, and she was also deprived of Idella's soothing presence and help. To ease her tension, Marjorie went on a drinking spree that began at the beach cottage and ended up at Cross Creek. When Gene Baro and a friend showed up for dinner that evening, she went into the kitchen with Gene, who did most of the cooking. By the time the meal was ready, she knew that her equilibrium and equanimity were sufficient only to get her to bed, where she immediately went to sleep. The young men ate dinner, washed the dishes, and slipped away, leaving a thank-you note for her. The next day she was only faintly shaky, and unrepentant. "The binge was the only thing that would have relaxed me," she told Berg. "If Moe and Bernard get into trouble again, I shall probably do the same over again, with absolutely no sense of guilt."

Marjorie used a part-time secretary in St. Augustine to help her keep up with her business and fan mail and hoped to finish the first draft of her book by the first of May. Then she planned to let Scribners see it and to move to Van Hornesville for the summer. But the writing continued to be difficult, and she had to change her schedule. She told Bernice Gilkyson:

> I should not be in such anguish if Max were here. He could have told me long ago whether or not I am on the right track, and there is absolutely no one else I could allow to see unfinished work. And even when it's done, there's no one I trust for an honest answer as we trusted Max. I have a list of questions ready to make out, as he might have asked them, and may be obliged to give the answers myself. I have lost all faith in my creative ability, yet there is nothing for it but to go on.

Clifford Lyons and others connected with the University of Florida persuaded Marjorie to give the university the original manuscripts of *The Yearling* and *Cross Creek*, and she revised her will to provide that her other papers and letters would come to the university after her death. On March 31, a new library was to be dedicated at the school, and it was decided that the announcement of her gifts should be made then. She agreed to speak for ten minutes, knowing that she would suffer almost as much over this short talk as over one of an hour. The Youngs and Norton came to Gainesville to attend the ceremonies, which began with a luncheon at the home of the university president, Dr. J. Hillis Miller, and ended with drinks and talk for the Youngs, Gene Baro, Norton and Marjorie at Cross Creek, with everyone staying overnight there.

When *Publishers Weekly* wired to ask that Marjorie review the collection of Max Perkins's letters, *Editor to Author*, she gladly undertook the task. John Hall Wheelock, Perkins's long-time associate at Scribners, selected the letters from the company's files and wrote the introduction to the book. He included more of Perkins's letters to Marjorie than to any other authors with the exceptions of Wolfe, Hemingway, and Fitzgerald. In her review Marjorie said:

> *Several of us who had the privilege of his counsel have asked one another, 'What was it that he gave us?' We agreed that his special gift was his ability, as creative as that of the author himself, to enter into the mind of the individual writer, to understand what that writer was attempting to do and to say, to direct all criticism and all help toward that writer's own best expression, whether Max himself agreed or not.*

She thought that the Perkins letters should become required reading for other editors and for troubled creative writers anywhere. "He cannot but help them all, as he helped three generations of Scribner authors, infinitely more than he would ever have admitted," she wrote. The review appeared in *Publishers Weekly* of April 1, 1950, under the title, "Portrait of a Magnificent Editor as Seen in His Letters."

Marjorie was gratified when her matchmaking talent resulted in a marriage that spring. She had become friends with Margaret Freeman, who had worked in the publishing business in New York and who had helped Marjorie locate some of the furnishings for her Yankee house. Now Marjorie decided that Margaret would make a good second wife for the lonely James Branch Cabell. Margaret and James were friends, but the idea of a romance did not seem to occur to the seventy-year-old author. Marjorie and Norton were fond of

Ballard, the retarded son of Cabell. Ballard, who was thirty-five, had the mind of an eight- or nine-year old, and he mimicked the mannerisms and dignified deportment of his famous father, who was devoted to him. Marjorie invited Margaret Freeman to come to St. Augustine at a time when she knew Cabell and Ballard would be there, and she and Norton became the babysitters for Ballard in order to give Cabell and Margaret leisure to do their courting. The result was that in April of 1950, the Baskins received an announcement that read:

> *Ballard C. Cabell and Mr. James Branch Cabell*
> *are happy to announce the*
> *wedding of*
> *James Branch Cabell and Margaret Freeman*

The date of the wedding was a year and a day after the death of Priscilla, Cabell's first wife. The tight social group of gray-haired ladies who lived at the Buckingham Hotel where James and Priscilla had stayed in the winters did not approve what they felt was too hasty a remarriage. They banded together and decided they would not receive the upstart new Mrs. Cabell. But Marjorie plotted to change the situation. She planned a tea for Margaret and invited all the ladies from the Buckingham and the crème de la crème of St. Augustine society. She got 100 percent acceptance with five requests to bring extra guests. After that reception, which was held in the Castle Warden, Margaret Freeman Cabell was not only accepted but eagerly sought after by St. Augustine society. Cabell told Marjorie that, although it was difficult to play Romeo at his age, he was truly grateful for her help. Since the stocking incident, most of his letters to her were addressed to "My Dear Hellion."

Affairs at the Creek, too, occupied Marjorie's time. She bought two hundred new orange trees to bring her grove to full production. She left the work of setting them out and watching over them to Chet Crosby, her faithful grove man. For a week she had as a guest Buddy Bass, the ten-year-old son of one of her neighbors. The father of the family was slowly dying from multiple sclerosis. Marjorie sent him to the Duke University medical clinic to make sure the diagnosis was correct, and his condition was confirmed by the Duke doctors. The mother ran a fish camp and café at Lochloosa and cared for her ill husband and their three boys. During Buddy's stay, Marjorie found that little boys not only collect dirt but also other little boys. She found them an interesting study, but when Buddy announced that he would like to stay with her permanently, she persuaded him he must return to his family.

On April 12 a terrible tragedy took the life of Marjorie's nearest Cross Creek neighbor. The Tom Glissons had been among the first friends Marjorie and Chuck had made at the Creek. The friendship had its ups and downs but in the end was steadfast. Marjorie enjoyed visiting with Tom's wife and was fond of his children. Tom had been planning to build a new house and had gone with his eldest son to look at the property. In his truck were two jugs that had held Coca-Cola syrup—one containing drinking water and the other a poison for killing trees. He took a drink of the poison instead of the water, spit it out, and rinsed his mouth with the water. The son begged Tom to take an emetic, but Tom laughed and refused. A few hours later he was in the hospital in Gainesville, suffering horribly, and in a few more hours he was dead. Marjorie went to the Glisson house immediately and helped in telephoning and wiring relatives. She took young Jake Glisson home with her and sat up until three a.m. with the boy talking with him about his dad, the Creek, and his art school.

Norton came over to attend the funeral with Marjorie. It was a soft spring day, and the birds in the trees surrounding the burial ground provided a lovely chorus. Her friend's death brought thoughts of her own mortality, and Marjorie turned to Norton and said, "I think I could find peace and rest here."

Just as Marjorie was preparing to pack up for the trip to Van Hornesville, Martha became ill and Idella left again to go to New York to take a job with her husband so they could hire on as a couple. Marjorie had to manage all the housework, laundry, packing away of winter blankets, and other chores, including mailing two large express boxes to Van Hornesville in order to save room in the car for Moe and Uki. She and Norton drove to New York by way of his home town, Union Springs, Alabama, where they stopped to visit his relatives for a couple of days. Norton stayed at the Yankee house for two weeks, and then she put him on a train in Albany. She engaged a local woman to keep house for her, and after the woman recovered from her astonishment at being required to fix Uki a scrambled egg to be served on Marjorie's breakfast tray, she proved to be quiet and efficient. Marjorie's goal was to get her first draft of *The Sojourner* finished by midsummer.

When Colgate University wanted to get Robert Frost to come to Hamilton to accept an honorary degree, the president of the college enlisted Marjorie's aid in persuading the poet to attend the ceremony. She gladly invited Frost to stay with her overnight and promised to take him to Albany to catch his train back to Vermont. That night in the Yankee house Frost told Marjorie tales of his early days and the stories behind some of his poems. He compared his experience when he lived on a farm in New Hampshire to hers in living on her farm at Cross Creek, telling her that he had the same sort of relationship with the village people in his area that she did in hers. Then the wealthy people on nearby estates began lionizing him and telling him that they could raise a great deal of money for the village school if he would give a reading of his poetry at a fancy lawn party. Frost objected that the local people wouldn't be able to afford tickets, but when he was assured that they would be there, he accepted the engagement. "They were there, all right," he told Marjorie. "They were there as servants. They waited on us. . . ." This incident, he told her, persuaded him to move on. So he just bought another farm and moved over into Vermont. "Seemed the best way out of it," he said. Like many other men Frost revealed intimate details of his life to his sympathetic hostess. He confided in her the jealousy he still felt when he remembered that his wife (some fifty-five years earlier) had become semi-engaged to another young man when Frost had thought she recognized that they "belonged together, forever." And the poet told Marjorie of his grief at the death of his wife in 1941, a grief from which he had never recovered.

When Frost asked Marjorie, "Don't suppose you want to say what your book's about?" she answered that it was pretty much the theme of his own short poem "Revelation," and quoted to him the last stanza:

> *But so with all, from babes that play*
> *At hide-and-seek to God afar,*
> *So all who hide too well away*
> *Must speak and tell us where they are.*

Her meaning, she said, was that "Each of us who knows, recognizes, the good, is at fatal fault when he doesn't 'stand up in meeting' and speak for it. And so, we let wars happen—there are enough of us to make a decent world if we were not individually cowardly and lazy."

The next morning before Marjorie drove Frost to catch his train, they walked up Mt. Tom together—and almost missed the train. She marveled at his vitality at the age of seventy-five. He insisted on carrying his own heavy suitcase, saying that if he was not strong enough to do that, he would not be strong enough to farm that summer.

Concerned over Marjorie's struggle with her manuscript, Carl Brandt offered to come to Van Hornesville to go over it with her; but she told him not to come," [Y]ou are sweet, as always, to want to help me, but with Max gone, it seems to me now only God can help me, and I doubt whether He's interested."

As the summer weather grew hotter, so did the news of the Korean War. Norton received an alert from the American Field Service, and Marjorie was in terror at the thought of his going off to another war. She felt menaced by time and was conscious of the depletion of her strength "physical, nervous, emotional." Yet it was more important than ever to her that she maintain enough serenity to complete her work. "Whether my book has the slightest value or not, and I am at least dealing with matters that transcend wars, my survival, self-respect, whatever makes a human being, depends on finishing the job to the best of my ability," she told Berg.

In the late summer, the Armenian piano tuner who had originally put her antique piano back in tune appeared again. After he finished the tuning he played Balkan music and sang, and while he rested,

Marjorie wound up her old Swiss music box for him to listen to. He rose from his chair and bowed from the waist, "Madam, shall we dance?" Marjorie loved to dance, and they waltzed and mazurkaed and polkaed. He was an excellent dancer and told her she was too. Carried away by the magic of the moment, Marjorie cried out, dramatically, "Strange Armenian, I love your soul! Play one more song for me and I shall let you go!"

The Armenian, too, was carried away and exclaimed, "Let me go, Madam? But must I go? Can you not find it in your heart to let me stay? You are so alone, Madam." Marjorie murmured that she was flattered, for as she told Bee, she had never been propositioned with "such grace and courtesy."

"You attract me strangely, Madam," the Armenian said.

"Thank you, but it is impossible."

"Eet eez a matter of preenceepul?" Not to offend him, she said, yes, it was a matter of principle. She had a charming husband. He responded, "I respect and regret, Madam. Let us congratulate each the other, that we have come through another year in a troubled world. Next year, I shall hope to tune you."

Marjorie's ability to charm men of all ages did not diminish as she grew older. At fifty-four she was described by her friends and by interviewers as "handsome" rather than "pretty." But it was her responsive and sympathetic nature that was the greatest attraction, a fact she was aware of. Earlier in the year she had written to Berg that it was almost a curse that she knew how men feel and react. "And then my half-female nature drives me on to protect that maleness, to want to make any man I care about, feel more the man. And that partly accounts for some of my own unhappiness, trying never to let a man down."

About the time of her birthday, Marjorie received a letter from Arthur Kinnan, saying that he had been married (for the third time) since March 25, and that his new bride was pregnant and the baby due in January. Pictures were enclosed of the new wife and a letter from her. Marjorie thought she looked attractive and sounded as if she had both "sense and sensibility." She fervently hoped Arthur had the right girl at last.

On September 29 she finished the first draft of her book and slept twelve hours that night. She looked forward to the editing and rewriting as she felt that the manuscript was "fearfully over-written." She had been discussing the plot with Norman Berg by mail for most of the year, bouncing her changing ideas off him. Her three main themes had always been clear to her. The first was that the fact that there are a few choice individuals in the world gives hope for a decent human evolution. The second was that every man has lost his brother. And the third theme, the one she had mentioned to Robert Frost, is shown when her main character, Ase, realizes that his inarticulateness has been an active harm in the eternal battle between good and evil, that to know the truth and not speak it at any cost gives aid and comfort to the enemy. But the exposition of these themes was much more difficult than the conception of them, and the revision went slower and harder than she had anticipated. "God, I'm *only* telling a tale of one puzzled man, a sojourner on the earth," she moaned.

In October she had another automobile accident. Turning from her country road to deliver magazines to a friend (who then passed them on to others), she was hit by a speeding car coming over a blind knoll. The state troopers listed it as an unavoidable accident, but her car was totally wrecked. With her phenomenal luck, she escaped with only a badly scraped and bruised left leg. She replaced the car with another Oldsmobile.

The weather began closing in at Van Hornesville when Marjorie was about a third of the way through her revision, and she had to make a choice as to whether to stay to finish her project, or to return to Florida before the weather cut her off. She actually enjoyed the snowstorms just as she enjoyed wild rainstorms in Florida, and coping without utilities she accepted as a challenge. However, on her icy hill she was dependent much of the time during cold weather on her neighbors to bring the mail, milk, and groceries, and it seemed unfair to Norton to remain alone all through the winter. Therefore she decided to call Norton to come to drive her and Uki and Moe back to the South. When he arrived, they took her new car to be serviced in snow and ice and slid into a snow-filled ditch, but her friendly neighbors brought a Jeep and cable and hauled them out undamaged. Marjorie and Norton watched for a weather break and got off the hill only to run into wind, sleet, and rainstorms. After the drive home in the terrible weather, Marjorie discovered that the new housekeeper Norton had hired for her had worked only in a café and needed to be trained not to dish up the meals on one plate and not to dump catsup and mayonnaise bottles on the table as well as in the finer points of housecleaning. And at the Creek she found that Martha was ailing and that the farmhouse was badly neglected.

In her Christmas letter to Bee McNeil, Marjorie wrote that she was about to go crazy because she couldn't get back to her work, but that it was gratifying that Norton was so happy to have her back in Florida. "The conflict between trying to be a writer and a good wife disturbs me as one calls for a completely hermit-like life and the other for gregariousness which I enjoy when through writing," she told Bee. As usual she exchanged cat news with Bee, telling her she envied her her cat, Cousin Hank, who put his arms around her neck, remembering that Benny had done the same thing, and also kissed her. Uki, however, had his own charms. He was a lap sitter and slept on her stomach or on Norton's—all ten pounds of him. From time to time Norman Berg received letters written in the persona of Moe, who complained to "Mr. Norman" about Marjorie's and Uki's treatment of him and sometimes bragged of his conquests among the female dogs at Van Hornesville and in Florida. Norman Berg owned Moe's offspring Hem (Hemingway), who sometimes sent messages in Norman's letters to his sire or to Marjorie.

Marjorie found an interesting proposal among the mail waiting for her in Florida. Irita Van Doren, the editor of the New York *Herald Tribune* book review and the wife of Carl Van Doren, the writer, wrote to ask if Marjorie would consider writing a biography of Ellen Glasgow. Irita and Frank Morley were Ellen's literary executors. They were holding the unpublished autobiography (which Ellen had specified not be published as long as anyone was living who would be hurt by it), and Irita told Marjorie there was only one man to whom this restriction still applied. She also said that a number of young people, particularly graduate students, were anxious to do the biography of Ellen Glasgow, but that she and Frank Morley wanted someone of distinction and understanding to do the book. "I do know Ellen had great regard for you and you seem to have not only great regard for her work but understanding of her personally," Irita wrote and urged that Marjorie consider doing the biography as her next major undertaking. Marjorie was intrigued but did not want to make up her mind about such a serious writing project until she was out from under the one that weighed on her so heavily at the moment.

In late February Norman Berg read through *The Sojourner* manuscript. He wrote four pages of general criticism and four more of specific line-by-line suggestions. "The valuable thing you have done for me is to make me think deeply," Marjorie told him. She reported that she was in a stage of "angry ferment" and knew she must "sweat hotter and darker blood" to answer endless unanswered questions about the book and to translate those answers into the combination of "reality and mysticism" toward which she was struggling. She planned to stay at the Creek, away from the winter visitors in St. Augustine, working hard for several weeks until she had a decent first draft to send to Scribners. Martha Mickens and her daughter Adrenna were there to help her. Although she was seeking seclusion, she welcomed a visit by Robert Frost, who came to lunch one day. After the meal, he recited some of his poetry for Martha, and she sang spirituals for him.

When Marjorie finally sent Carl Brandt and Charles Scribner the revised copy of her manuscript, Carl wrote her a cautious letter. "I see what you mean about its being only a rough draft and how hard it must have been for you to let go of it at this stage," he told her. Marjorie was aggrieved that he did not sense that she was writing a potentially major novel. She told Bernice Baumgarten that what she was trying to do was to write an "extremely serious book, with great overtones." It did not please her much more when Charles Scribner wrote that the book was certain to be "successful." "This curdles my blood!" she told Bernice. "I wanted to do a stark thing, a sort of minor Russian novel sort of thing. The hell with 'Success.'!!"

While the Brandts and Scribners' editors took time to examine her manuscript in depth, Marjorie had time to concentrate on other matters. Disturbing news came from Arthur. He was desperately unhappy with his third wife, who had had a baby boy. He told Marjorie that his wife had violent tantrums and he was threatening to take the baby and leave her. The three Kinnan aunts, Wilmer,

Grace, and Marjorie, who had settled in Phoenix, were completely on Arthur's side and were urging him to get out of the marriage. Marjorie's love for her younger brother was unwavering, but she did not see him in the same rosy light as the aunts and could see that his troubles were largely of his own making. She was deeply concerned and discussed with Norton the possibility that if Arthur got custody of the baby and could not care for it, they might take it to raise. She knew it would have to be on a permanent basis because she realized that if they took the child to live with them for a short time and then Arthur took it away, it would break her heart. In the end they decided not to make the offer to Arthur.

Marjorie was tempted by an invitation from Martha Gellhorn to come to visit her in Mexico. Martha, after her divorce from Hemingway, had continued her friendship with the Baskins, and had visited them in St. Augustine. Several years earlier they had helped her locate a cottage near theirs where she had spent some months working at her writing. She told them she never forgot their "lovely drink/talk evenings." Now, she was living in Cuernavaca and loving the free and easy life there. She urged them to come to see her and drink tequila until their "eyes bugged out" and talk all night in the blissful soft air. "Roam down here while there is still time to roam," she begged. But Marjorie was far from finished with her novel and did not take the opportunity.

In April she went to New York by train for a conference with her agents and her publisher about *The Sojourner*. She had been having pain in her eyes, which she at first dismissed as eyestrain. When it persisted, Norton insisted she take time to have her eyes checked at the Harkness Pavilion in New York, where it was found that she had glaucoma in an early stage. She was given drops to use and a prognosis that the trouble would not advance any further. Pleased with the results of the medication, she immediately prescribed it for Martha, who also suffered from glaucoma, and it was apparently helpful to her too. Playing amateur doctor was a role Marjorie often assumed and seemed to enjoy.

In New York, she spent a long afternoon with Charles Scribner and Jack Wheelock, talking over her manuscript, which they all agreed needed extensive revision. That night she had dinner with

Julia Scribner. On another night she went to Café Society to see Pearl Primus's opening there and to meet Pearl's husband, who was also her manager, and her mother and brother. She found Pearl's African dances and authentic costumes "magnificent" and was pleased that her friend's performances were well-received by the sophisticated New York audience.

In May Norton drove Marjorie and the animals up to Van Hornesville, and she prepared to redo her manuscript from the beginning. When Norman Berg offered to meet her in late June to discuss the manuscript changes, she refused his offer, telling him that "from now on, I am on my own." She also asked that he not send her sermons on her drinking, assuring him that she was perfectly capable of stopping completely when she was deep in her work and the drinking was interfering. But she told him, "I must have the satisfaction of absorption in the writing to make the deprivation worth-while."

Norton, too, was deeply worried over her tendency to turn to alcohol to relieve whatever was bothering her. "I try so hard not to preach or interfere, but I do get so distressed about your drinking," he told her. He assured her that if it brought her any comfort or relief or were in any way an answer to her problems he would not say anything. But far from being an aid to coping with her problems, he could see that it only complicated them. "None of the beauty of your writing comes from the bottle," he said, adding, "You must understand this is not nagging and just comes from my great love for you and worry over you." He was so conscious of her changing moods that he found it hard to write her "silly, chatty" letters that might hit her at the wrong time and infuriate her with their trivialities. He was thinking, he said, of putting notations on the outside of his letters with such directions as "To Be Read Before Breakfast," or "To Be Read in the Light of 'I love you,'" or even "To Be Read Thru a Bourbon Bottle Darkly."

The summer of 1951 was surprisingly happy for Marjorie, although her writing went slowly. She accepted the fact that she could only concentrate for half a day and make any real progress. She gave up liquor almost entirely and lost several pounds. Although a checkup at the Cooperstown Hospital showed her blood pressure was a bit too high, she had a sense of well-being. Louise Young found her a little Irish girl to be her housekeeper. The girl called Marjorie "Mother," and after taking her home in the afternoon, Marjorie picked up her mail, wrote letters, worked in her garden, or made jellies and jams, an activity that never failed to give her pleasure. She also liked picking the berries, and every evening she took a long walk with Moe.

She refused invitations to visit friends like the Gilkysons because such interruptions threw her off her stride. Having the Young tribe over for a buffet supper kept her away from her typewriter for six days. But for once she felt satisfied with her work. She was not just revising, she was actually adding a great deal of new material to her story.

In October she went to New York to talk over the manuscript with her Scribners' editors and to record a script she had written for a Voice of America program called "In This I Believe." A number of writers had been asked to contribute to the program, which was aimed at a worldwide audience. It was a request she couldn't refuse as it gave her an opportunity to express some of her ideas about the need for Americans to deal honestly and wholeheartedly with the problem of equality for blacks. She began the broadcast by tracing her writing career from the time she sat under a tree as a little girl, writing verses on scraps of grocery bag paper. She spoke of her father's influence in passing on to her a love of animals and of the world of nature. She told of her struggles with writing in her young adulthood, and described the new world that opened to her when she moved to Florida. She traced the evolution of *The Yearling* and pictured for her listeners her surroundings at Cross Creek—the mammoth live oaks draped with gray Spanish moss, the stately magnolia trees, the yellow jasmine, the mockingbirds and redbirds, the truck farms of beans and garden vegetables. She described the miles and miles of orange groves, where among the jade green leaves hung the golden globes, "surely the golden apples of antiquity."

Then she turned to the conditions of the Negroes in her area and spoke of her delight at having seen with her own eyes in one generation the change in the attitude in the South toward the Negro. She mentioned the advances in education and wages and said that her Negro friends visited in her home, and she was a guest in theirs.

"Today he [the Negro] is very close to full membership in the American society," she said. She concluded her talk:

> *But what of you who are listening[?] . . . Many of you are hungry, many afraid. We here also know these things. In writing of poor people and their family life close to the soil, I've tried to reveal the love and courage that sustain them and that love, that courage is ours and yours, the common heritage of every man and woman on earth.*

Telling Bee McNeil about making the broadcast, Marjorie complained that her voice sounded harsh. "Don't know what happened to the good voice I once had—or thought I had." The kindly Bee would not have pointed out that thirty years of heavy smoking might have had something to do with the change.

Marjorie decided to stay at Van Hornesville as long as possible to work on the manuscript, so Norton came up in October and met her in New York for a few days there and then returned to Van Hornesville with her for a ten-day visit. It snowed most of the time, and as it was only the fourth time Norton had been in snow, he had a thoroughly good time, picking the apples and putting out peanuts for the chipmunks.

After he left, Marjorie read Edwin Way Teale's *North with the Spring*. She wrote Teale enthusiastically that she hated to come to the end of his book and felt it could stand with Thoreau's work. Teale wrote back that Orange Lake and the Big Scrub were among the places he most wanted to return to. He recalled that the day spent with her while he was collecting material for the book had been one of the happiest experiences of his trip. In the book he described the food she had provided that day. First there was the wicker basket crammed with fried chicken, boiled eggs, potato salad, layer cake, and oranges for their picnic in the Scrub. That night back at Cross Creek she had fed them broiled halves of grapefruit, scrapple, string beans, baking powder biscuits, mangoes, and "special food for the gods," the white heart of a cabbage palm. After summarizing other regional food, Teale said that nowhere else in their travels did they meet "so many culinary stars" on a single table as at Cross

Creek. And nowhere else, he wrote, did they find "anyone more generous or directly sincere than Mrs. Rawlings."

CHAPTER 18

Another Beginning

M arjorie did not call for Norton to come to get her and the animals until almost Christmas of 1951. They set out at eight degrees below zero, and after days of driving in sleet and snow on icy roads, the warmth of the Florida sun was more agreeable than ever. After the obligatory round of holiday entertainments, Marjorie retreated to Cross Creek to finish her rewriting. "I have abandoned poor dear Norton once again to tuck in at Cross Creek to finish the bloody book, which nobody believes I'm even working on," she told Bee. Martha and her daughter helped her after a fashion, but their inadequacies were "too terrible" to report, Marjorie told Bee. But Adrenna did make wonderful coffee, was kind to all the animals, and kept the fireplaces filled.

On February 11 Marjorie received a wire from Julia Scribner Bigham telling of the sudden death of her father that day. Two days later, Marjorie received one of the last letters written by Charles Scribner. She had told him that she could see the end of her book and that she was not too dissatisfied with it. His letter expressed his delight and his belief that it would certainly be a good book. Since Max's death, Marjorie measured every loss against that greatest of all losses. She told Norman:

This loss, while severe, is not that of Max. Charlie was a dear friend. Max had become a part of my thinking. It was perhaps in losing Max that I became more or less inured to death. After too great a wound, there is scar tissue, and one can never feel in that region too acute a pain again.

By mid-February she had almost finished her rewriting, and she anticipated that less than a week's work remained to do. To catch her breath before the final surge, she drove over to the cottage one Saturday afternoon. On Sunday afternoon, she did not feel well, but thought she just had indigestion. Norton urged her to stay overnight, but she was anxious to be at her work early on Monday and left to drive back to Cross Creek about five p.m.

The pain got increasingly worse during the evening. By nine p.m. it was almost unbearable, but she had no way of calling anyone. There was no telephone in the farmhouse, and she was too weak to get to the door to call to the tenant house. Helpless, she lay and endured the pain until Adrenna came at seven the next morning to make breakfast. She did not expect to live through the night, and felt that death, cold and dark and lonely, was closing in on her. She seemed to be looking down a straight road overarched by trees, and the road went on and on with no end in sight, but she felt no fear or dread or terror at the thought of going down it.

Surprised to find herself still alive in the morning, she sent word by Adrenna to her neighbors to call a doctor from Gainesville. He arrived about 8:30 and gave her a shot that mercifully relieved the acute pain. Norton came over with a St. Augustine ambulance as soon as he got word of her condition. As she was being carried to the ambulance, Marjorie had the bearers stop so she could instruct Adrenna to leave the rear door of her car open so Moe, who was distressed by her absences, could jump in and out of the car, which seemed reassuring to him.

She was taken to Flagler Hospital in St. Augustine, where she remained for three weeks. The doctors told her she had had a coronary spasm, but that she could live a normal life if she gave up smoking permanently, limited her drinking, and never let herself pass a certain limit of exhaustion or tension. She felt fortunate, she told various friends, to have had this "much needed warning." Actually, she told Bee, she had been planning a luxurious few weeks of collapse when she finished the book, but she seemed to have got a little ahead of herself. Norton, she reported, was having the time of his life giving her orders. "I shall hate keeping myself composed," she told Bee. "How ridiculous to be sensible!" she said to Gene Baro. But, intellectually, she knew the importance of the doctor's advice. "I need never have another attack if I decide that living carefully is worth while," she told another friend.

After she was released from the hospital, Marjorie returned to the beach cottage in order to be near a telephone and her doctors. Catherine Mulligan, the little Irish maid from Van Hornesville, came to take care of her, and Norton went to the Creek to bring back some of her things and Moe and Uki.

During her convalescence, Marjorie was showered with flowers and books, and she had many visitors. One of the most welcome was Robert Frost, who delayed his return to Vermont to come over from Gainesville to see her. His visit did her more good than nitroglycerin, she told a friend. "How I love him!"

With the efficient help of Nike Grafstrom, her capable St. Augustine secretary, she was able to get her manuscript ready to send to Scribners in April. When word came back that it was being set in print, she was alarmed until she realized she could do a great deal of work on it in galley proof, as she had always done with her books.

Feeling nervous and irritable at her confinement, she began drinking again soon after her release from the hospital. However, by the end of April with the manuscript sent off and with the prospect of heading for Van Hornesville soon, she swore off "this time for good." One of the problems that added to her anxiety was a letter from her brother Arthur. He had kidnapped his son Jeffrey from his third wife and fled from Alaska to Seattle. Failing to get work as a photographer, he had joined a real estate firm and was working on commission, which so far had not yielded any income. His bank account was overdrawn, and he was asking for another "loan" from his sister. Marjorie complied with this request as she had always done in the past. From time to time, she also sent checks to her Aunt Ethel Riggs, who was in poor health, and to her aunts in Pheonix for birthdays and Christmas. The aunts did not improve Marjorie's state of mind by their predictions that "poor, dear Arthur" was likely to be jailed.

The second week in May Norton drove Marjorie and the animals to Van Hornesville. When the galley proofs of *The Sojourner* were sent to her there, Norman Berg came for a weekend to help her with them. As so often happened when these two volatile, opinionated people got together, they clashed, sparks flew, and shouting matches ensued. Marjorie told Jack Wheelock, "Anyone listening in would have thought we were mortal enemies or lovers, about to slay one another, for we yell so." She gave an example:

> *Norman shouted: "You don't need much! . . . just some little perfect sentence."*
>
> *I shouted back, "Do you think little perfect simple sentences grow on trees?"*
>
> *He turned purple and yelled, "I know God damn well little perfect simple sentences don't grow on trees, you have to work for them, well, work for it!!!"*

Max Perkins, she told Wheelock, was even more of a slave driver than Norman Berg, but he did it in such a beautiful, quiet way that you thought it was your own idea and "your blood pressure didn't jump."

As her editor, Wheelock tried to be encouraging and comforting, but he could never bring himself to criticize her work, and she told him, "Jack, I love you, but if you want me to adore you, you'll have to be a bit tougher with me." And she added that she needed to have her hand held until she was entirely done with the proofs. It crushed her that he hadn't written to her in a week. "I live a life, not of Thoreau's quiet desperation, but of overt and blatant desperation. . . ." she told Wheelock.

When Norman Berg admired her style in something she wrote and mused that he didn't know how she did it, she answered that she didn't know herself. It seemed absurd to her that anything creatively good came out of her, because the process was so "anguished and *messy.*"

Norton called on June 18 to say that Ida Tarrant had had a stroke and was in the hospital in a coma. Marjorie had promised her adopted aunt that she would come to her in case of serious illness and that when she died she would take her ashes back to Ohio for burial. So as soon as she could get a train, Marjorie started for St. Augustine, but Aunt Ida died without ever coming out of her coma. Marjorie rejoiced that at ninety-two Ida had been active until a week before her death, and yet she surprised herself by going to pieces over the death of her friend of thirty-five years. As always, Norton was her rock and helped her clean out the old woman's apartment of the paper bags and Christmas cards she had saved for decades. After a simple service at the undertaker's chapel, Marjorie took the ashes to Cincinnati by train. Her friend Lois Hardy met her, went to the cemetery with her, and then drove her up to Van Hornesville. A touching note came to Marjorie from Ballard Cabell, who had been fond of Aunt Ida. In it he said, "You were always her ray of sunshine."

The first week in July, Arthur showed up in San Augustine with his little son. They stayed with Norton at the beach cottage. Aunt Wilmer wrote from Phoenix that she was glad Arthur was with Norton, "who could straighten him out." Wilmer remarked that she hoped the boy would *not* grow up to be handsome like his father as Arthur's good looks had always got him in trouble with women. And she begged Norton and Marjorie to come to Arizona to visit, adding prophetically, "Time is running out." In September Arthur brought his eighteen-month-old son to Van Hornesville for a week's visit. He confided to his sister that his domestic situation was critical, and he was desperately afraid of not getting custody of the child. There had been no court order giving it to the mother, so his custody of the child was not illegal, he explained, adding that he had an awfully good case against the mother. Arthur's finances were also at rock bottom, and undoubtedly Marjorie supplied funds to enable him to take care of his and the baby's needs.

Marjorie's continuing fight for civil rights became personal in the fall when the driver of the school bus that went by her gate at Cross Creek refused to stop and pick up Betty Jean, Adrenna's daughter, because it was a "white" school bus. The nearest "colored" bus was twelve miles away. When Marjorie lost her fight with the county superintendent of schools to have the bus stop for Betty Jean, she wrote a moving account of the incident of the bypassed little girl for the New York *Herald Tribune*. The write-up brought her grateful letters from black and white civil rights leaders, and the next semester arrangements were made to have a bus pick up Betty Jean.

Now that *The Sojourner* had passed into the final printing processes and was completely out of her hands, Marjorie did not take long in deciding on her next project. She definitely wanted to do the Glasgow biography. But first she and Norton planned a leisurely six-week trip to England and Ireland. Desperate to clear up her correspondence before leaving, Marjorie accepted Owen Young's offer to loan her his secretary for two days of dictation. When the woman called to say she had some thirty letters ready for her signature, Marjorie got in the car with Moe and started out. Driving too fast around a gravel curve, she lost control of the car, jerked the steering wheel too hard trying to straighten out and skidded through her neighbors' barbed wire fence, over a stone wall, knocking down a telephone pole and snapping it in half. All of the telephones in the area were knocked out, so Marjorie accepted her neighbor's invitation to have coffee and cake while they waited for someone to send for help. When the bread truck passed by, Marjorie got the driver to notify the telephone company and a garage. With her incredible luck, she had only a sore nose and a few bruises and Moe was unhurt. But the left front fender and the headlights of the Oldsmobile were completely smashed.

They were due to leave on the *United States* on October 3, and a few days before Marjorie went to New York to shop for the trip. Julia brought her useful material on Ireland, and Marjorie had a long talk with Julia's brother, Charles Scribner, Jr., who was taking over his father's position at Scribners. Marjorie was impressed with "Young Charles" and told Berg: "Give him a few years, and I think you will have in him the leading American publisher. I expect to see some distinguished things appear under his aegis."

Gene Baro, who was in England trying to write, met the Baskins when their ship docked and traveled with them for two days. When he complained that he couldn't find a place to settle down and write, Marjorie offered him Cross Creek for the winter and spring. Baro caught the next ship for America. Norton and Marjorie spent four days in London, where she gave a number of interviews. Then they went to Oxford, where a mutual friend had given them an introduction to Neville Cogswell, the translator of *The Canterbury Tales*. He was charming to them and took them to visit the various colleges and afterward to his don's living quarters for tea. The next day he drove with them through the Cotswolds and was their guest for drinks and dinner. When they remarked that they were going to Ireland, he suggested they stay at Castle Townsend, which was owned by his mother, Lady Cogswell. The family took in paying guests but didn't advertise.

The Baskins fell in love with the beautiful house and gardens at Castle Townsend, and it was arranged that an apartment in one wing of the house should be fixed up for Marjorie to return to the next year to work on her biography. At Tara Hill, north of Dublin, Marjorie picked up some small stones from the Royal Enclosure, a bit of earth from the site of Cormac's house, and some lichen from the Stone of Destiny, on which the High Kings of Ireland were crowned. The soft Irish mist on Tara Hill had made them quite wet and damp, and when they returned to their car, they opened a bottle of John Powers Irish Whiskey and drank a toast to the dead kings of Ireland.

Marjorie sent gifts back to relatives and friends, including some beautiful Irish tweed to Bee, who told her that she had some very rich friends who would never think of doing anything so magnanimous. "I would be upset by your lavishness if I did not know that you get real pleasure out of doing things for others," Bee told her.

Aside from houses and furnishings, Marjorie was peculiarly reluctant to spend money on herself. She bought fairly inexpensive clothes from stores like Best and Company, even after she could afford to patronize the expensive shops at whose displays she had looked longingly in her early working days in New York. She was so upset that Norton had booked them first class on the *United States* that she threatened not to go on the trip, and it was her choice that they return on the more modestly priced *Mauretania*.

On the return trip Marjorie read John Steinbeck's *East of Eden*. She thought it "magnificent, beautifully and poetically written," and she felt that she had been trying to write the same kind of book in *The Sojourner*. She thought, however, that she had a slight edge on

Steinbeck in that he told his story through two different families and thereby dissipated the immediacy of his themes, while hers were coordinated by her use of only one family.

The *Mauretania* docked in New York; and on the way to Florida, Marjorie stopped off in Richmond to stay with the Cabells in order to make preliminary plans for her research for the Ellen Glasgow biography. Many of Ellen's friends were elderly and fragile as "spun glass," and she was afraid to delay interviewing them. She also wanted to locate a house to live in for the two or three months she estimated would be necessary for her research. It was a disappointment to her that the owner of the house she finally found would not permit her to bring Moe and Uki.

James and Margaret Cabell introduced her to various people who they thought could help her. One of her most important sources was Colonel Henry W. Anderson, a lawyer, Ellen Glasgow's one-time fiancé and the one survivor Irita Van Doren had mentioned as the only living person who might be hurt by a biography of the writer. Anderson had been overseas during World War I as head of the American Red Cross war relief for the Balkans and was rumored to have had a love affair with Queen Marie of Rumania. After his return to America the engagement to Ellen was broken. The Cabells had Col. Anderson to dinner so Marjorie could meet him. In turn he had her to lunch. She found him wary and distrustful of her motives in writing the biography, and she turned on all her persuasive powers to convince him that she had no intention of rushing into print with a "gaudy" book. Her book would have dignity, she told him, both for Ellen's sake and her own. "I have violent ideas about biographies, and next to the dry as dust ones, I most deplore the over-intimate ones, which are always in the most appalling bad taste," she said. She saw the story of Ellen Glasgow and her work as a permanent one for posterity—if she did her work well enough. For all her love and admiration for Ellen, she told the colonel, "I am an objective workman." She assured him she was committed to doing a creative job but needed to know as much as possible about Ellen's private life and emotions, even though she would use only a fraction of the material in the finished book. But she felt her biography would fail if she did not give a complete record written "within the bounds of good taste." Aside from his own relationship with Ellen, she thought he could explain other puzzles such as Ellen's hatred for her father and her "pseudo-love" for animals as a revolt against humans. After meeting several more of Ellen's friends and arranging to rent the house she had located on Paxton Road, Marjorie went to Florida for the Christmas holidays. And she wrote a short Christmas article for *Better Living* magazine and donated her check for it to the Foster Parents organization.

January 4, 1953, was the publication date of *The Sojourner* set by Scribners. When Brandt and Brandt had offered the novel to the book clubs, Book-of-the-Month refused it, but the Literary Guild accepted it as their choice for January 1953. The London publishing house of William Heinemann planned to publish their edition simultaneously. When the Literary Guild sent Marjorie a twenty-two page questionnaire for publicity use, she told Bernice Gilkyson it was driving her mad as they wanted to know everything from her weight to her solution to world problems. "I'm lying about the weight and ignoring the world problems," she told Bernice.

The Sojourner, which took more than a decade of anguished writing and rewriting, contained much of its author's philosophy about human relationships, time, alienation, loneliness, cosmic awareness, religion, and death. Ase (Asahel) Linden is her spokesman as Lant was in *South Moon Under* and Penny Baxter was in *The Yearling*. The time span of the novel is sixty years, and traces Ase's life from the time he is twenty until his death at the age of eighty. But the story begins further back in time with a betrayal of Ase's father by his own father and brother, who break a pact to help him establish a farm and home after he helps them establish their own places. This betrayal seems to Ase to have been a repetition of the biblical story of Jacob and Esau—one son beloved, the other despised. The pattern is repeated as Ase's father becomes hard and withdrawn from his family, and the mother centers all her half-mad, possessive love on Ben, Ase's older, adored brother. Gangling, homely and inarticulate, Ase finds spiritual communion with other aliens who are lost and lonely—a hard-drinking Irishman handyman, an old Fisher Indian, who is the last of his tribe, and a band of roving Gypsies. After Ben leaves to seek a richer fortune in the West, Amelia and Ase are left desolated, and Ase marries the girlfriend whom Ben has indifferently willed to him. Nellie, based on Marjorie's vivacious grandmother Traphagen, is pretty and practical and an excellent housekeeper; but she cannot share Ase's eternal longing to understand man's place in the cosmos. They have five children, but only his delicate daughter Dolly responds to Ase's love. She at the age of six is left out in a blizzard to die by the crazed Amelia. The three older children are selfish and materialistic, and the youngest son, who is sensitive but withdrawn, is killed at Château-Thierry in World War I. The coldness of his other three children intensifies Ase's inability to communicate with them. He longs to draw the five-year-old Nat close against him to say, "We have both arrived strangely on earth and shall depart strangely, and we are related for the moment, so let us try to speak together, alien as we may appear one to the other." But he hesitates too long and the chance is gone.

Besides his three friends, Ase has a flute and finds comfort in music, although as long as his mother is alive, he must go off to play it in hiding. With McCarthy the handyman accompanying him on the fiddle, he finds solace in sad, sweet songs. But Ase's main satisfaction comes from the land, which he (like Marjorie) feels can only be held in trust, not owned. The book is rich in descriptions of crops and animals, trees, plants, and flowers, of food and seasonal changes. Ase likes to read the biblical descriptions of shepherds and sheep abiding in the fields, for "it seemed to him that a man might meet God, if ever, in the fields, for so much of creation was there."

Like Marjorie, Ase read the Bible constantly, "for its profound study of men in trouble and in joy, for the relation of human living to other living, for the possibility of a man's reaching into the outer space for a comfort the earth did not provide."

Ase's feeling for the unity of time is an important motif running through the book. He is troubled by his feeling about time because it seems so different from other people's. While Nellie speaks of time as being "marked off in jumps, he finds it not clearly marked, but all one, forever whole. It seems to him that he can stand off at a distance and see his remotest ancestors side by side with his farthest descendants:

All life seemed to him contained in the beginning and the end,
if there had ever been a beginning and if there would ever be
an end. Time was, must be, timeless. As from a great enough
height a landscape would show no detail, so from a far enough
distance all time would be seen to exist simultaneously. He
felt this in his inner mind and spirit.

Consciously or subconsciously Marjorie must have had Arthur in
mind in her portrayal of Ben. Ase, despite his deep love and yearning
for his brother, comes to realize that Ben is a lost soul who will
always wander "strong and beautiful and admired, incompetent,
reckless and futile." Ase's journey to California to find his brother
has Jungian overtones. He realizes "It was in the faces of all men he
should have peered. He had been homeless, and knew that for such
men as he there was no home, only an endless journey."

As he is flying home with his brother's ashes, the stewardess tells
him that the aircraft will climb for another half hour before it levels
off. Ase longs for the half hour to last for half a millennium, "to
keep on and on, higher and higher, farther and farther, to the core
of the cosmos." And he wonders if man, like the birds, might be
intended to be migratory, since the battered planet beneath him could
not last forever. Ase feels his heart constrict and then the deadly
pressure of a severe heart attack. Recognizing the approach of death,
he is not afraid:

It had been so brief a sojourn, not even a full century. He had
been a guest in a mansion and he was not ungrateful. He was
at once exhausted and refreshed. His stay was ended. Now
he must gather up the shabby impedimenta of his mind and
body and be on his way again.

The reviews of Marjorie's last book were more mixed than for any
other of her writings. Her English publisher told her, "In it you have
put everything in you of wisdom, knowledge, love, and understanding." *Time* sneeringly called it a "revised Book of Job, and said it
was a "sententious smudge compared to her famed, finely drawn

1938 novel, *The Yearling*." The Los Angeles *Times* said that the coming year was unlikely to produce a finer novel and compared her writing to that of Thomas Hardy. The reviewer for the New York *World-Telegram* complained that the characters didn't come to life, while the reviewer for the Hartford *Times* found the characters real and human and the novel "powerful and poignant." In the *Saturday Review*, Louis Bromfield called it a good, solid book, but found the characters as well as the time and place "blurred." The Spokane *Chronicle* called the book "warmly written but exasperatingly tedious, totally lacking in dramatic intensity" and concluded that "Ase Linden is thoroughly dull and so is the book." *Newsweek* said that *The Sojourner's* appeal was in its warmth and wisdom and its revelation of "the slow growth of understanding." The New York *Post* called it a "lyrical farm novel," as long as the author was writing of the planting and the harvest, the animals, and Nellie's wonderful food, but felt it fell apart toward the end when the writer "begins to labor the point that money, if not the root of all evil, is the cause of much of it."

Perhaps the review that pleased Marjorie most, because the writer seemed to understand best what she was attempting, was the one in the New York *Herald Tribune*. The reviewer pointed out that the elements of Asahel Linden's life are as timeless as the "continuing search of mortal man for certitude and understanding and brotherhood." Explaining that the name "Asahel" means "God has made," the reviewer, Coleman Rosenberger, said:

> *Surely Mrs. Rawlings' Asahel, sojourner on earth, planting and harvesting the land with no title to it, inarticulate but hungering for communication, groping toward answers to man's ancient questions, coming to recognize good and evil in their many disguises—is man made by God.*

The story, the reviewer concluded, is a "luminous fable of man, affirmative and hopeful."

It was a comfort to Marjorie that she believed that the best work of most creative people—artists, sculptors, musicians, writers—was not appreciated when first presented. She was humble about her work, but had no "mock-modesty," she told Norman Berg. "*The Sojourner* is a major novel, for all its faults. I shall stand or fall on that."

Her friends, of course, wrote letters of lavish praise, sometimes of anger at the newspaper and magazine reviewers. Theodore Pratt wrote a letter of protest to the editors to the *Saturday Review* that began, "Of all the dreadful reviewing nonsense I've ever seen, Louis Bromfield's alleged review of *The Sojourner* is the worst exhibition extant." Then Pratt proceeded to tear the review to pieces.

James Cabell thought it her best book and suggested Norton should treat her with more deference "upon the double count of your newly attested genius—which isn't a word I use lightly—and your dangerous knowledge of men."

"If the brash young boy reviewers don't know what you've done, so much the worse for them," Bernice Gilkyson told her. "I think a million or more people will read your book with appreciation of the wisdom that is there." Bernice's figures may have been a little exaggerated, but two weeks after publication *The Sojourner* was number seven on the New York *Times* best seller list, following Hemingway's *Old Man and the Sea* and number ten on the New York *Herald Tribune* best seller list, with the Hemingway number eight.

In early January, while at the beach cottage, Marjorie fell on the steep steps leading up to the back of the house. Her leg was badly bruised and sore and she had to spend several days in bed. During the enforced rest she made plans for a trip to New York to fulfill several publicity engagements there. While there, between January 18 and 22, she gave two radio talks, had four interviews, and spoke at the Book and Author Luncheon, which Irita Van Doren had invited her to address. When a reporter asked her about her future plans, Marjorie said that it would probably take her four or five years to do the biography of Ellen Glasgow, who, she said, should take her place as a social historian alongside Jane Austen. Then, Marjorie told the interviewer, she wanted to work on a "northern novel" and do a number of short stories.

During her visit in New York she made time to visit Fania and Carl Van Vechten. Van Vechten, a writer and photographer, was a distant cousin of hers. He had sent her a copy of an essay he had written on James Cabell for the *Yale Gazette*, and she had sent him an inscribed copy of *Cross Creek*, and they began a correspondence in which they addressed each other as "Dear Cousin," and developed a warm friendship. Marjorie sometimes complained that few people had wanted to photograph her when she was young and "fairly fair" but when she became no longer young and "fairly fat" everybody wanted to take her picture. However, she had liked the pictures Carl had taken of James Cabell and of Truman Capote. She had agreed to let him photograph her in the reclining "Capote" pose. At fifty-six Marjorie, in spite of a constant battle with her weight, was plump; but she had kept her attractive features; her beautiful hands, her simply arranged dark hair, her tiny mouth, and her penetrating blue eyes. At times those eyes took on a cold, hard glaze when something or someone displeased her. When Carl Van Vechten's pictures were developed, she liked them much better than any taken of her by other photographers. Finding them "intelligent and sad," she told her cousin he elicited and captured "something of whatever it is that passes for the soul."

Although she felt overwhelmed by a sense of exhaustion, which should have been a warning, Marjorie plunged immediately into her research for the biography of Ellen Glasgow. During Ellen's life, the two writers had exchanged reciprocal admiration for each other's work. Marjorie considered Ellen's *Prefaces* masterly studies in the art of writing and in the relation of the artist to his work. And she recognized that even though their material was so different, they were both concerned with presenting human beings struggling against whatever enemy they faced—whether it was something inimical within themselves or in their background. It did not matter that Ellen's characters struggled within a sophisticated background and Marjorie's within a natural background.

Ellen Glasgow's work falls into three categories. First, a series of novels of social history of Virginia from the mid-nineteenth century to 1912. These first works include: *The Battle-Ground, Deliverance, The Romance of a Plain Man, Virginia*, and *Life and Gabriella*. Next she wrote three novels of the country: *The Miller of Old Church, Barren Ground*, and *Vein of Iron*. And finally, her novels of the city:

The Sheltered Life, The Romantic Comedians, They Stooped to Folly, and *In This Our Life,* for which she received a Pulitzer in 1942. She also published a highly acclaimed book of short stories, *The Shadowy Third,* in 1925. Marjorie was well acquainted with all these works and agreed with Ellen's statement that fiction should be "experience illuminated."

From New York, Marjorie went straight to Palm Beach to spend several days as the guest of Ellen's brother, Arthur Glasgow, who was collecting for her his correspondence with his sister. He, of course, had valuable reminiscences of their parents and of their childhood. He also offered to send to England for his voluminous correspondence with Ellen between 1905 and 1939.

On May 3 Norton drove her to Richmond to help her settle into the house she had rented at 5 Paxton Road. The house, which she rented for $37.50 per week, included linens and silver plus a cook for $20 per week, a yardman (who did the heavy cleaning), and a laundress. It was arranged between her and the Cabells that they would dine with each other twice a week—on Wednesdays at the Cabells and on Thursdays at Marjorie's house.

The local newspapers did interviews with Marjorie and in their write-ups gave equal attention to Ellen Glasgow, their local celebrity, and to Marjorie Rawlings, the famous author, who had come to do research for a biography of Glasgow. A woman who read an interview in which Marjorie mentioned that Uki, her beloved Siamese cat, had been lost over the holidays in Florida, offered to bring by her two Siamese kittens—just for Marjorie "to meet." Actually the woman was leaving for England to join her husband in the air force there and was anxious that the cats have a good home. Marjorie succumbed to their charms on first sight and Ditty (for Bandit) and Chi Chi (for Banshee) soon became a part of her life. Chi Chi, the female, was all charm, daintiness, and demureness, but a selfish conniver; while Ditty, the male, was shy and slow-witted, but starved for love. Since Moe had to be left in Florida, they filled the need in her life for animals to love, and furnished hours of entertainment and companionship. Marjorie wrote Norton long letters that included accounts of the antics of the kittens as well as details of her research activities. She asked him to keep the letters as she planned eventually to use them as reference when she began to write the biography.

In addition to acquiring pets, Marjorie made herself at home in the Richmond house by keeping it filled with flowers from her landlady's garden or with flowers from a florist's shop. And she bought ten pounds of birdseed for the feeder outside her window, which attracted song sparrows, redbirds, and turtle doves. Norton sent her a dozen red tulips and a dozen jonquils for Valentine's Day. Marjorie wrote Norton that she had gone alone to see the play, *Bell, Book and Candle*, mainly to see the Siamese cat in it. She got a seat close to the stage and was impressed by the cat's performance.

Aside from Col. Anderson, Anne Virginia Bennett, Ellen's longtime companion and secretary, was Marjorie's most important source for first-hand information. Many people came, after the publicity in the papers, to tell her tales and bring bits of gossip; but Marjorie, always meticulous in her research, was determined to verify every bit of information. And Anne Virginia was the ultimate source for the truth. The problem was that Anne Virginia, who was in frail health mentally and physically, had qualms about talking about her friend of so many years. After promising to tell Marjorie everything she knew, Anne Virginia had a nervous collapse, was hospitalized, and was given a series of electroshock treatments, which temporarily disturbed her memory. And Col. Anderson, in response to a direct question put to him by Marjorie about his relationship with Ellen, became short of breath and turned purple. Marjorie had to back off, for as she told Berg, she didn't want to go around Richmond "killing people."

One of Ellen's close friends who was extremely cooperative was Carrie Duke, a seventy-seven-year-old woman of great energy and zest. Duke gave a cocktail party for Marjorie in her attractive live-in antique shop, to which she invited a number of people who had known Ellen.

As Marjorie's circle of acquaintances in Richmond widened so did her social activities. For every luncheon, dinner, tea, or cocktail party she was given, she returned hospitality in good measure. On top of her intense research activities, it was extremely tiring mentally and physically. To save her strength, she worked mornings in bed with her typewriter on a tray. She told Norton that she must take a real rest when she had her material safely in shape. The trip abroad had really just begun to get her on her feet after the ordeal of finishing *The Sojourner*, and she admitted, "I wasn't ready to tackle anything like this." But she would not back down from the goal she had set of gathering all she could by the time she had to give up her house in mid-April.

As she discovered things in Ellen's background that shocked and dismayed her, she had moments when she wondered if she could do the biography at all. "It can only be brutal in many of its aspects," she told Norton. The way Ellen presented herself in her autobiography, *The Woman Within*, Marjorie came to feel was not a true nor a complete picture. The relationships within the Glasgow family reminded Marjorie of some little adders she had once seen living under a floribunda rose, and she decided she would use this symbol in the biography. Information supplied by friends and acquaintances of Ellen's ("because we know you'll be kind") revealed that she had had many feuds and was often a martinet. Marjorie agonized over how she could write the life story of her friend without revealing facts she would prefer not to discuss. Yet the body of Ellen Glasgow's works were so "unavoidably important" that she knew she would have to see it through. She vacillated over her approach, but she was sure that one strong theme would be the importance of Ellen as a social historian.

Col. Anderson gradually became more cooperative under Marjorie's skillful handling, and on one occasion he took her upstairs in his home where she saw two large signed photographs of Queen Marie of Rumania. Anderson introduced Marjorie to the woman who had brought Ellen and him together, and she told Marjorie that they were definitely engaged, and that his romance with Queen Marie had hurt Ellen. But after the breach healed, they remained platonic friends, having supper together every Sunday evening.

When Anne Virginia was finally able to see Marjorie, she proved at first disappointing. "I've always been able to draw people out," Marjorie told Norton, but Anne Virginia simply would not talk freely. She even went so far as to burn all but fourteen of the letters Ellen wrote to her.

On the whole, the time spent in Richmond was satisfying to Marjorie. Thanks to the efficiency of her secretary Nike Grafstrom, she had a large, well-organized file of material. She had received great cooperation and hospitality, but complained to Owen D. Young that the social duties took as much time as the actual research. Nothing could be done "except over chicken wings and a glass of sherry or a cup of tea."

Bertram Cooper wrote that he was proud of her; "*Grant* never took Richmond."

CHAPTER 19

The
Final
Betrayal

M arjorie's Siamese cats were a constant delight to her. As they matured, she kept Norton informed of their mating activities. Chi Chi seemed to know instinctively what it was all about, but the slower Ditty was greatly puzzled by Chi Chi's behavior and his own urges. Marjorie reported that she told Chi Chi, "Nothing so frightens away the boy friend as avidity," and that she tried to encourage Ditty, "Don't give up. You'll be pleasantly surprised." She reminded Norton of Paul Gallico's cat, "When in doubt, wash," and said that Ditty had almost washed his fur off. On March 7, she announced "Ditty is now a man." Although Chi Chi's pregnancy meant that Marjorie would have to delay her anticipated trip to Van Hornesville, she was pleased that Ditty's neuroses seemed conquered and he had gained in self-confidence and acquired an air of independence. He was obviously her favorite, and she wrote a poem about their rapport:

A Defensive Ditty for a Defenseless Ditty

I have a cat whose name is Ditty,
Admittedly uncouth, un-pretty.

I've been called names, so I have pity.
And ah, we both detest a city.

We have so many things in common.
We share indifference to Mammon.
We play at Scat, but not backgammon.
We both adore a nice fresh salmon.

We watch the birds. (Our reasons vary.)
We're alternately sad and merry.
O'er milk and gin we love to tarry.
We will not fetch nor will we carry.

We recognize our serendipity.
We think each other wise and witty.
What's in a name when one's a kitty?
He calls ME "Meowm." THAT'S worse than "Ditty"!

However, after Ditty had proved his manhood, Marjorie did reconsider his name, and decided to call him Edwardus Bogardus after her illustrious ancestor; but this title was soon reduced to "Bogie," a name that stuck.

In April Marjorie returned to St. Augustine to await the birth of the kittens. On April 13 she heard of an incident that angered her into writing a scorching letter to the editor of the St. Augustine *Record* to protest what had happened to the maid of Henry Seidel Canby, the head of the board of judges of the Book-of-the-Month Club. The Canbys were making one of their periodic visits to St. Augustine, along with their daughter, son-in-law, three grandchildren, and the children's black nurse. The nurse, past fifty years of age and originally from the West Indies, was a quiet and well-educated woman. She had gone alone for a dip in the ocean, unaware that it was the local custom for "colored" bathers to go to a different beach, several miles to the south of the "white" beach.

When a neighbor reported the woman's appearance on the restricted beach, a deputy sheriff appeared, seized the woman by the arm, and pushed her roughly into his car, telling her that she was under arrest. Terrified, she tried to explain that she was a nursemaid to the Canbys. Calling her "nigger" several times, the deputy told her he would take her to her residence only to get some clothes other than the bathing suit she was wearing and then would let her do her explaining to the judge. When they reached the Canbys' residence, Canby, after an unpleasant confrontation, managed to persuade the deputy to release the woman.

Marjorie wrote the editor condemning the treatment of the woman and said she was "most concerned with not to call it so harsh a name as brutality, the lack of simple courtesy and simple good manners on the part of the representative of the law." And she pointed out the damage such ungracious behavior did to the reputation of the city. In turn, Marjorie received grateful letters from blacks and civil rights leaders, including one who thanked her for "the many steps you have taken in behalf of members of my race." Not everyone agreed with her viewpoint, however, and she was called by some a "nigger lover." For a time the town was seething, with people taking one side or the other.

From April 26, 1953, through May 17, 1953, the Sunday editions of the Los Angeles *Times* carried a five-part "autobiographical" write-up by Marjorie. Compiled from the twenty-two-page questionnaire she had answered for the Literary Guild the previous year, it amounted to a summary of her life and work and contained much of her philosophy.

In it she mentioned Chuck only briefly ("My husband, a newspaperman, and I were amicably divorced in 1933,") and passed on to the lonely years of freezes and low prices for her oranges, and the desperate day when she was down to a can of soup and a box of crackers and stamped her foot and said, "Things will have to get tougher than this to run me away from the Creek," followed by the miraculous arrival in the mail that same day of the $500 check for the O. Henry first prize for "Gal Young Un."

She told of her marriage to Norton Baskin in 1941 and of his "puzzled patience" while she abandoned him for six summers to write *The Sojourner* in Van Hornesville. Crediting Owen D. Young with helping her find this northern retreat, where she could again live through a dramatic change of seasons, she said, "Cross Creek is

still 'home' but it has become a race between me and the robins in
our mutual yearning to return to quote Edwin Way Teale, 'North
With the Spring.' "

She revealed to her readers something of her creative process in
discussing the slow development of *The Sojourner*. It was Ase Linden's book, she said, but his wife Nellie kept threatening to take
over:

> *I began, as I did with Ma Baxter in "The Yearling," with an*
> *almost total lack of sympathy for her. Nellie did not appreciate*
> *Ase, nor truly love him. Her standards were materialistic. She*
> *kept saying extremely vulgar things that I was obliged to*
> *delete. I had to give up and let her be herself, a much nicer*
> *and kinder little soul than I had intended, "a good wife," after*
> *all, as Ase himself said of her in the end.*

Something of the same sort happened with Benjamin, the lost brother,
Marjorie wrote. He seemed cruel in his abandonment of Ase; he was
apparently heartless toward their mother, Amelia. "I meant Ase's
lifelong devotion to him to be unwarranted, a sign only of his capacity
for love, but I found almost with surprise as Ben lay dying, that he
had valid reasons, and that he was worthy. I remember exclaiming
aloud, 'Ase was right about him all the time.' " Her plodding agony
in the latter-middle part of the book matched Ase's feelings as he
met with one betrayal after another, as he failed in his articulateness
to speak for the good and against the evil, knowing himself that he
was failing. Her answer, she said, came only toward the end of the
final rewriting of the book. By this time she was so identified with
Ase that she felt the same soaring release that came to him. "I realize
now that was what I had always intended," she concluded.

In the second installment of her Los Angeles *Times* autobiography,
Marjorie discussed her working methods beginning with her need
for an almost exact topography in her writing, which necessitated
her drawing maps for her own use. Her note-taking she described as
being always voluminous no matter what her subject. In the case of
her books about the Florida Crackers, much of her research was done
by informal interviews, which were simply a matter of asking ques-

tions of oldtimers about hunting experiences, herbal remedies used by their grandparents, and the like. She told of living in the Scrub under the same conditions as the Crackers. Although she had worked from eight or nine in the morning to five or six at night and sometimes toward the end of a book into the night during most of her working life, she admitted that now she found herself able to work only half a day at her writing. She rewrote a book several times because infinite, apparently small, details required rewriting to give a final harmony of character and situation or even to accent the style. And she said she composed on a typewriter except for her "private verses" whose slow thought required pencil and paper.

The third installment contained a discussion of her favorites among the many characters she had created. Penny Baxter, whom she called "wise and tender and a little man against great odds," continued to be special to her. She told her readers that she enjoyed writing about Quincey Dover, the big, fat countrywoman who could take a joke on herself, and "who has a tolerance and understanding of the male that I like to think of as my own." Marjorie remarked that she was still too close to Ase Linden to know whether or not she would continue to care for him. "I rather think so," she said, "for there is perhaps more of every man's struggle in him than in any other of my characters." She admitted to being devoted to the Forresters in *The Yearling.* Their uncomplicated zest for life was a relief to her from some of the more serious and worthy characters she had invented. "They are a shocking family, vulgar, brawling, fiddling, dancing, drinking before dawn, unclothed, uninhibited." The only one of her characters Marjorie hated, she said, was Amelia Linden, Ase's mother in *The Sojourner.* "Because of her madness she cannot be held entirely responsible for her evil, but her very madness becomes centered, without the concern for others that alone redeems all egotistic humanity."

Mentioning her desire to write more short stories, Marjorie explained that a long novel calls for "so much carpentry and bricklaying," while a short story is conceived almost whole and is more amenable to being molded into "Robert Frost's 'roundness.'" She told the readers that Robert Frost's liking for her story "Benny and the Bird Dogs" had pleased her as much as any reaction to her work.

She especially like his insistence that it was a man's kind of humor, since she thought that the accident of a writer's sex should not obtrude on his work. "I long not to be of the 'lady-author' ilk who, as Dorothy Parker said of one of them, 'trails her petticoats through literature.' "

In the fifth and last installment, she mentioned the authors she admired, prefacing her list by saying there had been no such style "before or since" to equal the style of the King James version of the Bible. "I stand in awe of Marcel Proust, as a stylist first, for even the most involved of his sentences climb rhythmically to a superb climax, like Bach organ music," she said. And she praised her friend Sigrid Undset's sweeping range in her historical novels and her "bitter" understanding. The Russians—Tolstoy, Dostoevsky, Chekhov—moved her among the foreign writers as did the French novelists Stendhal and Balzac. As favorite English poets she named Shelley, Keats and "some of Wordsworth." In the short story genre, Guy de Maupassant had been her first mentor.

Discussing actors, she mentioned having had the good fortune to see the three Barrymores, Ethel, Lionel, and John, in their greatest character roles on the living stage. "Time has killed one of them, the exigencies of radio and movies have lowered a bit the acting standards of the others, yet the Barrymores still stand in the great tradition of acting." On the modern stage she named Marlon Brando and Judith Anderson as unique in maintaining a "complete integrity of acting." Fredric March, she said, also maintained that integrity. She excluded Helen Hayes, regretfully, because she had allowed herself to act in so many inferior plays and movies. Among screen stars, Marjorie's preferences were Katharine Hepburn, Greta Garbo, Gregory Peck, Henry Fonda, Gene Kelly, and Spencer Tracy.

She admitted that although she was once a wonderful cook, ten years of having maids to do the cooking had spoiled her, and she had lost a great deal of her knack. But nothing in life still gave her more satisfaction than making jams and jellies. "Here, perfection is attainable, results are tangible. I make a wild raspberry syrup the flavor of which has a more devastating effect on strong men than strong perfume."

Although she felt it presumptuous for a novelist to offer solutions to the problems of the world where world leaders, sociologists, and economists had failed, still since humanity itself was the writer's business, she ventured to say that the basic problem of man was a spiritual one, at home and abroad. Plain people seemed to her to be ahead of their leaders in some respects. As an example she mentioned the pressure that such people had put on the U.S. Congress to vote for wheat to be sent to the starving people in India. The immediate problem "is the enslavement of too many hundreds of millions of plain, decent people by a Soviet minority, the ideals of whose original revolution have been dissipated in a cruel inhumanity and blind lust for power, and who must be halted lest the whole universe be enslaved." But she concluded:

> *Yet the military defeat on the ideological containment of the ruling Soviet will not solve the continuing problem which might be reduced to that of man's arrogance, his lack of love and humility, tiny bit of dust that he is, in the face of God and the Cosmos.*

Bogie and Chi Chi became the parents of four charming Siamese kittens the first week in May, and the veterinarian advised the Baskins to wait at least three weeks before taking them on a long car trip. Accordingly, it was not until May 31 that Marjorie and Norton with the faithful Moe, two adult Siamese cats, and four three-week-old Siamese kittens set out for Van Hornesville. They had sent off by express all possible parcels and suitcases in order to leave the whole rear seat of the car for the grown-up animals, Moe and Chi Chi and Bogie. The four kittens were in a big box on the front seat. In the unair-conditioned car, the three in the back seat became increasingly wild. The cats decided to blame the dog for their condition and took turns picking on him, while Moe cowered in a corner, bewildered. They stopped several times to buy big bags of ice to cool the temperature and wrung out handkerchiefs in ice water to swab the kittens. By the time they stopped at a new tourist court at the end of the day, all were completely exhausted.

Talking fast, Norton persuaded the manager that the animals were well-behaved. But as soon as the man opened the door to the room,

Chi Chi climbed to the top of the drapes and Bogie followed her lead. Moe ran into the closet and refused to come out, and the kittens moaned pitifully. Norton assured the owner that as soon as he fed them, they would all be fine and perfectly behaved, and the man, obviously still dubious, let them stay. Twenty minutes later in the cool room with their stomachs full, all were feeling better, and Chi Chi and Bogie went into the closet and made up with Moe. When they reached Van Hornesville, Marjorie promised Norton that as soon as the kittens were old enough, she would find good homes for them. They both should have known her better. The most adventurous of the kittens, the one who was first in everything important to kittens, she named Marco Polo. By June Marjorie was telling Bee that the kittens were "so ravishing" she didn't see how she could give any of them up. "If you haven't had a Siamese, you haven't lived."

As Marjorie prepared for a summer that included lots of company, she felt fortunate to have Gertrude Sandvoldt, a neat, efficient Norwegian woman, as her housekeeper. She expected to work on some new short stories and to rework some old ones and to continue by correspondence her research on Ellen Glasgow. She fretted over when she should return to Richmond and where she needed to be during the winter. Norton wrote her, "Darling, you're a valley of indecision and a mountain of discontent. Why don't you relax and enjoy your cats and your garden and Gertrude and quit worrying about your winter?" She had certainly earned the right to a leisurely summer, he told her, but it wouldn't do her any good if she stayed in a constant stew. "Tell Moe I asked about him first and the cats second," he said and added he was overseeing the fixing up of the cottage and Cross Creek in preparation for her return.

One of Marjorie's concerns was that her Aunt Wilmer was in Boston, alone, having hip surgery for the fourth time. She took the train from Van Hornesville to Boston and, shocked at the drab tiny room her aunt was in, insisted on paying for a larger, more airy room with a view. She left a standing order with a local florist to deliver a bouquet of flowers every week to her aunt during her prolonged stay in Boston, and she also bought her aunt toiletries and a month's supply of reading matter. Before she returned to Van Hornesville, she gave her money to pay for a comfortable room close to the hospital after her release for as long as she needed to be there.

During this time Marjorie was sending Arthur regular checks to help him care for Jeffrey. And another cause to which she contributed was the Holland Flood Relief, which was supported by a committee that included Francis Cardinal Spellman and Walter Winchell, by turning over her royalties from the sale of her books in the Netherlands.

As usual Marjorie participated in the four-generation Young family annual show in which each person present prepared an exhibit to illustrate his or her accomplishment for the year. Marjorie's exhibit was a laundry basket covered with gilded chicken wire on top and laced with flowers and ribbons, with six cats inside. Naturally, all of the Young children voted for her exhibit as being the best, and she was pleased to win third prize in the show. At her annual buffet supper for the thirty or so Youngs, she served her famous jellied chicken and baked ham. As the summer turned to fall, Marjorie wrote to Bernice Gilkyson that the maples and sumacs were turning red and she had done no work. She felt "an appalling sense of guilt" when she was not writing, and she told her friend that she was feeling very tired.

Norton drove up in mid-September so he could take the animals back to Florida while Marjorie stopped off a few weeks in Richmond to finish up her research there. The first thing he saw in the Yankee house was six cats. Marjorie defended herself, telling him, "You live with them a day and you won't be able to give them away either." Norton answered, "In that case, they leave here today." Together they drove around the area until they found homes for three of the kittens. Norton agreed that Marco Polo was too special to give away, which was some comfort to Marjorie, who shed tears at each parting.

On the trip home, Norton and Marjorie caravaned part of the way, and then Norton took all the animals in his car so Marjorie could stay in Virginia. He had a vexatious trip back to St. Augustine with the three cats and Moe. One day Moe quietly ate the fried chicken out of Norton's picnic basket as they drove along, and at every stop the cats kept escaping. Once as he was sitting on a log eating lunch, Norton looked back to see the three cats stalking down the road, single file, tails stiff and high. At this point, he probably did not agree with Marjorie's declaration to Bernice that "Three Siamese cats are not a bit too many."

Marjorie herself went first to Lexington, Virginia, for a profitable visit with Ellen Glasgow's sister. Then she went on to Richmond where she took rooms at the Jefferson Hotel. Immediately she was caught up in an exhausting social round that seemed to be unavoidable in her research. She entertained Margaret and James Cabell for dinner in her rooms, and went to their home for long visits. Anne Virginia Bennett, whose health had improved, came for lunch at the Jefferson. She had dug up some more letters and was finally willing to talk freely, so Marjorie planned a series of visits with her. Carrie Duke and Marjorie entertained each other, and Marjorie bought a butler's table and a chair for Cross Creek from Carrie's antique shop. Marjorie entertained other friends and acquaintances of Ellen's at tea or lunch or for cocktails. "I am gradually getting some select dirt and also some sweet and charming stories," she told Norton. She also continued to write letters of inquiry and to send out feelers in connection with her research. She had decided she wanted to relate Ellen's personal life to her work in order to make the book a true biography. One of her lines of investigation was intended to uncover the early romantic involvements in Ellen's life that would account for her "sexual bitterness." Also she wanted to discover how much Ellen's increasing deafness affected her personal relationships. To track down some leads, Marjorie made a trip alone to Norfolk and Virginia Beach. The leads proved to be of little consequence, and the drive itself was a nightmare as she got into Norfolk after dark and ran into heavy football traffic. Several days after the trip, even though she spent the mornings in bed, she was still feeling extremely tired.

Just before she left Richmond, Marjorie had one hundred ten-pound bags of cat litter sent by freight to Crescent Beach. She left Richmond the second week in November in a driving snowstorm and was sideswiped by a truck on the highway. En route to Florida she stopped to spend a night with Norman Berg and Julie at Dunwoody, just outside Atlanta. Then she drove over to Union Springs, Alabama, to spend a night with Norton's family there. Leaving at 7:45 a.m. she reached the cottage by 4:30 p.m., "breaking all Baskin records." She found Norton and the animals in good condition, with Norton now completely under the spell of Marco Polo, who picked up his red collar when it came off and carried it to Norton to put on again.

On November 13, Marjorie wrote her editor, Jack Wheelock, that she had a quarrel with him. He had said that it was not often that the biography of a great writer is written by another great writer his or her peer. Marjorie scolded: "God damn it, Ellen Glasgow was not a *great* writer. Neither am I. You do not use adjectives loosely in your poems, do not use them so in writing about me and my work. I know my limitations."

A few days later, Marjorie wrote to Ellen's sister, Rebe Glasgow Tutwiler, to discuss her progress and certain similarities she had discovered between Ellen and herself. They were both born with a tragic sense, she told Rebe. But Ellen, Marjorie said, had a keener, more analytical mind and undoubtedly faced the "fatal reality" earlier. "I myself had intervals of this when young, but it did not overwhelm me until middle life." She was groping, she said, toward what the biography should be:

> *I can scarcely hope to write deathless prose, but if I can bring enough artistry to this book I may be able to bring Ellen to life again for those who did not have the good fortune of knowing her. I think she would have liked to have this done.*
>
> *But as with two other dear writer friends, Sigrid Undset and Margaret Mitchell, it is almost impossible to think of them as gone. I find myself thinking I must write so and so to Ellen or Sigrid or Margaret. . . .*

During November 1953, Marjorie was busy making many plans with Norton for the next year. News arrived that their apartment at Castle Townsend in County Cork, Ireland, was completed and ready for their arrival in spring. There was difficulty in taking the cats, as they would have to spend a long time in quarantine. Perhaps she could find a cat over there to live with her since a friend had written her that she "must have a familiar."

Before going to Ireland, they planned to make the long-promised visit to the aunts in Phoenix for the spring. The three were becoming increasingly excited over the prospect and wrote that for the rest of their lives, they would date things as happening "before" or "after" the visit. Marjorie also made plans to see the Van Vechtens in New York in the early spring for social and business purposes, as Carl had some letters from Ellen Glasgow for her to copy. And she planned to include a side trip to see the Gilkysons also.

Carl Brandt sent her a proposal from *Holiday* magazine that she do an article for them on Florida. She accepted the offer and planned to revisit the Scrub and the surrounding area to refresh her memory and to see what changes had occurred since she wrote *The Yearling*. And the Brandts had another offer for her that involved a television show. She was interested and told Carl, "I shall undoubtedly be in New York for a couple of weeks this winter or early spring and look forward to seeing you and Carol and Marcia Davenport."

With her usual Christmas munificence, Marjorie sent chocolates and other treats to overseas friends, Florida fruits and preserves to friends scattered over the United States, and carefully selected gifts to her close friends and relatives. Before the gifts had time to reach their destinations, the intended recipients heard the news by radio, telephone, or newspaper that Marjorie was dead.

On the night of December 12, 1953, while the Baskins were playing bridge with the Youngs, Marjorie complained of feeling ill but thought it was her old troublesome diverticulitis acting up. Later that evening when she became unable to walk, Norton realized something serious was wrong and took her to Flagler Hospital. The doctors told him that she had a ruptured aneurism, that a blood vessel had burst at the base of her brain. They told him that it could happen again but that it might not. If it didn't, she could probably lead a careful, normal life. It was a matter of chance. But life and time had loaded the dice against Marjorie. All of the factors that can add up to a fatal stroke were against her. She was betrayed by her genes (both parents had died young); by her own personal habits (heavy smoking and drinking); by her love of good food that led to excessive weight; and by her personality (high-strung and tense). The next day another blood vessel burst and she died. She was fifty-seven years old.

Numbly, Norton planned for the funeral with the help of nearby friends like Phil May. In distant cities friends like the Norman Bergs and Marcia Davenport heard the news on the radio with shock. The New York *Times* of December 15 not only ran an obituary but also devoted a segment of its editorial column to Marjorie, equating her loss to that of Dylan Thomas and Eugene O'Neill, both of whom had died recently. Telegrams and letters of condolence poured in to Norton. Pearl Primus, who fainted when told of Marjorie's death, asked that Norton place a single red rose for her beside Marjorie. In addition to old friends, recent ones like Carrie Duke wrote to express their sense of grief at not being able to continue their new but treasured friendships with her.

The most poignant letters, though, were from complete strangers, who wrote simply because they had been touched and helped by her books. As Norton read these spontaneous outpourings from many different countries, written by people of all classes, but all expressing gratitude and deep feeling for the woman who had been his wife, he began to formulate the epitaph he had been struggling with. Finally he found the one simple, perfect phrase he had been working for. The inscription read:

MARJORIE KINNAN RAWLINGS

1896–1953

wife of

NORTON BASKIN

THROUGH HER WRITINGS SHE ENDEARED
HERSELF TO
THE PEOPLE OF THE WORLD

Epilogue

The minutes tick so slowly,
  the years so fast
A long time now, minutes, unbearable
  slow minutes, until you come.
But the years when you were gone
  are (were) only an instant, a breath
of air across the oleanders,
  a butterfly on the one-day hibiscus blossoms.

So, it is life and love are slow,
  and death is fast (quick).

Found among Marjorie's papers after her death.

A final irony in Marjorie's life is that her tombstone in the Antioch Cemetery is only a few feet from that of Zelma Cason. Zelma came to Marjorie's funeral, and shortly thereafter she went into a nursing home, where she was often seen to be grieving and crying. Norton went to see her and told her that Marjorie did not hold any bitterness against her, that it was only a question of the right to write. Following the visit, he sent Zelma flowers, and she was touched, saying she knew they came from Marjorie.

In her will, Marjorie named a few specific bequests, including the original Wyeth painting of "The Dance of the Cranes" to Julia Scribner Bigham; their mother's silver to Arthur; and the desk that had been on her Cross Creek porch to Col. Otto Lange. She provided that Martha Mickens be allowed to use the tenant house in the yard at Cross Creek for life and that she be given a weekly income. The will provided that Arthur's indebtedness to Marjorie, which amounted to several thousands of dollars, be canceled.

Her library, manuscripts, notes, correspondence, and all literary property were to be turned over to Julia Scribner Bigham, whom she named as her literary executor, with the power and duty of destroying any of the notes, manuscripts, or correspondence that she thought should be destroyed. Julia was then directed to turn over the literary remains to the University of Florida.

All the rest of Marjorie's property was bequeathed to the University of Florida Endowment Corporation in trust. The income from the trust, after meeting the specific requests in her will, was to be divided equally between Norton Baskin and Arthur Kinnan. She asked that her home at Cross Creek and the land surrounding it be used to further "purposes of The University of Florida," and gave as examples of the type of use she had in mind: the occupancy of the house as a residence by faculty members; the use of the house as an auxiliary library; or the use of the land for agricultural experiments, particularly in the citrus field.

Some of the university's young faculty members who were billeted at Cross Creek left something to be desired as housekeepers. As the years passed, the property became rundown and unkempt, causing several people to write to the university in distress. Finally, the university turned the house and grounds over to the Florida Department of Natural Resources, a division of the parks system, which at present maintains and operates it as the Marjorie Kinnan Rawlings State Historic Site. It is conceived as a living museum, with vegetable and flower gardens and redbird baskets in the trees. The shelves of the pantry are lined with jams and jellies and often visitors will find a park ranger in the kitchen baking bread in the old wood stove. Some of Marjorie's books, clothes, and furniture are there, including the palmetto base table that Chuck made and at which she sat on a horsehide chair, sweating away at her writing. And there are cats that may be able to trace their ancestry back to the pre-Siamese days.

As Marjorie's literary executor, Julia Scribner destroyed some of the more personal and revealing letters in the voluminous correspondence about Ellen Glasgow. In accordance with Marjorie's wishes, she adamantly refused to allow "Mountain Prelude" to be published as a book. And Julia oversaw the publication by Scribners of two posthumous books of Marjorie's writing. The first was *The Secret River*, the book about Calpurnia, the little black girl with the poetic bent, which Marjorie had worked on with Max Perkins and then put away thinking she might someday develop it into a longer book. When it appeared in 1955, according to the custom then, it received small notice from reviewers because it was a children's book. However, a few journals took note of it because it was by Marjorie Rawlings. The New York *Herald Tribune* called *The Secret River* a "haunting, symbolic tale," and other reviewers said it was "a perfect gem," "charming," and "enchanting." Various reviews referred to it as an allegory, a folklore tale, and a fable. At the end of the book, Calpurnia, who has seen the secret river, makes up a final poem to say to her dog, Buggy-Horse:

> *The world is full of love.*
> *It sings like a turtle dove.*
> *The world will love me*
> *And under a cypress tree,*
> *On its knee,*
> *We will watch the secret river together.*
> *We will find a white bird's feather.*

The book was charmingly illustrated by Leonard Weisgard. Its publication was a reminder to some of how untimely Marjorie's death had been. In December of 1956, James Branch Cabell wrote to Norton:

> *I cannot but rage when I think of what the world has lost through* [The Secret River] *author's sudden death in her very prime. . . . But above all, my dear Norton, we lost her. I confess candidly that not until after her death did I comprehend how deeply I had loved Marjorie, just as a private person, and to the best of my knowledge, as a person whose like has not ever existed at any time elsewhere.*

In 1956, Scribners published *The Marjorie Rawlings Reader*, edited by Julia. It contained *South Moon Under*, four chapters from *Cross Creek*, two from *The Yearling*, the novella *Jacob's Ladder*, and five short stories, chosen to show the range of Marjorie's writing. The stories were "Gal Young Un," "Cocks Must Crow," and Marjorie's own three favorites: "Jessamine Springs," "The Shell," and "The Pelican's Shadow." A collection of her letters was published by the University of Florida Presses in 1983.

Her works have truly been read worldwide. *The Yearling* has been published in twenty-one languages, *Golden Apples* in ten, *The Sojourner* in eight, *Cross Creek* in six, and *South Moon Under* in five. *The Yearling* has fulfilled Max Perkins's prediction of becoming a classic, as have some of her short stories through their continued use in anthologies. A handsome new edition of *The Yearling* was published in 1985, with the illustrations of N. C. Wyeth, and the same year a new musical version of the novel opened in Atlanta.

Shortly after Marjorie died, Arthur Kinnan wrote to Norton, "I have depended on Marjorie all my life." He continued this dependence after her death, asking for an advance out of her estate to help him in his custody fight for Jeffrey. During an unpleasant trial, his third wife was made to appear insane, and Arthur won permanent custody except for one day a week visitation rights by his ex-wife and six weeks in the summer. The aunts in Arizona each lived to be around a hundred, and Jeffrey was grown when they died. Their estates, amounting to about $90,000, were all left to him. Norton gave Marjorie's car to the aunts and continued to send them gifts as long as they lived.

When Julia Scribner Bigham died of cancer in 1960, Norton became Marjorie's literary executor. He kept in touch with many of their mutual friends, including Bee McNeil. Several years after Marjorie's death, he wrote to her that life went on in a dull way, adding, "The spice is gone."

SELECTED BIBLIOGRAPHY

The following chronological listing of published works by Marjorie Kinnan Rawlings does not include most of her juvenile writing nor most of her writing as a newspaper feature writer and reporter during the eight years preceding her move to Florida.

BOOKS

South Moon Under. New York: Charles Scribner's Sons, 1933.
Golden Apples. New York: Charles Scribner's Sons, 1935.
The Yearling. New York: Charles Scribner's Sons, 1938.
When the Whippoorwill. New York: Charles Scribner's Sons, 1940.
Cross Creek. New York: Charles Scribner's Sons, 1942.
Cross Creek Cookery. New York: Charles Scribner's Sons, 1942.
The Sojourner. New York: Charles Scribner's Sons, 1953.
The Secret River. New York: Charles Scribner's Sons, 1955.
The Marjorie Rawlings Reader, Julia Scribner Bigham, ed. New York: Charles Scribner's Sons, 1956.
Selected Letters of Marjorie Kinnan Rawlings, Gordon E. Bigelow and Laura V. Monti, eds. Gainesville: University of Florida Presses, 1983.

SHORTER WORKS

"The Reincarnation of Miss Hetty." *McCall's Magazine* (August 1912), p. 27ff. Fiction.
"The Miracle." *Wisconsin Literary Magazine,* XVII (October 1917), p. 7. Poem.
Wisconsin Literary Magazine, XVII (April 1918), pp. 169–170. Editorial on Vachel Lindsay.
"The Monastery." *Wisconsin Literary Magazine,* XVII (May 1918),

pp. 205–206. Poem. Reprinted in Braithewaite's anthology, "Poets of the Future," 1919.

"Cracker Chidlings: Real Tales From the Florida Interior." *Scribner's Magazine*, LXXXIX (February 1931), pp. 127–134. Fictionalized anecdotes.

"Jacob's Ladder," *Scribner's Magazine*, LXXXIX (April 1931), pp. 351ff. Fiction.

"Plumb Clare Conscience." *Scribner's Magazine*, XC (December 1931), pp. 622–626. Fiction.

"A Crop of Beans." *Scribner's Magazine*, XCI (May 1932), pp. 283–290. Fiction.

"Gal Young Un." *Harper's*, CLXV (June 1932), pp. 21–33; (July 1932), pp. 225–234. Fiction.

"Hyacinth Drift." *Scribner's Magazine*, XCIV (September 1933), pp. 169–173. Nonfiction.

"Alligators." Written with Fred Tompkins. *Saturday Evening Post*, CCVI (September 23, 1933), pp. 16ff. Fictionalized anecdotes.

"Benny and the Bird Dogs." *Scribner's Magazine*, XCIV (October 1933), pp. 193–200. Fiction.

"The Pardon." *Scribner's Magazine*, XCVI (August 1934), pp. 95–98. Fiction.

"Having Left Cities Behind Me." *Scribner's Magazine*, XCVIII (October 1935), p. 246. Poem.

"Varmints." *Scribner's Magazine*, C (December 1936), pp. 26ff. Fiction.

"A Mother in Mannville." *Saturday Evening Post*, CCIX (December 12, 1936), pp. 7ff. Fiction. Condensed version in *Reader's Digest* (February 1968).

"Mountain Rain." *Scribner's Magazine*, CIV (July 1938), p. 63. Poem.

"I Sing While I Cook." *Vogue*, XCIII (February 15, 1939), pp. 48–49. Nonfiction.

"Cocks Must Crow." *Saturday Evening Post*, CCXII (November 25, 1939), pp. 5ff. Fiction.

"The Pelican's Shadow." *New Yorker*, XV (January 6, 1940), pp. 17–19. Fiction.

"The Enemy." *Saturday Evening Post*, CCXII (January 20, 1940), pp. 12ff. Fiction.

"In the Heart." *Collier's*, CV (February 3, 1940), pp. 19ff. Fiction.

"Regional Literature of the South." *College English*, I (February 1940), pp. 381–388. Nonfiction.

"Why I Am an American." Summer 1940. Radio broadcast, printed in various syndicated papers.

"Jessamine Springs." *New Yorker*, XVII (February 22, 1941), pp. 19–20. Fiction.

"The Provider." *Woman's Home Companion*, LXVIII (June 1941), pp. 21ff. Fiction.

"Here is Home." *Atlantic*, CLXIX (March 1942), pp. 277–285. Nonfiction.

"Who Owns Cross Creek?" *Atlantic*, CLXIX (April 1942), pp. 439–450. Nonfiction.

"Fanny, You Fool!" *Vogue*, C (July 15, 1942), p. 42. Nonfiction.

"Sweet Talk, Honey!" *Vogue*, C (December 1, 1942), pp. 77ff. Nonfiction.

"Cross Creek Breakfasts." *Woman's Home Companion*, LXIX (November 1942), pp. 72–73. Nonfiction.

"Trees for Tomorrow." *Collier's*, CXVII (May 8, 1943), pp. 14ff. Nonfiction.

"Florida: A Land of Contrasts." *Transatlantic*, XIV (October 1944), pp. 12–17. Nonfiction.

"Shell." *New Yorker*, XX (December 9, 1944), pp. 29–31. Fiction.

"Black Secret." *New Yorker*, XXI (September 8, 1945), pp. 20–23. Fiction.

"Miriam's Houses." *New Yorker*, XXI (November 24, 1945), pp. 29–31. Fiction.

"Miss Moffatt Steps Out." *Liberty*, XXIII (February 16, 1946), pp. 30ff. Fiction.

"Introduction," *Katherine Mansfield Collection*, John Middleton Murry, ed., Cleveland: World Publishing, 1946. Nonfiction.

Mountain Prelude. Six-part serial. *Saturday Evening Post*, CCXIX (April 26, 1947), pp. 15ff; (May 3, 1947), pp. 36ff; (May 10, 1947), pp. 38ff; (May 17, 1947), pp. 40ff; (May 24, 1947), pp. 36ff; (May 31, 1947), pp. 40ff. Fiction.

"About Fabulous Florida." New York *Herald Tribune* weekly book review (November 30, 1947). Review of *The Everglades* by Marjory Stoneman Douglas. Nonfiction.

"Writing as a Career." *Book of Knowledge,* 1948 Annual Supplement. Nonfiction.

"The Friendship," *Saturday Evening Post,* CCXXI (January 1, 1949), pp. 14ff. Fiction.

"Portrait of a Magnificent Editor as Seen in His Letters," *Publishers Weekly,* CLVII (April 1, 1950), pp. 1573ff. Nonfiction.

"Marjorie Kinnan Rawlings." Autobiographical sketches. *Los Angeles Times* (April 26, 1953; May 3, 1953; May 4, 1953; May 10, 1953; May 17, 1953; May 24, 1953). Nonfiction.

"Lord Bill of the Suwannee River." Gordon E. Bigelow, ed., *Southern Folklore Quarterly,* XXVIII (June 1963), pp. 113ff. Folklore.

UNPUBLISHED WORKS

The Rare Book Section of The University of Florida Libraries houses the extensive Marjorie Kinnan Rawlings Collection. In addition to handwritten material, it includes transcripts (typewritten), photocopies (positive), and microfilm (negative). Her voluminous correspondence is here, as well as manuscripts of her books, short stories, unpublished poems. Also included are newspaper articles, notes, journal entries, lecture notes, and speeches. The remaining information she gathered toward a biography of Ellen Glasgow is in this collection. There are several large scrapbooks containing newspaper and periodical clippings, genealogical material and family photographs. Maxwell Perkins's letters to Marjorie have been supplemented by microfilm copies of her letters to him. The collection contains many business papers relating to Marjorie's writing and to her personal affairs, including a copy of her will; and transcripts and correspondence about the trial in 1946, which was occasioned by a lawsuit brought against Marjorie by Zelma Cason. In addition to this collection, I have examined the Marjorie Kinnan Rawlings collections at these libraries:

> *University of Georgia Libraries, Athens.*
> *Alderman Library, Manuscript Department, University of Virginia, Charlottesville.*

Beinecke Rare Book and Manuscript Library, Yale
University, New Haven, Connecticut.
Scribners' Archives, Rare Book Department, Princeton
University Firestone Library, Princeton, New Jersey.

Also I have examined correspondence, clippings, business papers and
miscellaneous artifacts privately held by:

Norton Baskin, St. Augustine, Florida.
Martin Dibner, Casco Village, Maine.
Beatrice Humiston McNeil, Los Angeles, California.
Jean Kinnan Peterson, Phoenix, Arizona.
Henry W. Clune, Scottsville, New York.
Jake Glisson, Evinston, Florida.

The University of Florida Libraries has the following collection of
theses and dissertations pertaining to Marjorie Kinnan Rawlings:

Furlow, Carl Tim. "Folklore Elements in the Florida Writings of
Marjorie Kinnan Rawlings." Master's thesis, University of Florida,
Gainesville, 1963.
McGuire, William J., Jr. "A Study of Florida Cracker Dialect Based
Chiefly on the Prose Works of Marjorie Kinnan Rawlings." Master's thesis, University of Florida, Gainesville, 1939.
Peck, Joseph R. "The Fiction Writing Art of Marjorie Kinnan Rawlings." Master's thesis, University of Florida, Gainesville, 1954.
Robillard, Ambolena H. "Maxwell Evarts Perkins: Authors' Editor."
Ph. D. dissertation, University of Florida, Gainesville, 1964.
Saffy, Edna Louise. "Marjorie Kinnan Rawlings' *The Yearling*: A
Study in the Rhetorical Effectiveness of a Novel." Ph. D. dissertation, University of Florida, Gainesville, 1976.
Shaw, Peggy Jo. "Marjorie Kinnan Rawlings: Her Life in Cross Creek,
1928 to 1953." Master's thesis. University of Florida, Gainesville,
1982.
Slagle, Mary Louise. "The Artistic Uses of Nature in the Fiction of
Marjorie Kinnan Rawlings." Master's thesis. University of Florida,
Gainesville, 1953.

INTERVIEWS

I have discussed Marjorie Rawlings informally with many people in the Cross Creek area, and I have had more extensive interviews with the following:

Norton Baskin: April 12, 13, 1983; October 24, 25, 26, 1983; October 3, 4, 5, 1984. Telephone: June 1, 1985; October 20, 1985, St. Augustine, Florida.
Henry Clune: October 21, 1984, Scottsville, New York.
Jake Glisson: October 5, 1984, Cross Creek and Evinston, Florida.
Beatrice Humiston McNeil: May 6, 7, 8, 1984. Telephone: May 26, 1985. Los Angeles, California.
Charles Scribner, Jr.: October 9, 1984, New York, New York.
Stephen Nesbitt: October 22, 1983. Cross Creek, Florida.
Bob Lucas: December 24, 1982; October 27, 1983. Cross Creek, Florida.
Sally Morrison: April 11, 1983; October 27, 1983; October 1, 1984. Cross Creek, Florida.

SECONDARY SOURCES

The following list of published works about Marjorie Kinnan Rawlings and her environment and her writing includes only a few of the hundreds of articles that have been written about her.

"Ase's Agonies." (review of *The Sojourner*) *Time*, January 5, 1953, p. 74.
Baker, Carlos. *Ernest Hemingway: A Life Story*. New York: Charles Scribner's Sons, 1969. pp. 286–290; 295–296.
Bandler, Michael J. "Old-Fashioned But in Style." *American Way*, October 1983, pp. 30–33.
Bellman, Samuel. *Marjorie Kinnan Rawlings*. New York: Twayne Publishers, 1974.
————. "Marjorie Kinnan Rawlings: A Solitary Sojourner in the Florida Backwoods." *Kansas Quarterly*, 2 (Spring 1970), pp. 78–87.

Berg, A. Scott. *Max Perkins: Editor of Genius.* New York: Pocket Books, Washington Square Press, 1978.

Bickel, Mary. "Marjorie Kinnan Rawlings." *Demcourier,* 13 (December 1943), pp. 3ff.

Bigelow, Gordon E. *Frontier Eden: The Literary Career of Marjorie Kinnan Rawlings.* Gainesville: University Presses of Florida, 1966.

———. "Marjorie Kinnan Rawlings' Wilderness." *Sewanee Review,* 73 (Spring 1965) pp. 299–310.

Bromfield, Louis. "Case of the Wandering Wits." *Saturday Review.* January 3, 1953.

Brooks, Paul. "Oklawaha: 'The Sweetest Water-Lane in the World.' " *Audubon* 72 (July 1970), pp. 34–45.

Davenport, Marcia. *Too Strong for Fantasy.* New York: Charles Scribner's Sons, 1967.

Evans, Harry. "Marjorie Kinnan Rawlings." *Family Circle.* 2 parts, May 7, 1943, pp. 10ff.; May 14, 1943, pp. 20ff.

Fadiman, Clifton. "Books." *New Yorker.* May 4, 1940.

Figh, Margaret Gillis. "Folklore and Folk Speech in the Works of Marjorie Kinnan Rawlings." *Southern Folklore Quarterly,* 2 (September 1947), pp. 201–209.

Glasgow, Ellen. *Letters of Ellen Glasgow.* Blair Rouse, ed. New York: Harcourt, Brace, 1958.

Haines, Ned. "Marjorie Rawlings Lived Here." *National Retired Teachers' Journal.* March/April 1980, pp. 58ff.

Kinnan, Mary. "A True Narrative of the Sufferings of Mary Kinnan." *Garland Library of Narratives of North American Indian Captivities.* vol. 21. Compiled by Wilcomb E. Washburn. New York: Garland Publishing, 1977.

Morris, Lloyd. "A New Classicist." *North American Review,* 246 (September 1938), pp. 179–184.

New Republic, March 8, 1933.

Noble, Eva. "Southern Personalities." *Holland's Magazine,* October 1939, pp. 8ff.

Perkins, Maxwell E. *Editor to Author: The Letters of Maxwell E. Perkins.* John Hall Wheelock, ed. New York: Charles Scribner's Sons, 1950.

Pope, Vernon. "Marjorie Rawlings Hunts for Her Supper; Menu:

Alligator, Turtle, and Swamp Cabbage." *Saturday Evening Post*, January 30, 1943, pp. 26ff.

Porter, Amy. "Growth of the Yearling." *Collier's*, September 29, 1945, pp. 74ff.

Publishers Weekly, June 29, 1946, pp. 3328–3329.

"Rawling's Most Recent." *Newsweek*, January 5, 1953.

Teale, Edwin Way. *North With the Spring*. New York: Dodd Mead, 1951.

"Today's Woman." *Christian Science Monitor*. September 4, 1940.

Turner, Helen Humiston. "Old Madison Hi Remembered 1917–1921." *This is Madison*. June 1978, pp. 12ff.

NEWSPAPERS

Aberdeen (Scotland) *Press and Journal*, October 18, 1933.

Atlanta *Journal*, May 27, 1945; May 29, 1946.

Burlington (West Virginia) *Advertiser*, May 22, 1938.

Christian Science Monitor, September 4, 1940.

Chicago *News*, October 16, 1935.

Cincinnati *Inquirer*, January 11, 1953.

Daytona Beach (Florida) *Evening News*, May 20, 1946; May 24, 1946.

Dayton (Ohio) *News*, May 7, 1939.

Florida Times-Union (Jacksonville), June 5, 1938; November 29, 1942; December 2, 1942; May 23, 1946; July 18, 1946; August 10, 1946; November 3, 1946; July 24, 1966; November 13, 1966; January 27, 1971; May 5, 1972; October 19, 1972; March 25, 1973.

Gainesville (Florida) *Sun*, May 20, 1946; May 21, 1946; May 25, 1946; May 26, 1946; May 27, 1946; May 28, 1946; May 29, 1946; March 30, 1950; May 23, 1965; August 21, 1966; September 21, 1966; October 25, 1966; March 9, 1967; July 7, 1972; August 27, 1972; October 21, 1972; June 9, 1974; September 29, 1974; April 9, 1976; April 9, 1976; July 31, 1977; March 19, 1978; March 10, 1979; July 29, 1979; June 25, 1982; July 1, 1982; October 10, 1982.

Hartford *Times*, January 3, 1953.

Holly (Michigan) *Herald,* June 30, 1938.

Los Angeles *Times,* May 14, 1939; January 4, 1953; April 26, 1953; May 3, 1953; May 4, 1953; May 10, 1953; May 17, 1953; May 24, 1953.

Lakeland (Florida) *Ledger,* May 24, 1946.

Madison (Wisconsin) *Times,* October 27, 1935.

Miami *Daily News,* May 20, 1946.

Miami *Herald,* April 24, 1938; March 30, 1946; May 22, 1946; May 24, 1946; May 25, 1946; May 26, 1946; May 28, 1946; May 30, 1946; April 27, 1958; November 1, 1966; February 16, 1969; September 17, 1973; December 13, 1981; March 27, 1983.

Milwaukee *Journal,* March 10, 1974.

New York *Daily News,* Dec. 12, 1965.

New York *Herald Tribune,* March 5, 1933; June 8, 1933; June 18, 1933; April 28, 1940; May 19, 1940; June 9, 1940; February 2, 1941; February 9, 1941; January 4, 1953.

New York *Post,* January 4, 1953.

New York *Sun,* October 4, 1935.

New York *Times,* March 5, 1933; October 6, 1935; April 1, 1938; April 3, 1938; May 14, 1939; April 28, 1940; November 1, 1941; November 30, 1941; February 2, 1943; January 24, 1947; December 16, 1953; September 24, 1979.

New York *World-Telegram,* September 22, 1942; January 7, 1953; December 11, 1965.

Ocala (Florida) *Morning Banner,* June 21, 1939.

Ocala (Florida) *Star-Banner,* May 24, 1946; March 5, 1972; September 27, 1979.

Orlando (Florida) *Sentinel,* May 22, 1946; May 24, 1946; May 30, 1971; November 10, 1971; April 30, 1972.

Oxford (England) *Times,* October 6, 1933.

Pensacola (Florida) *Journal,* December 29, 1973.

People's Voice (New York), September 14, 1946.

Philadelphia *Inquirer,* February 23, 1975.

Philadelphia *Record,* March 5, 1933.

Providence (Rhode Island) *Journal,* April 21, 1939.

Richmond *Times Dispatch,* February 5, 1953.

Roanoke (Virginia) *Times,* January 4, 1953.

Rochester (New York) *Evening Journal*, Sept. 19, 1922; Nov. 2, 1922.

Rochester (New York) *Sunday American*, October 1, 1922; October 8, 1922; October 22, 1922.

Rochester (New York) *Times-Union*, May 24, 1926; May 25, 1926; May 26, 1926; May 27, 1926; May 28, 1926; June 1, 1926; June 2, 1926; June 3, 1926; June 4, 1926; June 5, 1926; June 7, 1926; June 8, 1926; June 9, 1926; June 17, 1926; June 18, 1926; June 19, 1926; June 30, 1926; July 10, 1926; July 12, 1926; July 13, 1926; July 14, 1926; July 15, 1926; July 19, 1926; July 20, 1926; July 21, 1926; July 22, 1926; July 23, 1926; July 24, 1926; July 26, 1926; July 27, 1926; August 7, 1926; August 9, 1926; August 14, 1926; August 16, 1926; August 17, 1926; August 31, 1926; September 21, 1926; September 22, 1926; September 23, 1926; October 26, 1926; October 27, 1926; December 13, 1926; December 14, 1926; December 23, 1926; December 24, 1926; December 27, 1926; February 26, 1927; February 28, 1927; March 1, 1927; March 2, 1927; March 3, 1927; March 29, 1927; March 30, 1927; March 31, 1927; May 16, 1927; May 17, 1927; May 18, 1927; May 19, 1927; May 20, 1927; December 15, 1927; December 16, 1927; December 17, 1927; December 19, 1927.

St. Augustine (Florida) *Record*, October 25, 1944.

St. Petersburg (Florida) *Evening Independent*, July 21, 1978.

St. Petersburg (Florida) *Times*, February 29, 1976; April 25, 1976; May 31, 1981.

Salt Lake Tribune, October 27, 1935.

San Diego *Union*, October 24, 1954.

Scotsman, The (Edinburgh), October 2, 1933.

Spokane *Chronicle*, January 8, 1953.

Tampa *Daily Times*, May 22, 1946; May 23, 1946; May 24, 1946; May 25, 1946; May 27, 1946; May 28, 1946; May 29, 1946; May 31, 1946.

Tampa *Tribune*, May 26, 1946; May 30, 1946; June 29, 1958.

Tampa *Tribune and Times*, March 10, 1974.

Utica (New York) *Observer-Dispatch*, September 2, 1951.

Washington Post, April 1, 1941; January 4, 1953.

Wisconsin State Journal, September 22, 1940.

INDEX